BEST AMERICAN
CRIME WRITING

BEST AMERICAN CRIME WRITING

GUEST EDITOR
NICHOLAS PILEGGI

EDITED BY **OTTO PENZLER**
AND **THOMAS H. COOK**

VINTAGE BOOKS
A DIVISION OF RANDOM HOUSE, INC. • NEW YORK

Library of Congress Cataloging-in-Publication Data
Best American crime writing / edited by Otto Penzler and Thomas H. Cook ; guest
editor Nicholas Pileggi.— 1st Vintage Books ed.
p. cm.
Vintage ISBN 0-375-71299-2
Pantheon ISBN 0-375-42163-7
1. Criminals—United States—Case studies.   2. Crime—United States—Case studies.
3. Crime and the press—United States.   I. Penzler, Otto.
II. Cook, Thomas H.   III. Pileggi, Nicholas.
HV6785 .B47 2002
364.973—dc21   2002066195

Book design by Debbie Glasserman

www.vintagebooks.com

CONTENTS

CONTENTS

Crime reporting begins with Cain's response to humanity's first interrogation. Asked the whereabouts of his brother, Cain answers that he does not know. His surly tone is duly noted. He barks back at the questioner, then takes what would become a common tactic of one determined to obstruct justice: he not only lies, but arrogantly attempts to put the interrogator in the dock. The question that Cain poses—"Am I my brother's keeper?"—chillingly reveals the murderer in all his unrepentant malice, and if the King James Version's account of these events accurately reflects the spare eloquence of the original Hebrew, then the crime reporters of ancient Israel were very deft indeed.

Samuel Johnson once defined a library as the final depository of all the great variety of human hope. The accumulated record of man's crime is a similarly varied depository; for crime, being human, runs along a continuum that steadily darkens, from the harmless folly of Mark Singer's "The Chicken Warriors" and Doug Most's "Judgment Day" to the deep harm of Julian Rubinstein's "X Files" and finally to the black malignancy of Nancy Gibbs's "The Day of the Attack." It may begin with the slightest misstep, as does a dedicated government agent's fall in Charles Bowden's "Our Man in Mexico," or—as revealed in David McClintick's "Fatal Bondage"—it may be the grim labor of a lifetime. But whether one records a good man's sudden veering or a bad one's long career, great crime reporting is always about human life and must essentially hold its subjects within the realm of human understanding. For the best crime reporters, no man is really a monster; he is just a monstrous man.

Of course, only a few criminals are truly monstrous, and because of that, crime reporting is usually less a record of psychopathic deeds than a journey down the winding road of human feloniousness and malfeasance.

One of the first lessons of that journey is that neither wealth nor power can cleanse a human heart. Indeed, as Peter Richmond so skillfully suggests in "Flesh and Blood," such great good fortune, in this case that of Rae Carruth, may serve only to generate an arrogance that, once emboldened, knows no moral limits.

But if wealth and power can spur criminal arrogance, so can the desire for more of each. The fatal flaw of greed has rarely been more aptly demonstrated than in "The Killing of Alydar," Skip Hollandsworth's riveting account of a horse breeder whose spiraling upward need generated a spiraling downward fall. The desire for control can be no less maddening than the desire for wealth and power, and when that desire is sexual, the criminal potential is terrifying. The murders of Nicole Simpson and Ronald Goldman were spun from that dark threat, but the O. J. Simpson portrayed in Pat Jordan's grimly comedic "The Outcast" demonstrates that acts of high criminal content do not require minds of equally high intellectual capacity. O. J. Simpson has never appeared more thoroughly damnable and moronic than in this piece, his own inconceivable obviousness cheerfully providing the only rope he needs to hang himself.

Intelligence (that is to say, the lack of it) is also the subject of Alex Prud'homme's "Should Johnny Paul Penry Die?" a fascinating account of a death row inmate who may have succeeded in faking his mental retardation.

Thus far we have talked of crimes and criminals, but the best crime reporters understand that there is no crime without a victim, and great crime reporting never forgets that the body sprawled across the floor was once a living human being, one who rested at the center of an extended network of relations, wives and husbands, friends and lovers, parents and children. In Robert Draper's "A Prayer for Tina Marie," a single hapless life is taken. In E. Jean Carroll's "The Cheerleaders," a whole community is ravaged by multiple murder, a crime that despite its heinousness still pales in magnitude beside the scores of lives laid waste in William Langewiesche's "The Crash of EgyptAir 990." Grief, however, is not measured in the number of the bereaved, but in the depth of the bereavement. A single mourner is a world, and the greatest crime reporters are never blind to the awesome and eternal wake of crime, its human debris, the terrible truth that certain wounds are doomed to bleed forever.

Crime's echo is a call for justice, one that is answered in two phases. The first is apprehension. The second is judgment.

Apprehension is the task of the police. Robert Kurson's "The Chicago Crime Commission" records one man's long effort to bring the last of the old-line mafia to justice, while Peter J. Boyer's "Bad Cops" details how an entire contingent of equally determined cops, in this case members of the Los Angeles Police Department, can be undermined by a few well-placed lies.

Judgment is the task of the courts, and coming to it is rarely easy. Atul Gawande's "Under Suspicion" suggests just how difficult it can be when even the best eyewitness testimony must be held suspect.

In the face of such difficulty, how, then, do we come to judgment? That is the compelling question posed, and to some degree answered, in "Anatomy of a Verdict," D. Graham Burnett's thoughtful account of jury service. In countless ways the men and women of any jury are no less human than the men and women whose fates rest in their hands. But in their modesty and dedication, their struggle for order and proportion, jurors prove themselves to be the shining opposite of criminals, and for that reason we have chosen to end this volume with their story.

Finally, we wish to note that this work was undertaken with no anticipation that one crime, that of September 11, would, in the sheer magnitude of its carnage and the utter depth of its malevolence, dwarf all others. The attacks upon Washington and New York immediately generated a vast number of articles and essays, many of which were profoundly moving, and thus worthy of inclusion here. In the end, however, we chose to remember the crime itself, those who suffered the blow or heroically responded to it, rather than any later work of analysis, opinion or consolation. Nancy Gibbs's harrowing "The Day of the Attack" is that account, and we offer it in memory of all who died, and in admiration of all who labored, and in support of all who yet stand firm in our nation's determination to end this scourge forever.

In terms of the nature and scope of this collection, we defined "American crime reporting" as any factual story involving crime written by an American or Canadian and published in the United States or Canada during the calendar year 2001. We examined a very wide range of publications, which included all national and regional magazines and nearly two hundred so-called little magazines, reviews and journals.

Finally, because this annual volume is the first of a series, we would welcome submissions by any writer, publisher, editor or other interested party for *Best American Crime Writing 2003*. Please send a tear sheet with the name of the publication in which the submission appears, the date of publication and, if available, the address of the author. If first publication was in electronic format, a hard copy must be submitted. All submissions should be sent to Otto Penzler, The Mysterious Bookshop, 129 West 56th Street, New York, NY 10019. Those wishing verification that their submissions have been received should provide a self-addressed, stamped postcard or envelope. Submitted material cannot be returned.

Thomas H. Cook
Otto Penzler
New York
January 2002

INTRODUCTION

I worry about nonfiction crime writers today, and reading the excellent stories included in this volume makes me even more concerned.

I am not concerned because these writers have chosen to track down unsavory types, from homicidal maniacs to cockfight managers. Nor is it because true-crime stories are difficult to find. In fact, almost all of these stories first appeared in county newspapers and on local TV news shows. My concern centers on an increasing number of problems that have slowly evolved and are now facing nonfiction crime writers.

For instance, true-crime writers today are unquestionably facing increased legal obstacles and sometimes even hard-nosed opposition from prosecutors and judges.

Earlier this year, Vanessa Leggett, a thirty-three-year-old writer, was jailed by a federal court judge because she refused to give a grand jury the notes and taped interviews she had collected while working on a book about a homicide case. In fact, she was freed only after the prosecutors got their homicide indictment—without her notes and tapes, incidentally—and there were no longer grounds to keep her in jail.

The prosecutors claimed that Leggett wasn't a "real journalist," because she was writing her first book, but that did not keep them from wanting to see Leggett's notes so badly that they convinced the judge to send her away for 168 days, longer than any American journalist had ever spent behind bars.

But, even if a true-crime writer isn't tossed in jail, there are still plenty of other obstacles around to create problems.

Ever since the federal witness program in the mid-sixties produced Joe Valachi, the first mob turncoat, writers and their publishers have been battling a proliferation of "Son of Sam" laws in various state courts across the country.

There is no question about the fact that the possibility of having to deal with Son of Sam litigation has had a chilling effect on publishers and writers, but most significantly on just the kinds of people, like Valachi, whom society should be encouraging to talk.

Doubtless Valachi's testimony and Peter Maas's book, *The Valachi Papers* (required reading for FBI agents dealing with the mob), was not only the first inside look anyone ever had into the Italian-American mafia, but also shed so much light on that secret criminal society that today the mob has fewer secrets than the Boy Scouts.

Another problem that nonfiction crime writers are beginning to encounter involves the Erin Brockovich syndrome. Definition: the minute a writer starts asking questions for an article or book, the people approached start calling their lawyers and looking for agents. Instead of paying attention to the questions, the subjects want to know who's going to play them in the movie.

"But I'm taller than Mel Gibson," they say, astonished at the studio's stupidity.

The subject's fifteen-minute fantasy of stardom is, of course, not the real problem. The real problem, which also arises when someone is paid to talk, is that it becomes very difficult to know how much of what they are saying is the truth and how much is being embroidered just a bit to increase their chance for celebrity and money. There's not much most writers can do about that except insist that there is no movie interest.

Another problem that has begun to emerge recently involves the increasing number of lawyers who have started chasing down magazine articles and nonfiction crime books instead of ambulances.

In a desperate search for contingency fees, these lawyers scour books and magazine articles looking for any kind of "aggrieved party," who they promptly call and notify that they have been maligned and might have a lawsuit. The lawyers then suggest that if they are permitted to file an action on behalf of the "aggrieved party," on a contingency basis, of course, chances are that the publishers will probably settle out of court rather than incur court costs. Their fee is usually between 30 and 50 percent of the settlement.

Unfortunately, the lawyers are often right about publishers giving in and the writers are stuck facing the horrendous cost of defending themselves or agreeing not to fight the charges in the suit. Writers need not be reminded that even a worthless defamation suit can be prohibitively expensive where $70,000 for photocopying costs is not excessive.

There are fewer publishers every year willing to fight for the truth. Most will now negotiate and urge the writers to settle these lawsuits without going to trial. This is a particularly grim situation for the writers, since it leaves them in the position of either going along with the publisher and living with the onus of capitulating to the false charges or continuing the defense on their own and somehow paying for a six- or seven-digit legal defense out of their five-digit writers' incomes.

It's not all bad. Freedom of Information laws have certainly helped writers gain access to files and documents, but for the writers to actually get their hands on those documents is another matter. For instance, court documents relating to federal trials in Chicago, Illinois, are not stored somewhere in Chicago; nor, for that matter, are they even stored anywhere in Illinois.

All the documents relating to the federal courts in Chicago are stored in the middle of Kansas farm land, hundreds of miles from the Loop and miles and miles from any Kansas airport. In fact, the Chicago documents are tucked away in such a remote area that they can be reached only after driving hours through endless two-lane state roads that slice through fields of Kansas corn that stretch to the horizon.

Finally one sees a huge, gleaming, stadium-size white-brick warehouse off in the distance, and the rutted state farm road is replaced by a smooth, six-lane federal highway that could easily handle Super Bowl traffic. The highway leads up to a football-field-size parking area, surrounded by a ten-foot-high security fence, where there are rarely more than five or six cars, two of them belonging to the two clerks on duty.

These problems, however, will not disturb the best of nonfiction crime writers in this volume because they all bring more to their work than can be found on the arrest sheets, autopsy reports or trial transcripts sometimes denied them. What bureaucrats tend to forget is that writing about true crime is always about much more than the crime. It is not about arrest sheets, autopsy reports, wiretap affidavits and the trial transcripts hidden away in cardboard boxes in Kansas. The story is about the environment in which the crimes take place, and the people connected to the events. While the character, environment, cops, lawyers and judges are all an important part of any narrative, the most important element of them all is the writer who brings it all to life.

On the following pages, you will encounter first-class journalists who are able to achieve that elusive quality and bring stories and the people who populate them to life.

Nicholas Pileggi

BEST AMERICAN
CRIME WRITING

THE CHEERLEADERS
E. JEAN CARROLL

Welcome to Dryden. It's rather gray and soppy. Not that Dryden doesn't look like the finest little town in the universe—with its pretty houses and its own personal George Bailey Agency at No. 5 South Street, it could have come right out of *It's a Wonderful Life*. (It's rumored the film's director, Frank Capra, was inspired by Dryden.) But the thriving, well-heeled hamlet is situated on the southern edge of New York's Finger Lakes region, under one of the highest cloud-cover ratios in America. This puts the 1,900 inhabitants into two philosophical camps: those who feel the town is rendered more beautiful by the "drama" and "poetry" of the clouds and those who say it's so "gloomy" it's like living in an old lady's underwear drawer.

If you live in Dryden, the kids from Ithaca, that cradle of metropolitan sophistication fifteen miles away, will say you live in a "cow town." ("There's a cow pasture right next to the school!" says one young Ithacan.) But Dryden High School, with its emerald lawns, running tracks, athletic fields, skating pond, pine trees and 732 eager students, is actually a first-rate place to grow up. The glorious pile of salmon-colored bricks stands on a hill looking out on the town, the mountains, the ponds and the honey- and russet-colored fields stretching as far as the eye can see. In the summer, the Purple Lions of Dryden High ride out to the fields and the ponds and build bonfires that singe the boys' bare legs and blow cinders into the girls' hair.

In the summer of '96, many bonfires are built. The girls are practicing their cheerleading routines and the boys are developing great packs of muscles in the football team's weight room; everybody laughs and everybody roars and the fields around town look like they've been trampled by a pride of actual lions. In fact, the Dryden boys display such grit at the Preseason Invitational football game that fans begin to believe as the players do: that the upcoming season will bring them another division championship. This spirit lasts until about 6:30 P.M. on September 10, when Scott Pace, one of the most brilliant players ever to attend the school, the unofficial leader of the team, a popular, handsome, dark-haired senior, rushes out of football practice to meet his parents and is killed in a car crash.

It is strange. It is sad. But sadder still is the fact that Scott's older brother, Billy, a tall, dazzling Dryden athlete, as loved and admired as Scott, had been killed in a car crash almost exactly one year before. The town is shaken up very badly. But little does anyone dream that Scott Pace's death will be the beginning of one of the strangest high school tragedies of all time: how, in four years, a stouthearted cheerleader named Tiffany Starr will see three football players, three fellow cheerleaders, and the beloved football coach of her little country school all end up dead.

At a home football game, Friday evening, October 4, 1996, three weeks after the death of Scott Pace, townspeople keep talking about the team and the school "recovering" and "pulling together," but the truth is, nobody can deal. To the students of Dryden High, it just feels as if fate or something has messed up in a major way, and everybody seems as unhappy as can be.

The game tonight, in any case, is a change. Tiffany Starr, captain of the Dryden High cheerleaders, arrives. The short-skirted purple uniform looks charming on the well-built girl with the large, sad, blue eyes. Seventeen, a math whiz, way past button-cute, Tiffany is on the student council, is the point guard on the girls' basketball team and has been voted "Best Actress" and "Class Flirt." She hails from the special Starr line of beautiful blonde cheerleaders: her twin sisters, Amber and Amy, graduated from Dryden two years before. Their locally famous father, Dryden High football coach Stephen Starr, has instilled in his daughters a credo that comes down to two words: "Be aggressive!"

And right now the school needs cheering. Though her heart is breaking for Scott, Tiffany wants to lead yells. But as she walks in, the cheerleading squad looks anxiously at her, and one of them says, "Jen and Sarah never showed up at school today."

"What?" says Tiffany.

Tiffany taught Jennifer Bolduc and Sarah Hajney to cheer, and her first thought is that the girls, both juniors on the squad, are off somewhere on a lark. Tiffany knows Sarah's parents are out of town and that Jen spent last night at Sarah's house. For a moment, Tiffany imagines her two friends doing something slightly wicked, like joyriding around Syracuse. "But then I'm like, 'Wait a minute . . .'"

"Being a cheerleader at Dryden is the closest thing to being a movie star as you can get," says Tiffany's sister Amber. "It's like being a world-class gymnast, movie star and model all in one. It is fabulous! *Fab-u-lous!* It's so much fun! Because we *rule.*"

The Dryden High girls have won their region's cheerleading championships twelve years in a row. The girls' pyramids are such a thrill, the crowd doesn't like it when the cheer ends and the game begins.

"I'm like, 'Hold on, Jen and Sarah would *never* miss a game,'" Tiffany continues. "So the only thing we can do is just wait for them to arrive. And we wait and we wait. And finally, we walk out to the football game and sit down in the bleachers. We don't cheer that day. Well, we may do some sidelines, but we don't do any big cheers because you can't do the big cheers when you're missing girls."

Jen Bolduc is a "base" in the pyramids (meaning she stands on the ground and supports tiers of girls above her), and Sarah Hajney is a "flyer" (meaning she's hurled into the air). At sixteen, Jen is tall and shapely, a strong, pretty, lovable girl with a crazy grin and a powerful mind. She is a varsity track star, a champion baton twirler, and a volunteer at Cortland Memorial Hospital.

"Jen is a great athlete and a wonderful cheerleader," says Tiffany. "Really *strong*. And she's so happy! All the time. She's constantly giggling. And she's very creative. When we make Spirit Bags for the football players and fill them up with candy, Jen's Spirit Bags are always the best. And she's silly. Joyful. Goofy. But she's a *very* determined person."

"Jen is always doing funny things," says Amanda Burdick, a fellow cheerleader, "and she's smart. She helps me do my homework. I never once heard her talk crap about people."

Sarah Hajney is an adorable little version of a Botticelli Venus. She's on varsity track and does volunteer work for children with special needs. "She's a knockout," says former Dryden football player Johnny Lopinto. "I remember being at a pool party, and all the girls, like Tiffany and Sarah, had changed into their bathing suits. And I was walking around, and I just like bumped into Sarah and saw her in a bathing suit, and I was just like, '*Oh my God*, Sarah! You're so beautiful!'"

As the football game winds down to a loss, and Sarah does not suddenly, in the fourth quarter, come racing across the field with a hilarious story about how Jen got lost in the Banana Republic in Syracuse, the anxious cheerleaders decide to spend the night at their coach's house. "And we go there, and we begin to wait," says Tiffany. "And we wait and we wait and we wait and we wait."

.   .   .

Before the game is over, a New York State trooper is in Sarah Hajney's house. "I get a phone call on Friday night, October 4, at about—I should say, my *wife* gets a phone call, because I'm taking the kids to a football game and dropping them off," says Major William Foley of the New York State Police.

Major Foley (at the time of the girls' disappearance he is Captain Foley, zone commander of Troop C Barracks, which heads up the hunt) is a trim man in enormous aviators, a purple tie modeled after the sash of the Roman Praetorian Guard and a crisply ironed, slate-gray uniform. The creases in his trousers are so fierce they look like crowbars are sewn into them.

Sitting with Foley in the state trooper headquarters in Sidney, New York, is the young, nattily dressed Lieutenant Eric Janic, a lead investigator on the girls' disappearance. "I know Mr. and Mrs. Bolduc because I lived in Dryden," says Foley. "Ron Bolduc calls me because he's concerned he's not going to get the appropriate response from the state police. A missing sixteen-year-old girl—*this happens all the time.* So I call Mr. Bolduc back and say I will look into it. And what I do is, I ask that a fellow by the name of Investigator Bill Bean be sent. This is unusual for us, to send an investigator for a missing girl. We'd normally send a uniformed trooper who'd assess the situation, but in this case [as a favor to Mr. Bolduc], Investigator Bean is the first to arrive at the Hajney residence. And he *quickly* determines there's cause for concern."

The Hajney house, a snug, one-story dwelling with a big backyard, is outside Dryden, in McLean, a hilly old village settled in 1796. The village houses are done up in a pale gray and mauve and preside over lawns so neat and green they look like carpeting. Wishing wells and statues of geese decorate the yards, flags flutter on porches and there's a farm in the middle of town.

"There are a lot of people, concerned family members, inside the house," says Janic. "And the first obvious fact is: there's a *problem* in the bathroom."

"There are signs of a struggle," says Foley. "The shower curtain has been pulled down; the soap dish is broken off." On the towel rack is Jen's freshly washed purple-and-white cheerleading skirt. Sarah's skirt is discovered twirled over a drying rack in the basement.

"We start treating it as a crime scene," says Janic. "Sarah's parents have gotten the call [they are in Bar Harbor, Maine, for a four-day vacation] and are on their way back."

The first break in the case occurs almost immediately: The Hajneys' Chevy Lumina, which was missing, is found about seven miles from the house in a parking lot of the Cortland Line Company, a well-known maker of fly-fishing equipment. "The trunk is forced open by one of the uniformed sergeants," says Foley, "because we don't know, of course: *are the girls in the trunk?*"

The trunk reveals that the girls have, in fact, been inside. Investigators tear the car apart and find, among other things, mud, pine needles, charred wood, blood and diamond-patterned fingerprints suggesting the kidnapper wore gloves, meaning this wasn't some freak accident or a hotheaded crime of passion. This was planned.

Outside the Hajney home, waiting behind the yellow police tape in the cold night, is the other flyer on the cheerleading squad, Katie Savino. Small, with sparkling dark eyes and the merriest laugh, more like a sylph than a human girl, Katie is Sarah's best friend. She watches the troopers go in and out of the house and waits—full of hope—to speak to an official. What no one knows yet is that Katie could have been the third girl in the trunk. She had made plans to spend the night with Sarah and Jen but, at the last moment, decided to stay home.

.   .   .

Saturday dawns with diaphanous skies. The day is so sunny, so clear, that the natives, accustomed to clouds, find the silver blue blaze almost disorienting. "It's a *beautiful* day," says Kevin Pristash, a student affairs administrator at State University of New York at Cortland, which is near McLean and Dryden. "And suddenly these posters go up all over town. GIRLS MISSING! It's very eerie. Rumors are rampant. State troopers are everywhere. Helicopters are flying overhead. I go to get gas, and an unmarked car pulls up, and two guys from different police units get out. They're *everywhere*."

Gary Gelinger, an investigator with the state police, is in McLean interviewing the neighbors of the Hajney family. The first kitchen table at which he is invited to sit on Saturday morning belongs to John and Patricia Andrews. Their six-year-old son, Nicholas, attends Dryden Elementary. From an upstairs bedroom, one can look down into the Hajney's bathroom.

"John Andrews is *not* behaving appropriately," says Janie. "Isn't answering questions appropriately, doesn't seem to be aware of what's going on in the neighborhood. Investigator Gelinger reports back and just says: 'Nah, this isn't good. The next-door neighbor isn't good at all.'"

Back when he attends Dryden High, John Andrews is a bashful boy. The love of his life is cars. His old man has won a Purple Heart during one of his three tours in Vietnam; he's a "U.S.A. all the way" kind of religious alcoholic who believes in the belt and is strict about his rules. He beats John and his sisters, Ann and Deborah.

At Dryden, John finds a sweetheart, classmate Patricia McGory. They marry, and John joins the air force. At his German base, John allegedly, on two separate occasions, dons a ski mask and gloves and viciously attacks women who are young, attractive and petite. They have long, fair hair and are his neighbors. He's found guilty of the second assault, dishonorably discharged, and sent to Leavenworth.

When John is released, he and Patricia (who, along with his family, insists on his innocence) buy a house in McLean, and he begins working the third shift as a lathe operator at the same company where his mother is employed, the Pall Trinity Micro Corporation, in Cortland. A year later, in August 1996, the Hajneys purchase the house next door to the Andrews, and John quickly becomes obsessed with their beautiful and dashing daughter.

While the troopers are trying to get ahold of military justice records and follow up leads on other suspects, the massive search has alarmed Tiffany Starr and the cheerleading squad. "We keep hearing different rumors all day Saturday after we go home from the coach's," says Tiffany. "The house where I live is five minutes from the place where Sarah and Jen have been kidnapped. Of course I go wild, thinking they're coming to get me next. We've been imagining that they're after cheerleaders. And Saturday night and Sunday it's just me and my mom at home [her twin sisters, Amber and Amy, are away at college], and everybody knows that. By Sunday, I'm freaking out. And I say, 'Mom, we have to leave *now!* We have to get *out* of here!' And my mom says, 'Okay, let's go.' And we throw our stuff in bags. I can't be in that house another minute! I'm *terrified.* I'm sure somebody is gonna break in and we just get in the car and *go.*"

To fully understand Tiffany's dread, we must turn the clock back two years, to 1994, when Tiffany is a sophomore, her sisters are seniors, and their father is the Dryden High football coach . . .

The Starrs live in a lovely two-story house at the end of a wooded cul-de-sac in the country village of Cortlandville, which, like McLean, feeds into Dryden High. In the backyard is a swimming pool where neighborhood kids scramble and laugh, and on the garage is a basketball hoop, where Stephen Starr shoots baskets with his girls. Coach Starr is admired; his wife, Judy, is clever and good-looking, and his three daughters are the goddesses of Dryden High.

"My family is perfect," says Tiffany. "Besides being the Dryden High School football coach, my dad is the assistant Dryden High girls' track coach, and he is a sixth-grade teacher at Dryden Elementary. With all his jobs, it's years and years before he finishes his master's degree, and I remember the day he comes home; he brings champagne, and he pops it, and my mother and he are so excited! They dream about growing old together and sitting out on our back porch. Mom wants to get one of these swings so they can sit out there while Amy, Amber and I are at college."

"Dad's so funny," says Amy Starr.

"Dad sitting at dinner —," says Tiffany, laughing.

"The hat backward," says Amy.

"One of those mesh hats," says Tiffany, "backward, kind of sideways backward—"

"He calls me Pinny because I was so skinny," says Amy.

"Amber he calls Amber Bambi," says Tiffany, "and I'm Shrimp or Shrimper."

"And mom's Turtle, and he's Turkey," says Amber.

"Dad loves cookies," says Amy. "You come down to the kitchen, and there he is in the middle of the night, standing with the refrigerator door open. He can eat a *whole bag* of Oreos or Nutter Butters. He loves peanut butter."

"He dips the peanut butter out of the jar," says Tiffany, "and then dips the spoon into the vanilla ice cream. He's a *very* happy man."

"So I'm on my way up to bed," says Amber, "and he's on his way downstairs, he has a glass of milk and a plate of cookies, and for some reason this really overwhelming feeling comes over me. And I say, 'Dad! Wait!' And I say, 'Stop! I love you!' And I give him this *really* big hug, and he's like, 'I love you too, kiddo.' And he goes on downstairs. And that's the last time I see him alive."

In the fall of '94, a moody young boy from Truxton, New York, appears on the scene. A sulky rogue with dead-poet good looks, his name is J. P. Merchant, and needless to say, he's irresistible to young women. But romance has a trick of turning ugly when it comes J.P.'s way, and his last high school love affair ended in catastrophe.

Then he meets Amber Starr. She is not like the clingy, docile girls he'd known before. Amber is a Dryden cheerleader and a queen. They start dating. He falls in love; she doesn't. She breaks it off; a hole is burned into his life.

Merchant starts calling. He shows up. He knows Amber's schedule, her whereabouts, her friends. He tells her if they do not get back together he will kill himself. Amber is kind; she speaks with him for hours on the phone, "letting him down gently." In late December, he threatens to kill Amber's new boyfriend. Coach Starr is out of town, playing in a basketball tournament at his old high school, so Tiffany and her mother, Judy, go to the Cortland County sheriff on December 27 and file a complaint.

"Merchant is stalking my daughter!" says Judy. She asks for an order of protection. The sheriff arrests Merchant. Merchant's family posts bail: $500. Upon his release, he calls Amber and threatens her. Again, Tiffany and Judy go to the sheriff's department, this time with Amber. It is December 28. Judy begs the sheriff's department for help and protection.

On December 29, a sheriff's officer watches the Starr house. The officer goes home when his shift ends. No officer replaces him.

"Our dad raised us to be aggressive," says Tiffany. She lowers her voice in an impression of her father: "'Where's the aggression? *Dive* for the ball! Get in there!'"

"I don't know how many times I heard *that!*" says Amy.

"'I don't want to hear the word *can't,*'" says Amber, imitating her dad. "'That's not part of our vocabulary in *this* house.'"

Late on December 29, Stephen Starr returns home, eats a plate of cookies, drinks a beer, and goes to bed. Early the next morning as the family sleeps, J. P. Merchant shoots the locks off the Starrs' back door, climbs the stairs and is startled to see Tiffany standing in her bedroom doorway.

He aims the Ithaca twenty-gauge shotgun at her. "I am ready to die," Tiffany recalls. "I think for sure this is it. But something as simple as shutting my door keeps me alive. He is not after me. He wants Amber. He just isn't going to let anyone get in his way. And I don't try. I shut my door and let him go."

Forever after, Tiffany dreams of stepping into her closet, retrieving her baton, surging up behind him and striking him over the head. But J. P. Merchant moves on quickly—a matter of mere seconds—to Amber's bedroom. As he tells Amber to wake up, her father comes running to protect her.

J.P. shoots Stephen Starr dead with two blasts of the gun.

Somehow the girls and their mother manage to flee the house in their nightclothes. Merchant reloads his shotgun and follows. He fires into the woods at the edge of their house, believing they are hiding there. But the family goes in the opposite direction instead, racing across the yard to a neighbor's. J.P. starts to follow . . .

Amy Starr suddenly grabs the tape recorder out of my hand and yells into it. "This is reality, people!" she says. "This *really* happened! Okay? We were straight-A students! We had friends. We were cheerleaders. We played sports. We had great lives!"

The Starr sisters are visiting my room at the Best Western hotel outside Dryden. We have been out for an Italian dinner at the A-1 restaurant, and now the girls are sitting on the huge, double-king bed in my room, looking through their high school scrapbooks, doing their best to sort through the painful memories. They've since moved on, entered college (Tiffany is graduating this month from the University of Maryland), and they work every day. "We've not done one thing to mess up," says Amy, who is engaged to marry a "terrific" young man next spring.

But the girls carry scars. They do not talk to strangers now. They do not give out their telephone numbers. They fasten their seat belts to drive one hundred yards across a parking lot. They bolt their bedroom doors. If Russell Crowe appears with a sword, they walk out of the theater. It's six years later, and they still wake in the middle of the night, their hearts beating wildly. But the Starrs are prevailing. Not the growing-up sort of prevailing that most twenty-one-year-olds experience, but the kind of prevailing that comes from being trampled and standing back up.

As for J. P. Merchant, he leaves the cul-de-sac by the Starr home and drives to the grave of his high school sweetheart, Shari Fitts. Shari had committed suicide three years earlier, while she was dating Merchant. There, he puts the gun to his head, pulls the trigger and kills himself.

"The biggest mistake I made was not cutting off contact with J.P.," says Amber, who is dating now and seems quite happy. She takes the tape recorder out of Amy's hand and starts looking for the volume control. "Now I know, and I can tell other people." She finds the control, turns it up as high as possible, and yells: *"Cut off contact and get professional help!"*

There is silence for a moment. The girls are huddled together over the recorder, surrounded by pictures of themselves in their purple-and-white track uniforms, basketball uniforms and cheerleading outfits, their long *Alice in Wonderland* hair tied up in white ribbons. But one picture, from early 1997, is different. It is of Tiffany's cheerleading squad. On each of their uniforms the ribbons are black.

So is it any wonder Tiffany and Judy pack their bags and drive all the way to Tiffany's grandparents' house in Pennsylvania when Jen and Sarah disappear? As they're driving, the police are narrowing the suspects down to four—the Hajneys' neighbor John Andrews and three others. The hour is now approaching 10 P.M. on Sunday. A call comes in . . . like hundreds of other calls. It's a woman in her early thirties named Ann Erxleben, and she holds the key that will solve the case.

Ann is a pleasant brunette, a former class officer, yearbook editor and member of the softball team at Dryden High. "I'm working at the hospital with Cheryl Bolduc, who is a nurse," says Ann. "And when I hear about the girls missing, I can't even *begin* to imagine the pain Mrs. Bolduc's going through. Then something strange happens.

"My fiancé, Bruno Couture, and I own a hunting camp out in Otselic. [In this part of the country, the word *camp* is used to describe a cabin or lodge on rustic acreage.] A friend of ours, Marcus Hutcheon, has gone up to stay there Friday night. And when he walks in, the place is dark, but he notices a puddle on the floor. A friend of his comes and shines a flashlight on it and says it looks like blood.

"So I say, 'I think we need to go up there and check it out.' So we get ahold of Marcus, and we drive up to the camp. It's a small place—a basic hunting camp, one room, a loft, a wood stove. Marcus shows us the spot on the floor. It looks like somebody—" Ann's voice falters. "There's been a puddle, a dried puddle, and I'm scared.

"So we drive to the troopers' barracks in Norwich. There isn't anybody there, so we have to call somebody to come. I'm the one who calls. I say, 'Look, we've found blood in our camp.' I feel suddenly guilty. Call it instinct.

"So a trooper arrives, and we drive back to the camp. The trooper goes inside. He's very nonchalant. He comes out and asks, 'Do you know any people from McLean?' Well, obviously. Bruno has been raised there, and I grew up around there. And he asks us if anybody from McLean has been up there. And I answer, 'friends and family.' And the trooper says, 'Well, I've called the barracks in Cortland, and we need to wait for them to come.'

"The Cortland troopers come. It's very dark now. They take a look in the camp and start interviewing Marcus. Then they interview Bruno. Then they turn to me and ask who I am. I say I'm Bruno's fiancée. And one of the troopers asks if any of my family and friends live near the girls.

"Both Bruno and Marcus took at me. They're waiting for me to make the call as to what to say. I've decided beforehand—it's the only way I can live with my conscience—that I will volunteer no information unless they ask me *directly*. And I look at the trooper and I say, 'Yes, my brother.' And the trooper says, 'Has anybody you know that lives near the girls been up to this camp?' And I say, 'Yes, my brother.' And he says, 'Who is your brother?' And I say, 'John Andrews.'

"And the trooper flies by me so quickly he almost knocks me down. He runs into the camp and starts screaming for the senior investigator. And at that point I just want to vomit. Because my gut instinct is right. I love him, but the kidnapper is my brother, John."

"Ann's done the right thing," says Major Foley from behind his oak desk in the state trooper headquarters. "When the sun comes up at the camp, of course, it's obvious. Because we start to find . . ."

He stops.

"Parts of the girls," says Lieutenant Janic. "Body parts."

Foley adjusts himself in his chair and tilts his head away with a rush of emotion. "Well, I will tell you what," he says, quietly. "Here is something we will never go into. The details of the torture of those two lovely girls."

Silence.

"We arrested John Andrews," concludes Janic. "Monday at work."

Three days earlier, the day the girls never show up at the football game, John Benjamin Andrews, wearing a dark T-shirt and jeans, ducks under the Hajneys' garage door. He cuts the phone wires. Over his thinning dark hair and fleshy cheeks, he pulls a brown ski mask. He knows there is going to be a mess, so he puts on yellow rubber gloves, the kind people wear to wash dishes. The door to the kitchen is unlocked. He enters, turns and creeps down the steps to Sarah's room.

What does this grotesque, greasy-eyed nightmare carrying a bag holding duct tape, extra yellow gloves and six knife blades look like to her? He weighs close to 250 pounds. His bulk must overpower the small, vibrant girl. He binds the little flyer with black plastic ties and seals her mouth with duct tape.

Is he surprised to hear the shower running? Does he realize *two* girls are in the house? Does he know that Jen Bolduc—whose might and muscle have tossed entire squads of cheerleaders in the air—does he know that courageous Jen will stand and fight? He must be amazed when he lurches into the bathroom and Jen claws him, kicks him and, who knows, slams him in the face with the shower caddy. John Andrews is out of shape, but he has many knives; she is naked and outweighed by well over a hundred pounds. Sarah and Jennifer are soon trapped in the trunk of the Lumina.

Going the speed limit, the trip to the Otselic camp takes an hour. It is a curvy, up-and-down road. One of Sarah's greatest pleasures in life is to lie down full-length in the back of her brother's pickup, gaze up at the stars and, as he drives round and round, guess where she is. Now they are passing June's Country Store in Otselic. Now they are turning up Reit Road. It is bumpy. They are passing a farm. The farmer's dog must be barking. The girls are disciplined athletes, trained to think under pressure. Are they planning an escape? Are they making a pact? They are folded together like fawns, and no matter what, as Tiffany and the cheerleading squad say, "These two girls are *there* for each other."

The cabin and its pond are about a thousand yards off Reit Road in Otselic, on the edge of Muller Hill State Forest. At some point John Andrews builds a bonfire. At some point he tortures the girls. He cuts Jen and Sarah into small pieces. He drives back down Reit Road, throwing bloody body parts out the window. He heads toward a state game land and disposes of more. He sloshes motor oil over himself, the front seat and the dash to conceal clues, and leaves the car at Cortland Line Company. He tosses the yellow gloves in a trash can.

"Well, what can I tell you?" says Major Foley. "There's a driving force. A lust. A desire. Mr. Andrews was *going* to attack those girls.

Whether he knew Jennifer was there, we'll never know. But he was *going* to commit this crime. What drove him to do it? The easiest answer is a three-letter word: *sin.* People do things that are wrong because they *want* to. That's all."

"What makes us do things?" says Ann Erxleben. "What makes us *not* do things? What pushed my brother over the edge? The police tell us it was some kind of woman-hate crime. Because of the way the bodies were mutilated. But John *idolized* my mother."

In 1985, John Andrews's father, Jack, was accused of sexually abusing young girls. He killed himself three years later with a twelve-gauge shotgun. Did the son blame the girls? Was he so ashamed and angry that he took revenge against young women for his father's suicide?

Looking for answers about her brother and father has not been easy for Ann. But she is not grim, not somber. She smiles and says what doesn't kill her makes her stronger. She has baked delicious blueberry muffins for me to eat during this interview. She is relatively happy now, the mother of four comely young daughters—a toddler, twins who are athletes and her oldest daughter, now in college, who was a cheerleader. "It's a little scary for me to think that, in a lot of ways, we both were caring, giving people," Ann says of her brother. "We both were raised the same way; we both were taught the same values, we both were told to do unto others as you would have them do unto you. I said it's scary because I don't know what would make him do what he did."

When word comes on Monday, October 7, Dryden High decides to send notes to the classrooms. "Each teacher has to read to the students that Sarah and Jen have been found and that they are definitely dead," says Tiffany. "When the teachers read the notes to the classes, people jump out of their seats and run down the hallways, screaming. Everybody gathers in the gym and just screams and just cries and cries. And then people speed out to the parking lots, and they just, like . . . *leave.*"

Superintendent of schools Donald Trombley is quoted in the *Ithaca Journal:* "It is unbelievable hysteria."

"I'll never get over it," says Tiffany. "As a female, it's the most terrifying thing to imagine happening to you. Sixteen! They are sixteen. Young women are so protective of their bodies, about being touched . . . and then the way they're killed is so bad. And the question we keep asking is: *Why does it keep happening to us, our town, our group of people?"*

Before the school makes the announcement to the students, Katie Savino, Sarah's best friend, the raven-haired, high-bouncing flyer, the *third girl,* is taken out of class and told privately. On hearing the news, she runs toward Sarah's locker and collapses.

On Saturday, November 2, one day after being indicted on twenty-six counts of murder, kidnapping, aggravated sexual abuse, auto theft, burglary and criminal possession of a weapon, John Andrews hangs himself in his jail cell with his shoelaces.

Scott and Tiffany's class graduates in 1997. Sarah and Jen's class graduates in 1998. In June 1999, Gary Cassell, the young Dryden High athletic director and the man who became a surrogate father to the Starr sisters, dies of a sudden heart attack. Three days later, Judy Starr comes home from work and softly knocks on Tiffany's bedroom door. She asks Tiffany to get Amy and to come out to the living room. One glance at her mom's pale, twisted face, and Tiffany is terrified.

"And we come out in the living room and we sit down. And mom just says . . . 'Katie Savino.'"

.   .   .

Only two prisoners are receiving visitors today at the Tioga County Jail in Oswego, New York. One prisoner is a young curly-haired woman who is accused of killing her three-year-old child. The other is Cheryl Thayer, who has pleaded guilty to killing Katie Elizabeth Savino.

Katie graduated from Dryden and went on to the State University of New York at Oswego. When news of her death roared across the Finger Lakes region on the morning of June 11, 1999, the home of the Purple Lions was forced to shut down completely. Students simply could not *believe* Katie was dead.

"We felt like we're living in the Village of the Damned," says a student who described Katie as "the most popular girl who ever lived." "We were mad," says Tiffany. After standing strong through her father, Billy, Scotty, Sarah and Jen this one was "just *way* too much"—she became physically ill upon hearing the news. "We're like, '*When is this going to stop?*'"

Twenty-three hundred people attended the memorial service for the cheerleader who pulled a whole school back to something like normality after Jen's and Sarah's deaths. "She really believed Sarah and Jen were with her," says her mother, Liz Savino. "She was always smiling. I mean, she always *glowed*. Katie didn't make friends: she took hostages. She never left a room without a hug and a 'Bye. I love you.' I miss her terribly. I miss her horribly."

"Before Jen and Sarah died, Katie was so innocent," says Tiffany. "I don't think she'd kissed a boy until she was a senior in high school. *If* then. She was very smart, did really well in school, and she was friends with *everybody*. Then when Sarah died, Katie took a lot of her clothes and wore them. She wore Sarah's belt every day. I think it really terrified her that she was supposed to have been [at

Sarah's house the night of the kidnapping]. And then on top of it, she lost her best friend in the most painful way that you could possible imagine."

Katie's killer is tall and slender with lovely, dark, deep-set eyes, black eyebrows, and dark hair pulled high in a ponytail. Long wisps fall across her forehead as she sits very straight on her stool, her narrow shoulder blades drawn back elegantly. She is nineteen and pretty enough that, even in her orange prison pants and top, she looks like she stepped out of a Tommy Hilfiger ad.

"Katie was my best friend," Cheryl says, and immediately a large tear fills the corner of her eye. "I was leaving for California the next day, so Katie stayed and partied with me at a place in Cortland that serves kids drinks."

The tear falls against the side of her nose and begins to roll down—not down the type of burly, pockmarked face one sees in prison movies, but the face of a young girl with her hair pulled up in a scrunchy. It is disconcerting. "Katie and I were refused service because of our age," Cheryl says. "So we both just drank out of our friends' drinks. We left around two o'clock in the morning. When we got to the car, I could feel alcohol in my system, so I called shotgun. And Katie would *never* drive if she's even had one sip of a drink.

"I told the three guys we were taking home that one of *them* should drive," she continues. "But the guys all said they were too wasted. So that's how I ended up behind the wheel, even though I'm from Ithaca and didn't know the roads. Also the seating arrangement was weird. Katie was sitting in the seat behind me. The guy in the middle was huge. Normally, Katie would have been in the middle.

"I was driving her home first. She told me to take the back roads because they were quicker. I had no idea where we were going." It was so dark. Cheryl had the creepy feeling that if she stuck her arm out the window she would never see it again. Curves appeared suddenly, but even worse were the hills. She missed a turn. Katie laughed and made her stop the car and turn around. Cheryl lost all sense of direction but dutifully took the road Katie told her to take. A minute later . . .

"I didn't see the stop sign," Cheryl says, "and we got hit by the truck. It was so *dark!*" It's half a cry, and it strikes terror in my heart to hear it. "I didn't know the roads! I didn't see the sign! It's two-thirty in the morning. The roads are deserted. And here comes this *truck* out of nowhere! We were dragged a couple hundred yards under the truck, and the car caught on fire. As soon as the truck got stopped, the three guys climbed out. There were flames. My door was wedged closed. The truck driver pulled me out. The moment I was taken out of the car, it exploded."

"Cheryl," I say, "people in Dryden are saying Katie's screams could be heard as the flames shot through the car."

"No," Cheryl says. She waves her hand in vigorous denial. A yellow plastic ID band circles her thin, girlish wrist. Burns are still visible on her slender arms.

"I know Katie didn't die afraid," says Liz Savino. "But I have many, many nightmares about whether she was awake at the end. If she was, that would have been horrific. Absolutely horrific."

"Was Katie conscious at the end, Cheryl?"

Her upper lip trembles, but she speaks with certainty. "I think she was killed the moment the truck hit us. Katie was my best friend. I loved Katie. Everybody loved Katie. Katie was always laughing or shouting. We would have heard her if she were alive."

Liz, a small, personable woman, says she does not want to punish Cheryl Thayer. She remembers that when Katie was applying to colleges, one of her essays talked about sitting at Scott Pace's funeral and holding Jen and Sarah's hands. Liz Savino would like to think "that Katie's life was not in vain," and she believes that if Cheryl is given a chance, she will "teach others a lesson": don't get in a car with someone who's been drinking. So Liz and her ex-husband, Jim Savino, working with the Cortland district attorney, have asked that Cheryl be released from prison in six months and begin five years' probation. (She was released last summer and is taking classes at Tompkins-Cortland Community College in Dryden.)

"I tried to do what Katie would have wanted," says Liz. "Katie was a true, loyal friend. My way of handling my daughter's death is to live the legacy she would have wanted . . . to try to open myself up to others and be less judgmental. I'm not certain I'm as success-ful as she was, but I'm certainly trying. I believe she is guiding me."

Visiting hour is over. Cheryl must return to her cell. She stands with reluctance. She squares her slender shoulders and turns to go. There is a half moment to ask one last question: Katie escaped fate the first time by not spending the night at Sarah's . . .

"But fate made *sure* it met Katie," says Cheryl.

Three months after attending Katie's memorial service, her good friend Mike Vogt, the class clown and Dryden High's IAC Division All Star middle linebacker, walks out to a cabin in the woods. Mike is red-haired, big-muscled, fast, born to play football. He's funny, a musician and absolutely notorious in Dryden for his pranks. Mike drinks real beer onstage in a school play. Mike takes Chris Fox's car, parks it at the school's archery center and covers it with condoms he steals out of the nurse's office. Mike loves "mudding" and buries all kinds of vehicles up to their axles in the big open fields around Dryden.

"Mikey's my best friend since first grade," says Johnny Lopinto, who played football with him. "I never remember doing *anything* without him. We could be in the shittiest place in the world, and we would hate to be there, but as long as we were together, it was like everything was a big show and we were the only ones watching it. But Mikey was complicated," Johnny adds.

Mike was depressed by Katie's death and probably never got over the loss of his Dryden teammate Scott Pace three years earlier. "Maybe he wanted to protect us from his pain," says Johnny. "The morning after my twenty-first birthday, he walked out to the woods to the cabin that we built when we were younger, and he put a twelve-gauge to his head."

"Jill [Yaeger, Tiffany's best friend and fellow Dryden cheerleader] called me at school," says Tiffany. "She was hysterically crying. She was like, 'I'm gonna tell you straight out: Mike killed himself.' It was the *last* thing I thought I was ever going to hear. I *never* prepared myself to have one of my friends kill themselves." She sighs. "When I think about Mike," she says with a sad chuckle, "I can't think about anything but his red hair."

That is the end of the story.

The last Dryden High class that really knew Billy, Scott, Sarah, Jen, Katie and Mike is graduating this year. And the town? "It's weird, but young death almost seems to be the norm here," says the mother of a Dryden Elementary School student. The town's dead boys and girls live on in legend now. How mythic, how beloved they've become is seen at the graves of the three cheerleaders. They are buried together high on a hill outside McLean.

The graves are simple, but they're laden with a blanket of every kind of memento the townspeople can carry up to the cemetery—stuffed bears, angels, flowers, lighted candles, crosses, butterflies, letters wrapped in see-through sandwich bags, photographs, lip balms (Katie was known for wearing three or four different flavors at a time), poems, ribbons, purple lions, megaphones, sparkle nail polish and on and on.

On a cold, gray day, Tiffany and Jill agree to take me on a drive. As we go, Tiffany and Jill stare dejectedly out the windows.

"It's gloomy here," says Tiffany.

"It has to do with the elevation or something," says Jill.

"It's usually overcast," says Tiffany.

"Too many cornfields," says Jill.

"Tiffany," I say, "when you get married, do you want to live here?"

"No!" says Tiffany. She smacks the steering wheel lightly.

"Jill, do you want to live here when you—"

"*Absolutely not!*" says Jill.

Indeed, when Tiffany pictures the future—she's a 4.0 student with several job offers—the town of Dryden doesn't even enter into it. She can't afford to buy a car at present, but her "biggest freedom thought," she says, is this:

"I see myself flying down some highway in my new Mustang convertible with the Verve's 'Bitter Sweet Symphony' blasting. I can just see myself flying down the highway, far away, with my hair blowing and just being happy and free! That will be the day that I take this cleansing breath. And life will have been good for a while. And it will be forever."

✳   ✳   ✳

Looking so beautiful, and wearing a romantic storybook dress so sweeping that tears sprang into people's eyes just looking at her, Tiffany was married on the sunny Saturday of November 17, 2001, in the chapel of the University of Maryland. Tiffany's sisters, Amber and Amy, were bridesmaids. Jill Yeager, her best friend and fellow cheer-

leader, was her maid of honor. Her mother, Judith Starr, looking almost as young and pretty as the bride, walked Tiffany down the aisle and when the minister asked, "Who gives this woman away?" Judith Starr replied, with a radiant smile, "I do."

The groom, a young cinematographer and screenwriter named Berry Blanton, my nephew, was so besotted with happiness he did not utter one intelligent word all day. White carnations were worn in memory of Stephen Starr.

OUR MAN IN MEXICO
CHARLES BOWDEN

Time to go. He carefully picks up a shirt, smoothes it with his hand and then holds it away from his body. Afternoon light seeps through the east window of the storage room and catches the particles of floating dust. Sal stands there in the stale air and studies the shirt. It is short-sleeved, white with black stripes. Yes, he decides, he will want this shirt in seven years, and so he carefully places it in the moving carton. Before him, a mountain of brown boxes holds all the things he and his wife had before. A woman's hand has written clearly on each box: UNIFORMS. GUEST BOOKS. HONEYMOON STUFF.

Here in the house by the copper mill in El Paso, these are Sal's last days of freedom. Nine months ago, Sal was a Drug Enforcement Administration agent operating in Mexico. Now he is about to spend eighty-seven months as a convict.

For years, Sal was the perfect drug agent; he did what DEA expects an agent to do, which is to play loose with the law. But on December 14, 1999, he was arrested by the FBI. Two months later, he pleaded guilty to one count of arranging a murder for hire. Last May he was sentenced in federal court. Now, in August, he is days away from entering prison. He knows he must report with nothing, not even his contact lenses, will earn 15 cents an hour and must pay for his own plane ticket to get there—$238, one-way.

He pulls a snapshot out of storage, and there he is, the devoted agent, in camouflage pants, a black sleeveless T-shirt. His hair is long. He crouches in the dirt behind a car, a semiautomatic pistol holstered on his hip, a submachine gun firing from his shoulder. His body shows the ease of an athlete; there is a natural grace rising from the lethal pose.

A pile of papers labeled TRIGGERFISH sits on one of the boxes. The name refers to a device that intercepts private cell-phone conversations. Sal's work lives in these pages of transcripts. Voices whisper from the sheets, voices explaining that "Hey, this is the guy who killed Reuben." Or the voice is desperate: a snitch calling from Juárez, Mexico, reporting that he has come down a cobblestoned street and is now inside some house without furniture. There are eight guys in the house, he continues, but he can't tell if they are armed. Sal and some other agents race through Juárez tracing this call. But the agents never find the place; they can't triangulate the signals fast enough. The man's body turns up later. The whispers, of course, cease.

Sal has no interest in the transcripts. He is into figuring out what shirts he will want in eighty-seven months. He keeps talking, a steady patter. "Once I got the notice," he says of his prison assignment, "the clock was ticking. I gotta explain to the family that it will be OK."

The case against Sal Martinez is open-and-shut. As far as the government is concerned, he crossed a line and now he must pay.

Sal holds up a plastic milk bottle of holy water. He and his wife made a pilgrimage to a Texas church to get the water in the hope that it would help. Now the thing is leaking onto his shirt.

"Shit," he says.

This is a bad sign. And he knows it.

Sal was no angel. There is no room for angels in DEA. I ask him about his Mexican informants.

"One got shot in the head a couple of times, bro," he says. "Another was knifed a bunch of times in the heart." He gives me a look that says, why these questions? People die all the time in this work.

"Did you ever tell your wife?"

"No, bro."

He points to a book he wants to take with him to prison: *The Way of a Pilgrim.*

It's on top of a box that says JOGGING SUITS. WINTER STUFF.

He remembers his childhood as a cage, a time when "nobody took me out to show me things." He was in his junior or senior year of high school before he ever saw the good side of the city. He shakes his head at the thought, his shirt slowly drying from the holy water. His father was a butcher and bus driver. His mother had a job helping out down at the school. But there were four kids, and money was always tight. His Mexican grandmother lived in back, flying an American flag on holidays because, she explained, "this is where my hunger ended."

Football saved him. At 160 pounds, he became an all-city halfback. He suddenly was out with the guys—no drugs, of course; he's never tried any drugs; but rock music, a few beers, the crowd. He loved heavy metal, and he still has a Led Zeppelin tattoo on his shoulder.

But the thing that sticks in his mind is Sunday, and Sunday was always blue. His dad and older brother would be off playing softball, and Sal just didn't like being in the park while the men played and drank beer. The women in his family would be off visiting his mother's people. He'd be home alone, left with his chessboard in the barrio, and that made Sunday something to dread, made it the blue day when the smallness of El Paso closed in yet more and seemed to choke him. His body becomes rigid as he remembers those Sundays.

He was a good student and went to college. At first he figured he'd be an accountant, but then he read they had a high suicide rate. Because of a teacher in a crime course, he wound up majoring in criminology. After graduation, he joined the Texas Highway Patrol. He was out of the house, and there would be no more blue Sundays for him.

The Texas Highway Patrol led Sal to a small Texas town where he met Gloria, a schoolteacher, at Mass. They married, and he transferred to Customs, learned to fly a plane along the border looking for smugglers. But he missed the action of the street. When DEA beckoned—an outfit on the lookout for Spanish-speaking agents—he leaped at the chance. His cousin Phil Jordan was a big administrator in the agency, and Sal had thought about working there for years.

Soon Sal was in El Paso, making buys, doing busts.

He knows he's a natural, once he takes down a guy in a heroin buy in a parking lot with five minutes between the first hello and the cuffs biting into the guy's wrists. He loves the work, the streets, the quiet satisfaction of putting bad guys in jail. This is football without referees. He lives outside the rules.

DEA in El Paso is supposed to stay on the American side. But the action is just over the river, in Juárez, at that moment the biggest drug city on earth, with tons of coke, heroin and marijuana floating around. Sal and his partners dive in with the joy of young guys making their bones. There is no official paperwork recording these jaunts. Everything is verbal—the assignments, the reports. Things happen but in a sense do not happen.

Shit, he enters a bar and sees one of his informants sitting at a table with some cartel guys. He takes the kid aside, warns him. The kid says, "Ah, don't worry." The next morning, his body is on the street, an overdose. The kid didn't use drugs. Keep moving, Sal tells himself. Don't think about it. Do the deal.

Rolling and tumbling, the blues ringing in his head—he always loved the blues—that steady bass and then the harmonica riffing and then over the bridge into Juárez, where the music in his head changes. Life becomes heavy metal, full of electric moans. Into the cartel, into a city of one or two million, into the dives, his hair long, that fucking earring, a nine-millimeter tucked into his waistband. Now *he* is the drug dealer, at your service, sir. Park the car, keep the submachine in there, walk the walk, walk alone, without backup. They call the joint the Electric Q, walk in, yes, a double on the rocks, hey, they're here, all the assholes with their fine threads and chains, all the guys packing heat, part of a machine that earns $200 million a week, moving those loads. And the killing—shit, bodies in the *calles* each dawn, hands tied, duct tape across the mouth, a single slug in the skull.

Those are the lucky bastards, not like the ones buried alive or taken apart piece by piece or that bitch with the kid still sucking on her tit, the one who was plopped in the barrel of acid, she looked so fine once, *muy guapa.* Forget about that. Keep talking the talk. Hey, *cómo estás?* He glides into Juárez, into heavy metal, shuffling and jiving, and one mistake and . . .

There is no paperwork. What happens never happens.

Back to the ranch, debrief, say hello to the boss, a few drinks with the guys, then home, and how was your day, honey? Classes go all right? Me? Naw, nothing much, just checked on some things, same old same old. Huh? Sure, let's go get some ribs; you look beat, honey.

·   ·   ·

Sal never lives without a plan. He is never going to waste time again, never be trapped in the house on Sundays. His hours must be accounted for, just as at this moment, he carefully sorts through the clothes and makes use of his few remaining days. Others in his town are thinking about him; more than two hundred people in El Paso have formed a prayer circle devoted to his fate.

"Now I need to explain what happened," he blurts out. "And I don't know how to do it. Before, I had regular forms and outlines to fill in and file, agency case reports, a system of order."

No one will hear your screams. In Mexico, when the thugs come, they come as the police. Every DEA agent knows this fact. Before Enrique Camarena, a DEA agent stationed in Guadalajara, vanished into torture and death in 1985, he was last seen at noon getting into a truck DEA is convinced was full of Mexican cops. All the Sals know this tale.

The cops stride right up, seldom wearing uniforms. A shiver passes through your body, but a single thought forms: I have faced this before and nothing has happened. Just a few seconds ago, you felt so safe. Safe in your home, safe on the streets, safe in your favorite bar. As they approach, the drink sits before you, beads of moisture forming on the glass. A great thirst calls out inside you, a desire to hear ice cubes clink together, to feel the cold liquid course across your tongue. Safe, just an instant ago, safe.

Once, a few years back, they came at 4:30 A.M., at the time the gray light was just seeping over the city, came for that woman who had given birth eight weeks before. They carried automatic rifles, rode in the Dodge Ram Chargers they so often prefer, the kind with darkly tinted windows. The woman, who may have been a snitch or just a woman who got in the cartel's way, was swiftly taken from her home. The neighbors noticed her being dragged down the sidewalk in her bra and panties, arms held by men with masks who had the look and moves of police. The baby was left behind. The authorities insisted they had no record of officers on such a call. A few weeks later, the woman—ah yes, she's that one—is found packed into a barrel of acid floating in a sewage canal. Safe, so safe before, with the babe in arms sucking at the tit, the reassuring tug at the nipple, the soft flow of the milk—and then the knock and a brief scuffle.

So this is how you know you will go: You will turn from the bar, and they will say you must come with them. Your arms will be grasped and you will be out the door before you can even remember to grab that drink, the faces of the customers blurring as you go by. Later you will remember all those faces turning away or looking down at the floor. The wrists will be instantly taped together, the legs will possibly also be bound at this time and maybe the mouth taped. You land hard on the floor of the vehicle, the engine starts, you sense movement, then the kicking begins, and all you notice is the cracking of your rib cage. You have begun to disappear, and yet you still exist, exist in your mind and in your pain, but back there where the drink sits waiting on the bar, back there you no longer exist. In fact, back there everyone is beginning to understand that you never existed. A stab of pain, a white sheet of flame, reaches up and burns your head as a boot smashes your testicles.

Sal flips me another snapshot. He was sent down to Mazatlán, Sinaloa, a beach city, on agency business. And he bagged a few hours' spare time. Sal smiles, remembering the trip. Suddenly, a sea breeze cuts through the room. In the photo, he's lying on his stomach on the chaise lounge, the Led Zep tattoo there on the shoulder, a baseball cap on his head. The face is turned to the camera and smiling with the look of a cat who just swallowed a canary, and there in the background the deep blue sea is crashing on the sand, a white surf line rumbling home.

Who wouldn't do a deal with such a friendly face? Hell, sure, fifty keys? Done, man.

I look up, and he's back sorting out the clothes, the yellow light from the window glowing around his face.

"How many guys have you sent away?"

He pauses for a moment.

"Hundreds, man, hundreds and hundreds."

The room keeps getting smaller as the boxes press in, but Sal never skips a beat in the careful sorting and hanging of his clothes. He talks to me without turning his head. He talks right into the boxes stacked floor to ceiling.

"I had that tunnel vision," he offers, "that tunnel vision every cop has. I was always thinking things are black and white. I need to explore the gray areas."

I think this is the moment to put out the question.

I ask, "How often did you do that?"

And he knows what I mean, knows I'm talking about how DEA agents in Mexico take care of some of their problems. There is, say, a guy who is dirty, a fucking drug dealer, and you can't nail him in the United States, and the Mexican cops pretend they know nothing. And you feel pressure to get results from your bosses. And so finally, you go to the Mexican cops, and you give them the plate numbers and make of the guy's car, his address, a photo even, and you say, "This guy is causing me trouble. I'm hearing about him, and I gotta do something." And that guy, if he's not too big and powerful, that guy disappears.

"So how often?"

"Maybe twice a year."

And then he pauses; he's giving it real thought.

"No, more like three or four times a year."

"And you had to know," I say, "what would happen to them."

This pause is longer, and when the voice comes, it is soft.

"Sure, we knew."

The job starts to get to him. In early 1995, Sal came close to the hole where men lose themselves, so close his body still feels the danger. It is the thing men do not talk about. Not the risk—they love to talk about risk—but this peculiar flavor, this taste of fear rising in their gorges and choking them to death. This feeling that reveals to them what they always know and deny: they are weak; they are not brave.

It happens on a routine day when Sal crosses the bridge into Juárez. The Electric Q, been there the day before, time to check it out again. The long hair, the earring, the nine-millimeter under the shirt, the submachine gun on the passenger seat. Go alone, no time to find backup, go alone all the time anyway, go into Mexico armed, which is illegal, go into Juárez as a DEA agent, which is against regulations. No paper, never paper. Just go, things need to be done, no time to wonder. Sal drives the same rig, that flashy pickup once seized by DEA he's been hauling ass in; he parks by the Q and saunters in and makes the scene and becomes large ears and quick eyes, all this with a drink in hand and Spanish dribbling from his lips. After a while he is ready to leave, gets up and goes to his truck and finds it is blocked by a guy in a big rig. He has been made, he knows instantly, knows it in his bones, feels the fear in his body, knows he came back once too often, somehow looked too obvious. He starts waving his arms at the guy in the rig, speaks English, pretends he is a tourist, babbles as one hand creeps toward his nine-millimeter, and his eyes flicker to the submachine gun on the

seat; he shuffles and jives and wonders if his number has finally
come up, if this is the moment he never thinks about but always
keeps in mind. The guy in the rig stares, hesitates and then pulls his
machine back just a bit, enough so Sal can back out and get to the
street.

Now there is no time, not a second to wait. Hit the pedal, get the
fuck out of here; the truck is following, careening down crowded
streets, finally the big bridge, and shit, there's a line, stalled lanes of
cars waiting to cross and crawl through American customs, fuck
this, hit the pedal, yes, right into oncoming traffic, storm through
cars screeching off to the right and left, just get across that bridge,
there. Customs is racing out to stop this mad invader, ah, slow
down, flash the badge, do everything but kiss the ground. Back at
the office, file no report. The other agents have picked up radio traffic from the cops in Juárez, chatter about trying to stop this fucking
pickup truck, laughter that "Hey, next time we'll plant a couple
keys on the asshole."

Sal is still reeling from the incident, still replaying it in his mind,
when two weeks later, something happens. Sal is watching the
evening news in El Paso and sees that a man has been killed in a
carjacking. An hour later, the phone rings and Sal learns the man is
his cousin Bruno, a twenty-seven-year-old men's clothing salesman.
They are roughly the same age and share a lifetime of family gath-
erings and random beers after work.

Bruno's oldest brother, Phil, is scheduled in three days to take
over the three-hundred-man El Paso Intelligence Center, DEA's
narc-intelligence bunker and the biggest such facility on earth.
Phil, who has been running DEA's Dallas bureau, has recently gotten an indictment of one Amado Carrillo Fuentes, the head of the
Juárez cartel, just across the river. Could the murder have been a
retaliation from the cartel? Within thirty minutes of the killing, a
thirteen-year-old street kid from Juárez is arrested. He confesses

twice to police and jailers but refuses to talk further. His confessions are inadmissible. Few who've looked at the case doubt his guilt or that he was anything more than a stooge for the cartel. Thirteen-year-olds in Juárez don't get nine-millimeters easily. The boy eventually gets twenty years for the killing. The stolen vehicle and the murder weapon are never recovered.

At the funeral, Sal breaks down into helpless sobbing, begins to sink to the ground and has to be supported by the wife of a fellow DEA agent.

He thinks, Why is Bruno dead? He just sold suits, for Christ's sake.

He picks up the small box and opens it and shows off a harmonica. He's been trying to learn to play the blues for years. But somehow he gets going every six months or so, and then his practice is broken off by his work. Now, he thinks, he can really get down with the blues. Next to the harmonica, he's stacked a bunch of blues CDs. When things settle down in prison, he'll send for them.

In the summer of 1997, Sal is transferred to Monterrey, Mexico. Serving in a foreign country helps his career track, and he gets more pay for the danger. The house is two stories, and the furnace never works. Two German shepherds patrol outside. The walls and phones are bugged. Sal and Gloria whisper or speak in code when at home or on the phone. She is not working and spends her time being pregnant and then losing babies to ectopic pregnancies. Sal leaves early and comes home very late. He works out of an office at the consulate and has a string of informants to pay, Mexican cops to drink with into the night and pump for information. He sits in while the Mexican cops torture prisoners—the file drawer busted over the head, the head shoved into a toilet of shit and piss, the electric prods. Sometimes, when "special" techniques are required, the cops say, "Hey, Sal, how about making a beer run?" And when Sal gets back, all the questions have answers. The president of Mexico creates a new, incorruptible federal drug force, and DEA immediately begins paying the new, incorruptible drug cops, with Sal as the paymaster in Monterrey.

He finds this life dull, too much office, not enough street. Down the hall are some CIA guys, and God only knows what they are up to. But if he does three years, he has his ticket punched with DEA.

He's got one guy, Comandante Yañez, on the pad for about two grand a month. Yañez runs plate numbers for DEA and has been in and out of their files as an informant for at least fifteen years. DEA agents who have dealt with Yañez consider him dirty, a killer. Perfect.

On May 14, 1999, Yañez is in Sal's office on business when a call comes from family in El Paso. The caller tells Sal that Bruno's alleged killer has been released after an appeal won him a new trial and two more trials ended in hung juries. He's been extradited across the bridge to Juárez.

The guy who whacked Sal's cousin is now a free man.

Sal puts down the phone and blurts out some obscenities.

The way to fix this is right before Sal's eyes, the way he has learned to fix things, the way the agency fixes things. The thing not written down on paper.

Sal hears the comandante say he has friends in Juárez, that he can take care of this matter.

Sal says, "Do whatever the fuck you want."

Sal holds the Vulgate Bible in his hand and riffles the pages, stares down at the holy words in this room in which he packs away his life. Gonna read it in the joint, he's sure of that.

He does not feel guilty, not at all. Stupid, but not guilty. He regrets the misery he's caused his family. But he can't feel guilt.

A week or two or three ago, a Mexican federal cop, one of those guys in the new, incorruptible drug force that Sal tended to, well, this guy came to El Paso. Sal had ignored his calls; hell, must mean trouble, he thought. But the guy crosses the bridge and tracks him down. They go to a bar. The guy tells Sal he'd been good to them. And Sal *had* been good to them, putting them on the DEA payroll when their tiny checks from the Mexican government kept failing to arrive. Now that Sal is down-and-out and headed for prison, the guy wants to thank him, help him out. The guy says, "Let's go somewhere private." They huddle in the men's room. The guy reaches into his pocket and gives Sal a thick wad of bills. Sal is grateful for the help now that he is broke and ruined as an agent. But he knows a wad this size can only fall into the hands of a Mexican cop from the drug world.

Still, Sal asks, "Where'd you get this?"

The Mexican agent looks at him and says, "You know better than to ask."

Spring turns to summer, Yañez keeps bringing up how he could do a hit in Juárez, no problem. Sal and Yañez talk often. The talk is a small matter in the flurry of normal business. There are phone calls, a lot of the calls initiated by the comandante. In late September, under the prodding of Yañez, Sal meets him at an Exxon station in McAllen, Texas. Sal hands him a photograph of the kid who was charged with killing Bruno.

The official record insists that at this point, after months of talk, Yañez went to the FBI. But it is more likely that Yañez was already on the FBI's pad, just as he was on DEA's and the drug cartel's. Efforts are made by Yañez to bring Sal's cousin Phil Jordan into the scheme, efforts Sal dismisses and ignores. The phone calls are taped by the FBI. There is a meeting in Laredo, Texas, in November with other DEA agents to go over a case. Sal has been drinking. Yañez suddenly appears out of the blue, hands Sal a photo he says is the kid's corpse, and Sal blurts out clear words about how he doesn't care about the kid, just wants him killed. One video camera and four microphones are running.

The FBI takes him down a month later. The whole thing was a scam. Yañez never seems to have talked to anyone in Juárez, maybe had no connections there. There was no physical plot. Just talk.

There are details and the whiff of FBI entrapment (why does Yañez's relationship with the FBI suddenly enter records after months of talk about the murder plan? why did the FBI wait a month after receiving the tape of a drunken Sal talking about the murder plan before making the final bust?), a whiff now locked and buried in the FBI's files. Normally, an agent who crosses the line like Sal did gets sent to a shrink or tossed out of the agency. Not sent to jail. There is the possibility that the bust is political, part of the longtime turf battle between DEA and the FBI for drug-budget money. There is a clue that the real target was his cousin Phil, a constant critic of the FBI and DEA and U.S. drug policy on national television. Phil is told by his government contacts that the arrest comes from the very top, from Janet Reno and from Louis Freeh, the head of the FBI, and from Donnie Marshall, the then acting head of DEA, a guy just dying to get a permanent appointment. After the bust, even after Sal pleads guilty, the FBI comes to Sal and says a deal is possible if he implicates his cousin Phil. There is no question that Sal's case became political, and there is no way to prove this absolutely until that day when the FBI's and DEA's files are opened to the light of day.

Then the justice machinery kicks in, and by May 5, 2000, Sal is out $80,000 in lawyer fees and sentenced to eighty-seven months in prison on a plea bargain. Yañez cuts a deal, vanishes into the world of federally protected witnesses and now lives peacefully in the United States with his wife and kids. The kid—the one in Juárez who beat the rap on Bruno's murder, the one Sal shrugged off to Yañez, saying, "Sure, kill him, I don't care"—is alive and well.

I have fumbled for months to try to explain Sal's actions to people, and I always fail on the same point. I admit to them that he meant to kill the kid who murdered his cousin. And then I say that this is hardly novel given the known culture of the agency. Just one more wink and nod to a Mexican comandante, just one more problem solved by DEA. At this point, people almost always turn away from me.

I'm sitting in a bar with one of Sal's sisters just before he ships out to the joint, and I ask her what she thinks of his behavior. She's been around agency guys for years, dated some of them.

She says, "It is within the job description at DEA."

I'm sitting at a dining room table with his wife, Gloria, and she says, "What we are doing down there in Mexico nobody should be doing."

The government maintains that none of this matters, that it does not change the bottom line: Sal Martinez was willing to have a Mexican cop commit murder.

But I want a drink, because I've spent a lot of time in the world in which Sal operated, and I know the rules, and nothing he did or thought of doing surprises me.

Gloria is calm. Her young face smiles, her smooth skin denies problems, as she tends things in the kitchen. She remembers when it all became real for her, at a U.S. consulate Fourth of July party in Monterrey in 1999. Another agent came up to Sal and said, "Hey, we just found one of your informants. Of course, he hasn't got any legs now."

These days she goes to Mass. She bites her tongue about the

what-ifs of the case: What if Bruno had not died? What if Phil had not criticized U.S. drug policy to the press? She puts it all aside. She's into contracts, the sanctity of the marriage contract, and she abides by the terms she vowed to keep.

And Gloria clings to a dream.

She had the dream weeks before Sal's sentencing in Laredo, and it was very real to her. In the dream, she is divorced from Sal, and he has his arm around some chick. Gloria does not care. She looks up at the sky and sees seven and a half tornadoes, and she thinks this is odd, seven tornadoes and then over there, half a tornado. She must get her purse; the tornadoes are coming. And then they all find shelter: Sal, this chick hanging off him and Gloria with her purse. And in the shelter, Sal puts his arm around Gloria, and suddenly she feels real peace.

She knows the dream cold. The purse is money, security, everything that has been destroyed by Sal's arrest. The chick is the blows against the marriage. And the seven and a half tornadoes are easy for Gloria. Sal was in DEA exactly seven and a half years.

Sal is gone now, gone from the room where the clothes hang neatly, gone from the boxes that hold chunks of his life. TRIGGERFISH is silent, back in a box where all the intercepts and the killings can be hidden and eventually forgotten. Sal is doing time.

I am clearly out of step with the nation. I don't understand why Sal Martinez is in prison when the heads of the agency remain free after sanctioning his actions and those of others just like him for years. I remember sitting in court as the judge cast Sal into the gulag of our federal prison system. The judge said, "Lord have mercy on us if that's how our law enforcement is going to act."

I bristled at the judge's smug words. Just how did he think our law enforcement acts on the line or outside the country?

The women know better than the boys. There is a note Gloria gave Sal a few days before he left. She signed it *Vatos Locos*, something like "crazy motherfuckers" in English. Her clear, schoolteacher hand flows across the paper and whispers, "Come back when you become the man you want to be. I'll be there waiting."

Sal still speaks proudly of DEA, of his work. "I put bad people away," he says. Now he runs his prison life on a schedule, reads his Bible, practices his blues harmonica. Gloria works, reads in the papers about all the presidential pardons, and she thinks, why not some mercy for a guy who risked his life for years for his country?

Sal stays alive by remembering a motorcycle night ride down a Texas interstate in a thunderstorm. He comes up on a wall of water created by a semi, moves to pass, accelerates to over ninety, slams blind into the cold torrent. And he comes out the other side on his bike. Every time.

✻   ✻   ✻

When the story appeared in the June 2001 issue of GQ, *Sal Martinez was immediately put in maximum security for his own protection and then, after some weeks, moved to another prison. Phil Jordan, along with Sal's wife and the Martinez family, continues to seek his release or a reduction of sentence. Historically, Comandante Jaime Yañez had kept his wife and children in Laredo, Texas, and it was reported that he had entered the witness protection program. However, he evidently did not want to give up his lucrative work. On July 9, 2001, at half past three in the afternoon, Yañez took five bullets, mainly in his head, as he sat in his police car in Matamoros, across the bridge from Brownsville, Texas. Two other bullets entered his aide's body. They were instantly killed. The police found $20,000 in twenty-dollar bills in a black briefcase by Yañez's side. The Mexican state police announced that Yañez was a model officer and was murdered* *because of his relentless war against the drug cartels. The FBI announced that he was a fellow officer who cooperated in building the case against Salvador Martinez for nothing. DEA sources indicate that Yañez received somewhere between $30,000 and $200,000 for delivering Sal Martinez, and that he was murdered at the orders of the Mexican federal police for his greed in taking drug money, an avarice that naturally cut into their share. As for the Mexican state police, they insist the $20,000 found in his briefcase was planted by the Gulf Cartel in an effort to smear Comandante Yañez. Some DEA agents believe the killers would have taken the money if they had known of it.*

SHOULD JOHNNY PAUL PENRY DIE?
ALEX PRUD'HOMME

J ust before three o'clock last November 16, the warm afternoon
and creeping sense of inevitability in Huntsville, Texas, were suddenly interrupted by the shrill sound of ringing cell phones. Then
people all over this small town — women, mostly — began to cry out.
Some cried in relief, others in anguish.

At 6 P.M. that evening, forty-four-year-old Johnny Paul Penry was
scheduled to be strapped to a gurney at the Walls Unit, an old red-
brick prison building known as the "death house," and executed by
lethal injection. He'd been convicted for the brutal 1979 rape and
murder of Pamela Moseley Carpenter, a twenty-two-year-old housewife in the east Texas town of Livingston. But Penry was no ordinary
convict. He had an IQ somewhere between 51 and 63 (the intelligence level of a six- or seven-year-old) and had been horribly abused
as a child. He still liked to draw with crayons, and he believed in
Santa Claus. As a result, Penry was at the center of a raging controversy: should the mentally retarded be put to death for capital
crimes?

All afternoon Huntsville had swelled into a kind of macabre carnival filled with pro- and anti-death-penalty protesters and TV news
cameras. Inside a holding cell, Johnny Paul Penry—a man of
medium height with black brush-cut hair and wide-set eyes behind
the thick black-framed glasses—nervously wolfed down the pickles
and cheese left by the previous tenant, who had been executed.

"Execution isn't so simple to explain to someone like Johnny," recalls Father Stephen Walsh, Penry's spiritual adviser. "We talked it over in terms of sleeping, and he eventually calmed down."

It seemed inevitable that Penry would soon become the third inmate executed in Texas that week—and the thirty-eighth that year. Then everyone's cell phones began ringing; at virtually the last minute the United States Supreme Court had imposed a stay on Penry's execution.

Ring. Kathy Puzone—one of Penry's pro bono lawyers from Paul, Weiss, Rifkind, Wharton & Garrison, the powerful New York law firm famous for having defended Michael Milken—answered her cell phone with a shaky hand. "We got the stay!" she cried; overcome, she dropped the phone.

Ring. At a nearby hotel the family of Pamela Moseley Carpenter went into a collective state of shock. Rossie Moseley, Pam's mother, crumpled to the floor. Jack Moseley, Pam's father, a tough man who'd spent his life working heavy equipment, broke down in tears. Ellen May, Pam's niece, flung her cell phone across the room. Storming outside, she ran smack into a TV crew and unleashed her fury on it. "The Supreme Court had the stupid case for *thirty days,*" she says now. "So why did they wait until just *three hours* before the execution to tell us about the stay? It was one of the most devastating moments in my life—right up there with Pam's murder."

Ring. When prison officials informed Penry of the stay, he shouted, "Thank God I'm alive!" Then he asked if he could still have his final meal: two cheeseburgers, french fries, soda and cheesecake. The answer was no. The guards quickly returned Penry to death row at the Terrell Unit in Livingston. Penry irritated a fellow inmate named Gary Etheridge by asking, about twenty times in a row, "Hey, Gary, is it okay to unpack my things now? Is it over?"

"I don't know," Etheridge answered, again and again.

. . .

It's far from over. In fact, the debate over executing the retarded is now one of the hottest legal topics in the nation. On March 26, in a surprise move, the Supreme Court decided it would revisit whether such executions are constitutional. This fall the court will hear the case of Ernest McCarver, a convicted murderer with an IQ of 67; a ruling is expected in 2002. The turnabout came exactly one day before the Supreme Court heard the case of Johnny Paul Penry for a rare second time. In Penry's case the justices are looking at a narrower slice of the law: did his murder trial jury receive enough information about Penry's retardation to make a reasonable judgment about his fate? The court is scheduled to give its answer in June.

Whether the brouhaha over the Penry case caused the Supreme Court's surprise move, only the justices know. But if the court does at some point rule against executing the retarded, it will be one of the most significant revisions in law since the reinstitution of the death penalty twenty-five years ago.

Like Norma McCorvey, the woman called "Roe" in the landmark 1973 *Roe v. Wade* decision that legalized abortion, Penry has become the focus of a sharply divisive issue. As in *Roe*, large political forces are arrayed on either side, and the rhetoric is emotional. Indeed, Howard Cosell once called for Penry's execution during a broadcast of *Monday Night Football*, and last year Bianca Jagger wrote an open letter on behalf of Penry for Amesty International.

And like Norma McCorvey, Penry is a flawed icon. Although he's been portrayed in the media as an amiable naif, he has a long history of violence, and there are questions about how retarded he actually is. Both times his case has gone to trial, juries have ruled unanimously to have him put to death.

If the Supreme Court agrees with Texas, Penry could be executed within a matter of weeks. "People don't want to hear it, but

Mr. Penry will be gone soon," predicts William "Rusty" Hubbarth, an attorney for Justice for All, a pro-death-penalty and victims advocacy group. Anti-death-penalty groups believe the case will be remanded back to Texas for a third trial. Furthermore Penry is now technically eligible for parole. Although the possibility of his walking free appears to be distant, the Moseley family is not reassured by that. "Who knows?" says Ellen May. "Governors change, laws change, his sentence could be commuted—anything could happen over time. It scares the living daylights out of me that he could walk out those doors."

Although he declined to comment for this article, President George W. Bush has a long history with the Penry case. Last November, as governor of Texas, Bush was awaiting the Supreme Court's ruling on the presidential election. He had run as a "compassionate conservative" and was being criticized for having overseen 150 executions, including at least three of mentally retarded prisoners, in six years—a new record. Indeed, a purportedly retarded inmate named Mario Marquez was executed on the morning of Bush's gubernatorial inauguration in 1995. When the Supreme Court agreed to rehear the Penry case, it saved Bush from having to decide between granting Penry a reprieve and putting him to death.

In an odd twist, Penry's sister Belinda Gonzales claims that President Bush is related to her family. For evidence she points to a detailed genealogy, self-published by a cousin, about the Bushes in America. Penry is certainly related to *a* Bush family, but it's unlikely that family is the presidential Bushes. If a link exists, it is probably a shared ancestor in England centuries ago.

When I asked Penry about the president he said, "Mr. Bush, I think he's a good man. But he made some mistakes. And he kept on making them and making them, and then he had earned him a new name: executioner! He ain't no Christian like he says."

.   .   .

This past February I talked to Johnny Paul Penry at the Terrell Unit, a modern prison only a few miles from the scene of Carpenter's murder. Penry seemed eager to please, and he had a certain offbeat charm. But I found the conversation disconcerting.

Dressed in a white uniform, he smiled at me through the plexiglass and in a soft voice said, "Hello. What are we going to talk about today?"

Penry was shy at first; then he opened up. He pronounced his *r*'s as *w*'s—as when he said, "My momma made me eat my own number two and dwink my own uwine." His stories wandered, he was distracted by a buzzing noise in the ceiling, and he happily admitted he didn't know the meaning of some of the words he used— "Some people in here look at me like an outcast," he said, "which I don't know what that means." He said he dreams about getting out of jail and getting a job as a busboy.

Yet Penry didn't appear nearly as retarded as he has been portrayed in the reams of press coverage about his case. He was able to carry on a fairly normal conversation, could tell the correct time from his digital watch, and said he could read and write "a little bit." Suddenly I understood why some prison guards and practically everyone I met in Livingston suspect his claim of retardation is disingenuous.

"The Supreme Court knows I'm not faking," Penry said. "They know I'm not playing with a full deck. I am for real. And I thank them so much for that."

Penry has denied committing the rape-murder of Pam Carpenter; he has also said he doesn't remember it. When I asked him about the crime, he answered, "I'd better not get into that because my attorney told me not to." Later, when I asked why he was in jail, he looked confused and replied, "I really can't figure that out. I thought it was a dream, but it's real."

As I stood to leave he waved good-bye, and his grin reminded me of a smiley face. Then a TV crew began to set up lights and a camera for an interview. "Hello," he said to the frosted-blond reporter. "Why are you here? What are we going to talk about?" I felt a twinge of something cold, like a suspicion that I had been manipulated. Maybe he greets all visitors this way, but after giving jailhouse interviews for twenty-two years I thought he must have known why she was there with her lights and camera.

As I left the gates and razor wire of the Terrell Unit, I wondered which version of Johnny Paul Penry to believe: the sweet and tormented retarded man who didn't understand why he was in prison, or the manipulative psychopathic killer.

Prosecutors say that Johnny Paul Penry attacked at least two other women before he killed Carpenter. In 1976 he broke into the house of Julia Armitage in Goodrich, Texas, and tried to rape her, but Armitage screamed and Penry ran off. In a statement provided by the police, Penry is quoted as saying, "I went to the house to get a piece and some money." For reasons that are not clear, he was never charged for this alleged attack.

In February 1977 Penry slipped into the front seat of Diana Koch's car in downtown Livingston. He told her that his brother had been in an accident and persuaded her to give him a ride to a back road. She grew nervous, but when she reached for her CB radio she discovered that the microphone cord had been cut. According to Koch's testimony, Penry pulled out a switchblade and forced her down a dirt road. He raped her there and told her that if she was good he wouldn't hurt her. After the assault he got the car

stuck and they had to walk. Two hunters in a pickup offered them a
lift. Penry and Koch climbed into the truck's bed, and when the
driver stopped at a convenience store Koch began screaming. The
hunters held Penry at bay with a shotgun until sheriff's deputies
arrested him.

When I asked him about this incident, Penry insisted, "That was
something I didn't really do." Then he said, "She wanted it. But her
mother made her testify against me."

In any event, Penry pleaded guilty to rape and was sentenced to
five years in prison. He served about half his sentence and was
released on parole in August 1979. He was twenty-three. He returned
to Livingston, where he quickly found a job as a day laborer for
Harold Stubblefield, an appliance dealer. In mid-October he helped
deliver a stove to the home of Pamela and Bruce Carpenter.

Pamela Moseley Carpenter was a vivacious, slim woman with
long, straight, brown hair. At twenty-two, she did not have kids yet,
but she showered her nieces with attention, she devoted a lot of
time to the Central Baptist Church and she loved to water-ski. "She
was beautiful, full of spunk, a real go-getter," recalls Bruce. The
couple met at Livingston High School, got married and then lived
in Houston for two and a half years. After their apartment was
robbed they decided to return to their quiet hometown, which was
considered so safe that most people never locked their doors. In
1979 Pam and Bruce moved into a house owned by Pam's parents,
and "life was really going good," says Bruce, his voice cracking.

On the morning of October 25 Pam Carpenter was at home
making Halloween costumes and decorations. Sometime around
9 A.M. her mother called and asked her to join a prayer breakfast.
Carpenter said she'd rather finish her project but would meet her
mother for shopping at Wal-Mart and lunch.

At about 10 A.M. one of Carpenter's best friends, Cindy Peters, got a phone call. "This is Pam," said a strained voice that Cindy didn't recognize at first. "I have been stabbed and raped. Help me, and hurry."

Penry later told investigators that after delivering Pam Carpenter's stove he had often thought of her. On October 25 he had seen a woman in town who had reminded him of her; he started to think about her some more. "He told us, 'I was going to get the money and get me some,'" says Joe Price, the district attorney who has prosecuted Penry since 1979.

Penry bicycled over to Carpenter's house, on a quiet, tree-shaded street near the high school. He later told authorities that he knocked on the screen door and asked if the new stove was working. Carpenter said it worked fine. Then he forced his way inside and grabbed her. She screamed and managed to knock a pocketknife out of his hand. They struggled, and Penry slapped her face and threatened to cut her throat. When he turned, Carpenter grabbed the orange-handled scissors she'd been using to make paper jack-o'-lanterns and stabbed Penry in the upper back. He knocked the scissors away and dragged her into the bedroom. Frantic, Carpenter tried to get her terrier to bite the attacker. Penry kicked the dog under the bed. Carpenter was lying on the floor. He told her to remove her clothes, and when she refused he stomped her very hard with his big, brown work boots.

"She had a perfect heel print on her side, below her rib cage, where he'd stomped her," says Price. "It ruptured her kidney. She had massive internal bleeding."

According to his confession, Penry raped her on the bedroom floor. Then he picked up the orange-handled scissors, sat on her stomach, and said something like, "I love you, and I hate to do this, but I have to kill you so you won't squeal on me." Carpenter didn't say a word. He raised the scissors over his head and plunged them into her chest. The blades missed her heart but punctured her lung, which collapsed. "He thought that would kill her instantly," says Price. "But she sat up and pulled them scissors right out like it was easy. Well that scared him, and he ran out of the house." Then he biked home.

Carpenter managed to drag herself over to a telephone. She called Cindy Peters and then she called an ambulance.

Livingston police officer Edgar Paige arrived to find Carpenter "with blood bubbling from her mouth." She managed to describe her attacker: he wore glasses and blue jeans and a red plain shirt.

Carpenter was rushed to the Livingston hospital, where Corky Cochran, the local ambulance driver and feed store owner, continued to ask questions about the attacker and broadcast her answers over the police radio.

Sheriff's Deputy Billy Ray Nelson heard the description and couldn't imagine anyone from Livingston committing such a crime; nothing like that had ever happened there before. He drove around, looking for a hitchhiker or a vagrant. Then he thought of Penry, whom he knew from around town. (Julia Armitage, whom Penry allegedly attacked in 1976, is Nelson's sister.) Nelson radioed the hospital: "Did the suspect have extremely dark hair?" "Yes," came the reply.

Nelson drove up the hill to Penry's house and knocked on the door. Penry came out wearing work boots and jeans but no shirt. He had a radio tuned to the local news station, playing very loudly. "What you want?" he shouted.

Penry was sweaty, as if he'd been working out, Nelson recalls, and he seemed hyper. "He was in a different state," says Nelson. "Previously he'd always want to come up and talk to me. Now he backed into the bedroom and wouldn't turn his back to me."

When Nelson asked Penry where he'd been, Penry said he'd

been home all morning. Then he said he'd been riding his bike. Nelson asked him to come down to the police station, and Penry agreed. He put on a shirt, and as they walked out to the car Nelson noticed a bloody spot on Penry's back. Penry explained that he'd fallen off his bike onto a stick. Nelson hadn't heard about the scissors yet and let the comment pass.

At the police station they met Price and his investigator, Ted Everitt. They all drove to the Carpenter house, and while Price and Everitt went inside, Penry sat in the patrol car, "watching us real inquisitive-like, real squirmy," Nelson recalls.

Nelson walked around the house looking for evidence, and Penry kept calling to him, "Billy, come here! I want to talk to you!"

"Shush," Nelson said. "Be quiet."

"No! No!" Penry shouted. "Come here!" Then: "I done it."

Nelson says he almost had a heart attack when he heard those words. He remembers the moment with absolute clarity.

"I want to tell you about it," Penry insisted.

The lawmen read Penry his Miranda rights, then brought him into the house, where, they say, he willingly walked them through the rape and murder of Pam Carpenter. Back at his house, Penry led them to his red plaid shirt. It was in the washing machine; it had two holes in the upper back and was covered with blood.

At the hospital, emergency room doctors treated the stab wound in Carpenter's chest, unaware of her crushed kidney. A Life Flight helicopter was circling overhead, preparing to airlift her to Houston. The doctors thought they had her stabilized, but when they inserted a catheter the damaged kidney hemorrhaged and Carpenter went into shock and died in a flood of her own blood. The blood washed away any semen there might have been, so no usable DNA evidence was recovered.

Even so, at Penry's first trial, in 1979, it took the jury only two and a half hours to find him guilty of the rape and murder of Pam Carpenter.

"Penry changed the town of Livingston," says Lee Hon, who was in the eighth grade at the time and is now an assistant district attorney working on the case. "From then on everyone started to lock their doors."

Johnny Paul Penry's problems started on May 5, 1956, when he came into the world in a difficult breech birth. While his mother, Shirley, abused all four of her kids, she reserved her most venomous rage for Johnny Paul, the second of her children, because she believed he was illegitimate.

"I used to say, 'Momma, I love you,' but she'd say, 'Shut up, I don't want to hear it,'" Penry recalls, frowning. "She was a little bit overboard with the abuse. It was horrible, horrible." In a monotone he recounts, "She threatened to cut off my penis. She whupped me with a baseball bat and a big old belt buckle. She burned me real bad on a hot water heater. Tried to drown me in the bathtub. . . . She padlocked me in my room and covered up the window with plywood. The 'buse kept going on and on, stronger and stronger. She bit my heels, gouged out my eyes with her nails. Why? I always wonder why my momma treats me like this. . . . It's like a scar deep on my brain."

Shirley Penry, who died of cancer in 1980, spent time in mental institutions, was suicidal and drank heavily. "She was a very sick woman," affirms Penry's sister Belinda. "And she saw her momma commit suicide by drinking rat poison."

Penry's father, John, worked several jobs and was hardly ever at home. He has since remarried and suffered a stroke, and he reportedly no longer communicates with his children. The eldest daughter, Trudy Ross, lives in Livingston; Belinda Gonzales was once arrested for burglary and now lives in Houston; and son Jesse is serving a ten-year sentence in an Arizona prison for child molestation.

At the 1979 Carpenter murder trial Shirley testified that she did not abuse Johnny Paul. But Belinda vouches for her brother and says she saw her mother "making him eat his own feces out of his pants. I'll never forget that."

A baby-sitter testified about the burns she saw on Penry's back when he was two: "She had him in the kitchen sink giving him a bath, and he supposedly turned the water on. But the burns were down his backside, and it didn't seem logical." A neighbor testified that she heard "terrified screams" coming from the Penry house, and when another neighbor called a child welfare agency, the Penrys moved away.

In 1962 Penry attended first grade at an elementary school in Bacliff, Texas. After only a few days he got into trouble for climbing a flagpole and refusing to come down. After scoring 60 on an IQ test he was placed in classes for the retarded and then taken out of school by his parents. "Momma just locked him in his room and left him," Belinda says. "Sometimes we'd let him out, feed him, get him some sunshine. If she caught him out we'd all get beat."

At the age of twelve, Penry was placed in the Mexia State School for the mentally retarded, where he stayed for about three years. The school's intake summary reads, "Both parents were rigid when parting with subject and showed no affection. The mother did not say anything to subject, but hurriedly went to the car, crying and sobbing aloud for a few seconds. I got the impression that she felt this was expected of her." When his wards at Mexia gave Penry a haircut, they noticed that the boy's scalp was covered with scars. He said they were from the cuts made by a large belt buckle that his mother whipped him with.

John and Shirley Penry separated in 1971. Shirley moved to

Humble, Texas, and John and the kids relocated to Livingston. In December of that year, John arranged for Johnny Paul's release from Mexia. "Daddy felt like he should be with family," says Belinda. "We tried to teach him how to read and write at home."

During the next six years, Penry was twice committed to state mental institutions and was accused of a number of offenses, including fighting, sexual abuse and arson. In 1976, when he was twenty, he allegedly attacked Julia Armitage. He had turned down a dark alley from which he would never emerge.

There were no witnesses to the Carpenter murder, so it has not been definitively proven that Penry was responsible. But Penry's lawyers are arguing the fairness of his trial rather than his innocence. "Neither myself or any person working to stop the execution of Mr. Penry in any way minimizes the tragic crime that lies at the heart of this case," writes lawyer Bob Smith. "The question . . . however, is the appropriate punishment."

One of the central questions is just how culpable Penry actually is. If a defendant can demonstrate that he did not know right from wrong when committing a crime, he is judged insane and is automatically exempt from the death penalty. Retardation is different. Experts consider a person retarded if he has an IQ of less than 70. State authorities have tested Penry's IQ as low as 51 and as high as 63. Prosecutors, however, contend that Penry has scored as high as 72 on certain parts of the IQ test, which might suggest he sabotaged his performance.

"There is no doubt he is retarded," says James Ellis, a leading expert on mental retardation and the death penalty at the University of New Mexico School of Law who wrote the amicus brief for Penry's Supreme Court hearing. "He puts up a good front. He wants to appear to know more than he actually does."

But the prosecutors and the family of Pam Carpenter do not believe that Penry is retarded, and they doubt he was abused as badly as he claims. The want him put to death as quickly as possible.

"Penry is the wrong poster child for the issue of mental retardation," says Ellen May, who has a child with learning disabilities and has coached retarded children. "When the media come around, he starts with the stuttering and baby talk, but he's just faking to avoid the consequences of his actions. He must face them. He is not a sweet little boy."

"He knew enough to plan the crime and the getaway. He knows what he did was wrong," says Price. "He's a cold-blooded killer. And every jury that has ever considered the facts has agreed with that unanimously."

Mark Moseley, one of Carpenter's three brothers and a former all-pro placekicker for the NFL's Washington Redskins, says, "I could have used my sports celebrity to say more about our side of the case, but we wanted to let justice run its course. Instead it's dragged on and on, with no sense of closure. All the special interests are jumping in—mostly to promote themselves. It's a farce. And it's just torture for my parents."

Jack and Rossie Moseley have been crushed by the loss of their only daughter. Rossie writes, "There has never been a night that I didn't go to bed and cry for her pain. . . . I envy other mothers with daughters. I don't mean to be jealous, but it is an aching feeling. . . . I bought her [a leather jacket for her birthday], and her first time to wear it was in her casket." After Carpenter's murder the family moved from Livingston to a farm; her parents' marriage almost foundered. "It's been real, real hard," says Jack in a hoarse whisper. "We've waited so long for justice, and I'd hate to go to the grave and him still alive. . . . I'm a firm believer in the rope they used in the old frontier days as a deterrent to crime. When they used that, it had a real quick effect on people."

Carpenter's husband, Bruce, has been through two failed marriages since her death. Choking back tears, he says, "I just wonder what life would've been like if this hadn't happened."

Today Johnny Paul Penry has supporters around the world, some of whom insist that he is innocent.

"The problem is, it's very easy to get Johnny to confess to almost anything," says Father Walsh. "He had delivered a stove to [the Carpenter] house, and his fingerprints could have been left over. There is at least the possibility of his innocence."

"I personally do not believe his confession," says John Wright, the Texas lawyer who has defended Penry for more than twenty years. "Penry had no advocate at the scene of the crime, so you have to take the sheriff's word. They asked him yes/no questions. That is *not* the way to get a reliable statement from a mentally retarded person."

Penry's sister Belinda insists he was framed: "The Livingston police railroaded him."

Others say Penry's guilt or innocence is not the point.

"The Supreme Court has established that only the most blameworthy of convicted murderers can be executed. So how can those who have the lowest level of understanding fit that criterion?" asks Ruth Luckasson, professor of special education at the University of New Mexico. "What is the purpose of executing him? Is it rehabilitation? The mentally retarded can't be rehabilitated. Is it to set an example? Executing someone with an extremely low IQ will not [change the behavior] of those with low IQs, or those with high IQs. So what's left? Some kind of extremely simplistic retribution? That is not permissible under the U.S. Constitution. It is illogical to make the jump from finding Penry guilty to executing him."

"Johnny is a child trapped in a man's body, as he was the day he committed the crime," says Bonnie Caraway, a pen pal who has created a pro-Penry Web site. "Executing someone who doesn't know what he's doing is the greatest sin Texas could ever commit."

The first time Penry's case went before the Supreme Court, in 1989, his lawyers not only challenged Texas law, they also claimed that executing the retarded is unconstitutional. Writing the majority opinion, which ruled against unconstitutionality, Justice Sandra Day O'Connor said that there was no "national consensus" about the issue. Instead the court determined that Penry deserved a new trial because the Texas jury had not been told that he might be retarded. That ruling, now referred to as the "Penry instruction," forced Texas to rewrite its jury instruction in capital cases. Ironically, Penry was not a beneficiary. By the time he was retried, the new jury rules were not yet in place; his attorneys used this point to convince the Supreme Court to hear his case a second time.

In the meantime, the context of the case has shifted dramatically. In 1989 only two states (Maryland and Georgia) of the thirty-seven with the death penalty banned executing the retarded. Today thirteen of the thirty-eight states with the death penalty prohibit such executions, as does the federal government. Combined with the twelve states that don't have the death penalty, that means half the nation now forbids executing the retarded. Even conservatives are lining up against the practice. Florida governor Jeb Bush is opposed to executing the mentally retarded. George Ryan, the Republican governor of Illinois, has put a moratorium on *all* executions. And a number of condemned prisoners—McCarver in North Carolina and others in Mississippi, Virginia and Maryland—have been granted temporary reprieves until the Supreme Court issues its decision on Penry in June.

In April the Texas legislature took a new look at the state's policy on capital punishment. At this writing, the House had passed a bill banning executing the retarded and sent it to the Senate. (If the bill becomes law it will not be retroactive and thus not affect Penry.) Governor Rick Perry remained neutral on the debate, saying that Texas should take its cue from the Supreme Court.

On the cold, blustery morning of March 27, the white Supreme Court building stood out sharply against a blue sky. Inside, the temperature was considerably warmer as the justices pelted the lawyers with tough questions. This time Penry's attorneys had decided to bypass the larger issues and focus instead on two legalistic points: whether Texas's new jury instruction is still flawed and whether a state psychiatrist's report violated Penry's right against self-incrimination.

O'Connor called the jury instruction "awkward, to say the least." But Justice Antonin Scalia maintained that it was perfectly clear: "We assume that even if the defendant is mentally deficient, the jury is not."

Although no one mentioned the McCarver case, it was clearly on everyone's mind. For years organizations from around the world have been urging the court to rule on the issue of executing the retarded. The American Bar Association, opposed to such executions, notes that only the U.S. and Kyrgyzstan carry them out. The European Union has outlawed them entirely.

The effect of the McCarver case on Penry is unclear. "I'm no constitutional legal scholar," says Joe Price, "but the two cases are arguing different points, so I don't see how they're related." Bob Smith disagrees: "[McCarver] certainly benefits Penry."

The subject of death remains abstract for the man at the center of the debate. Johnny Paul Penry seems more afraid of images of death—the gurney, in particular—than of death itself. "I have heard that the injection of a drug makes your eyes roll back in your head," he says in wonder. "They put a needle in your arm and put you to sleep and you don't wake up. But I think there's a little bit more to it than that." He's aware that his case is important, and he understands what is at stake. "I've been over [to the death house] two times now. I'm pretty damn lucky to get a stay. I've outlasted a lot of those guys. I'm a survivor."

The Moseley family, meanwhile, struggles with conflicting impulses. "As a Christian I believe it is our responsibility to forgive those who harm us," says Ellen May. "I have been trying to forgive Penry in my heart of hearts. But it's hard. For a long time I didn't. Now I truly believe that one day he will walk through the gates of heaven and my aunt Pam will greet him with open arms."

*   *   *

This is one of the most interesting stories I've ever written. And it seemed to hit a nerve: we got a number of letters from people expressing their own ambivalence about Penry and the death penalty.

After its publication, the U.S. Supreme Court ruled six to three in favor of Penry, saying that the Texas jury instruction was flawed. The opinion, written by Justice Sandra Day O'Connor, called the instruction "ineffective and illogical" and noted that it did not allow jurors to consider mitigating evidence of Penry's retardation. He remains in jail in Texas.

As more and more states change their laws to ban executing the mentally retarded, the high court intends to consider whether this practice is unconstitutional.

THE OUTCAST
PAT JORDAN

E arlier this year, on three separate occasions, I spent a total of
about fifteen hours with O. J. Simpson. I met him through his current attorney, Yale Galanter, who is representing him in an assault
case that is scheduled to go to trial this fall, and who has become his
"official spokesperson." Simpson now lives in Pinecrest, Florida, a
bedroom community fifteen miles south of Miami, on the Atlantic
Coast. He moved there in June 2000, four and a half years after he
was acquitted by a Los Angeles jury for the murder of his former
wife, Nicole Brown, and her friend Ron Goldman. Simpson was, of
course, famous years before the trial, as a professional football
player, as a corporate spokesman for the Hertz car-rental company
and as an actor in popular movies, most prominently *Naked Gun*
and *Naked Gun 2½*. Since Simpson's acquittal in the murder case,
his income as an actor and celebrity has greatly diminished; he now
lives on his N.F.L. pension and the returns from his investments. In
February 1997, he was found liable for the deaths of Nicole Brown
and Ron Goldman in a civil suit brought by the victim's families,
who were awarded $33.5 million in damages. Three years later,
probably as a means of sheltering his remaining assets from that
judgment, he moved to Florida.

I first met Simpson on a sunny day in late winter. I spent most of
the day as a passenger in his car, a black Lincoln Navigator SUV.
He talked obsessively. As a running back, Simpson used to over-

come tacklers with his merciless will. "I let them push me around for three quarters," he said. "They were exhausted by the fourth quarter. I wore them out." He came at me the way he used to come at tackles, talking from the time we met for breakfast until late that afternoon.

Galanter had directed me not to ask Simpson about Nicole Brown's murder, but Simpson repeatedly brought up the topic. "The press created this guy who was hurting because his wife left him," he said, still spinning his story, seven years after the chase in the white Bronco. "That's bullshit! It was Nicole who wanted to come back to me after the divorce. She stalked me! Trust me. She'd send home cookies with the kids, and once she showed up at my house with a tape of our wedding and began to cry. 'Please, O.J.! I wanna come home!'"

We turned the corner and drove down a residential street. Housewives in spandex shorts were jogging on the sidewalk. Simpson glanced at them and said, "I loved the way Nicole looked. If I saw her on that sidewalk right now, I'd pull over and hit on her. If she had a different head."

Simpson is used to playing the character he created over the years—the genial O.J. we saw in the broadcasting booth, in TV commercials and in films—and he seemed ill equipped to play a man tormented by tragedy. His features rearranged themselves constantly. His brow furrowed with worry; his eyebrows rose in disbelief; his eyelashes fluttered, suggesting humility; his eyes grew wide with sincerity. All of this was punctuated by an incongruous, almost girlish giggle.

It was Simpson's will, as much as his talent, that enabled him to become not only a great football player but also one of America's most beloved black athletes. ("When I was a kid growing up in San Francisco, Willie Mays was the single biggest influence on my life," Simpson told me. "I saw how he made white people happy. I wanted to be like Willie Mays.") Over the course of his life, Simpson had gotten virtually everything he has wanted—fame, wealth, adulation, Nicole Brown and eventually, acquittal. It was widely reported that Nicole told friends that if her husband ever killed her he'd probably "O.J. his way out of it." Today, at fifty-three, almost six years after his acquittal, Simpson seems to be free of doubt, shame or guilt. He refers to the murders of his wife and Ron Goldman, and his subsequent trials for those murders, as "my ordeal." Now he wants vindication. Only that can erase the stigma that has transformed him from an American hero into a pariah, living out his days in a pathetic mimicry of his former life. And he appears to believe that he will get it, as he got everything—by sheer will—and with it a return to fame and wealth and adulation.

"O. J. Simpson is the most misunderstood person on the planet," Yale Galanter told me some months ago. To remedy this, Galanter said, he has a "grand plan."

"I want people to get to know the real O.J.," he said. "How giving he is. What a great family man, father and neighbor he is. I envision a day when O.J. will again be a celebrity spokesman in the mainstream of commerce."

Galanter is a forty-four-year-old Miami–Fort Lauderdale criminal-defense attorney who prides himself on his ability "to take either side of a case." His clients include the former W.W.F. wrestler Terry Szopinski, who was arrested on a drug charge, and Scott Campbell, a motorist whose car allegedly pushed the car of an eighty-three-year-old woman named Tillie Tooter into an Alligator Alley canal.

"But there's celebrity, and then there's O.J.," Galanter said. "O.J. was an American hero. And in a blink of an eye all his champagne-and-caviar dreams were taken away from him. I would like to see him back on top. Americans are very forgiving. They forgave Marv Albert and Frank Gifford. Not that I think O.J. did anything that needs to be forgiven! Personally, I am humbled that O.J. put his trust in me. My parents are walking on cloud nine because O.J. picked me to be his spokesman."

Simpson's civil lawyers recommended that he hire Galanter last December, after he was involved in a "road rage" incident in Kendall, Florida, south of Miami. Simpson was accused of cutting off another driver, confronting him and ripping off his sunglasses. The resulting felony and misdemeanor charges are scheduled to be heard in the First Circuit Court of Dade County.

Galanter asserts that Simpson is "a terrific father and family man" who drives his children — his daughter, Sydney, fifteen, and his son, Justin, twelve — to and from school each day, and who is in bed by eight o'clock. Be that as it may, Simpson has been constantly in trouble over the past year. In addition to the road-rage arrest, Simpson has been involved in three incidents that required the police's attention. All of them have been tied to Christie Prody, a female friend and companion of Simpson's. Prody, who is twenty-six, is a former "esthetician" (a giver of facials) who is now a waitress. In October 1999, before Simpson moved from Los Angeles to Florida, he flew to Miami after a panicked long-distance call from Prody. He later called the police from Prody's home and reported that a friend was "loaded out of her mind" on drugs, and driving around. In September 2000, Prody called the police to report that Simpson had let himself into her home. (Simpson claimed that he had entered Prody's home to do his laundry.) In another incident, the police were called to Miami's Wyndham Hotel to quell a disturbance. The management ended up asking Prody to leave the hotel, reportedly for physically assaulting "the victim," O. J. Simpson. The previous fall, Prody had sold a story to the *National Enquirer* for $50,000, in which she divulged what she described as details of her five-year relationship with Simpson, including two abortions, Simpson's obsession with Nicole's murder and numerous public brawls, which Prody told me had been fueled by cocaine binges.

All this may explain why Galanter is desperate to control what the media writes about his client, who, he insists, is a victim of his own celebrity. "Everything that happens to O.J. is news, and everything the media writes is inaccurate," Galanter said. "You'll see. You'll love him."

At seven-thirty in the morning, Simpson hobbled into the Kendall branch of the Wild Oats Supermarket, an organic-health-food store and juice bar. He has bad knees, the result of arthritis and his years in the N.F.L. He wore a gray shirt and black slacks. He sat down, smiling, and ordered what he said was his morning drink, leafy green vegetables and garlic, which reminded him of the time he had to hug Leslie Uggams, who was taking garlic pills—"all that garlic on her breath," he said, grinning. "But it helps my arthritis, so I can play golf again. Although I didn't play golf when I moved to south Florida, eight months ago, because I didn't want to leave the kids alone."

Yale Galanter arrived and sat down with us. He was dressed in a blue oxford shirt, gray slacks and black loafers. He is a good-looking man, with short brown hair and a chiseled profile.

"I love L.A.," Simpson said. "L.A. is my home. It's still the best place to be—the weather, the golf, my friends. I had a nice life in L.A., even after my ordeal."

His life in Los Angeles was not without incident, however. "Once someone keyed my car," Simpson said. "But when I was incarcerated I read the Koran, which said everyone goes through some ordeal, everyone's persecuted and overcomes it. I still had friends who wanted me to play golf at the Riviera Country Club, but I didn't want to bring any controversy there. One time, on another course, a helicopter followed us on the fairway and I hid under a tree. And another time this big ol' guy calls out to me, 'You're a murderer!' I said, 'You've got a right to your opinion.' He said, 'You better watch out, there are snipers on this course.' I said, 'I hope they can't shoot straight.' Then he calls me an asshole and I threw my clubs down and came up on him fast, looking for leverage so I can fuck him up a little bit, my face real close to his, spittin' in his face while I'm saying to him, 'You call me a fuckin' murderer I got to live with that, but "asshole"—come on, let's get it on.' He backs down. And now I'm a hero to all the little old ladies on the course, who thought I handled it great."

After Simpson finished, we went to the checkout line and I paid for his drink.

"Thanks," he said, laughing. "I ain't got any money anymore."

We got in the Navigator and Simpson drove to Roasters N' Toasters, a deli in a strip mall just across the street. "I like to eat breakfast here, hanging out with judges and lawyers," he said.

The deli was crowded and noisy with people talking and the clatter of dishes. As we walked to our table, they looked up, went silent then turned away. After we ordered, Simpson sat against the wall and looked around the crowded dining room. "I never sit with my back to the room," he said.

The waitress brought our food and we began eating. Simpson ate hunched over, his face low to the plate, looking up expectantly from time to time.

"I didn't picture my life like this," he told me. "I thought I'd retire at fifty with enough money, on my own terms. It's hard to retire this way. But I did it for my kids."

"O.J. is a devoted single parent," Galanter said.

"As a father, I was just a disciplinarian before, and now I'm everything to my kids. People ask me what's the hardest thing for me, and I tell them I was always a great dad but I'm a horrible mom. I don't cook. . . . A man's natural instinct is to solve problems. Like when Jason said Sydney did a lot of things and I never caught her. I said, 'That's one of the reasons why I love her. She's smart enough not to get caught.' She's her mom all over again, she's got those German genes—her grandmother, my wife, now my daughter. Those bitches'll wear you out."

Simpson said that he likes south Florida because "everyone's got a history here." He meant a history they were trying to escape: that people come to south Florida to create a new life. He added, laughing, "They got funny laws in this state." He was referring to two state laws, the bankruptcy and head-of-household laws. The former says that one's home can't be taken to pay off debts. The latter prevents creditors from garnisheeing the wages of any head of household; Simpson, as the father of two children, counts as a head of household. This is convenient for him, given the judgment levied against him in his civil trial.

"It's a bonus I didn't expect. I don't have to turn over anything to the Goldmans. They have to find out and get a court order for me to send them money. It's a cat-and-mouse game."

Pedro, the deli's cook, sat down with us. "I seen you come in, Juice," he said. He was a burly, unshaven man wearing a Yankees cap. "Me and Juice are good buddies," he said to me. "Juice had Christmas Eve dinner with my family."

Most of Simpson's friends here are what some celebrities might call "the little people." He plays golf on public courses. It doesn't seem to bother him that he has lost his celebrity friends, like Marcus Allen, as long as he has someone to listen to his monologues and jokes. The basic structure of his life—golf, restaurants, women—hasn't changed much.

A woman in her seventies stopped by our table. She had a bouffant of lacquered, pinkish-blond hair and wore heavy makeup and gaudy jewelry.

"I just wanted to say I wish everyone would leave you alone," the woman said in a faint, unplaceable European accent.

"Well, thank you," Simpson said, grinning. The woman held out her arms. Simpson stood up and hugged her over our table.

"Can I get your autograph?" she said.

"Certainly." The woman handed him her card. There was a photograph on it of a much younger woman with the name Rossette. Simpson signed her card and handed it back.

Simpson sat down and said, "I never got hugs before. Now the public shows me so much love. Women are my biggest defenders. It's that bad-boy syndrome. Now girls chase me. But if a girl wants to be with me I tell them they have to be number three, behind my kids."

"Being a father comes first with O.J.," Galanter said.

"I mean, I like gorgeous girls, but I can't walk around naked around my house or jump in the pool with a friend, because of my kids."

"When you say the name 'O.J.,'" Galanter said, "a lot of words come to mind, but not 'family man.'"

We drove south, toward Mount Sinai Medical Center, where Simpson was scheduled to visit some patients. According to Galanter, he does this in his spare time.

At Mount Sinai, we met with Pat Stauber, a registered nurse and a licensed clinical social worker. Pat is tall, slim and attractive, with straight black hair and an earnest demeanor. She led us down the hall to a hospital room, and stopped at an open door.

"This is all I could arrange on such short notice," she said to

Galanter. "I wanted O.J. to visit this man coming out of a coma, but I couldn't arrange it."

"When I played in Buffalo," Simpson said, "I used to visit these kids with inoperable cancer. The newspaper ran stories all the time about the kids I visited before they died. Then I had to visit another kid with cancer who was a huge O.J. fan. The minute I arrived, the kid flipped out. He said, 'If O.J.'s here, I must be dying.' That blew me outta the water."

Simpson went into the room and spoke to an old man in a wheelchair with a breathing tube in his mouth. He sat on the man's bed and talked softly to him while they watched a golf match on TV. Simpson pointed to the screen and tapped the man on the shoulder. The old man just nodded as Simpson talked.

When Simpson came out of the room, a half hour later, he said, "The guy was totally alert, he just couldn't talk, so I talked about sports."

Pat said, "Thanks," and gave Simpson a hug.

Simpson said, "Like I got anything else to do."

Simpson, Galanter and I drove to the Calusa Country Club, a public course, in Kendall. "I told ya, now I get hugs," Simpson said. "At the Holyfield fight in Vegas I got all the play." He grinned. "The tabloids were saying I was the reigning King of Porn. That I had sex with two girls four times each in two and a half hours. If I could do that I'd be in a porn film! A guy fifty-three. But I ain't need no Viagra yet. Thank God it's still there." Then, flashing his O.J. grin, he repeated an old joke. "I met this girl once and she tells me she only dates guys with ten inches. I said, 'Baby, I ain't cuttin' off two inches for no one.'"

Simpson parked his Navigator in the nearly deserted parking lot of the golf course. Two men came out of the clubhouse and met us by the golf carts. Simpson introduced me to Stephen Lee, a music distributor from Jamaica, and Delvon Campbell, also from Jamaica, formerly a steward in a Miami airport lounge.

"Hi, mon, how ye be doin'?" Delvon said to Simpson.

Simpson laughed and shook his head. "I have no idea what Delvon is saying."

"O.J., he's been a friend of mine since I met him at a golf tournament in the Bahamas seven years ago," Delvon said. We were in a golf cart following Galanter and Simpson to the first tee. Simpson lined up his drive. He hunched over, biting his lower lip, and began his backswing. His knees buckled and he lunged at the ball with his driver. The ball bounced up the fairway about a hundred and fifty yards. Galanter and Lee teed off next. The rough along the fairway was barren of trees and exposed to the afternoon sun, and the fairway itself was full of dirt and clumps of dried grass.

The foursome played in silence. Although Simpson had told me that golf is his "passion," this particular round, at least, seemed joyless. At the sixth hole, Simpson's game began to improve, just as storm clouds moved in.

"It looks like rain, mon," Delvon called from our cart as Simpson prepared to tee off. "We best be gettin' back to the clubhouse."

"I'm weak, I'm crippled and I'm old," Simpson said. "But I'm getting my game back now. I ain't going nowhere."

Delvon turned our cart around and we motored toward the clubhouse. I looked back over my shoulder and saw Simpson bent over in the rain, lining up his next shot.

A few minutes later, Simpson, Galanter and Lee, all dripping wet, came into the clubhouse. "You should've stayed out there," Simpson said to me. "I had my best hole."

The bar and dining room of the Calusa Country Club were quiet, except for a table of older women having lunch by the window, a bartender polishing glasses and the club pro drinking a Coke at the bar.

Galanter's cell phone rang and he answered it. A friend of his was in Los Angeles and needed to know about restaurants. "Here, let me put O.J. on," Galanter said.

Simpson took the phone and said, "You wanna go to the Ivy at the Shore, or maybe Chinois, or Schwarzeneger's place, Schatzi." He listened, then said, "It's like Laguna Beach. That's where my wife grew up. Nicole." He hung up.

"O.J., did you see Johnnie when he came to Florida the other day?" Galanter said.

"No," Simpson said.

Johnnie Cochran, Simpson's former lawyer, was now representing a fourteen-year-old black boy from south Florida, Lionel Tate, who is serving a life sentence for the first-degree murder of a six-year-old black girl.

"I wish Johnnie would just focus on the life sentence and not make it a racial thing," Simpson said.

A woman was reading the news on CNN on the overhead television when our food came. Simpson looked up at her and said, "Man, she got old quick. When you think the last time that woman got laid?" He shook his head. "Who knows? You never know in this world what rings your bell. Now, that Heather Graham girl is fine. And that Jennifer Love Hewitt—that girl got booty for days."

The CNN reporter was now reading a story about the breakup of Meg Ryan and Russell Crowe. Simpson watched until the report was over. Then he said, "You think if Crowe and Quaid"—Dennis Quaid, Ryan's estranged husband—"ever met they'd fight?" He shook his head. "As a man, you gotta punch the guy that fucked your wife."

. . .

It was late afternoon, and Simpson was driving again.

"For the last few years, I wasn't really looking for work," he said. "I got an offer to be a TV spokesman in Europe, an *Inside Edition*–type thing, but I'd have to be there eight days a month, and I can't leave my kids."

"O.J. is a wonderful father," Galanter said from the backseat.

"Now I'm gettin' active again. I got Galanter to help me. This is the first time I'm really ready to take advantage of offers. Yesterday, a guy wanted me to be the director of a youth program. A year ago, I'd have said, 'In the future.' But basically the future's here."

I asked him if he ever gets depressed. "I'm not prone to get depressed," he said, "but sometimes . . . the weight on me reaches a point and I just wanna go home and—" His cell phone rang. He answered it and listened for a moment. Then he said, "I ain't no advice for the lovelorn," and hung up. "Christie," he said.

"Your girlfriend?"

Simpson gave me a pained look. "Aw, man, she ain't my girlfriend. She's just, you know . . ." He made a thrusting motion with his hips. "Find me a girl owns a golf course and will pay all my bills and I'm pretty sure I'll marry her."

Later, I spoke to Cathy Bellmore, Christie Prody's mother, who told me, "O.J. wanted to get rid of her when she lived in L.A., so she went to Florida a year ago without him." Once she was gone, Simpson wanted her back. Apparently, Simpson was unable to give up even a girlfriend he was bored with, because he considered her his private property. A friend of Simpson's discounted any threat to Prody's life, saying, "O.J. was really in love with Nicole, but he doesn't care enough about Christie to kill her."

. . .

A few weeks after my first meeting with Simpson, my wife and I had dinner with him and Prody at the Palm, a steak house in North Miami Beach. Galanter and his wife, Elyse, arrived a few minutes after we did. While we waited for Simpson, Galanter leaned over and told me that Christie liked to stay out late. "Wait'll you see her," he said, "If you or I ever walked into a restaurant with her, our stock would go up."

Simpson and Christie arrived late. Christie is an attractive woman with the rounded features of a tomboy. She has lank, reddish hair that she once dyed blond because, as Simpson put it, "what woman doesn't want to be a blonde at one time?" Even as a blonde, however, Christie is not, as the tabloids would have it, a "Nicole look-alike."

Simpson apologized for being late. He looked at the three women, who were talking, to make sure they weren't watching him, then he grinned and made a thrusting gesture with his hips.

Christie said she and Simpson had met when she was nineteen, when she'd moved to Los Angeles after attending the University of Minnesota. This was shortly after Simpson's trial. One day, on a lark, she drove by Simpson's house, on Rockingham. "Like everybody else, I thought he did it," she said. She saw Simpson outside riding an electric bicycle and called to him, "Hi, O.J.!" He came over and they talked for hours. She gave him her telephone number, and the next day he called and invited her to the house. They have been together, on and off, ever since.

"He was charming and charismatic, and kind of intriguing," she said. "I always liked older guys. I got enough problems myself so why hang out with young people? O.J. forgets I have a typical twenty-six-year-old's problems. I have my whole life ahead of me. But I live for today and don't worry so much about five years from now." She laughed. "I might not be here."

We were seated at a round table in the far corner of the dining room, barely noticed by the other diners. Simpson began to tell a story about when he was a teenager and everyone fell silent.

"I smoked dope with this white chick I was trying to make it with, and then after we smoked I thought, I'll never become an athlete now, so I ran all the way home to get the pot out of my system." Then he began another story.

I asked Christie what attracted her to Simpson.

Christie glanced nervously at Simpson. Then she turned back to me and said, "I'm mature for my age, and he's an immature older guy who likes to play golf. That's a game for retired guys who want to escape reality." She looked at Simpson, who was talking. "O.J.'s into denial. He loved L.A. I hated L.A. It corrupts your soul. I loved growing up in Minnesota."

Simpson stopped talking and glared at her. "Yeah, that's why you couldn't wait to leave." He turned toward me, grinning lasciviously, and said, "You're into Christie, huh?" He raised his eyebrows. "Did you ever fool around on your wife? Everybody fools around and lies about it. Everyone lies. Look at Clinton. Deny, deny, deny."

Christie didn't speak again for the rest of the evening.

A few days later, on the telephone, Christie said, "I'm sorry I was very uncomfortable. O.J. told me to watch what I say with a writer." She paused. "O.J. feels he has to construct these elaborate lies. He tells me he went to the doctor when he was really playing golf. Why bother? I don't care if he plays golf."

She told me that she no longer believed that Simpson murdered his wife, but she did stand by everything she had said about him in her *National Enquirer* exposé. "I was angry," she said. "I had given up my life for him and had nothing to show for it. He told me there was no room in his life for a wife, or more kids. I want kids. And then someone offered me fifty thousand dollars to tell the truth. So I did it. I don't deny my drug use, or anything I said in it."

.   .   .

On the first day I spent with Simpson, he drove me back to my car late in the afternoon. "The thing I'm most proud of," he said, "is that the girls I dated were offered two hundred and fifty thousand dollars by the tabloids and not one single one of them said anything bad about me. . . . I expected the cops to lie. They were told not to investigate the case because no one in L.A. wanted to hear it. . . . And the media. They let me down the most. They got lazy and relied on police tips instead of investigating. During my trial, the truth was known, but no one would write it. It's a much better story if I'm guilty. They didn't look at anybody but me. I was set up."

Simpson stopped his Navigator at a red light across the street from the Wild Oats parking lot, where I'd left my car. He said, "I wonder if I've run into this person who killed Nicole. Have I talked to them? Do I see them every day?"

*   *   *

Ever since O. J. Simpson moved to south Florida (my home since '83) a few years ago, he has been in the news repeatedly for public fights with his girlfriend, for assaulting a motorist (he was acquitted) and, most recently, as the subject in an investigation of an ecstasy and money-laundering ring. Like a vampire, it seemed, O.J. and his public presence could not be killed until someone drove a wooden stake into his heart. Ironically, he seemed to relish his notoriety, as did his new attorney, Yale Galanter. A friend of mine at the Miami Herald *told me that Galanter was anxious to have a nationally prominent magazine do a profile of his client. So I called Galanter, and he told me he'd agree to my interviewing O.J. for a profile as long as I didn't ask him about Nicole's murder and guaranteed that the piece would run in either* The New York Times Magazine *or* The New Yorker. *I immediately called David Remnick, the* New Yorker *editor, and he gave me the assignment. I then spent over fifteen hours with O.J., on three different occasions, and never had to ask him a question. He talked nonstop, pathologically, about everything in his life, including his wife, Nicole, who, he assured me, had stalked him and been physically abusive to him. He also assured me that he was still searching for Nicole's murderer, but had yet to find him.*

FATAL BONDAGE
DAVID McCLINTICK

I have a feeling that inside you somewhere, there's something nobody knows about.
— *Shadow of a Doubt,* Alfred Hitchcock and Thornton Wilder

John "J.R." Robinson, a fleshy man of forty-one with wavy brown hair and a winning smile, left his four-acre estate in the horsey exurbs southwest of Kansas City, Missouri, and drove to an apartment in the city where he kept the woman he called his mistress. The trip from the rolling Kansas prairie across the Missouri border to the gritty, urban precincts of Troost Avenue took barely half an hour. It was still early on this Saturday morning in late May of 1985.

Robinson let himself into the brick apartment building—he had his own keys—and then into the apartment itself, a two-bedroom unit on the third floor. The woman in residence, Theresa Williams, twenty-one, had been asleep but bolted awake when Robinson barged into her bedroom.

J.R. grabbed Theresa by the hair, pulled her over his knee and started spanking her.

"You've been a real bad girl," he snarled. "You need to learn a lesson."

Theresa, momentarily speechless, started screaming. J.R. threw her to the floor and drew a revolver from a shoulder holster.

"If you don't shut up, I'll blow your brains out." He put the gun to her head and pulled the trigger. There was a loud click. The chamber was empty.

Cowering and crying softly now, Theresa stiffened as J.R. slid the gun down her torso and stuck the barrel into her vagina.

"I'll bet you've never had a blowout," he said.

"Don't do that!" she pleaded.

J.R. withdrew the gun from Theresa's body, holstered it and left the apartment as suddenly as he had entered. The terrified woman, her sobs slowly ebbing, did not summon help. She felt helpless. One did not cross J. R. Robinson.

J.R. drove from Troost Avenue back across the state line to his Kansas home, where he arrived in time to attend his teenage son's regular Saturday soccer game. To all appearances, J. R. Robinson was a doting father and husband. A skilled handyman, he had built a soccer goal in the family's spacious yard so his son could practice at home. He attended his daughter's flute recitals and band concerts, and refereed school volleyball games.

His neighbors knew J.R. as a successful businessman and entrepreneur, always talking of new ventures. He was a neighborhood activist, an officer of the residents' association and chairman of its rules committee. He was also a founding elder of the nearby Presbyterian Church

Neither his neighbors nor his children knew that J. R. Robinson led a second life—secret and sordid—dating back nearly two decades. (How much his wife knew was unclear, even years later.) J.R. was a swindler, an embezzler and a forger. He was a sexual predator, a deviant and a pimp. And in the mid-eighties in Kansas he was becoming something much more sinister—a murderer of women.

Indeed, J. R. Robinson is rare in the annals of American crime: a genial con man and a homicidal monster all in one. Unlike Ted Bundy or John Wayne Gacy, who chose their victims impulsively and killed them with dispatch, Robinson developed relationships with his. Using the Internet and his own considerable charm, he lured them to Kansas with offers of employment and sadomasochistic sex. He exploited them financially, enticing them into giving him their life savings and retirement accounts, cashing their disability checks and, in one case, selling a victim's baby to his brother and sister-in-law. Then, prosecutors allege, he beat at least five women to death with a blunt object, most likely a large hammer.

"I've dealt with a wide variety of characters, but never anyone like Robinson," says Stephen Haymes, forty-nine, who has been a probation officer for twenty-six years and who saw through Robinson far sooner than anyone else in law enforcement. "He's just chilling. There are so many sides to him. There is the con man after money. There is the murderer. There is the sexual deviant. There is the cover-up artist—the lies, endless lies."

The real Kansas belies its image. I know because I grew up there, as did my parents and grandparents. Kansas isn't nearly so flat as it appears from thirty-five thousand feet; the Flint Hills of eastern Kansas are craggy and stark. Kansas isn't bland; *Come Back, Little Sheba* and *Picnic*, by William Inge of Independence, Kansas (where my mother was born and her uncle was district attorney), reveal as much elemental human strife in small-town Kansas as in the urban East of Eugene O'Neill and the South of Tennessee Williams.

Kansas isn't peaceful either; murder and mayhem stain its history and stain it today. The cattle centers of Dodge City and Abilene (my father's hometown) were as violent as any other towns west of the Mississippi in the nineteenth century. In 1892 four members of the Dalton Gang were shot to pieces in Coffeyville, after trying to rob two banks in the same day. Staggering quantities of blood were spilled along the Missouri border in the 1850s when Missouri, a slave state, tried to impose its ways on Kansas. The antislavery zealot John Brown and his allies clashed so violently with proslavery forces that the region became known all the way to

Washington, D.C., as "Bleeding Kansas." In the twentieth century, too, Kansas saw more than its share of violence. The Ma Barker and Pretty Boy Floyd gangs crisscrossed the state in the 1930s. When Perry Smith and Richard Hickock drove to western Kansas in 1959 and slaughtered the Clutter family, chronicled in Truman Capote's *In Cold Blood,* they left from the town of Olathe (pronounced "Oh-*lay*-thuh"), Hickock's hometown, just a few minutes from where J. R. Robinson lived two decades later.

Still, Kansas retains a know-your-neighbor, help-your-neighbor quality of life that makes it seem different—even from adjacent Missouri—and gives the atrocities of John Robinson a special horror. This story presents the case against Robinson as reflected in a three-month *Vanity Fair* investigation, which includes detailed evidence gathered by Kansas and Missouri prosecutors and law-enforcement officers and set forth in court.

John Edward Robinson was born not in Kansas but in Cicero, Illinois, a blue-collar, mafia-tinged enclave on the west edge of Chicago, in 1943. He was the middle child of five. His father, Henry, was a machinist for Western Electric and a binge drinker. His mother, Alberta, was the family disciplinarian and turned young John into a teenage star—at least briefly. When he was thirteen in the fall of 1957, he enrolled in the Quigley Preparatory Seminary in the heart of downtown Chicago, a five-year academy for Catholic boys. That same fall he made the rank of Eagle Scout and flew to London to lead a group of 120 Boy Scouts onto the stage of the Palladium theater to appear in a command performance of a Scout variety show before Queen Elizabeth II. According to a *Chicago Tribune* article at the time, unearthed much later by the *Kansas City Star,* Robinson was selected for the honor "because of his scholastic ability, scouting experience, and poise. . . . He also has an engaging smile." Backstage he met Judy Garland. "We Americans gotta stick together," young Robinson told her.

Robinson's smile and choirboy mien were on display in that year's Quigley yearbook. He did not appear in subsequent yearbooks, however, and seemed to disappear for a time, according to investigators who have probed his background. Robinson attended a Cicero junior college in 1961 and studied medical X-ray technology. He did not graduate, and next surfaced three years later in Kansas City, Missouri. He was twenty-one and had married a woman named Nancy Jo Lynch.

It wasn't long before John Robinson ran afoul of the law. He was employed as a laboratory technician and office manager by a Kansas City physician, Wallace Graham, who had been President Harry Truman's personal doctor. In June 1967, Graham reported to the Kansas City police that Robinson had embezzled about $33,000 from him by manipulating checks and deposits. Robinson was prosecuted and found guilty by a jury of "stealing by means of deceit." He avoided jail, but was placed on probation for three years.

While on probation, Robinson got a job as a manager of a television-rental company. He stole merchandise and was fired but not prosecuted. In 1969 he went to work as a systems analyst for the Mobil Oil Corporation, which wasn't aware that he was on probation.

In choosing not to inform Mobil of Robinson's background, his probation officer said in a memorandum to the Missouri Board of Probation and Parole that Robinson "does not appear to be an individual who is basically inclined towards criminal activities and is motivated towards achieving middle class values." Another officer stated on August 13, 1970, that Robinson was "responding extremely well to probation supervision" and she was "encouraging [him] to advance as far as possible with Mobil Oil."

Precisely two weeks later Mobil Oil discovered that Robinson had stolen 6,200 U.S. postage stamps from the company. He was fired, reported to the police, and charged with theft. The following month, Robinson and his wife moved back to his home city of Chicago, where he got a job with a company called Illinois R. B. Jones. Within a month he was stealing again; he embezzled $5,500 over six months before he was caught and fired. Robinson's father gave him the money to make restitution, so Illinois authorities dismissed criminal charges.

Robinson and his wife moved back to the Kansas City area, where he was arrested for violating the terms of his probation and thrown in jail "to provide a strong motivation for a complete reversal in his behavior," wrote Gordon Morris, a Missouri probation officer. Robinson was released after only a few weeks and his probation was extended five years—to 1976.

Probation authorities still believed that "prognosis in this case is good," as they stated in an April 1973 report. They did not know that Robinson was already stealing again, this time from his next-door neighbor Evalee McKnight, a retired schoolteacher who gave Robinson $30,000 to invest, according to police records I reviewed in Kansas. She never saw the money again.

Oblivious to all of this, Missouri probation authorities discharged Robinson from probation in 1974, two years early.

Around this time Robinson started a company he called Professional Service Association Inc. (P.S.A.), purportedly to provide financial and budget consultation to physicians in the Kansas City area. Two groups of doctors at the University of Kansas medical school hired him to manage their financial affairs. The doctor who interviewed Robinson later told the *Kansas City Star*, "He made a very good impression: well-dressed, nice-looking . . . seemed to know a lot, very glib, good speaker." The doctors dismissed Robinson after only a few months, however, because of irregularities in his handling of their finances.

But that didn't stop Robinson, who was sending letters to potential investors in P.S.A., portraying a growing, healthy company. One letter suggested that Marion Laboratories, founded by Ewing M. Kauffman, then owner of the Kansas City Royals baseball team, was negotiating to purchase P.S.A. It wasn't.

Federal authorities got wind of the scheme, and a U.S. grand jury indicted John Robinson on four counts of securities and mail fraud. In June 1976 a federal judge fined him $2,500 and placed him on three years' probation. It was his third such sentence in six years. He had served only a few weeks in jail. And authorities didn't even know of all the crimes committed by Robinson, a pathological thief dodging easily through the system.

In 1977, John Robinson, now thirty-four, moved his growing family—he and Nancy by this time had four children—a few miles across the state line into Kansas. They bought a nine-room house on four acres in a neighborhood called Pleasant Valley Farms, in the southern reaches of Johnson County, which stretched south and west into Kansas from the Missouri border. It was one of the richest counties in the United States, 480 square miles of sleek suburban affluence—some of the towns had Shawnee names, such as Lenexa (for the wife of an Indian chief), and the county seat, Olathe ("beautiful"). The people of Johnson County felt a bit superior to their Missouri neighbors, and once you crossed into Kansas there was a different feeling. The light seemed brighter, the landscape less dingy. The Kansans were richer, smarter, nicer, gentler.

Pleasant Valley Farms, with its vistas across rolling hills, stands of elm and maple trees, bridle path and lake stocked with fish, felt rural and remote, even though it was less than an hour's drive northeast to downtown Kansas City. The Robinsons' new home was a modern asymmetrical structure of wood, brick and stone on four levels with two big stone fireplaces. It nestled in the middle of the property, with a horse stable and corral at the back, against a tree line along the ridge of a low hill. The Oregon and Santa Fe Trails, along which thousands of settlers had made their way west in the nineteenth century, coincided in eastern Kansas, and their route traced the back of the Robinsons' property.

John Robinson had a new career to go with his new home— hydroponics, a method of growing vegetables in a controlled nutrient-rich indoor environment. He started a company, Hydro-Gro Inc., and produced a sixty-four-page booklet, *Fun with Home Hobby Hydroponics:* "We hope that as you read this book you will form an acquaintance with John Robinson as a sensitive and stimulating human being," the introduction said, portraying Robinson as "one of the nation's pioneers in indoor home hydroponics" and a "sought after lecturer, consultant and author."

Whatever they thought of hydroponics, Robinson's new neighbors found him intelligent and energetic, conversing knowledgeably about international finance and other business matters at local picnics. In addition to helping run the neighborhood association, he was a visible neighbor, working in his yard a lot, installing a rail fence and a pond. His children—John junior, who was fourteen years old; Kimberly, twelve; and twins Christopher and Christine ("Chris" and "Chrissie"), who were eight—were well behaved and popular. John junior helped his father with work around the property. Chris and Chrissie took care of the dogs and cats of their neighbors Margaret and Jim Adams when the Adamses traveled. Margaret Adams enjoyed having Chrissie come over and pick strawberries in the garden.

John Robinson's neighborhood activism extended to civic activism, or so it appeared. GROUP FOR DISABLED HONORS AREA MAN headlined the *Kansas City Times* on December 8, 1977. The article reported that John Robinson, president of Hydro-Gro Inc., had been named "Man of the Year" for his work with the handicapped. He headed the board of a "sheltered workshop," which employed disabled people, the newspaper said. The award, a "proclamation" signed by the mayor of Kansas City, turned out to be one of the more bizarre episodes in Robinson's checkered career. Two weeks after the newspaper report, it was revealed that Robinson had orchestrated the award himself through a complex sequence of fake letters of recommendation he had sent to city hall. The *Kansas City Star*, then the afternoon counterpart of the *Times*, revealed the ruse in a story headlined MAN-OF-THE-YEAR PLOY BACKFIRES ON "HONOREE."

As his neighbors in Pleasant Valley Farms got to know John Robinson better, they noticed that he could be prickly and even mean when upset. Margaret Adams, an avid gardener, recalls that she once asked him to demonstrate his hydroponics system. He gladly complied and was pleasant until she told him that she felt his price for the system was too high. "You've wasted my time—you're small potatoes," he snapped, abruptly terminating the encounter.

Robinson nearly came to blows with another neighbor over a misbehaving dog. And he became disenchanted with the neighborhood association, accusing it in a formal letter of being "invalid" when, in his opinion, it failed to enforce some of its rules. "He was cocky and arrogant," another neighbor told me. "You needed to walk on eggs around him."

Robinson liked to control his surroundings. Neighbors occasionally heard him yelling at his wife and children, ordering them about like a drill sergeant. The children followed his orders and seemed to thrive on the discipline, becoming model citizens who adored their father. Nancy, however, began divorce proceedings, and the marriage survived only after counseling.

In 1980, Robinson, while continuing to run Hydro-Gro, took a job as the director of personnel at a Kansas City subsidiary of Borden Inc., the global food company. Borden did not check Robinson's background. Within a few months the company caught Robinson stealing—again by manipulating checks and bank deposits to divert funds to his financial company, P.S.A. The losses totaled more than $40,000, part of which Robinson spent on an Olathe apartment where he conducted sexual liaisons with two women who worked for Borden, police records and internal Borden documents show. "John kind of swept me off my feet," one of the women told a police detective in a formal interrogation. "He treated me like a queen. . . . He always had money to take me to nice restaurants and hotels."

Fully cognizant of Robinson's criminal record, the Missouri authorities still coddled him. He faced a maximum sentence of seven years, but spent only two months in prison and was again placed on probation, this time for five years.

The Borden scandal caused hardly a ripple in Robinson's neighborhood, where he managed to bluff it through as a misunderstanding over a business matter. He went on running Hydro-Gro and set up another company, Equi-Plus, which purported to offer management-consulting services. One of Equi-Plus's first customers in the early eighties was a company called Back Care Systems, which ran seminars for corporations on treatment of back pain. Back Care hired Equi-Plus to develop a marketing plan. When the company began getting invoices from Equi-Plus that appeared to be inflated or in some cases bogus, it reported Robinson to the Johnson County district attorney's office, which began a criminal investigation. Robinson's lawyer advised him to obtain sworn affidavits attesting to the legitimacy of the invoices. Robinson did so. He faked the affidavits.

Undaunted by the investigation of Equi-Plus, John Robinson created another company, Equi-II, as an umbrella corporation to absorb Equi-Plus and engage in a variety of business and "philanthropic" ventures. He had used his previous companies to perpetrate financial fraud and theft, but his new company would serve an additional, more sinister purpose: luring young women to their deaths.

One of the people he hired to work for him, in 1984, was Paula Godfrey, a pretty dark-haired young woman who had graduated from high school in Olathe the previous year. Robinson told Godfrey, an honor student and accomplished figure skater, that he would enroll her in a training course in Texas and pay all her expenses. On the day of her scheduled departure, Robinson picked her up at her parents' home in Overland Park, a Johnson County suburb, to go to the airport. After not hearing from her for several days, the Godfreys reported to the police that their daughter was missing. The police checked with Robinson, who disclaimed any knowledge of her whereabouts. Shortly thereafter, the police received a letter purportedly signed by Paula Godfrey stating that she was "OK" and that she did not want to see her family. Having no contrary evidence, the police suspended their investigation. It was a decision they would come to regret. Many people now believe that Paula Godfrey was Robinson's first murder victim.

Robinson soon offered help to other young women. In December 1984 he presented himself to social workers at the Truman Medical Center, the leading public hospital in Kansas City, and to an organization called Birthright, which counseled unwed, pregnant young women and aided them after delivery of their babies. Robinson told both groups that he and several other businessmen in Olathe and Overland Park had started an organization called Kansas City Outreach. It provided housing for young unwed mothers and their babies, Robinson said, as well as job training and baby-sitting. Robinson invited Truman Medical Center and Birthright to submit candidates for the services and said the program would likely receive funding from Xerox, IBM and other major corporations.

In early January 1985, Truman Medical Center put Robinson in touch with a nineteen-year-old woman named Lisa Stasi, who had just given birth to a daughter, Tiffany. Lisa and her husband, Carl, had separated. Robinson indicated that he would house Lisa and Tiffany at an apartment he had rented on Troost Avenue, an area of small businesses and apartments in south Kansas City. When Robinson spoke to Stasi directly, he told her that his name was John Osborne and that he could help her get a high-school equivalency diploma and job training not only in Kansas City but in Chicago and Denver as well. Instead of putting her up at the Troost Avenue apartment, Robinson installed Lisa and Tiffany at a Rodeway Inn in Overland Park.

On January 8, Robinson told Stasi that he had arranged for her and the baby to travel to Chicago in a day or two. In preparation, Robinson had Stasi sign four blank sheets of stationery and give him the addresses of her relatives. He would notify them of her whereabouts, he said, because she would be too busy in Chicago to write letters.

Stasi spent several hours that day and the next with Kansas City relatives who tried to dissuade her from going to Chicago. How well did she really know John Osborne? they asked. "He is a gentleman," she replied. On the afternoon of January 9, Robinson drove from Overland Park through a heavy snowstorm to pick up Stasi at the home of her sister-in-law, Kathy Klinginsmith, in Kansas City. Angry that she had left the Rodeway Inn, he insisted that they leave immediately. Stasi, carrying Tiffany, accompanied Robinson, whom she still knew as John Osborne, to his car, leaving most of her belongings and her own car at her sister-in-law's. As Klinginsmith watched the man take Lisa off into the snow, she would later say in court, "I was *afraid* of him. I knew deep down that was the last time I would see Lisa."

The next morning Klinginsmith telephoned the Rodeway Inn where Stasi had been staying. A clerk said that she had checked out and her bill had been settled by a John Robinson, not John Osborne, with a corporate credit card in the name of Equi-II. Klinginsmith's fear deepened into panic.

There was a festive party that evening at the Robinsons' home in Pleasant Valley Farms. John Robinson's brother and sister-in-law, Don and Helen Robinson, had been trying for years to adopt a baby. John had told them that he had connections in Kansas City who might help. That morning they had flown from Chicago to Kansas City, where John met them at the airport and took them to the offices of Equi-II in Overland Park. Don and Helen signed what looked like official adoption papers and paid John $5,500 in cash. He then drove them to his home, where Nancy awaited them with a healthy female infant in her arms. John had brought the baby home unannounced the previous evening, Nancy recalled later in court. A photograph of the occasion shows the happy extended family celebrating in John and Nancy's living room. At the center of the picture, looking every inch a godfather, is John Robinson with the baby on his lap.

John confided to Don and Helen that the baby had become

available for adoption when her mother had committed suicide. The new parents named the baby Heather and the next day, January 11, flew back to Chicago, not knowing that Heather already had a name, Tiffany Stasi.

That same day Kathy Klinginsmith's husband, David, appeared at the offices of Equi-II in Overland Park and confronted Robinson on the whereabouts of Lisa Stasi and Tiffany. Robinson physically ejected David Klinginsmith from the office. Kathy, meanwhile, drove to the Overland Park Police Department and reported her sister-in-law and the baby missing.

Robinson's approach to Birthright had been more problematic, because Ann Smith, the Birthright employee to whom Robinson had first spoken, grew suspicious. Robinson had told her that Kansas City Outreach was supported by the Presbyterian Church he had helped found near his home in Pleasant Valley Farms. He also told her that his program's supporters included an Olathe bank on whose board of directors he sat.

Smith called both the church and the bank. The church acknowledged that Robinson was a member, but said it had no connection to any program to help unwed mothers. The bank said Robinson was not on its board; it had never heard of him.

Smith made more inquiries, which eventually, on December 18, 1984, led her to a district supervisor of the Missouri Board of Probation and Parole, a slim, mustachioed, soft-spoken man named Stephen Haymes, then thirty-two years old. Missouri born and bred, he had majored in sociology and criminal justice in college. When poor eyesight had barred him from many jobs in law enforcement, he had settled on a career as a probation officer.

Haymes, taking Ann Smith's call in Missouri, had never heard of Robinson, who was supervised by a Kansas probation officer in

Olathe. He pulled Robinson's file and perused his lengthy criminal record. After checking with his Kansas counterpart, who reported no problems with Robinson, Haymes sent a letter to Robinson ordering him to report to the Missouri probation office on January 17, 1985. Robinson did not show up. Haymes sent him another letter, registered this time, ordering an appearance on January 24.

Haymes also telephoned a contact in the Kansas City field office of the Federal Bureau of Investigation, a supervisor with whom he had worked in the past, to ask if the FBI was investigating Robinson or was aware of any "baby selling rings" operating in the Kansas City area. The answer to both questions was no, though the supervisor said the bureau was "aware" of John Robinson.

Robinson arrived at Haymes's office promptly at 1 P.M. on January 24. At five feet nine and two hundred pounds, Robinson reminded Haymes of the Pillsbury dough boy, though he was more nattily dressed. He was friendly and deferential and had an answer for just about everything. Yes, he had met with Birthright, as part of an effort by several of his "business associates" to "help the community." No, he had not told Birthright that the Presbyterian Church was behind the effort. The Birthright people had misunderstood; they had asked him what church he attended and he had told them. Robinson volunteered that he also had met with social workers from the Truman Medical Center and that they had placed two young women in an apartment he had rented on Troost Avenue. Haymes was welcome to visit the apartment and speak with the residents, Robinson said.

Robinson's mention of Truman Medical Center was the first Haymes had heard that Robinson's efforts had gone beyond Birthright, according to contemporaneous notes Haymes kept and I reviewed. In subsequent days, the probation officer spoke to the Truman Medical social workers and learned that their clients in the Troost Avenue apartment were doing well. However, another young woman, Lisa Stasi, whom Truman had referred to Robinson, seemed to have disappeared, and the Overland Park police were looking for her. Truman Medical was concerned.

Haymes called an Overland Park detective, who said they had found no evidence of wrongdoing in the Stasi case and weren't pursuing it. The detective mentioned, however, that a second young woman who had worked for Robinson, Paula Godfrey, had been reported missing a few months earlier. The detective recounted the letter the police had received, purportedly from Godfrey, saying she was OK and didn't want to see her family. The police weren't pursuing that case, either.

Steve Haymes was skeptical. From Stasi's relatives he learned that Robinson had her sign four blank sheets of stationery. Two letters arriving shortly after she disappeared looked suspicious. They didn't sound like Lisa. And they were typed. Lisa didn't know how to type.

Haymes asked Robinson where Stasi was. Robinson claimed she had run off to Colorado with a guy named "Bill."

Haymes was now deeply concerned. It was conceivable that Robinson, already a pathological con man, had metastasized into a killer of vulnerable young women. Haymes called the FBI supervisor again. "You need to take a look at this," Haymes said. "We've got two women and a baby missing. We've got Robinson crossing state lines." The supervisor assigned two agents to begin an inquiry.

Over the next few weeks, Special Agent Thomas Lavin, a veteran of the FBI, and his young partner, Special Agent Jeffrey Dancer, who had been an agent less than a year, began pooling their efforts with the now relentless Haymes. They discovered that Robinson was involved in an astonishing variety of ongoing criminal activities in the Kansas City underworld. Robinson and a fellow ex-convict, Irvin "Irv" Blattner, were under investigation by the U.S. Secret

Service for forging the signature on and cashing a government check. Haymes and the FBI learned as well of the investigation in Johnson County, Kansas, where the district attorney was building a case that Robinson's company Equi-II had defrauded Back Care Systems.

It was around this time that Robinson developed a strong taste for sadomasochistic sex—generally defined as sexual activity between two people who agree that one will be dominant and the other submissive in seeking enhanced sexual pleasure through bondage and the infliction of pain through such means as spanking and whipping of the submissive by the dominant.

Sadomasochistic sex, or S&M, is also known by the abbreviation BDSM, for "bondage discipline sadomasochism," or simply D&S, "dominance and submission." Some 5 to 10 percent of American adults regularly engage in some form of D&S, according to Gloria and William Brame and Jon Jacobs, the authors of the 1993 book *Different Loving: The World of Sexual Dominance & Submission.*

J. R. Robinson not only engaged in BDSM himself, he saw it as a means to make money. He apparently was organizing a ring of prostitutes for customers interested in S&M, and using a male stripper, nicknamed M&M, to find women for him. In this circle of people, Robinson was known as "J.R."

None of the investigative trails led to Lisa Stasi and her baby, or to Paula Godfrey. Still, it was clear to Haymes and the FBI agents that Robinson was up to no good on several fronts. Haymes ordered Robinson in for another visit.

"Why is everyone making such a big deal when I'm only trying to help people?" Robinson complained, according to Haymes's notes. "By the way," he told Haymes, "Lisa Stasi has been found. She's okay. Tiffany, the baby, everybody's okay."

Robinson claimed he had heard from a local woman for whom Stasi recently had baby-sat. She and Tiffany definitely were in the Kansas City area. That story collapsed, however, when FBI agent Lavin and an Overland Park detective spoke to the woman in question. After rigorous questioning she admitted that the story of Stasi baby-sitting for her was false: Robinson had asked her to tell the lie if the police asked. Her incentive to cooperate: she owed J.R. money, and he had photographed her nude as a prospective prostitute.

The FBI decided to deploy a female agent to contact Robinson and pose as a prostitute looking for work. Wired to secretly record their conversation, the agent met Robinson for lunch in an Overland Park restaurant. He told her that his clients were mainly lawyers, doctors and judges, and that she could earn $2,000 to $3,000 a weekend traveling to Denver or Dallas to service them, or $1,000 a night in the Kansas City area. As an S&M practitioner, she would have to undergo pain such as having her nipples manipulated with pliers, Robinson said. After hearing the recording of the conversation, the FBI decided against proceeding with the undercover effort for the time being out of fear for the agent's safety.

Irv Blattner, however, agreed to help the authorities make a case against Robinson in exchange for lenient treatment in the government-check-forgery investigation. The FBI advised Truman Medical Center to remove its two young women from Robinson's Troost Avenue apartment, but to give Robinson a plausible excuse.

One of the women whom the male stripper M&M had introduced to Robinson as a candidate for prostitution was Theresa Williams, an attractive twenty-one-year-old itinerant from Boise, Idaho, who had been working odd jobs around Kansas City and looking for the main chance. Robinson took her to an Overland Park hotel room, where he photographed her nude and offered her a position as his "mistress," a job that would involve sexual services not only for him but for others as well. He would put her up in an apartment and pay all her expenses, plus prostitution fees. He would supply her with marijuana and amphetamines. Williams took the job.

On the night of April 30, 1985, J.R. gave Williams $1,200 in cash, outfitted her in a fancy, alluring dress, and told her to wait in a park across the street from the Troost Avenue apartment. A limousine picked her up. The driver blindfolded her and took her to a mansion somewhere in the Kansas City area. She was turned over to a distinguished looking, sixtyish gray-haired man who was called "the judge." He escorted her to the basement, which was outfitted as a "dungeon" for sadomasochistic sex, or "brutality and other unnatural sex acts," as Williams later put it. The man had her disrobe, and then began stretching her on a medieval rack. She screamed in panic and demanded that he allow her to leave. She was blindfolded again and returned to the Troost Avenue apartment, where, a few days later, she was forced to return the $1,200 to an angry John Robinson.

She incurred J.R.'s wrath further when he found out that she had been entertaining a boyfriend—not one of Robinson's customers—at the apartment. It was behavior such as this that prompted his early-morning visit on a Saturday in late May when he allegedly assaulted her with his gun.

They made up, however, and J.R. promised to take her on a trip to the Virgin Islands in mid-June.

On June 7, Lavin and Dancer paid an unannounced call on Williams. At first she told the agents a cover story—that she worked for Equi-II and was being trained in data processing. But after Lavin and Dancer told her that they had reason to believe Robinson had been involved in the disappearance of at least two young women, Williams began to cry, and the agents were able to coax a more believable story from her—how Robinson had assaulted her with his gun, and how he now planned to take her to the Virgin Islands. And one more thing: at J.R.'s insistence, Williams had been fabricating a diary accusing his friend Irv Blattner of committing various crimes and of threatening her life. Robinson seemed to have sensed that the police were going to use Blattner to implicate him in crimes, and he wanted to use the fake diary to discredit his partner. J.R. had written it out, and Williams had copied it as her own.

As Lavin and Dancer were questioning Williams, they heard a key unlocking the front door. Robinson entered the apartment. The FBI agents identified themselves. Lavin held up J.R.'s draft of the diary and asked if it was his handwriting. Robinson acknowledged that it was. The agents frisked him for weapons but found none. Robinson said he was in a hurry and left the apartment. The agents made no move to stop him. After he had gone, however, they insisted on moving Williams to another location to be kept secret from Robinson. They felt her life might be in danger. Like Stasi and Godfrey, Williams had been asked to sign blank sheets of stationery.

Lavin and Dancer summoned Steve Haymes, who helped interrogate Robinson and then filed a formal report with the Missouri court that had jurisdiction over Robinson's probation. Haymes alleged that Robinson had violated the terms of his probation by carrying a gun, supplying drugs to Theresa Williams and lying to his probation officer. Haymes asked the court to revoke the probation and jail Robinson.

A judge did just that after a hearing, but Robinson was released on bail pending appeal. The FBI kept Williams hidden, gave her money, and finally bought her a one-way plane ticket out of town. The Missouri Court of Appeals later overturned the district judge's ruling on the ironic grounds that Robinson's constitutional rights had been violated: he had not been allowed to adequately confront his accuser, Theresa Williams.

It was amazing to the frustrated Haymes and the FBI agents that J. R. Robinson was free. To the world at large, he was still a thriving Kansas business entrepreneur with a sumptuous office in Overland Park and a four-acre estate in Pleasant Valley Farms. Just days after the probation-violation hearing, which received no publicity, Robinson was featured on the cover of *Farm Journal,* a nationally circulated, widely read monthly agricultural magazine. He had persuaded the editors that he was an expert on agriculture finance.

In Kansas, however, Robinson finally came a cropper. After a long investigation, the Johnson County district attorney charged him with fraud in bilking Back Care Systems. A jury convicted him in January 1986. He was then convicted of a second fraud, against an Overland Park man in connection with an Arizona real-estate deal. Because of Robinson's extensive prior criminal record, a Johnson County judge sentenced him to serve between six and nineteen years in prison as a habitual criminal. After appeals, he finally went to prison in Kansas in May 1987.

At about this time, another young woman whom Robinson had employed in the early months of that year was reported missing. Catherine Clampitt, twenty-seven, had moved to Kansas from Wichita Falls, Texas, after answering a newspaper ad in which Robinson had promised a "great job, a lot of traveling and a new wardrobe," according to Clampitt's brother, Robert Bales, with whose family she lived in Overland Park. Clampitt, whom Bales described as intelligent with a "wild side," often stayed at local hotels for several nights at a time. In mid-1987, after she inexplicably disappeared for weeks, Bales called the police. There was insufficient evidence to link her disappearance to Robinson, who was on his way to prison in Kansas.

Robinson found that his intelligence and persuasive manner worked as well in prison as out. He was an exemplary inmate. After psychological and mental testing showed his intelligence to be well above average, he was put to work as the coordinator of the prison's maintenance-operations office. There he developed computer programs that would save the Kansas prison system up to $100,000 a year.

Robinson suffered a series of minor strokes while in prison, and during treatment he made an exceptional impression on the prison medical staff. In a nine-page "Report of Clinical and Medical Evaluation," dated November 1, 1990, two ranking doctors, Ky Hoang, M.D., director of medical services, and George M. Penn, M.D., supervising psychiatrist, wrote that John Robinson was a "model inmate who . . . has made the best of his incarceration. . . . He is a non-violent person and does not present a threat to society. . . . He is a devoted family man who has taught his children a strong value system."

Kansas paroled Robinson in January 1991 after less than four years, but he still faced prison time in Missouri for violating his probation from the Borden fraud a decade earlier. His probation officer was still Steve Haymes, who now stood alone, as the FBI had moved on to other cases. Haymes hadn't forgotten Robinson, nor had he forgotten Paula Godfrey and Lisa and Tiffany Stasi. Though Missouri prison doctors agreed with their Kansas counterparts that Robinson should be freed, Haymes warned against it.

"I believe him to be a con-man out of control," Haymes wrote in an official memorandum to a colleague in 1991. "He leaves in his wake many unanswered questions and missing persons. . . . I have observed Robinson's sociopathic tendencies, habitual criminal behavior, inability to tell the truth and scheming to cover his own actions at the expense of others. . . . I was not surprised to see he had a good institutional adjustment in Kansas considering that he is quite bright and a white-collar con-man capable of being quite personable and friendly to those around him."

Haymes predicted that Robinson would use his medical problems "to his advantage." Robinson was imprisoned in Missouri, and sure enough, two of the people he promptly befriended in the penitentiary were the prison doctor, William Bonner, and his forty-seven-year-old wife, Beverly, the prison librarian. She gave Robinson a job in the library.

Missouri kept Robinson in prison for two more years. He was released in the spring of 1993. He was forty-nine years old. Since his income had stopped during his six years in prison, his wife, Nancy, had been forced to sell their estate in Pleasant Valley Farms. She had taken a job as the manager of a mobile-home development in Belton, Missouri, a suburb south of Kansas City. The development was called Southfork, after the large family home on the *Dallas* television series, popular in the seventies and eighties. All its streets were named for *Dallas* characters: Sue Ellen Avenue, Cliff Barnes Lane, and so forth. J.R. joined her there when he left prison.

It was a real comedown from Pleasant Valley Farms, but the Robinsons soldiered on. Their two older children were grown, and the twins were in college, so J.R. and Nancy could make do with less room. They rented lockers at a nearby storage facility for their overflow belongings.

Despite his model behavior in prison, Robinson soon reverted to his old ways. A few months after his release from the Missouri penitentiary, Beverly Bonner, the prison librarian, left her husband, filed for divorce and in 1994 moved to the Kansas City area and joined forces with Robinson. He gave her the title of president of Hydro-Gro Inc., his hydroponics company, which he had reconstituted. Her mother began getting letters, apparently from Beverly, saying her job with Hydro-Gro was taking her to various cities abroad. She never gave a return address, but directed that all her mail, including her alimony checks, be sent to a post-office box in Olathe. Unbeknownst to William Bonner or any of Beverly's relatives, J. R. Robinson picked up the checks.

No one heard from Beverly Bonner after January of 1994.

Sheila Faith told friends she had met her "dream man" in John Robinson, though she didn't give his last name. Robinson likely found Faith through a personal advertisement in a newspaper. Her husband had died of cancer, leaving her with a teenage daughter, Debbie, who was wheelchair-bound with spina bifida. Sheila and Debbie lived in Pueblo, Colorado, on disability payments from Social Security. Sheila was a "very lonely person—she needed companions," a friend later told the *Kansas City Star*. John "promised her the world. He told her he was going to take her on a cruise, that he would take care of her daughter, that she'd never have to work, that money was no problem," the friend recalled.

The Faiths had planned to travel to Texas in the summer of 1994 and stop in Kansas to see Robinson on the way. But without warning early in the summer he drove to Colorado and picked them up in the middle of the night. They were never seen again. It was later learned that their disability checks were being delivered to a postal box in Olathe, Kansas. As with Beverly Bonner, John Robinson picked up the checks.

Pursuing his interest in S&M, Robinson began placing and monitoring advertisements in the *Pitch Weekly*, a so-called alternative newspaper in Kansas City, whose back pages feature personals columns called "Romance—The Dating Connection" for people seeking conventional relationships, and the "Wildside" for those who prefer the unconventional.

Around September 1, 1995, Robinson spotted an ad which read, "MASTERFUL, SUCCESSFUL, ENTREPRENEURIAL SWM, 35–50, sought by successful, rubenesque beauty."

Robinson left a voice mail and the "rubenesque beauty" called him back. She went only by the name Chloe Elizabeth to conceal her identity as a successful, well-known, college-educated businesswoman in Topeka, Kansas. A driven careerist, never married, accustomed to "dominating" in her business life, she had "decided it was time to seek what [I] truly wanted in [my] personal life—a Dominant with whom I could give up control of the personal side of my life and obey a worthy man who would advance my sexual and personal journey beyond what I was willing to admit wanting on my own."

Chloe Elizabeth tells me her story, referring to notes, in front of a fire in her spacious home on a cold January day in Topeka.

"I was looking for someone who was in business for himself because I believe that provides a dynamic and a personality that I'm seeking—one that I understand, one that I'm like. [J.R.] made me feel he was pretty close to the type of man I like to date. We had many phone conversations before we actually met for the first time."

Chloe Elizabeth asked Robinson to send her documents to prove he was who he said he was. "I'm not at all a paranoid person, but in a relationship of D&S, where you're sincere about what you're doing, you really need to know the person you're going to give the control up to is someone who will take good care of you."

J.R. sent Chloe Elizabeth (by now she had told him her real name and address) an array of material designed to portray him in

the best possible light—Chicago newspaper accounts of his appearance before the queen in London as a thirteen-year-old Eagle
Scout; his hydroponics booklet; a Kansas University brochure pic-
turing two of his attractive children; his appearance on the cover
of *Farm Journal*; and the "proclamation" naming him "Man of the
Year."

Of course, there was no indication of J.R.'s criminal past, no hint
that the "Man of the Year" award had been arranged by fakery.
Chloe Elizabeth was impressed, and invited J.R. to come to her
home at 2 P.M. on October 25, 1995. By then, nearly two months
after their first conversation, she and J.R. had discussed their sexual
preferences extensively by phone, and she knew what he, as her
"dominant" or "master," expected of her: "I was to meet him at
the door wearing only a sheer robe, a black mesh thong pantie, a
matching demicup bra, thigh-high stockings, and black high
heels. My eyes were to be made up dark, and lips red. I was to kneel
before him.

"He was wearing a dark-navy, single-breasted business suit, a
starched light-blue shirt with gold cuff links, burgundy striped tie
and polished shoes. Once inside the door, he took a leather studded
collar from his jacket and placed it around my neck and attached a
long leash to the collar.

"I took him first to the library and a large king chair in front of
the fire. Next to it I had put his drink of choice—scotch on the
rocks. He drew me to him and we kissed for the first time. After
some relaxed small talk, I led him through the rest of the house,
ending up in my bedroom on the third floor. There he asked me to
remove the few items of clothing I was wearing—one at a time,
except for the stockings.

"He then took from his pocket a 'contract for slavery' giving my consent to use me as a sexual toy in any way he wished and to punish me in any way he saw fit.

"I read the contract and signed it. He asked if I was sure. I said yes—very sure.

"He put the contract back in his pocket and asked me to remove all of his clothes except his pants. Then he asked me to lie facedown on the bed and spread my arms and legs as wide as I could. Using rope he had brought, he tied my wrists to the head of the bed and my ankles to the foot of the bed.

"Once he had me tied, he asked me to try to move. I couldn't. He then removed his belt and began to whip me across my bottom, slowly and lightly. I could feel excitement flowing across my skin. Then the blows got harder and closer together. It was painful and I cried. He then lay down beside me and cuddled me and comforted me and told me he loved me.

"He untied the ropes around my wrists and ankles and instructed me to kneel on the bed in front of him. My punishment training for the day was not over. He took a spool of smaller rope as he talked about 'training' my large breasts. I wanted to please him. He said that the breasts to be pleasing and well trained must be able to endure pain and to wear marks. He began to wrap the rope tightly around the base of the breast. He wrapped it so tightly that it bulged and turned reddish purple. He crossed the rope in the middle of my chest and began wrapping the other breast. Now both my breasts were like large ripe tomatoes . . . red and ready to burst. The nipples were erect and brown. He took clamps and put one on each nipple. The pain was severe. He thrust the solid leather strap of his belt down upon the top of my breasts. The pain caused the nipples to expand and become unimaginably restricted by the clamps. Engorged to about three times their normal size, the nipples turned purple and blue. He strapped my breasts again. Only those swats, there would be no more today. To show my gratefulness to his attention, he required one more duty. He stood before the bed and removed his pants. He required that I perform oral sex.

"That was the first date. It was sensational! He had an ability to command, to control, to corral someone as strong and aggressive and spirited as I am."

I asked Chloe Elizabeth if pain is always part of a BDSM relationship.

"It depends on what you consider pain. I wasn't interested in being beaten. I don't love pain. Some women in this lifestyle love pain. For me, there comes a physical state that you're in where what one might consider pain on your body isn't painful. It's exciting."

Before he left, Robinson told Chloe Elizabeth she had been "stupid" for allowing him to do all he had done. "I could have killed you," he said. Though she hadn't told him, Chloe Elizabeth never felt threatened by J.R., even when she was tied defenseless to her bed. That's because she had stationed a male friend in the house to be alert for any sign of excessive behavior. He made a note of J.R.'s license-plate number while Chloe Elizabeth and J.R. were upstairs.

J.R. and Chloe Elizabeth began seeing each other at least twice a week. But she gradually became suspicious of him. Through a contact in state government, she ran his license plates and found that his car was registered in his wife's name as well as his own. He had told her he was divorced. After they had pledged their love for each other repeatedly, J.R. suggested to Chloe Elizabeth that they should exchange lists of all their assets. She balked, suspecting this was a first step by J.R. to get his hands on her money.

In BDSM relationships, dominants sometimes take control of submissives' financial assets. A sample master-slave contract featured on a BDSM Web site stipulates, "All of the slave's possessions . . . belong to the master, including all assets, finances, and material goods."

"It is not unusual for [the relationship] to include financial decisions," says Jes Beard, a Chattanooga, Tennessee, lawyer who has represented four clients in BDSM relationships, including a woman who had a relationship with Robinson. The woman, who met him on the Internet, says she gave him $17,000 from an IRA to invest for her and never saw it again. "The dominant will tell them, Here's where you need to do your banking, here's the insurance you need, here's the whatever," Beard told me.

Another lawyer for BDSM clients, Lloyd E. N. Hall of Atlanta, who practices BDSM himself, says that, while relationships vary widely, total financial dominance is unusual. "It's fairly the exception that a person actually transfers their personal assets or anything like that when they enter into a master-slave relationship."

Chloe Elizabeth was determined to avoid any financial relationship with Robinson. He invited her to travel to Europe with him. After she tentatively agreed, he suggested that she sign several blank sheets of stationery and give him a list of her relatives' addresses so that he could keep them informed of her whereabouts. She balked and never traveled with him.

He told her he would be away in Australia for a while. She discovered that he had not left Kansas. She telephoned his office. Someone answered but said nothing. An hour later her phone rang.

"How dare you check up on me!?"

"J.R., what are you talking about?"

"You're checking up on me. You know I record every phone call that comes in to any of my businesses. I know that was you. I'm really pissed that you would check up on me after all we've gone through."

"I don't have a clue what you're talking about."

"Don't ever check up on me again!"

She finally learned about his criminal record and told him in February 1996 that she wanted to stop seeing him. Their relationship fell off to occasional e-mails.

In 1996, J.R. and Nancy Robinson moved from the Southfork mobile-home development in Missouri to a similar development in Olathe called the Santa Barbara Estates, where all the streets were named for California cities. The Robinsons took up residence at 36 Monterey. They installed wind chimes near the front door and a statue of St. Francis of Assisi in the front yard. Their Christmas decorations were considered the most spectacular at Santa Barbara, where Nancy was the manager, as she had been at Southfork.

The Robinsons also bought sixteen acres of farmland with a fishing pond an hour south of Olathe. They put a mobile home and shed on the property, and he occasionally took friends fishing there.

Thanks to the Internet, J.R.'s sexual horizons expanded dramatically beyond the personal ads of the *Pitch Weekly* and other newspapers. He maintained five computers in his Santa Barbara home, three desktops and two laptops, and trolled the BDSM Web sites for hours. His handle was "Slavemaster."

Robinson met Izabel Lewicka on the Internet in the early months of 1997 while she was a freshman at Purdue University in Indiana. Born in Poland, Lewicka had come to Indiana with her parents when she was about twelve. At Purdue she was studying fine arts but also took a great interest in computers and often was at her monitor late into the night.

In the spring of 1997, Lewicka announced to her parents that she had been offered an "internship" by a man in Kansas. She wouldn't give details, except that she would be able to use her artistic training. Though her parents tried to dissuade her from going, she drove to Kansas that June, taking clothing, personal items and nearly all her paintings. She left an address in Overland Park, Kansas, on Metcalf Avenue, a main north-south artery. Her parents wrote letters to that address but received no reply. In August they drove to Kansas to look for their daughter and found that the address on Metcalf was that of a Mail Boxes Etc., whose manager refused to give them Izabel's address or telephone number. They returned to Indiana without contacting the police.

In fact, Robinson had installed Lewicka in an apartment in south Kansas City where they regularly engaged in BDSM sex and he photographed her nude in bondage, all in accord with a "slave contract" enumerating 115 provisions of his dominance and her submission. He paid her bills, and when they weren't having sex, she led a life of leisure, spending a lot of time reading gothic and vampire novels she purchased at a rare-and-used-book shop in Overland Park. Usually dressed in black, sometimes with a black leather dog collar with metal studs, she told the owners that she was proud to be from Dracula's part of the world.

In January 1999, J.R. moved Lewicka into an apartment in Olathe. He referred to her variously as his adopted daughter, his niece and a graphic designer who worked for his new company, Specialty Publications, which covered the modular-home industry. The following summer, she introduced Robinson to her bookstore friends and told them he would be buying her books in the future because she was moving away.

Though the Olathe apartment was leased through January 2000, Lewicka suddenly disappeared in August 1999. Robinson told one of his business associates that she had been caught smoking marijuana with her boyfriend and had been deported. When Robinson released the apartment to the managers so they could prepare it for the next tenants, they found it remarkably, immaculately, memorably clean.

Suzette Trouten, a twenty-seven-year-old home-care nurse who lived in Monroe, Michigan, near Detroit, amused herself by collecting teapots, playing with her two Pekingese dogs, and engaging in BDSM sex. Trouten was so deeply involved in the BDSM lifestyle that she carried on relationships with four dominants at once. She had pierced her nipples, her navel, and five places in and around her genitalia, piercings which could accommodate rings and other devices used in BDSM rituals. A photograph of Suzette Trouten with nails driven through her breasts had circulated on the Internet.

Trouten and J. R. Robinson met on the Internet in the fall of 1999, just weeks after Izabel Lewicka disappeared. J.R. invited Trouten to Kansas. He might have a job for her, he said, as a companion and nurse to his elderly father, a rich man who liked to travel but needed constant care. (J.R.'s father had actually been dead for ten years.)

J.R. flew Trouten to Kansas City and had a limousine meet her at the airport. The job interview went well, she told her mother by phone. J.R. and his father, whom she did not meet, had a yacht, and she would be sailing with them in the Pacific off California, possibly going all the way to Hawaii. Suzette and J.R. agreed that he would pay her $60,000 a year and provide her with an apartment in the Kansas City area and a car.

Back in Michigan, preparing to return to Kansas, Suzette told her mother, Carolyn Trouten, that she feared homesickness but hoped the money she would earn from Robinson would enable her to complete her nursing degree. She drove to Kansas in a Ryder truck, paid for by J.R., on February 13 and 14. In the truck were her clothing and books, plus her teapot collection and her two

Pekingese dogs, Harry and Peka. She also took along her BDSM equipment—whips, paddles, canes, collars and the like.

J.R. had registered Trouten at the Guesthouse Suites, room 216, in Lenexa, a Kansas City suburb just west of Overland Park and north of Olathe. J.R. boarded Trouten's dogs at a local animal shelter. She could take them on the trip to California and on the yacht, he said, but the Guesthouse Suites didn't allow pets. J.R. told his new employee to prepare to leave two weeks hence. He directed her to get a passport. He had her do some computer work at his office. He had her sign a slave contract covering their BDSM relationship. He also had her sign more than thirty blank sheets of stationery and address more than forty envelopes to her relatives and friends; she would be too busy while they were traveling to worry about correspondence, which he would take care of.

Suzette kept in close touch on the Internet with a BDSM contact, a woman named Lori who lived in Canada and who knew about J. R. Robinson and Suzette's job in Kansas. Suzette also spoke to her mother, Carolyn, every day by phone. Suzette called Carolyn at around 1 A.M. on Tuesday, February 19.

"Everything's fine," Suzette said. "John is nice, I'm not as lonesome as I thought I'd be." They were leaving for California Wednesday or Thursday. Suzette would call frequently while they were traveling.

On the afternoon of Wednesday, March 1, J. R. Robinson paid Trouten's final bill at the Guesthouse Suites and checked her dogs out of the animal shelter. Neither the hotel clerk nor the animal-shelter attendant had seen Trouten. Later that afternoon, an animal-control officer was dispatched to Santa Barbara Estates, where someone had left two Pekingese dogs without identifying collars in a portable kennel outside the main office.

Carolyn Trouten heard nothing from her daughter in early March. Nor did Suzette's Canadian friend Lori. Both telephoned J. R. Robinson, who toyed with them. He told them that at the last minute Suzette had decided against taking the job he had offered her and had run off with a man named James Turner. Neither Carolyn nor Lori believed the story. Around the middle of March, they began receiving e-mails and letters that were signed "Suzette" but, they knew, were not from Suzette. They didn't sound at all like her.

"I believed this person [Robinson] had done something to Suzette," Lori would testify later.

Suzette's family contacted the Lenexa Police Department and reported her missing. Unlike the neighboring Overland Park department, which had received similar reports of missing women associated with John Robinson in the eighties, and had given them less than full attention, Lenexa detective David Brown immediately began a thorough inquiry into the disappearance of Suzette Trouten. Brown obtained Robinson's rap sheet, got in touch with Overland Park detectives and saw the possible connections with other cases of missing women. A task force of representatives of several local, state and federal law-enforcement agencies, including the FBI, was urgently organized under the supervision of Johnson County district attorney Paul J. Morrison, an eminent prosecutor in the Kansas City area. A native of Dodge City, Morrison, forty-five, had been Johnson County's chief law-enforcement officer for eleven years and had convicted several high-profile murderers.

One of the task force's first moves was sending two detectives to Missouri to see Steve Haymes. "You seem to have had this guy pegged from the beginning," one of the detectives remarked after Haymes briefed them on Robinson's criminal history, going back to the sixties. Detective Brown instructed the family of Suzette Trouten to tape their conversations with Robinson and send all e-mails to and from him to the Lenexa police. Brown coached them on inducing Robinson to divulge details that might be clues to Suzette's whereabouts.

In February 2000, as Suzette Trouten had been getting settled in Kansas and preparing, she thought, to leave with Robinson for California, Robinson had begun conversing on the Internet with a woman named Jeanne, a professional from the Southwest. Divorced and thirty-four years old, Jeanne was looking to establish a BDSM relationship with a man who might also be able to employ her professionally. Robinson identified himself to Jeanne as James Turner. After they explored their BDSM likes and dislikes extensively via phone and Internet, Robinson invited Jeanne to come to Kansas. She visited for a long weekend, Thursday, April 6, until Tuesday, April 11. He put her up in a hotel, where they engaged in various kinds of sexual interplay ranging from intercourse to fellatio to flogging.

Toward the end of her stay, they agreed that Jeanne would move to Kansas and work for Robinson's companies Hydro-Gro and Specialty Publications. When she returned to Kansas in mid-May, Robinson installed her in the Guesthouse Suites in Lenexa, where he had kept Suzette Trouten in February. They had sex on the afternoon of Tuesday, May 16, and intermittently thereafter. One day that week he didn't show up. On Friday, May 19, however, Robinson telephoned Jeanne, told her he was on his way and instructed her that when he arrived she should be nude and kneeling in a corner of the room with her hair pulled back.

When he entered the room he grabbed her by the hair and began flogging her across her breasts and back. He then insisted that she pose for photographs, even though she had told him she didn't want him to take pictures. He was particularly interested in photographing the marks his floggings had left on her body.

Robinson then told Jeanne that he didn't like her attitude and that if she didn't change she would have to move back home. He left the hotel room, saying he would return.

Jeanne became hysterical. She had moved to Kansas to be with this man and work for him. But he seemed interested only in punishing her and pleasing himself. Her body burned from his beatings, and he was threatening to banish her.

Jeanne ran to the front desk of the hotel, sobbing uncontrollably. She insisted on seeing the registration card for her room. She discovered that the man she had been seeing was named John Robinson, not James Turner. She tried to call the police but was too upset to complete the call. The desk attendant did it for her.

Within minutes, Detective David Brown arrived at the Guesthouse Suites. Two months into his intensive investigation of John Robinson, Brown knew his subject intimately. After hearing a brief version of Jeanne's story, told through tears, he collected her belongings and moved her to another hotel.

Brown interviewed Jeanne the next day, Saturday, May 20, and on into the following week. She explained how Robinson had beaten her far beyond her desires. She didn't like pain or punishment or marks on her skin. "I'm a submissive, not a masochist," she said.

The long-overdue investigation of J. R. Robinson was reaching its climax. A little more than a week later, on Friday, June 2, a convoy of nine police vehicles entered the grounds of Santa Barbara Estates in Olathe and surrounded the Robinsons' residence, at 36 Monterey. Police detectives placed a dumbstruck John Robinson under arrest, charged him with sexual assault and took him in handcuffs to the Johnson County jail. Other detectives began executing a warrant authorizing them to search the house. They seized all five computers, They also found a blank sheet of stationery signed by Lisa Stasi more than fifteen years earlier — in January 1985 — and receipts from the Rodeway Inn in Overland Park showing that Robinson had checked Stasi out of the hotel on January 10 of that year, the day after she disappeared with him into the snow.

As the search of the Robinson house continued, Lenexa detectives Dan Owsley and Dawn Layman, armed with a second search warrant, were wielding a bolt cutter on a padlock securing Robinson's ten-by-fifteen-foot locker at a nearby storage facility in Olathe. Inside they found a trove of items linking Robinson to Suzette Trouten, now missing two months, and Izabel Lewicka, who had not been seen since the previous August. There were Trouten's birth certificate and Social Security card; sheets of blank stationery signed "Love ya, Suzette"; a two-page slave contract signed by Trouten; and a stun gun. There were Izabel Lewicka's Kansas driver's license; photographs of Lewicka nude in bondage; a six-page slave contract listing 115 rules, sexual and otherwise, she was obliged to obey. And there was a pillowcase and several BDSM sex implements.

The next morning, Saturday, June 3, another convoy of police vehicles made its way an hour south from Olathe to the remote sixteen-acre plot of land that the Robinsons owned off a country lane near the town of La Cygne.

There, with yet another search warrant, Detective Harold Hughes, a forensic crime-scene investigator for Johnson County, located two yellow fifty-five-gallon metal barrels near a toolshed across from the mobile home. Using a pair of heavy pliers, he pried open one of the barrels. Inside was a female body, nude, with its head down, immersed in about fourteen inches of fluid, the result of decomposition.

Hughes opened the second barrel. He first saw a pillow and red-and-green pillowcase. He removed them and found another female body, this one clothed, also soaked in the fluid of its own decay. Hughes photographed and fingerprinted both barrels and resealed them, leaving the contents inside. Using a black Magic Marker, he labeled the barrels "Unknown 1" and "Unknown 2." The Robinson property was sealed and placed under guard.

The investigation was still top secret. However, a detective telephoned Steve Haymes at home that Saturday evening to confide that they had found bodies. He wanted Haymes to know before it hit the newspapers. Haymes was stunned. "It confirmed what I had always believed," he recalls, "but the move from theory to reality was chilling."

Early Saturday evening, as Detective Hughes was completing his search of the Robinson property, a pager beeped in the home of Mark Tracy, the deputy prosecuting attorney of Cass County, Missouri, a few miles across the state line. It was the county sheriff's communications center asking Tracy to telephone Johnson County D.A. Paul Morrison.

"Morrison himself, not just his office?" Tracy asked.

"Morrison himself."

Tracy felt a bit intimidated. Paul Morrison was a towering figure in Kansas City law-enforcement circles.

Tracy dialed the number and Morrison answered.

"I'm working a case," Morrison said. "It's kind of a big deal. I need your help to get a search warrant to look in a storage locker in your county. . . . I won't go into details, but you might want to alert your boss."

On Sunday morning Mark Tracy received a delegation from Morrison—his deputy Sara Welch and several detectives—at the Cass County prosecuting attorney's office. The affidavit they gave Tracy was the longest search-warrant affidavit he had ever seen. It indicated, among other things, that John Edward Robinson Sr. was believed to have killed several women; that he had used the Internet to lure them to Kansas for BDSM sex; that he maintained a locker thought to contain evidence at Stor-Mor-for-Less in Raymore, Missouri, a Kansas City suburb; and that he had paid for the locker with a company check so as to conceal it was his.

Back across the state line in Kansas that Sunday, at the medical examiner's office in Topeka, Donald Pojman, M.D., the deputy coroner, a bespectacled man with black hair, mustache and beard, removed the body from the barrel marked "Unknown 1." Across the face he found a large swatch of cloth secured by a rope around the head, possibly a blindfold. The hair was tied in an eighteen-inch ponytail. There were several rings on the body—one on a little finger, one on a ring finger, one through piercings in each nipple, and five rings through piercings in and around the genitalia.

Dr. Pojman determined that the woman had received a massive blow, probably with a large hammer, to the left side of the head between the forehead and the temple. The skull was fractured and a circular section of it was actually driven into the brain. The woman could have died from any one of three causes: bleeding, damage to the brain tissue, or swelling of the brain following the blow. There was no sign that she had had an opportunity to defend herself. Dr. Pojman estimated that she had been dead anywhere from a few months to a year.

Unknown 2 also had died from a blow to the left side of the head that had fractured her skull. In fact, there appeared to have been two blows, overlapping, forming an oval indentation. The left side of her jaw also had been fractured. Again, there was no sign that she had been able to defend herself.

It was late Sunday night when Dr. Pojman finished. Forensic odontologists would attempt to identify the bodies with dental records the next day.

.   .   .

Deputy Prosecuting Attorney Mark Tracy of Cass County served the search warrant at Stor-Mor-for-Less in Raymore at 8 A.M. Monday. It was much colder than normal for early June, and no one was dressed for it. Tracy led the Kansas task-force detectives to John Robinson's locker, E-2, and opened it. It was ten by twenty feet, even bigger than the locker in Olathe, and filled with clutter. The shivering detectives began gingerly removing the contents and either inventorying items as potential evidence or putting them aside.

After forty minutes, Tracy could make out what appeared to be three barrels in the shadows at the back of the locker. He also began to smell the unmistakable odor of rotting flesh.

Tracy halted the search and called his boss, Cass County prosecuting attorney Chris Koster, who was in his car en route to the Kansas City airport to catch a flight to Florida on another case. Tracy had been briefing Koster by phone since Paul Morrison's call on Saturday, but it had not appeared until now that bodies would be found in the Missouri storage locker.

"There are barrels and there are going to be bodies in them," Tracy told Koster. "You've got to come back."

Koster canceled his trip and was at Stor-Mor within the hour. There was an intense discussion of whether Kansas or Missouri authorities would control the investigation from then on. Koster and Tracy determined that the likely presence of bodies on Missouri soil meant the case was no longer just a search for evidence related to Kansas homicides. Missouri would control the crime scene. Koster summoned a team from the Kansas City crime lab's major-case squad. Its leader looked the scene over and said, "Has anybody ordered food? It's going to be a long day."

As it happened, a police van loaded with pizza, soft drinks and coffee was already there as the investigators resumed their slow work. It was afternoon before they had emptied the locker of everything but the barrels, which were made of metal and had been wrapped in clear plastic. Sealed with gray duct tape, they were sitting on piles of kitty litter, which apparently had been intended to minimize the odor.

A crime-lab technician opened one of the barrels. The first things he saw were a light-brown sheet, a pair of glasses and a shoe. He removed the sheet and then grasped the shoe, only to find that it was attached to a human leg. It was decided to reseal the barrel and take all three containers to the Kansas City medical examiner's office. One of the barrels was leaking fluid, and it was feared that their bottoms might have corroded and would give way when lifted. A police officer was sent to a nearby Wal-Mart to purchase three plastic children's wading pools. They were slipped under the barrels before they were placed aboard the crime-lab van.

Thomas W. Young, M.D., the chief Kansas City medical examiner, a veteran of 3,800 autopsies, opened the barrels. Chris Koster and Mark Tracy watched from behind two panes of glass. "When they opened those barrels . . . ," Tracy told me later. "I've been around homicide scenes before, and I've smelled pretty old, decayed bodies, but they'd been exposed to the open air. These had been in barrels. And, *man*, it was an extraordinarily strong smell and very uncomfortable."

Each barrel contained the severely decomposed body of a female who had been beaten to death, probably with a large hammer. They obviously had been dead for several years. The first body was fully clothed. On the second body was a T-shirt reading, CALIFORNIA STATE OF MIND. In the mouth was a denture broken in half. The third was the body of a teenager wearing green pants and a silver beret. There were no defensive wounds: none of the victims had been able to defend herself.

.   .   .

Earlier that Monday, a forensic odontologist in Topeka had identified the two bodies found on Robinson's property in Kansas as
Suzette Trouten and Izabel Lewicka. Later in the week, a Missouri
forensic odontologist identified two of the bodies found in Robinson's storage locker as Beverly Bonner, the former prison librarian,
and Sheila Faith. Sheila's wheelchair-bound daughter, Debbie, was
identified with a skeleton X ray.

Johnson County district attorney Paul Morrison and Cass
County prosecuting attorney Chris Koster charged John Robinson
with the murder of all five, as well as of Lisa Stasi, who has been
missing since 1985 and whose body has not been recovered. (Her
daughter, Tiffany, now sixteen and named Heather, still lives with
Don and Helen Robinson. DNA tests recently proved that Carl
Stasi is her biological father. She is aware of the current investigation into John Robinson's past.) Both Morrison and Koster will seek
the death penalty.

In the face of the evidence against him, Robinson, at a March
hearing, "stood silent," and Judge John Anderson III, son of a former Kansas governor, entered a not-guilty plea on his behalf. Asked
by *Vanity Fair* for a response to any or all charges against Robinson
dating back to the 1960s, his lawyer Ronald F. Evans, chief attorney
of the Kansas Death Penalty Defense Unit, said he had no comment.

As for Paula Godfrey and Catherine Clampitt, also missing since
the eighties, authorities are still investigating their disappearances
and haven't charged Robinson in those cases. He was placed in
solitary confinement in the Johnson County jail. No trial date has
been set.

.   .   .

A few days after Robinson's arrest, a spokesman for his family issued a written statement defending him: "We have never seen any behavior that would have led us to believe that anything we are now hearing could be possible. . . . While we do not discount the information that has and continues to come to light, we do not know the person whom we have read and heard about on TV. . . . [John Robinson is a] loving and caring husband and father. . . . We wait with each of you for the cloud of allegations and innuendo to clear, revealing, at last, the facts."

*   *   *

Had the Robinson case unfolded anywhere other than Kansas, I might never have been drawn to it. But its Kansas setting enabled me to write about a unique criminal in my home state, a historic crossroads that is widely misunderstood and often ignored, a kind of hole in the middle of America. Little of note has been written about crime in Kansas since Truman Capote's In Cold Blood, *which was published in the mid-1960s. I saw the crimes of J. R. Robinson as an opportunity to take a new look at mayhem in a special place I know well.*

The evidence detailed in this piece withstood cross-examination in a weeklong hearing in the Johnson County Court House in 2001. Robinson was scheduled for trial in late 2002.

FLESH AND BLOOD
PETER RICHMOND

One by one, day by day, they'd glide to the witness stand, this procession of improbable women, a spangled harem of them, drifting into the courtroom and out again, leaving the scent of their perfume and the shadow of their glitter and the echo of their cool. Week in, week out, they never stopped coming.

That was the extraordinary thing. How many there were. The final count stopped short of thirty—that was the number of photographs of women Rae was said to keep in a box at home—but there were more than enough of them to make each and every morning worth my springing out of bed for, worth walking down to the courthouse for, worth getting frisked at the doorway for: in the hope that a new one might illuminate the somber courtroom with its smoked-glass view of the jailhouse across the street.

And sure enough, in the middle of a gray day of testimony filled with the babble of a psychologist or the grunt of a jail guard or the platitudes of a coach, out of the blue Rae's attorney would suddenly say, "The defense calls Dawnyle Willard," and next to me the TV guy would arch an eyebrow at the local columnist—who's this one? what's the angle? lover? friend? cleaned his apartment? helped him jump bail?—and they'd both shrug, because no one had heard of Dawnyle Willard.

Then everyone would turn to the back of the courtroom to get a look at the newest entrant, because we just knew she was going to be beautiful. And honestly, she just about always was.

Dawnyle certainly was. Stately, slim, a dancer. Former girlfriend, now confidante. Wept on the stand, at the pure goodness of the man.

Amber was cool, slim and fiery and a favorite among those of us who spoke of such things during breaks in the action, although Starlita was easily the most exotic; she looked like an African princess dropped into a Southern murder trial. Michelle was the pretty little girl next door. Monique was innocently cute. Tnisha, Rae's current squeeze, was . . . well, a tad young looking. But she was pretty enough for you to understand why Rae would nod at her each day when, sandwiched by grim bailiffs, he left the courtroom—nodding as if to say, Hey, babe, don't worry: *You're* the one now. And I swear, she believed it.

Sometimes, though, Rae nodded at the woman in the front pew. She was there every day. By some measures, she was the most handsome of all: high forehead, piercing eyes, coiffed and jewelried to the highest. Some newcomers to the courtroom thought she was another female friend. But this was Rae's mother, Theodry Carruth, anchoring the Cult of Rae from the center of the home-team bench.

Really, there was no other way to think of them—other than as a cult—at least not after the mother of one of Rae's former girlfriends took the stand near the end of the trial, and the *mother* was gorgeous. Not only was she beautiful, but get this: after her daughter testified against Rae, the mother testified glowingly *for* Rae.

And then, as she left the stand, she looked right at Rae—a man facing the death penalty for taking out a hit on a pregnant woman—looked right into his eyes and, all sweet and wet, mouthed the words *I love you.*

As the weeks passed and the women came and went, I would

look over at Rae and stare at his profile, which never changed, because Rae never changed expressions, even during the closing argument, when the lead prosecutor played the 911 tape of Cherica Adams's moans: sounds from beyond the grave, all sputtering utterances, atonal syllables so skin-crawling that throughout the courtroom shoulders heaved in sobs. But Rae's face flinched not at all. Animated and emotional and expressive as the women were—weaving and looping their tales of goodness and his charity—Rae remained a well-tailored sphinx.

And so, day in, day out, I'd ask myself a question. Not what they all saw in him; the first look at Rae explained that: this baby face, the contours all smooth and rounded, the outward downslant of his eyebrows giving him this puppy-dog-swatted-with-a-newspaper look. Girls loved to take care of Rae even before he became a millionaire. No, the question I kept asking myself was this: If Rae Carruth loved women so much, why did he keep threatening to have them killed? How, if he gathered women around him like a cocoon, if he thrived on them and fed on them and drew sustenance from them, could a man get to a point in his life where he routinely considered disposing of them? And how could such a man wind up finding a home—even flourishing—in the National Football League?

Well, because he really didn't like women at all. (He liked to fuck them, and he liked their attention, and he liked the *idea* of them, but he didn't like them.) And because he was accustomed to violence. And because he was making a living in a league in which a man and his basest instincts are encouraged to run wild. Well, he was until recently, anyway; Rae doesn't play football anymore. He's in prison up in Nash County, where he won't have to worry about women and women won't have to worry about him, and as his crime swiftly seeps into the background noise of the culture, we're already starting to act as if we didn't have to worry about Rae Carruth anymore. As if the whole episode were an aberration.

Of course, it's anything but. Take even a cursory look at how Rae Carruth went from first-round NFL draft pick to ward of the state of North Carolina, serving a quarter century of hard time for conspiring to commit the most horrific crime in the history of professional sports, and the question is not how it could happen but when is it going to happen again.

Football is a violent sport, growing far more violent and mean and attitudinal every year, and it has been played by men who have traditionally been violent against their women. This has been the case since Jim Brown, the greatest running back ever to play the game, garnered the first of a half dozen charges of violence against women, ranging from spousal battery to rape to the sexual molestation of two teenage girls. Brown, who has never been convicted of a single charge, begat O.J., the second-greatest running back, who, at this writing, continues to seek out Nicole's true killers. O.J. begat Michael Irvin of the Dallas Cowboys, who, prior to one of his frequent cocaine-sex bacchanals a few years back, cavity-searched one of his girls a little too hard for the liking of her cop boyfriend, who then took out a hit on Irvin. It wasn't just Irvin who dodged a bullet that time. It was the NFL, which retired Irvin with pomp and circumstance.

This year, of course, Super Bowl MVP and murder defendant Ray Lewis, who has twice been accused—but not convicted—of hitting women, commanded headlines and earned full forgiveness at the hands of a most understanding media machine. Wearing a Giants uniform in the same Super Bowl was Christian Peter, a man accused of so many crimes against women in college that public outcry forced the Patriots to drop him within days of drafting him in 1996. Lost in the shuffle but not forgotten, Corey Dillon and

Mustafah Muhammad and Denard Walker contributed, each in his own way, to this long-standing tradition. On the day he ran for a record 278 yards, Cincinnati's Dillon, now arguably the game's best running back, was facing charges of striking his wife; after the season, he plea-bargained to avoid trial. His uniform was sent to the Hall of Fame, where it now keeps company with the memorabilia of Brown and Simpson. As for Walker, he played for Tennessee last year after being convicted of hitting the mother of his son. He then declared himself a free agent and was courted by several teams until the Denver Broncos anted up a cool $26 million. Muhammad, a cornerback with Indianapolis, led his team into the play-offs last year after being convicted of hitting his wife. And let's not forget the domestic-assault conviction of Detroit's Mario Bates or former Packer Mark Chmura's troubles surrounding his dalliance with his seventeen-year-old baby-sitter.

And what about the more subtle misogyny embodied by the late and revered Derrick Thomas of the Kansas City Chiefs, who was killed in a car wreck two years ago? He left behind seven kids by five women, and no will—thus no guarantees of money or consideration for any of the children or any of the women.

The NFL claims it is doing more than ever to educate its recruits. Its preseason three-and-a-half-day symposia are supposed to make its rookies duly aware of their newfound responsibilities to their fans and their leagues and the kids who put their posters on the wall: To avoid the sleaze joints. Steer clear of the hucksters. Grow up quick.

But what is it really doing? When the NFL parades its first-round draft picks to a podium on national television and slathers them in their first frosting of celebrity, its message effectively and immediately neutralizes all the good-behavior seminars. On that day, the commissioner is not only handing each of the players a guarantee of several million dollars; he is also giving them the whispered assurance that the league likes them just the way they are. No need to grow up too fast.

Ultimately, the league refused to ban Ray Lewis and his brutal peers because it needed them on the playing field, and that mandate speaks more loudly than a lecture about good citizenship—especially to a remarkably immature kid like Rae. After all, little boys don't like little girls, and what was Rae Carruth other than an overgrown boy, a bundle of muscle and fiber jerry-rigged to play a game? Of course, most kids grow out of that stuff. It's the rare one who is allowed to harbor his playground sexism until it blossoms into monstrosity.

He came from the place so many seem to come from; only the details vary from kid to kid. Rae didn't grow up with his biological father. As a child, Rae split time among several houses, including his mother's, set in a neighborhood of squalor and dismay on the south side of Sacramento—on an avenue where vandals routinely set cars aflame—and her sister's place in a nicer part of town, absent the bars on the windows. Even then, even before he was showered with privilege, Theodry worried about the sharks and the vultures preying on her son, "the guppy."

This is how she describes him. This is why she describes herself as "the piranha" when it comes to protecting her son. To know Rae Carruth and to understand the course he chose to take, to divine the nature of his particular rebellion—because isn't that what all our adolescent contrarinesses are? rebellion against what was lacquered onto us beforehand?—you must first know Theodry Carruth. There is a hardness and a strength to her, and they seem like the same thing; she seizes the space she is in and commands it from on high.

But if one may be tempted to call Rae's mother domineering, one ought not to, because she will not tolerate being described as overbearing, and she will tell you so. Describe her instead, she warns in a voice that brooks no argument, as simply having been raised by a Southern mother, and then say she is raising her son thusly.

Theodry Carruth's vigilance over her only son's upbringing paid off, at least in the short run: Rae's grades at Valley High School were solid, he stayed out of trouble and big colleges came calling. In 1992 Rae went off to the University of Colorado. Back on the infernal block on Parker Avenue, Theodry Carruth turned one of the rooms into a miniature shrine where family and friends gathered to sit in mock stadium chairs and watch Rae's games from Boulder. It was called the Rae of Hope room. Neighborhood kids would set it on fire a few years later.

At Colorado, Rae's coach Bill McCartney was a demagogue. On the field, McCartney was known for teams that played hard and thuggishly. Off the field, he was known for the conversation he'd had with God. One day God told McCartney to found the Promise Keepers. Soon thereafter, at McCartney's urgings, tens of thousands of fathers and husbands took to gathering in football stadiums across the land to beat their chests and flagellate their souls and collectively recommit to their gender. The subtext of the Promise Keepers was a patently sexist one, of course: portraying women as worthy beings but regarding them, ultimately, as secondary, as biblical chattel.

But beneath the roar of McCartney's fire and brimstone, his daughter was getting pregnant by two different football players in four and a half years—the first, the star quarterback, wanted her to abort the fetus; the second sired his child during Rae's freshman year. This only proved that when you climb too high in the pulpit, it's easy to ignore the funky stuff going on under your nose. Especially if you're a member of the sinning crowd: McCartney himself quit on his Colorado contract after Rae's third autumn in Boulder. Broke his promise, if you will.

Rae's college athletic achievements were legendary—in one game alone, he had seven receptions for 222 yards and three touchdowns. In 1997 he entered the hallowed fraternity of first-round draft picks under the watchful wink of the NFL. The Carolina Panthers took him as their first selection, number 27 overall. Like all rookies, he would be instructed on how to behave. But like his first-round peers, he knew what had actually just happened: he'd been ushered into a land of entitlement, where the only promise he'd really be held to was the promise he'd shown thus far on the playing field.

The Panthers gave him a four-year contract worth $3.7 million and a $1.3 million signing bonus, and it wasn't so much the amount of money that was stunning but the ease with which it came. Within days of being signed, Rae got a check for $15,000 in the mail from a trading-card company. Just for being Rae. How sweet was that?

He immediately signed it over to his seventeen-year-old girlfriend in Boulder, Amber Turner, and told her to go ahead and set up house for them in Charlotte. Amber was a stylish and precocious beauty, a high school senior (even as a fifth-year college senior, Rae's tastes still tended toward postadolescence). His girlfriend in high school, Michelle, had been a sophomore when he was a senior, and she'd just turned eighteen when Rae got her pregnant on a visit back home from college. He'd waffled about whether or not to have the baby from day to day. Michelle wasn't surprised at his indecision. She says she knew him as a man of many moods. He could be a real joker, or he could be a cipher, or he could even be, in the dark moments, the devil himself.

Amber Turner knew about the baby back in Sacramento. Amber also knew Rae said the boy might not be his, and even if it were his baby, he said, there were ways to fix the blood tests.

And what of the parents? Amber's mother had no problem with Amber setting up house with Rae in a distant city, right out of high school. She loved Rae, too. He was polite and civilized and kind. He called her Mrs. Turner even after she said he could call her Barbara.

Rae's mom, Theodry, was pleased, too—pleased that her only son would be living in a Southern town with family values. But it wasn't family values that Rae found in Charlotte. It was what all young, wealthy, transplanted men find there, these strangers in a strange land: nightclubs, comedy clubs, strip clubs. Charlotte is full of gentlemen's clubs, peopled by men who are anything but. On the high end, there's the Men's Club, Charlotte's topless palace nonpareil.

The Men's Club, planted right off the interstate, like everything else in a town laid down like a new quilt of plywood and Sheetrock, is a sumptuous palace of fiction. What the Men's Club lacks in poetry it makes up for in excess. The red-felt pool tables are illuminated by hanging lamps ensconced in blue glass. The lobby boutique is filled with expensive clothes for men and women. The kitchen will serve you a fillet medallion sautéed in a mushroom demiglace.

In the center of the place, beyond the sunken bar, is the main stage. But the dancers are not the only attraction; above the stage looms a huge television screen, like Oz's mask, eternally tuned to ESPN, so that the allure of even the most seductive sirens competes with huge images of men being tackled and talking heads blathering about blitzes. In a very real sense, the women at the Men's Club are just another product, with this exception: there is nothing real about them. The tattoos on the soft planes south of the hipbones are frosted over with pancake makeup. Their names are as false as their chests. They are stage actors. They are not meant to be the stuff of reality.

This, of course, explains why Rae sought them out. Because they seemed to be less than real women yet possessed of the necessary female attributes. So that considering their feelings was a less complicated process.

Despite a terrific rookie season on the field—Rae earned a starting position at wide receiver and finished with an impressive forty-four receptions—Rae's home life soon proved rocky. Amber went home after that first season. He found her too possessive: she was jealous of all his other female friends. And there would be many female friends. There was Starlita, whom Rae had so charmed in a barbershop one day that before she'd finished having her hair done, Rae had taken her young son down the street for pizza. Soon Starlita thought Rae was the best thing in Jacobe's life. Rae was worried that Starlita was turning her son into a mama's boy. (Rae always harped on that. And what was Rae if not a mama's boy?) There was Fonda Bryant, who kept a picture of her son on her desk at a radio station Rae visited one day, and before long the boy was spending nights at Rae's. Rae was exactly what the boy needed; Rae was firm about staying away from alcohol and drugs, firm about making sure the boy did his homework. When they played, Fonda couldn't tell who was the kid and who was the adult.

And yet Rae hardly ever visited his own child. He gave Michelle grief about breast-feeding the kid and hugging him so much—he worried she was making Little Rae soft. So Michelle sued him for child support: a judge granted her $5,500 a month. She offered to lessen it if Rae would come home and visit more. He promised. He didn't. In the meantime, Amber went back to Charlotte for a quick

visit. She got pregnant. As Rae's responsibilities and missteps threatened to collide, as his little-kid appetites met his stunted ability to
cope with adversity, he began to consider a solution both novel and
bizarre on the surface but certainly logical in the context of a man
who regards his women as disposable and dispensable: anytime
he'd get a woman pregnant, he'd threaten her with death.

He didn't carry out all the threats, of course. He was a joker. He
just talked about it a lot—about having Michelle and Amber killed.

Like the time Michelle called him in March 1998. She'd been
unsuccessful in persuading Rae to come back home to visit their
son. Rae had another idea. He suggested the two of them fly east to
Charlotte. Fine, she said. I'll rent a car and see the sights while you
play with your son.

"Don't be surprised if you get in a fatal car accident," Rae
answered, according to Michelle. He spoke very quietly, nearly in a
whisper.

"What did you say?" asked Michelle.

"It was a joke," Rae said.

"It's not funny," Michelle said.

"That's why it didn't work out," he said. "You never know when
I'm joking."

Back in Charlotte one day, Rae got off the phone, turned to
Amber and said, as she recalls it, "Would it be messed up if I had
somebody, you know, kill Michelle and my son? Or just my son, so
that I wouldn't have to pay her any money? Or if she just got in,
like, a car accident, or something happened to her, I could have my
son and I wouldn't have to pay her money?"

He said it jokingly. Amber had overhead him talking about the
same thing to a friend. Yeah, she said. It'd be messed up, Rae.

So some months later, when Amber called from Boulder to say
she was pregnant after her five-day visit and Rae insisted she get an

abortion, insisted he was not going to have any more kids by women he had no intention of being with, well, how could Amber be surprised when he said what he said to her?

"Don't make me send someone out there to kill you," Amber remembers him saying. "You know I would."

This one didn't sound funny at all. She had the abortion. Barbara Turner hadn't raised her daughter to be no fool.

Cherica Adams worked in the Men's Club boutique. She also danced under an alias at a different bar — over on the stages of the Diamond Club, a slightly more frayed entry in the topless-club genre, a place where a dancer is likely to be visiting from her home club in Buffalo for the long weekend, to pick up a couple of bucks, leaving the two-year-old back with her grandmother. Cherica Adams was a very attractive, baby-faced young woman who moved with a glittery crowd and felt equally at home backstage at a Master P concert or courtside at the 1998 NBA All-Star Game in Madison Square Garden, where several players, including Shaquille O'Neal, came by to say hello to her.

They never really dated, Rae and Cherica. They had sex a few times. Rae was also having sex with an exotic dancer who was having an affair with Charles Shackleford, a former Charlotte Hornet who happened to be married with three children, but it was Cherica whom Rae got pregnant, in March 1999 — exactly one year after he and Amber conceived their second child.

Rae was ambivalent about this one. On the one hand, he kept a new set of baby furniture in a storage facility under his name and took Cherica to Lamaze classes. On the other hand, it was at a Lamaze class that Rae first leaned Cherica's last name.

Rae's second season had been a disappointment. He'd broken

his foot after a forty-seven-yard catch, and he'd missed most of the year. When Cherica got pregnant, his world began to close in.

He was taking grief from teammates and friends about letting a stripper use him, about her boasting all over town that she was carrying Rae Carruth's baby and wasn't going to have to work anymore. By now Rae's circle of male friends had expanded. Tired of the slick jocks in the Panthers' locker room, he was glad to finally meet some people who were real. This new coterie included a man named Michael Kennedy, who had dealt crack, and a man named Van Brett Watkins, who had once set a man on fire in the joint and stabbed his own brother. Watkins, too, had unusual ways of showing love to his women. He'd once held a meat cleaver to his wife's face.

Frequently injured, no longer a starter, Rae had by now become that singularly sorry football phenomenon: a first-round draft pick gone bust. Taxes and agents had taken half the bonus. He'd invested in a car-title-loan scam that had promised the trappings of easy living—and lost his money. He'd hired former wide receiver Tank Blank, later indicted on fraud charges, to manage his money. He'd signed a contract on a new house, but he'd had to pull out when he couldn't get the financing, and the owners had sued him.

And he had hired Van Brett Watkins, for $3,000, to beat up Cherica Adams so she'd lose the baby, but Watkins hadn't delivered.

He was tired of being victimized, tired of having these women sucking out his sperm, tired of being rewarded for all his kindness by predators and gold diggers. Tired of taking the ragging. Panicked at the money situation.

So Rae did the only thing he could do, the only option they'd left him.

. . .

It's as dark as Charlotte gets, the two-lane stretch of Rea Road a few miles north of the movie theater where Cherica and Rae went that night, in separate cars, and it's so silent, so still in the hour after midnight on a weekday, that if you stop your car in the dip in the road and kill the engine, you can imagine yourself back in the South when the farmland was creased by rambling stone walls and the woods were thick with kudzu.

There are houses here, a few of them, a light or two winking through the trees, but none has a clear sight line to the spot. No one could have known the exact location, even if anyone had been looking, even if someone had been awake and heard the hush of tires on pavement down the road.

No one could have seen Rae's Ford Expedition slowing down in front of Cherica's BMW, blocking her path. No one could have seen Michael Kennedy's rented Nissan Maxima pulling up alongside Cherica.

But they' have heard the five distinct cracks of the .38, when Watkins sent five metal-jacketed bullets through the tinted glass of the driver's window of the BMW. Four of them hit their target, burrowing through Cherica Adams's lung, bowel, stomach, pancreas, diaphragm, liver and neck, one of them passing within an inch of her fetus, leaving behind two distinct clusters of star bursts in the glass.

They'd have heard Rae's car pull forward and disappear up Rea Road, and Kennedy making a U-turn to go the other way, and Cherica's BMW weaving down a side street until it crawled to a stop on someone's lawn and she bled out her life onto the front seat. They'd have heard the moans. They *did* hear the moans, in fact; the woman who lives in the house where Cherica ended up that night told me she'd never forget the moans. But she wouldn't give me her name, and she wouldn't open the door more than a few inches, just far enough to flick out her cigarette ashes.

But she did remember one more thing: how after Cherica

repeated Rae's license-plate number to the 911 operator, after she pleaded with the operator to save her life, Cherica had had the presence of mind to carefully place the cell phone back on the dashboard.

One other detail of the scene escaped the woman's notice. The way Rae looked back at Watkins, the shooter, in his rearview mirror. As Watkins remembered it, for the briefest moment, their eyes met.

Cherica was conscious when the ambulance arrived at the hospital. Unable to speak, she motioned for a notepad and described the way Rae slowed down in front of her. "He was driving in front of me," she wrote. "He stopped in the road. He blocked the front."

Cherica gave birth to a son named Chancellor, who survived. Then the mother went into a coma from which she never awoke.

Nine days later, at dawn on Thanksgiving, police investigators drove to Rae's house in the Ellington Park subdivision. They rang the doorbell. Rae came to the door naked. A woman was in the bedroom. They arrested him. He made bail. Three weeks later, when Cherica died, and Rae now faced first-degree-murder charges, he skipped town.

They found him lying in the coffin-dark trunk of a gray '97 Toyota Camry in the parking lot of a $36-a-night motel in Tennessee, surrounded by candy bars and two water bottles filled with urine and a cell phone and a couple thousand in cash. His mom had turned him in: Theodry had given him up to the bail bondsman. When FBI agents popped the trunk, Rae kept his eyes closed, and he didn't move.

Soon he opened his eyes, raised his hands and climbed out. This seemed curious at the time, but it doesn't seem curious anymore. Knowing Rae as we do now, we know that he simply reasoned thusly: if he didn't see them, then the agents weren't there at all.

.   .   .

Michelle Wright watched the trial on television, watched as Candace, Starlita, Dawnyle, Monique, Fonda and Amber took the stand, and told Little Rae about all the pretty women.

"How many girlfriends did my dad have?" Little Rae asked his mother.

"I don't know, Rae," she answered. "I'm learning just like you."

"But you can't marry that many women, can you?"

"No," said Michelle. "You can't."

The creak of the knee braces Rae wore beneath his pants to keep him from fleeing was the only sound in the courtroom when he was led in to hear the verdicts, one day shy of his twenty-seventh birthday. Out the smoked windows in the back of the courtroom, black clouds huddled on command and great Gothic spills of water tumbled out of the Southern sky as Judge Charles Lamm pronounced the verdict of a jury of Rae's peers: Guilty of three of four counts, including conspiracy to commit murder. Innocent of first-degree murder.

The weeping of the women on Cherica Adams's side of the courtroom was immediate and audible and joyous. In a state with no parole, a murder-conspiracy conviction means that Rae will be off the streets for decades. He'll serve nineteen years minimum, twenty-four maximum.

Rae took the news of the verdict the way he'd taken everything for seven straight weeks: with no discernible emotion or expression. Just, as the bailiff led him for the last time past his women, a slight nod—at Tnisha, whose expression was confused, and at Theodry, who was already steeling herself to be strong, and at the rest of the women, who were looking toward him with whatever expressions they could muster.

Rae seemed, if anything, distracted, as if it had just occurred to him for the first time: the only intimate adulation he'd get for the next quarter century would be from men. The women were finally out of his life.

*   *   *

We've become accustomed to our athletes running afoul of the law. But even in a society jaded by the sight of outlaws on its athletic fields, Rae Carruth's crime stood out: a former first-round draft pick of the National Football League had been accused of taking out a hit on his pregnant girlfriend. It seemed too brutal to be true. But a jury in Charlotte, North Carolina, found it entirely plausible—as I did. Having spent three weeks in Charlotte during the trial, then journeyed to Carruth's hometown of Sacramento, I ultimately discovered that the most chilling piece of evidence in the Carruth case was not the sound of the dying woman's voice on the 911 tape but the charges by two other women whom Carruth had previously impregnated: that he had threatened them with physical harm, too. In the end, the third time proved the macabre charm.

But "Flesh and Blood" is an indictment of more than one man. It is a commentary on a system that has allowed sports to become larger than a cultural diversion or a branch of entertainment. It is the fable of a culture whose worship and enabling of its athletes has bred a warped breed of immature men whose brutality, misogyny, greed and arrogance now must prompt us to ask, as Rae Carruth sits in a jail cell for twenty years, not, "Why did he do it?" but, "When will it happen again?"

A PRAYER FOR TINA MARIE
ROBERT DRAPER

Gentlemen, here is your girl.

Twenty-two, with a soft, round face you could hold in one hand and chew like a peach muffin. Drowsy eyes that see right through you but give in all the same. Lips braced in a nursery-school pout. Gleaming dirty-blond hair swinging like a Thoroughbred's tail against the small of her back. She laughs easily, both at her own expense and at all your jokes. Though she loves a good time, her tastes are not expensive. She will have sex with you on the first night. She works at a gentlemen's club in Austin, Texas, known as Exposé, but you do not have to tell your friends this, as she is also studying to be an auto mechanic. She is a tomboy at heart and thus will endure your male obnoxiousness with sporting aplomb. And when you eventually edge away, unnerved by her obvious quest to find a father figure for the two young children who tag along with her on sleepovers, and jittery about her views against abortion, she will not put up a major fight. Instead, she will gamely move on to the next gentleman studying, from his lofty barstool perch, the litter of pleasure givers, judging who among them will give ever so much and demand ever so little—and who, at the very, very least, knows what to do when she misses her period.

Here, gentlemen, are two children lying still in a shallow creek. The blond-haired boy is facedown, his hands curled just above his shoulders. The girl lies on her back. Her overalls are unstrapped, and she is barefoot. Her lips are braced in a nursery-school pout. Their small bodies are just slightly swollen but otherwise perfectly preserved by the cool creek water and the temperate April air. If it weren't for the laceration on the boy's skull and the redness around the girl's mouth, one could almost imagine that the two of them are playing some obscure game. Pretend We're Fish. Pretend We're Water Angels. On this clear spring afternoon of April 19, 1999, the little figures in the Brushy Creek wilderness seem strangely aglow, like fallen moon rocks, radiant with mystery. For forty-eight hours, nothing more is known of them—until a day-care worker at the center the children attended learns from a news report that the girl was wearing a four-leaf-clover pendant and gasps as if the two kids were hers.

Gentlemen? Citizens? Good people? Here is your yellow-maned devil, garbed in white, the mark of the beast carved across her back: Texas Department of Criminal Justice inmate number 905058. She killed her two children. Chucked them off a limestone embankment like twenty-one- and twenty-seven-pound sacks of garbage. While the word *Mommy* slowly died on their lips over the course of the next five days, she was dancing for tips with her clothes off, smoking pot at a reggae festival, dining at a yacht club, snorting speed and sleeping with three different men, two of them total strangers. Upon recovering the bodies of three-year-old Amanda and two-year-old Dominick, the family delayed the funeral for the sake of the children's missing mother. They should not have bothered. The mother was in Corpus Christi, spending her days on the beach and her nights at a carnival riding something called the Zipper over and over, spinning in a pleasure cage suspended high over the Gulf of Mexico.

Behold Tina Marie Cornelius in her new cage: six by nine feet, cemented in the central Texas flatlands of Marlin, at the TDCJ Hobby Unit, where she will spend somewhere between thirty and sixty years. She will be in the company of approximately 1,300 women who live like pigs and vent their sexual jealousies with piercing wails and occasional homemade shanks. She will eat her breakfast at three-thirty in the morning, her lunch at ten, dinner at four. Starch and more starch—it will play hell with her once fetching frame, just as the dank institutional air will lend a porridgelike hue to her flesh and the stresses associated with living among howling thugs will gray her hair well before its time. As the years mount, she will eventually bear no resemblance to the blond-tressed wild child whose talent for finding a warm bed was exceeded only by her abysmal taste in bedmates. That girl will be disfigured into yet another hunched and haggard walking corpse, demolished from the inside out. Tina Marie Cornelius will die the slowest death there is. The people's will be done.

And the best part, gentlemen? "I can't blame anyone but me." Those are her words—unambiguous, uncoerced, emphatic, final. Only her. So there it is. Justice is served. We're off the hook. What a girl.

Tina Marie frowns and says, "The stuff about the baths I don't really want published."

She is not without a measure of feminine authority, even here and now, reposed in baggy prison whites on a metal stool behind a layer of Plexiglas and a few smudges of cheap eyeliner. A flip of her mane, a bemused undulation of the pursed lips, a singsong of laughter, and one is reminded of men as powerful as the president of the United States weakening, sinking—then up and away again, leaving the Monicas and the Tina Maries to brood in the wake of spent testosterone. Still, they had their moment, did they not? Their fleeting hold tells us far more than we would ever wish to know about malehood. In the country jail that held Tina Marie prior to her guilty plea, male officers were forbidden to have contact with her. Jail officials did, however, tour church groups past her cell. They gawked at the baby-killing succubus with fascinated horror, as if in the presence of Satan's personal hooker. "I'd talked to a lot of guys who'd been with her," chortled one of her arresting officers, "and they had nothing but high praise." Rather than live with the primally threatening notion that a mother can love her children all the way up until the day she kills them, we prefer to regard Tina Marie Cornelius as a creature not of love but of wholly impure appetites. When I informed one of the individuals connected with her prosecution that I would be visiting her in prison, he sternly warned me, "She will want to have sex with you."

There is more than Plexiglas to prevent such an overture. The charm offensive Tina Marie exerts today is more like a turn on the dance floor for old time's sake. She did not initiate these interviews and agreed to them only when persuaded that clarity on the subject is badly needed. But she does not wish to dwell on the baths. The subject is irrelevant, she tells me. The baths took place more than a decade before she left her babies to die. "I'm here because of the road I chose." Plus, it's a family matter, and her people have been dealt enough misery. She and her sister no longer speak. Her mother has written only one letter and has yet to make the seventy-five mile drive to visit Tina Marie. Her former stepfather (who did not respond to requests for an interview) remains in the west Arizona town of Parker, where he used to give her the baths, but Tina Marie does not yearn for vengeance. He provided well enough. Big house, a pool, a boat. In fact, she considers aloud in a soft drawl tainted with self-disgust, "Maybe I was just spoiled. I mean, every family has their faults."

A close relative remembers walking in during one of the baths — remembers the sudden swirl of bathwater, the stepfather recoiling in shame. At this point, Tina Marie is perhaps eleven. She has confided in the school principal about the baths, but nothing changes. Name-calling, beatings—and then, as a kind of balm, the baths. She carries her sense of alienation to school, where the boys grab her breasts and the girls laugh at her acne. Parker is small, a square mile of a town. There's talk. Problems at home. An adult friend observes her growing moodiness and asks carefully, "Are things going on in your life, Tina Marie?" When she finally tells her stepfather, "I don't want you bathing me anymore," he goes bananas. Tina Marie begins her pattern of running away.

"All my life, I've run away from things." The baths are no excuse for a bad habit. Today, while sewing the rips in inmate uniforms, Tina Marie Cornelius ponders the year in her life she would most like to have back. Fifteen. That's when she hops a bus to Las Vegas with $13 in her pocket. Upon arrival, she huddles on a bench and tries to sleep while shivering. A biker takes her home. For two months, she's his girlfriend. "Sex, sex, sex," she remembers wearily. "That's all he wanted." She runs from him too. The biker is pissed. He finds her address and guns it over to Parker. But Tina Marie has been sent to Mesa, to a little home for troubled girls. For a while, anyway. One day she walks out the door. A few hours later, she's sitting on top of a small mountain, looking down at her new home, the streets.

You can learn a lot at age fifteen. In the groves of Mesa, oranges and grapefruit are there for the taking. You can sleep under the shrubs along the roadways. You can take showers at the truck stops. And if you have a peach-muffin face and a skirt that shows off your sinewy gams, you can meet all sorts of people. Some have speed and heroin. Others have a nice bed and a few bucks they'll leave on the nightstand in the morning. One night in a filthy motel, she's shooting up when the cops materialize. She freaks out, and they hog-tie her. In her very first cage, at the Mesa police station, she shows the cops a little skin in return for Cokes and potato chips.

Sent to a rehab center in Flagstaff, which of course she runs
from, Tina Marie learns a neat new trick. People's houses are usually empty in the morning; you can crawl through an open window,
eat what's in the fridge, wash the dishes, take a shower and then
snatch up some clothes from the spoiled little daughter who doesn't
even know, much less appreciate, what's in her closet. She sleeps in
some kid's van at night, and one day she goes with him to school,
just to break the routine. A girl there says, "That's my coat you're
wearing! It's one of a kind!" Tina Marie obligingly hands it over, but
at that point someone brings up the recent string of burglaries in
the neighborhood. The judge lets her serve her intensive probation
in Parker, the square-mile town. She is put back a grade. Now she's
the girl you don't want your kinds hanging around with. Will fifteen never end?

"I was waitressing. I was trying to do good in school. Trying to
make people realize that, OK, I made a mistake. You know what I
mean? I don't know. It was weird. I stayed there in town, but I ran
around. I wanted a house of my own. So I found this place, no one
was in it, it was boarded up. So I went in. There's all these pictures
in there of the sheriff and his wife. And I'm like, fuck! But I stayed
there. I didn't care. And so at sixteen they sent me to a DOC."

At the Department of Corrections unit in Mesa, the counselors
ask her to engage in a psychodrama, a reenactment of some awful
moment in her life. Replaying the business about the baths only
makes her angrier. Her parents are brought in for a family-therapy
session. "It just did not work. We just didn't want to face it." The
next two years are spent variously in penal institutions, in halfway
houses and especially on the seedy streets of Sunnyslope in northern Phoenix. Meth is what's for breakfast. A month will go by without a decent night's sleep. She prostitutes herself whenever she
needs the cash. Her runaway pals in Sunnyslope go by names like
Warlock and Spiderman. They might as well be imaginary: One

week they're all she sees, and then they vanish. A few of them are actually decent. While they're getting high, she says to one of them, a guy with a real name, Jesse, "I wish I could have met you before all this." This is before Jesse takes a fatal turn at Russian roulette and subsequently disappears like the rest of them.

At a pay phone, Tina Marie calls her aunt, who makes the three-hour drive to the street corner in Sunnyslope and then brings her back to Squaresville.

At eighteen, Tina Marie resolves to clean up her act. No more shooting up. No more turning tricks. She works as a waitress in Parker while living with her aunt just across the Colorado in Big River, California. She fits anybody's definition of a pretty girl. Among these drawn to her is an unemployed forty-something named Corey who lives in his parents' trailer. He and Tina Marie are smoking weed one summer afternoon in 1995, and it leads to sex, which leads to pregnancy. To anyone with eyes, it is apparent that Corey will not be in this picture for very long. But Tina Marie Cornelius has reached an adult decision. She will not abort. The girl will be a mother.

"I really thought," she says today, with absolute sincerity and a chilling absence of irony, "this was what I needed to turn my life around. To have someone to care for."

How to understand? Her eyes explode with light as she speaks of Amanda (whom she named after a fellow runaway) and Dominick (after the boy in the movie *Kindergarten Cop*). "They make it out like I didn't love my children—and I did." Such unmistakable finality, but how can it be? She begins to cry as she recalls Amanda's first months of life, in a hospital with damaged lungs. "I've never been so scared in all my life." A photograph of her children's grave site arrives by mail. "I've never seen from my eyes that they're gone," she murmurs. And then: "I don't want to let them go!" How to describe the puddling in her throat, the sledgehammered face, in a way that proves beyond a shadow of a doubt that this grief is a mother's?

Impossible. "She is an evil person who needs to be locked up," said Williamson County district attorney Ken Anderson after Tina Marie Cornelius took his plea offer. Today the lead investigator on the case, Belinda Thompson, scoffs at the crocodile tears: "It's all 'Poor Tina, I got caught.'" Another officer predicts with enormous satisfaction, "I don't think she'll ever make parole." Their theory of the motive, that her two kids were simply getting in the way of a good time, is inconvenienced by thirty-nine months' worth of evidence to the contrary. The phenomenon of maternal filicide would not be so popular a topic for psychological discourse were it merely the rogue expression of a cold heart. True, we have Melissa Drexler, the infamous Prom Mom, who, at eighteen, gave birth during her senior prom, tossed her newborn in the bathroom garbage can and then returned to the dance floor. We have New York's Eva Campos, who beat her five-year-old daughter to death with a shoe after the girl soiled her pants. And we have Debra Jean Milke, an Arizona woman who hired two men to take her four-year-old son, who thought he was going to see Santa Claus, out to the desert, where he was shot three times in the back of the head.

Beneath these tabloid monstrosities lie the despairing, self-loathing remainder, each surely unaware of the template she so snugly fits. Young, white, meagerly educated. Single or unhappily married. Broke or about to be. Nearly two-thirds of them were sexually abused. In this somber camp, we find Susan Smith, the most notorious of all baby killers, whose stepfather fondled her seven years before she drove her two boys into South Carolina's John D. Long Lake at the age of twenty-three, roughly the same age at which Tina Marie Cornelius committed her unspeakable act. We find Christina Riggs, who claimed to have been molested by a male relative, pregnant at sixteen, depressed and deeply in debt the day she suffocated her two boys, ages two and five, for which the state of Arkansas executed her last year after she pleaded with it to do so, saying, "I want to be with my babies." Some kill themselves as well, whereas others deny their culpability to the end—both extremes thoroughly understandable, for what in this world can we trust, if not a mother's love? Would that we could write off maternal filicides as the acts of baby haters. Instead we find, far more often than not, women who viewed motherhood as an opportunity to find the love denied them elsewhere and who in turn had love, if not much else, to offer.

We find nineteen-year-old Tina Marie pushing two strollers through Parker—one containing Amanda; the other, Amanda's oxygen tank. We find her pregnant again, this time by her restaurant manager, who declines any interest in fatherhood. It occurs to her that she and her son will have something immediately in common: they will never know their fathers, but, yes, each will have a mother. In her third trimester, she follows her own mom, recently divorced, to Austin, where Tina Marie has neither a record nor a reputation. "I could start clean," she says. "Erase the past."

At this crucial juncture, let us pause to consider Tina Marie Cornelius's judgment in the matter of sexual relations. During her thirty months in Austin, a variety of men enjoy the pleasure of her company, but the only ones who profess to love her are already married. She meets one of them in a traffic jam. For a full year, he tells her his divorce is imminent. Another is her supervisor at an auto shop, who will neither leave his wife nor be denied Tina Marie's attentions, until one day she is forced to have a policeman chase him away from her parked car. A third fellow, also a coworker, calls her at night, saying his marriage is on the rocks, and asks if they can get together. The day after their rendezvous, he tells her he loves his wife after all. The wife later pays Tina Marie a visit at the shop and gives her an earful.

Strangely, the Texas authorities insist upon viewing Tina Marie's dirty-laundry list of boyfriends as the handiwork of a manipulative black widow. The coworker who stepped out on his wife for an evening begs to differ: it was entirely at his initiation, he admits, and, furthermore, his impression of her remains not that of a skillful man-eater but of someone "with an extremely low opinion of herself." He and the other suitors remained married while Tina Marie Cornelius, twenty-one and mother of two, drifted from one doomed romance to the next. The *tsk-tsks* fly. Of course, most of us remain grateful that thinking with one's hormones is not in and of itself a crime. A good number of us are the fruit of unplanned pregnancies. Yes, but it is murmured: a young woman with no means of support, she should know better. Better than anyone else? Who wishes to come out and say that abstinence is for the single, underemployed woman while sexual misadventures are for the rest of us?

Still, to this day she does not get it. Until imprisoned, she had scarcely a day without a man—even married, even unredeemable—and all the explanation she can offer is a shrug and a chirpy "I just thought that's the way it's supposed to be. And I like the closeness, the companionship." The lore of maternal filicide is rife with references to "poor-self-concept" women who define themselves by how the men in their lives—beginning with their abusive fathers—have regarded them. Just as it is easy to forget that their children had progenitors who failed to come to the rescue—who, in many cases, were nowhere to be found—it is similarly overlooked that the perpetrators struggled not only as mothers but also as women. It happened that Tina Marie Cornelius had moved to a city widely regarded, even among well-educated and childless young women, as a mecca for hopelessly narcissistic young males. In fast-track Austin, even her peach-muffin face and shimmering locks could only get her through a back door. So in and out of back doorways she shuffled, without complaint. "Some of them," she insists in her soft drawl, "were nice guys."

The point, she says, is this: "I can't put a rational explanation to why I did it. There is none. People say it was the drugs—but I don't want to do that. And I don't want to blame it on my not having enough support. I wasn't strong enough. That's what it is. I wasn't strong enough. I had no business even trying to be a single parent."

All of this through trembling lips as the cheap eyeliner runs. But the words are clear enough. Lads, you're free to go. And so on to Wednesday, April 14, 1999.

It has not begun well. Tina Marie has been up all night snorting coke, a drug she seldom used until seven days prior, when she moved into her younger sister's apartment and started dancing at Exposé. There is her dream, to open her own auto shop, and then there is $600 a month in day-care bills and used-car payments. Eight dollars and 32 cents an hour at the auto shop—say no more. The ponytailed guy at Exposé told her she could start as soon as she bought the right dance attire, thus prompting a few days' worth of hot-check writing. She had never worn high heels before; the nice salesperson showed her how. Her new boss coached her, "Now, what do you say when a customer offers to buy you a drink?" Tina Marie's list of vices has never included alcohol. Now she drinks five or six Bloody Marys a shift. From day one she is a hit—how ageless, that naughty-little-girl look. A hundred fifty to $300 for five hours of work. One of the customers enjoys shooting a syringe full of meth into a cotton ball and stuffing it into her mouth. Another is an RV salesman named Lance. As soon as he becomes her boyfriend, he tells her to quit dancing.

She will not. At last she has cash, enough to send Amanda to visit

her daddy. Corey says, Sorry, there's no room. Coked up, she snarls
into the phone, "What do you mean, no room for your own daughter!" Amanda has been acting out of late. She cries out, "I want to
see my daddy!" She bites herself. She bangs her head against the
wall, and Dominick, thinking it some kind of game, mimics his
older sister. Tina Marie can't find it within herself to discipline her
kids, a fact ruefully noted by the men in her life. She brings the kids
over to Lance's place on their first two evenings together. When she
tells him that she's late with her period, Lance hits the roof.

Though it turns out she's not pregnant, they are still not speaking
by Wednesday morning, and Amanda is having one of her acting-
out episodes in the car on the way to the day-care center, which is
north of town, fifty minutes from Exposé. At work she makes good
money, drinks a fair amount to take the edge off the coke she did
before coming in. That the day is no better or worse than those preceding it—that this is her life now and in the days to come—res-
onates only dimly at first, as a thunderstorm would to a fish at the
bottom of a lake. She does not catalogue her grievances: that her
mother will no longer help with the children; that she is living with
her kid sister, whose boyfriend beats her; that her daughter, who is
so much like her, screams out for her absent father; that yet another
man who was only too happy to sleep with her at first sight now says
they need to slow down. She does not have to recite the pressures
aloud for them to count. On this day, they are spinning inside her
like rotary blades.

She fights the crosstown traffic to the day-care center. A dollar a
minute is the late fee. The kids are already acting up. She sees a
woman step out of the day-care center. It's Kristie, the wife of the
guy at the auto shop whom she slept with that one night. She's
working at the day-care center! What is this about? Why is she tor-
menting her? And Tina Marie is furious—trembling even on the
day she recounts it. No escape! Not from anything! And the chil-

dren are hollering in the car like savages, and when she reaches around to swat at them, they laugh. Laugh at her! They know she won't get the better of them! They know there's no escape! She drives off, the kids in tow.

Except . . .

Today she asks it in a whisper: "Do you ever have times when your mind just goes blank? Just snaps?"

What plays out next is like a silent film, paced like a dream. Her sister's apartment is off Highway 79, but she drives past it—way past it, to a little town called Hutto, where she turns onto a dirt road and finds a cemetery and knows that this is the place. She parks on the roadside just past the last plots. Now her children obey, as if it has already happened and they are ghosts. She leads them down a slope to a limestone overhang. Some twenty feet below lies Brushy Creek. Somewhere behind her, the occasional car drives past. To do the unfathomable cannot take long at all.

She sits Dominick down beside her on the limestone. "I love you," she says, hugging him. Then she calls Amanda over. "I love you, princess," she says to the child's nursery-school pout through her own.

"I love you, too, Mommy," says Amanda. And then the three-year-old girl is thrown off the cliff.

And then Dominick is thrown. The mother sees her son's head bounce against a rock.

And then, from the creek bed below, Amanda manages to stand and calls out: "*MOMMY!*"

And in her car, driving westward into the smoldering dusk, Tina Marie is shaking, talking to herself as if to a passenger: What have you done? What the hell have you done? She wants to throw up. No one is home at her sister's apartment. She jumps in the shower. She gathers some belongings. And then she drives to Lance's. The kids are with relatives, she tells him, and they sleep together.

That night she hears the whistle of a gusting wind. Her children
are shivering. She cringes against the pillow. In her sleep, she cries
out their names, waking Lance. Then there is silence, the deathly
kind.

What follows cannot be explained. It can only be retold.

The next day she acquires some speed and returns to Exposé.
She sleeps with Lance again that night, but he is emphatic that he
is not ready for commitment. On Friday she checks in to a motel, as
seedy a place as any she has encountered since her days as a runaway. Her neighbor is a woman with an eye the color of spoiled
milk. The Bob Marley Festival takes place the following afternoon
in an Austin city park. Kids are smoking pot right in front of the
police officers. The reggae music is equally intoxicating. She has
needed to forget; she is in the right place. A guy she meets among
the pot smokers takes her back to his place to snort some speed. His
name is Lee, and he is cute and fun—the kind of guy that, but for
the immediate past, she would have liked to have built a future
with. The following afternoon, while parked near Lake Travis, she
tells Lee that she once had children but their father had thrown
them off a cliff.

On Monday, April 19, one of the other dancers, an outgoing
blond, notices that Tina Marie has been working later hours and
deduces she has lost custody of her kids. *Girl, check out of that
motel; you're coming with me.* She lets her new friend think whatever she will. They drive out to the lake, to a restaurant, where
yachts are parked. Tina Marie has never seen such a crowd. The
blond dancer knows two of the well-heeled men. They all go back
to her place. The guy who pairs off with Tina Marie makes her cry.
Outside, Tina Marie tells the blond dancer, "He keeps asking me

questions about my kids!" And yet she leaves with him, insisting to the blond dancer, "I need this." That night she tells her new companion that her children fell off a cliff. But the only details that rivet him are these: it's his birthday and this hot young thing wants his bones.

Tuesday at work, there's phone call for her. "Where have you been?" exclaims her sister. She's been worried—all the more so since it was reported late yesterday that two unidentified children were found dead in a creek. No, the kids are fine, Tina Marie insists. She finishes her shift. Then she checks in to a motel across the street from Exposé. She dials Lee's pager, but he does not return the call. All cords are now cut. The following morning, she is southbound in her battered used Pontiac. In San Antonio, a sign indicates a route to Corpus Christi. Her mother has been there. She said she liked the beaches. How long has it been since Tina Marie heard the waves?

By Wednesday afternoon, her skin is blistered. But she returns to the beach the following day. Flipping her visor down, she sees, fastened to it, a photograph of her daughter. There is a haunted aura about the girl's face. Now Tina Marie knows it: her daughter is dead. Back in the city on Thursday, she gravitates to a carnival, as she did on Wednesday and will again on Friday. A carnival worker says he can get her a job. They sleep together in a motel on stilts above the water. She avoids him the next evening at the carnival. In line for her favorite ride, the Zipper, she makes eyes at a Hispanic guy named Maurice, who thinks, *That's one fine-ass bitch looking at me*, while his sister Becky stands next to him thinking, *That little slut doesn't know I'm not his girlfriend!* They ride the Zipper together. Later, Maurice and Tina Marie check in to the Padre Motel. Why'd you pick me? he wants to know. You looked safe, she replies. She explains that she left her boyfriend in Austin after a fight, and, well, here she is. When his sister asks her the following day how she could just show up in town with barely a dollar to her name, Tina Marie Cornelius shrugs. "You've got to think positive," she says.

Soon she is living with Maurice and Becky and confiding to her new boyfriend that she is in some kind of trouble: She has warrants out of Lubbock for participation in a car-theft ring. But then she also speaks of having given up her children to their father because nobody wanted to be with a twenty-two-year-old mother of two. "I don't know if they're dead or alive," she murmurs. Then, with refreshed urgency, her peach-muffin face commands his attention. Will he help her get phony identification, send her car to a chop shop and run off with her to Mexico to start over together, maybe even have a baby?

Yes. Yes. He says he will, even though his sister is warning him that something's not right, that policemen keep driving by their house at all hours. "The honest truth," he says today, "is I was pussy-whipped."

But her new life is stillborn. On Wednesday, April 21, 1999, the two children in Brushy Creek are identified and an all-points bulletin is issued for their missing mother. Soon the police determine, through a trail of hot checks, that the mother is alive. When Lee from the Bob Marley Festival comes forward, they learn she is no one's captive. And when a Corpus Christi welfare office notifies the police that a Tina Marie Cornelius has submitted a new local address, the police confront the unfathomable, that a mother has killed her children and simply moved on.

Four days later, they burst into a Corpus Christi apartment, where they find her seated on a bed, watching television. A friend's baby is on her lap. Noting their horrified stares, she almost wants to laugh and say, Come on! You think I'm some kind of monster?

·   ·   ·

A woman would have to be crazy not to want out. From her very first day at the Hobby Unit, when a disembodied voice snarled down a corridor, Hey, baby killer, you ain't gonna be safe *anywhere*, there have been taunts, women jumping out of the darkness to kick her in the back and yank out a handful of dirty-blond hair, threats to bludgeon her with a hoe. In August she will be twenty-five and she is already at least ten pounds overweight, with at least twenty-eight more years' worth of starch ahead of her. A lonely-hearts guy named Joe had been sending her money for the commissary, but now that has ceased. The prison system will not let her complete her high school education: the few classroom seats available are reserved for those who will soon be returning to the free world. And she stopped attending the twelve-step meetings at step five, in which one is required to confess. She does not trust the counselors. They will tell the staff heretofore untold details, and the guards will resume their torments afresh. One of them wrote her up for supposedly rigging a door, and when Tina Marie laughed at the absurdity of such a charge, the guard responded, "Well, you deserve a case just for being who you are!"

A year has passed without her setting foot in the law library. That will probably change soon. She is on shaky ground here, having consistently admitted her guilt. But a lesser sentence would be nice. Ten years. Fifteen even. The only hard evidence prosecutors could take to a jury was Tina Marie's written confession. Absent a motive, a means, a witness or a specific time frame, and with every state witness sure to testify that Tina Marie Cornelius was a loving mother, the prosecutors freely admit today the unlikelihood of her receiving the death penalty she believed she was avoiding by signing her sixty-year plea agreement. Poor and ignorant, Tina Marie rested her fate in the hands of a court-appointed attorney who showed little bravado. In Minnesota, twenty-four-year-old Khoua Her accepted fifty years for strangling her six children. In Arizona, Lynn Cox

stabbed her four-year-old son more than 150 times and pled out for thirteen years. Then again, as of last December, eight women, including two in Texas, awaited death for the murder of their children. Rarely does a maternal filicide touch a juror's heart. Yes, there is mercy on earth. We look to our mothers to give it.

There are no back doors anymore, no street shadows to take her in. She misses none of that, anyway. No, she is living precisely as her persecutors would wish. She is hearing her children's voices at night—sometimes imagining driving with them, careening down anonymous byways, other vehicles in close pursuit. By day, when she could be poring over the appellate cases, she reaches for the Texas newspapers and studies the classified ads, reviewing the alternatives that were there. Adoption homes. Lots for sale, one with a log cabin—$4,000, *I could have paid for that.* She attends church, and it will please her detractors to know that she is not altogether certain of her salvation. Yes, her children are in a better place. But do they forgive her? *How can they possibly understand what I've done?*

She could help others. She really thinks that. Who knows runaways or abused kids better than she? Or mothers in, well, similar situations? "Talk to them, you know? Help them to where they'll have a support. Let them know there are choices." It would be something to live for, the ability to turn her twenty-two-year headlong disaster into a positive. But why should the world give her that chance now when it never did before? She says it herself, factually, plain as her prison whites: "Parole's not gonna allow me to have some kind of children's shelter or home for battered women."

Tina Marie has seen many a winding road. The one ahead is like a ball of yarn that never stops unspooling. It disappears beyond a colorless horizon. The here and now is her colony of fellow lepresses, a sorry, unloved sight. In her cell, she feels the Texas heat two times over. Lately, it has been wet and frigid. She feels the hard

wind, hears the rain turn the flatlands to mush. "But then," she says in a thinning voice, "I'll think, What right do I have to say I'm cold? Whenever I start feeling pain, I tell myself it's nothing compared to the pain I've caused.

"And so," she concludes, as any mother would, "I don't have a right."

*　　*　　*

I'm drawn toward stories that beg the question "Why would a person do such a thing?" The good-or-evil paradigm doesn't address the human condition, in my view: decent people routinely commit indecent acts. I was living in Austin when Tina Marie Cornelius left her infant children to die and then fled to Corpus Christi. It struck me that none of those who demonized her in the local press said, "If only she had left the children with me." Wholly unexplored was the possibility that Tina Marie, and only Tina Marie, truly loved her two offspring all the way up until the moment when she violently did not. Were maternal love and maternal filicide mutually exclusive? Uncomfortable as it may have made some readers, the facts were unassailable: mother and murderer were one and the same.

I was especially pleased that such a story would appear in Gentlemen's Quarterly *(where I've worked for the past five years). It's worth reminding seekers of a more perfect manhood that their lurid pursuit of the girl seated at the next bar stool may have unintended consequences.*

BAD COPS
PETER J. BOYER

On September 8, 1999, a thirty-two-year-old Los Angeles police officer named Rafael Perez, who had been caught stealing a million dollars' worth of cocaine from police evidence-storage facilities, signed a plea bargain in which he promised to help uncover corruption within the Los Angeles Police Department. Perez hinted at a scandal that could involve perhaps five other officers, including a sergeant. Later, Perez began to talk about a different magnitude of corruption—wrongdoing that he claimed was endemic to special police units such as the one on which he worked, combating gangs in the city's dangerous Rampart district. Perez declared that bogus arrests, perjured testimony, and the planting of "drop guns" on unarmed civilians were commonplace. Perez's story unfolded over a period of months, and ignited what came to be known as the Rampart scandal, which the *Los Angeles Times* called "the worst corruption scandal in L.A.P.D. history."

Eventually, Perez implicated about seventy officers in wrongdoing, and the questions he raised about police procedure cast the city's criminal-justice system into a state of tumult. More than a hundred convictions were thrown out and thousands more are still being investigated. The city attorney's office estimated the potential cost of settling civil suits touched off by the Rampart scandal at $125 million. A city councilman, Joel Wachs, said that it "may well be the worst man-made disaster this city has ever faced." The Rampart scandal finally broke the L.A.P.D. in a way that even the Rodney King beating, in 1991, and its bloody aftermath had not, forcing the city to accept a federal role in overseeing the police department's operation. Yet in the view of the lead investigator, Detective Brian Tyndall, members of the task-force team investigating Rampart have come to believe that Rafael Perez is not just a rogue cop who had decided to come clean but a brilliant manipulator who may have misdirected their inquiry. "He's a convict," Tyndall says. "He's a perjurer. He's a dope dealer. So we don't believe a word he says."

I—"HE'S GOT A GUN!"

One of the early signals of coming trouble for the L.A.P.D. arose from the palm-lined boulevards below Universal Studios, where an officer named Frank Lyga worked undercover narcotics in the Hollywood division. Lyga became the central figure in an episode that exposed deep ruptures within the L.A.P.D., and within the city it polices—dynamics that would, in large measure, define and propel the developing Rampart scandal.

In 1986, when Lyga joined the department, he was already an old-timer, a twenty-nine-year-old transplant from an Adirondack valley that his family had farmed for generations. He'd been on a local sheriff's force upstate, but he hated the cold, and he believed what he'd heard about the L.A.P.D. "It was professional . . . the best police department in the world," he says now. "I'm used to the East Coast police—not to knock the East Coast . . . a big fat cop sitting in a car eating doughnuts, drinking coffee. They couldn't get their gun out if their life depended on it."

Lyga embraced the ethos of the L.A. street cop, a breed distinguished not so much by race, or even by gender, as by distinctness from the "insiders," or "bun boys"—officers who make their way to command positions through desk jobs and adjutancy. Street cops haven't necessarily read the police novels of Joseph Wambaugh, but they've seen the movies, and they believe that in *The New Centurions* Wambaugh got it just about right. Officers of the L.A.P.D. may become cynics, depressives, drunks or bad husbands, but they believe that they form the outer membrane of civilization, and that chaos lies just the other side of the "thin blue line"—a term, as it happens, that was coined by the towering William H. Parker, an Eisenhower-era police chief whose distant memory is still revered.

The street cops' language is something like the voice of arrested adolescence. The suspects they engage ("jam") are "knuckleheads" and "assholes," and their encounters are "capers." They refer to themselves as "coppers." Frank Lyga's description of a good day at work is "rockin' and rollin', putting people in jail."

For Lyga, March 18, 1997, was not a good day at work. He and other members of his team were staking out a suspected methamphetamine dealer, and Lyga was the point man, which meant sitting in his unmarked 1991 Buick Regal and waiting for a drug deal to happen, so that he could follow the suspects back to their source. He'd sat there for three hours trying to look like an inconspicuous badass—with a Fu Manchu mustache and a ponytail, and dressed in jeans, a tank top and a baseball cap adorned with a marijuana-leaf logo—when the deal was called off and the team agreed to reconvene at the Hollywood station.

Lyga pulled his car onto Ventura Boulevard. While he was stopped at a red light, he heard the thumping beat of rap music at high volume emanating from a green SUV that had pulled up next to him. Lyga says he glanced at the driver, a black man with a shaved head. The driver stared back. When Lyga rolled down his window and asked, "Can I help you?" the man made a menacing gesture and said, according to Lyga, "Ain't nobody looking at you, punk." Lyga, who prided himself on his Aryan Brotherhood cover—"All I lacked was the lightning bolts on my neck"—was surprised by the confrontation. He assumed that the other driver was a gang member, especially when, he says, the driver of the SUV shouted, "Punk, I'll put a cap in your ass."

"He was a stone gangster," Lyga recalls. "In my opinion, in my training experience, this guy had 'I'm a gang member' written all over him. He had a shaved head, he had a goatee, wearing a nylon jumpsuit, driving a sport-utility vehicle." Lyga mentioned the "hand motions" the man had given him.

Lyga says he accepted a challenge from the other driver, suggesting that they pull over and have it out it right there. The driver of the SUV did pull over, but Lyga bolted into traffic and drove off, chuckling as he glanced at his infuriated adversary in the rearview mirror. "I'm thinking, What an idiot, thinking I'm going to stop," Lyga recalls. "And I'm laughing, and I'm watching him in the mirror and he looked like he was going to rip the steering wheel off."

But the other driver pulled back into traffic, and a slow-motion chase ensued, with the SUV edging through heavy traffic until it neared Lyga's car. Hoping that his partners were just a few blocks behind, Lyga radioed for help: "Hey, I got a problem. I've got a black guy in a green Jeep coming up here! He may have a gun."

Soon, Lyga was at another stoplight, and the SUV started to pull up beside him on the left. Lyga swore, then unfastened his seat belt, anticipating a street fight. He again called for help—using a hidden radio microphone, activated by a foot pedal—and took out his gun, placing it on his lap facing the SUV. Lyga could plainly see the other driver now, and saw his arm extend across the passenger seat toward Lyga's car, his hand clutching what looked to Lyga like a steel-cased .45-caliber handgun. Lyga leaned forward, out of the line of fire, and radioed again: "He's got a gun!"

Lyga says he again heard, "I'll cap you," then he raised his weapon, a nine-millimeter Beretta, and fired into the SUV, missing the driver. Two seconds later, Lyga fired again, and this time, he says, "I almost could hear the impact, the thud of the round hitting him, and I definitely saw it in his face." The SUV wheeled away in a U-turn, then rolled into a gas station, and stopped. Lyga radioed a last transmission: "I just shot this guy! I need help! Get up here!"

Lyga pulled into the gas station and, holding his badge in his hand, yelled to a customer coming out of the station's mini mart to call 911. Soon, a California Highway Patrol unit arrived, followed by Lyga's boss and the others on his stakeout team. Lyga had been right about his second shot—the bullet had struck the driver on his right side, puncturing his heart before stopping in his lung. Lyga had been right about the gun, too; the highway patrolmen found a stainless-steel nine-millimeter pistol on the floorboard of the SUV.

The other officers, following standard procedure, took control of the scene. A few minutes later, one of Lyga's partners approached him, and Lyga asked, "Is he dead?"

"Oh, yeah," his partner replied, "he's dead."

Good, Lyga thought. In eleven years on the force, he'd fired only two rounds, and had never before hit anybody; he was a brawler, not a shooter. But he figured that the guy in the SUV had left him no choice.

Lyga returned to the station and awaited instruction—there would be paperwork, and investigators would want a reenactment of the shooting. A little over two hours later, Lgya's boss, Dennis Zeuner, told him about the man he'd shot, whose name was Kevin Gaines. "The guy was a policeman," Zeuner said. "One of ours."

The next day, Lyga found media trucks parked near his home, in Ventura County. A group of African-Americans, led by Gaines's former partner, Derwin Henderson, showed up at the scene of the incident and began conducting an unofficial investigation. It was a provocative move, challenging the L.A.P.D.'s fairness in dealing with racial incidents—which is what the Lyga-Gaines shooting had now become.

Three days after the shooting, Johnnie Cochran Jr. stepped into the case, having been hired by Gaines's family to investigate a potential claim against Lyga and the city. Cochran's first act was to commission a private autopsy of Gaines's body, which revealed, a Cochran aide suggested, that there might be problems with the official version of Gaines's death.

Headquarters instructed that Lyga's "package" be pulled, meaning that the records of his job performance were being examined. On Lyga's second day back on the job, he was assigned to a desk by the narcotics-division commander, and was told that he had a bad package—some forty use-of-force incidents. The department, in one attempt at reform, had defined "use of force" to include, in some situations, even the use of a "firm grip" to apprehend a suspect; in eleven years, Lyga had arrested many drug suspects who required more than a firm grip. Of those use-of-force incidents, however, four had prompted complaints of unnecessary force, but in each case Lyga was exonerated or the charges were classified as "unfounded" or "not resolved." Now, however, every use-of-force incident was examined demographically, and tested for signs of racial bias. No apparent indications were found.

A week after the shooting, Kevin Gaines was buried, and his funeral was itself the cause of discord. The biggest association of black officers, the Oscar Joel Bryant Foundation (named after a policeman killed in 1968), requested an official police funeral with full honors, a ceremony reserved for policemen killed in the line of duty. The demand posed a dilemma for the chief, Willie Williams, a black outsider who had been brought in from Philadelphia to head the L.A.P.D. in 1992, after the Rodney King riots. If Lyga's account was accurate, Kevin Gaines had brandished a weapon at someone he thought was a civilian motorist, and he hardly warranted an honors funeral. On the other hand, the black officers were an important constituency for the besieged Williams, who was widely disliked by the L.A.P.D.'s old guard. In the end, Gaines received a semiofficial police funeral, attended by both Williams and Deputy Chief Bernard Parks.

Two months later, Cochran filed a $25 million claim against the city, charging that Lyga was "an aggressive and dangerous police officer who had failed to summon immediate medical assistance for Gaines, contributing to his death, and that he had conspired to "hide and distort the true facts concerning the incident." District attorney Gil Garcetti, whose office had lost the O. J. Simpson case, opened a criminal investigation into the shooting. Lyga noticed the stares now directed his way from black cops. " I was labeled an out-of-control, racist white cop with a history," he recalls. There was talk of an official cover-up, and rumors that Gaines had been the victim of an L.A.P.D. "hit."

Witnesses to various moments of the event confirmed Lyga's account, as did a surveillance camera at the mini mart, which recorded the sound of Lyga firing two shots, 1.8 seconds apart. Three months after the incident, the unit investigating the shooting found that Lyga had acted according to department policy. The department's shooting board recommended no disciplinary action. But that ruling was postponed, pending results of a three-dimensional digital re-creation of the shooting.

In November 1997, Lyga appeared again before the shooting board, which reviewed the evidence and the 3-D re-creation, and in December Bernard Parks, who had succeeded Williams as chief of police, reported that the shooting was within department policy; no action would be taken against him. The district attorney's inquiry also eventually ruled that Lyga "acted lawfully in self-defense."

Meanwhile, Cochran's case against Lyga and the city on behalf of Gaines's family was drawing closer to a trial. Lyga, who was represented by the office of the city attorney, James Hahn, could hardly wait. "My only hope was to go to trial. I wanted to go to trial, win, lose, or draw," he says. "I wanted the facts to come out—I did not do anything wrong."

But it was not Lyga's call. Even though the re-creation of the shooting supported his story, the city and Cochran agreed to a settlement conference the following October, mediated by retired judge R. William Schoettler, who first met separately with both sides. Cochran had reduced his request from $25 million to $800,000; Lyga didn't want to settle at all. Cochran dropped his figure to $250,000—and the city accepted.

Lyga felt betrayed. "My career, my life, is over," he recalls thinking. "I'm labeled a racist killer who was protected and covered up by the department."

Judge Schoettler wrote a letter to Parks telling him that he thought Lyga and the city would have won the case had it gone to trial. "Had the matter been submitted to me for a determination, I would have found in favor of the City of Los Angeles," Schoettler wrote. He added that a settlement had been proposed primarily to avoid adverse publicity, and said, "As you are aware, the settlement can be termed 'political' and neither the fact of the settlement nor the amount involved should in any way reflect upon the conduct of Detective Lyga." The "political" reason for settling the case seemed obvious: city attorney Hahn was preparing to run for mayor, and black voters made up his principal base.

Lyga had been allowed to return to undercover work in June of 1997, and he did so harboring a measure of bitterness. He knew well why the shooting had become such an inflammatory episode. "Four little words—'No justice, no peace,'" he says now. "Bottom line, four words. That's the political environment in the city of Los Angeles."

.   .   .

If the L.A.P.D. seems perpetually vexed by racial politics, it is not without historic cause. In the 1920s, the department had a chief, Louis Oaks, who was a member of the Ku Klux Klan. The modern L.A.P.D. was created in the image of William Parker, whose sixteen-year reign (1950–66) was driven by two overriding priorities, neither of which was the building of a racially sensitive police force.

In coming up through the ranks of the L.A.P.D., Parker had been a clean cop in a department so dirty that even the fictional treatments of police corruption, from Raymond Chandler to Hollywood's gangster pictures, did not defame it. The department's vice unit protected whores, its exams for promotion and hiring were sold by the mayor and his brother out of City Hall, and one head of the L.A.P.D.'s intelligence squad was sent to San Quentin for bombing the car of an investigator working for civic reformers.

Parker's first imperative was to create a police force that was impeccably clean. He was compulsive about police honesty; the everyday transgressions winked at in some East Coast police departments were often grounds for instant dismissal in the L.A.P.D. In Los Angeles, police officers even bought their own coffee.

The department was, and is, startlingly small, reflecting a political culture disinclined to spend tax money on its civic structure. For much of the last half century, the city's police force averaged about seven thousand officers, meaning that it could deploy only fifteen officers per square mile (New York's forty-thousand-strong force deploys 129 officers per square mile). By necessity, Parker's L.A.P.D. became a highly mobile strike force, whose operational signature was aggressiveness. Its officers intervened first and asked questions later.

"I will admit, we were a very aggressive police department," says Daryl Gates, who was once Chief Parker's driver and protégé, and who became one of his successors. "We went after crime before it occurred. We didn't sit back. . . . Our people went out every single night trying to stop crime before it happened, trying to take people off the street that they believed were involved in crime."

The force had a distinctly militaristic character, inculcated at an academy styled after a marine corps boot camp, and reflected in a department whose SWAT team was so proficient in urban-warfare tactics that it helped train American troops who snatched Manuel Noriega from Panama.

But the L.A.P.D. was not necessarily perceived as a benign presence in the city it policed. Its mission to "stop crime before it happened" felt to some like racial profiling before that term had currency, the more so because the force was for so long glaringly white. The L.A.P.D. didn't integrate its patrol force until 1961. As the demographic profile of Los Angeles changed—the black population quadrupled between 1940 and 1960—certain sections of the city began to view the police force as an occupying army. The illusion of a dreamy, well-ordered, monochromatic Los Angeles, as projected by the L.A.P.D.-approved *Dragnet* series, was pretty well shattered by the Watts riot, in 1965.

That year, Johnnie Cochran filed his first claim against the L.A.P.D. By the time of the Rodney King incident, twenty-six years later, Cochran had become the dean of a flourishing "police brutality bar," which portrayed the department as a congenitally brutal force given to victimizing minority citizens. There was a saying that the New York Police Department was corrupt but not violent, and the L.A.P.D. was violent but not corrupt. Critics of the L.A.P.D. coined a term to describe the type of malfeasance they discerned in the department—"force corruption."

As the criticism increased, the department found itself defending even its fundamental tactics, such as the upper-body control hold that was drilled into every recruit at the academy. This technique, used to subdue a resistant suspect, was also known as a choke hold, and became controversial in the early eighties with the revelation that fatalities occurred disproportionately among black arrest subjects. Chief Gates suggested in 1982 that the hold was killing blacks because their "veins or arteries do not open up as fast as they do in normal people." That statement, along with a couple of publicized choke-hold deaths that year, produced a ban on the technique. Gates, who complains that the ban left cops with only a gun and a club, predicted that the number of injuries would rise, and they did.

Racial issues upset the department from within, as well. In 1980, the city settled two discrimination lawsuits against the L.A.P.D., one private and one federal, by signing consent decrees mandating minority and female hiring quotas. Women, blacks and Hispanics joined the department in sizable numbers, but the hiring program seemed only to heighten racial tensions on the force. In 1986, the *Los Angeles Times* published the results of a three-month study showing that women and minorities felt they were being denied promotion and assignment opportunities, and that some white male officers felt the department had degraded its standards.

When a plumbing-supplies store manager named George Holliday videotaped the arrest of Rodney King, in 1991, he captured a scene that only confirmed a view of the L.A.P.D. that some in Los Angeles already held. A year later, a jury without blacks acquitted the officers who had beaten King, and the city burned for three days. By 1995, black disaffection had reached such a point that Cochran and the rest of O. J. Simpson's defense team correctly guessed that it could be exploited to contest a murder rap. Their cause was helped immeasurably by Detective Mark Fuhrman, whose serial utterances of the word "nigger" fortified the defense theory that Simpson was framed in a racist police conspiracy.

II—GANGSTA COPS

Such was the atmosphere in Los Angeles when Frank Lyga and Kevin Gaines crossed paths—an atmosphere that perhaps obscured some troubling information that arose from that incident. While Frank Lyga's background was being examined, investigators also pieced together a profile of the cop he had killed, and what they found startled them. Off duty, Kevin Gaines was apparently given to violent outbursts, causing his wife to file several domestic-abuse complaints. Investigators learned that he had been involved in other road-rage incidents, and in at least one case he had allegedly threatened to "cap" a motorist who had annoyed him.

The most bizarre event in Gaines's recent past had occurred the summer before his run-in with Lyga, when cops responded to a 911 report of a shooting on the grounds of a Hollywood Hills mansion. Gaines, off duty, pulled up to the scene and got involved in an altercation with the responding officers. Their account was that Gaines became verbally abusive and provocative, and had to be hand-cuffed. "Tell these motherfuckin' assholes to take the cuffs off of me, motherfucker!" Gaines shouted. He taunted the officers, saying that he hated "fucking cops." Gaines's account was that he'd been mistreated by the police. He hired an attorney and filed a notice of claim against the city. When the incident was investigated by the L.A.P.D.'s Internal Affairs division, it was discovered that the 911 call had been made by Kevin Gaines himself. "The evidence suggests that he did that to engage L.A.P.D. in a confrontation and basically wanted to secure a pension or whatever by filing a lawsuit," Russell Poole, a former L.A.P.D. detective, says.

Poole, a robbery-homicide detective who was assigned to investigate possible criminality in the Lyga-Gaines shooting, later wondered why that 911 incident had not been more thoroughly pursued by Internal Affairs, which was at the time directed by Deputy Chief Parks. Falsely reporting a crime was against the law, and would likely have warranted Gaines's removal from the force. Even more significant was the identity of the person who owned the Hollywood Hills home: Sharitha Knight, the estranged wife of the jailed gangsta-rap impresario Marion (Suge) Knight, who founded Death Row Records. In the course of investigating the road-rage incident, Detective Poole discovered that the SUV Gaines was driving—a green Mitsubishi Montero—was registered to Sharitha Knight. It was soon learned that Sharitha had been romantically involved with Gaines for some time, and that he was living with her at the time of his death.

Investigators had been struck by the lifestyle that Gaines had somehow managed on his salary of about $55,000 a year—he wore expensive suits and designer shirts, and drove a Mercedes—and the connection to Knight and Death Row began to explain it. Detectives found that Gaines had nine credit cards, and among the receipts they found in his belongings was one for a $952 tab at Monty's, a Westwood steak house that was a hangout for people who worked for Death Row Records.

Poole had heard talk around the force that cops earned big money off-duty working security for Death Row; their badges and gun permits made them especially valuable. But to many cops the gangsta-rap scene as epitomized by Death Row was, on the face of it, a crime scene. Gangsta cool glorified street violence, and Suge Knight's legend as a rap kingpin was notoriously colorful; the three-hundred-and-fifteen-pound record executive had, in building and maintaining a hundred-million-dollar enterprise, supposedly dealt with business associates by dangling one man by his ankles from a hotel balcony, smashing another's face with a telephone and forcing another to drink urine from a champagne glass.

More troubling to law enforcement were the apparent connections between Death Row and violent street gangs. The FBI had been investigating Death Row since 1993, and Knight, who had grown up in Compton, was said to be a member of the Mob Piru Bloods gang, associates of which were among the permanent crowd around Death Row.

Within the L.A.P.D., the Lyga-Gaines shooting took on a new dimension. "All those things begin to reflect on his off-duty associations, how he's conducted himself," Parks says of Gaines. "We hold our people accountable for their off-duty and on-duty behavior. It's very difficult to have a life outside of the L.A.P.D. that deals in the criminal element and then come back to work and put on your badge and your uniform and say, 'I'm now protecting the community and enforcing the law.'"

On the morning of November 6, 1997, two black men entered a Bank of America branch near the University of Southern California campus, and one of them, dressed in a jacket and tie and wearing sunglasses and a beret, made his way behind the bank's security shield and, showing a nine-millimeter handgun, demanded money. The robber and his associate—a "layoff man," whose task was to serve as lookout—walked out of the bank and joined their getaway driver in a white van that had been stolen near the airport the day before. They escaped with more than $700,000 in two bags.

Detective Brian Tyndall, who was then working the robbery-homicide division, concluded that the bank heist had been an inside job. The stolen money was freshly "shrunk"—compressed to fit an automated teller machine—and had just been delivered by armored car that morning. The money had been ordered by the assistant manager, a young woman named Errolyn Romero. Under questioning several weeks after the robbery, Romero, who was visibly nervous, told Tyndall, "You know who it is." When Tyndall pressed her for a name, she was so nervous that she could not say it. "I suggested that it might be easier for her to write the name down on a piece of paper," Tyrndall recalls. "And she tried to do that and her hand shook, and she couldn't complete the signature." Instead, Romero reached into her purse and produced a business card bearing the shield of the Los Angeles Police Department. The name on the card was David Mack.

Mack had grown up in the same Compton neighborhood as Suge Knight, and, like Knight, he'd escaped to find success in the world beyond the old neighborhood. He was a brilliant athlete, and had won a scholarship to the University of Oregon, where he ran track and made the United States national team running the eight hundred meters. He joined the L.A.P.D. in 1988. He was married, had two kids and, by all accounts, was a good cop. But investigators discovered that, like Kevin Gaines, David Mack had a secret life off-duty. He was a club crawler, a gambler and a womanizer. After one of the women he was involved with, Errolyn Romero, became an assistant manager at the bank, Mack saw his chance at the big score.

When Mack was arrested, in December 1997, he refused to cooperate with police. He didn't tell them who his accomplices were, or what had happened to the money. "Take your best shot," he told Tyndall. He was apparently content to serve out his term — fourteen years in federal prison — and have the money to look forward to upon his release. When Mack was in custody, his jailers began to notice a gradual transformation in him. He started using a red toothbrush, then wearing a pair of red socks, and soon he was adorned by as much red as could be obtained, given his circumstances. David Mack renounced the L.A.P.D. and aligned himself with the Bloods. "It appears he has completely divested himself of all relationships of his life as a police officer," Parks says, "and he is basically a gang member. He has taken on the role of being a gang member in jail."

During their investigation, Detective Tyndall and his colleagues found that, on the force, Mack had kept to a tight circle of friends, mostly African-Americans. They also discovered that, two days after the bank robbery, two of those friends had accompanied Mack to a weekend blowout in Las Vegas, and that one of them was Mack's ex-partner from the narcotics beat, a former marine named Rafael (Ray) Perez.

Three months after Mack's arrest, on March 2, 1998, six and a half pounds of cocaine were checked out from the property room at L.A.P.D. headquarters downtown and not returned. The coke, evidence in a drug-seizure investigation, had been stored in case it was needed as an exhibit in trial, but there was no trial and thus no legitimate reason for the evidence to have been checked out.

The evidence had been checked out under the name Joel Perez, and there was an officer with that name on the force, but investigators determined that someone else had signed his name. When a clerk at the police property room recollected that Rafael Perez had once checked out a large amount of cocaine, investigators began zeroing in on him. The cocaine theft, on top of what had been discovered about Kevin Gaines and the David Mack bank robbery, suggested a picture of corruption more ominous than any of the misdeeds alone. In any case, it was a possibility that had to be put before Chief Parks.

Unlike his predecessor, Willie Williams, Parks had spent his entire career on the force; he was a straight arrow who managed to avoid being ensnared by the department's political controversies without ignoring them. He was a founding member of the Oscar Joel Bryant Foundation, the black officers' organization, but he wasn't a group activist. He rose steadily in a department that had quelled the aspirations of many black officers. "Bernie Parks is L.A.P.D., and he's a cop through and through," Daryl Gates says.

Parks had been Gates's driver (as Gates had been Parker's), but as he rose to command level, he had sometimes been said to be a cautious critic of Gates's style, and even of the L.A.P.D. culture. After Gates was eased out of the job, in 1992, and it became obvious that the next chief would be black, Parks was a natural choice. When the job went to the Philadelphian Williams, Parks did not go out of his way to help the new chief to succeed, and when Williams failed to win reappointment, in 1997, Parks finally got his chance.

Gates reflexively defended the force whenever controversy arose, and an important lesson Parks took from the decade preceding his appointment was that Gates had done the department a disservice by failing unequivocally to condemn the Rodney King cops. Parks bristled whenever he heard cops argue that the King beating had been, strictly speaking, within policy. "When we did not have the ability to send a message to the community that we were going to be objective in evaluating the set of circumstances, it caused the community to have less trust in us," Parks says. "And I think that's the real issue; how we addressed it is as important as what occurred."

Now, faced with a budding scandal on his own watch, Parks was determined to act decisively in exposing and eliminating what he and his investigators believed might be a crew of gangsta cops.

"Perez is a good friend of David Mack's, both were good friends of Gaines's," Parks says. "I think the picture reflected that we had some people on this department that were, in a coordinated effort, involved in some very serious criminal misconduct."

Parks ordered the formation of an investigative task force to solve the cocaine theft, and to see if it was connected to the bank robbery or to other criminal activity. The task force decided to focus its investigation on Rafael Perez.

When Perez was a boy and was living near Philadelphia, where he and his mother settled after leaving Puerto Rico, he would watch the cop shows on TV and imagine himself one day having a badge and a gun. He went from high school to the marines, and from the marines to the police academy in Los Angeles, where he breezed through, and in 1989 joined the force. After his rookie tour on patrol, Perez was assigned to a special narcotics unit, where he teamed up with a veteran cop whom he came to idolize, David Mack.

Perez and Mack were on a "buy and bust" team, which meant that they traveled undercover throughout the city buying dope on the streets, working with the narcotics squads in different divisions to make arrests. Frank Lyga remembers working with them several times in the Hollywood division, and being struck by the fealty that Perez accorded to Mack. "Ray Perez was the underling and a wanna-be David Mack," Lyga recalls. "David Mack was the supreme leader, and Ray Perez was the supreme follower. Where one was, the other one was, always."

Perez later cast his loyalty to Mack as a case of combat bonding, citing an incident in 1993, when Perez says he found himself staring down the barrel of a drug dealer's gun, pleading for his life, and Mack shot the assailant. (This account has since been disputed by eyewitnesses.)

In 1995, Perez was transferred to the department's élite antigang team, CRASH (Community Resources Against Street Hoodlums), in the Rampart division. The custom at special units such as CRASH was that a prospective member needed to have a sponsor on the team. Perez's sponsor was an officer named Sammy Martin, a close friend of David Mack's. (Mack is a godfather to Martin's son.) It was Sammy Martin who accompanied Perez and Mack on their Las Vegas spree.

Based on those connections, and the statement from the property-room clerk, the task force put Perez under surveillance and began to profile him. It found a pattern in his off-duty lifestyle that was strikingly similar to Mack's. "Again, a very outgoing, charismatic type person, likes the finer things in life, liked to party a lot," Detective Tyndall, who was assigned to the task force, says. "Both were womanizers, had a very active social life. . . . On a policeman's salary, you can do that as long as you're single. But Ray was married and has a child, so we're starting to put together the picture now that his extracurricular activities are going to have to be supplemented in some way."

Investigators subpoenaed Perez's telephone records and were surprised to find that he sometimes made more than a hundred phone calls in a day. On the day that the cocaine was checked out, Perez called an unidentified person in the Rampart neighborhood just after the transaction. Detectives traced the number to a Bella Rios, one of several aliases used by a Honduran woman more commonly known as Veronica Quesada. She was a sometime nightclub singer with a drug record, and when detectives called on her they got lucky. Inside Quesada's apartment were the accoutrements of the drug trade—a razor-marked table, and chemicals for converting powder cocaine into rock. As the detectives were interviewing Quesada, the front door opened and in walked Quesada's brother, Carlos Romero, who was the subject of two outstanding felony-arrest warrants for drug dealing. The officers frisked Romero and found in his right-front trouser pocket a quarter pound of cocaine, freshly cut from a brick.

Romero was arrested, and while the cops were questioning Quesada she said that she needed to fetch something from a side table. When she opened the drawer, one of the detectives, Mike Hohan, noticed a startling photograph. "Sitting on top of everything," Hohan recalls, "is a picture of Rafael Perez in what we call in policeman's parlance a 'two-eleven suit.'" In the California Penal Code, two-eleven is the section for robbery, a crime that seemed to be committed by an inordinate number of people partial to nylon running suits. There was something else about the photograph that struck Hohan, something about Perez's pose. Perez was "throwing gang signs," Hohan says.

It was possible that Perez had been clowning around with the hand signs, engaging in some cop humor, but at the least, detectives could now connect Perez to both ends of the cocaine theft—the witness at the evidence room, and a dealer who could put the dope on the street. Richard Rosenthal, a deputy district attorney, who was now assigned to the task force, became even more convinced of Perez's guilt when he discovered that Perez had intervened in drug cases against Quesada and Romero, telling prosecutors that they functioned as his informants. "That evidence on top of everything else conclusively made me believe we had the right guy, and we had a provable case," Rosenthal says.

Perez was served with a search warrant on August 6, 1998, as he was reporting to the Rampart captain's office. When he was confronted with the news, he asked, "This is about the bank robbery, isn't it?" He was arrested three weeks later.

Rosenthal believed in the case he had against Perez, but as the trial began, in December, he knew that getting a conviction would not be easy. Perez was something of a courtroom legend, a witness who could sway jurors with an air of utter credibility—even, as it turned out, in those cases when he was baldly lying. "What we had with Perez was somebody you would look at and feel that, if I were in his position and I were innocent . . . that's the way I'd act, that's when I would cry, that's when I would stammer. And that was the kind of defendant we were against," Rosenthal says.

Rosenthal got an early hint of how formidable a presence Perez was when, during the jury-selection process, one prospective juror stood up and commented on how handsome Perez was. She was excused. During the trial, Perez admitted that he'd had an affair with Quesada, that he'd even been at the property room the day the cocaine was taken—but denied that he was the one who had taken it. The jury was unable to reach a verdict—the vote was eight-to-four for conviction—and on December 23 the judge declared a hung jury.

The prosecution team immediately went back to work, trying to build a stronger case against Perez, who remained in custody. Rosenthal, who had spent most of his career prosecuting fraud cases, had a study of Perez's financial records drawn up, with charts and graphs showing Perez's unexplained income. Meanwhile, Quesada, who was now in prison, indicated that the missing six and a half pounds wasn't all that Perez had stolen. Investigators followed up on another pound of cocaine that had gone missing the previous year—dope that had been seized in an arrest made by Frank Lyga. For a time, the investigators theorized that Perez had targeted Lyga's evidence in retaliation for Gaines's death. Then Detective Hohan had an idea: what if Perez had been stealing cocaine by checking dope out of the evidence locker, replacing it with another substance, and then returning the package?

The detectives went through hundreds of pieces of evidence in the storage rooms, eventually finding eleven transfers with suspicious paperwork. They had one package of cocaine analyzed. The department chemist found Bisquick instead of cocaine. Six of the other suspicious packages had been destroyed, according to routine department procedure, but four more proved to contain "bunk"— more Bisquick. Handwriting analysis and the recollections of another property clerk showed that some of the swapped evidence had been ordered by Perez.

The task force now had Perez connected to eight pounds of cocaine, which made him what the cops call a major dealer. "I had him," Rosenthal says. "I had him nailed to the wall." On April 6, 1999, Rosenthal got a grand jury to indict Perez on the missing pound and, increasing the pressure, added more complaints as he accumulated new evidence. Rosenthal kept hearing that Chief Parks and the department desperately wanted to deal with Perez, to "flip" him and gain his cooperation in exposing other dirty cops, and in May Rosenthal approached Perez's attorney with an offer.

Perez was represented by Winston Kevin McKesson, a lawyer who knew his way around police cases, but not from the orientation of defending cops. McKesson, who is in his forties, was born and raised in South Central Los Angeles, a neighborhood where violent crime and a fear of police were the hammer and anvil of daily life. His younger brother was killed in a fight outside their parents' home; McKesson's first college research paper was on the subject of police misconduct. After graduating from U.C.L.A. law school, he became a protégé of Johnnie Cochran's, and a notable figure in the police-brutality bar. The only cops he had previously represented were plaintiffs in discrimination suits filed against police departments.

On September 8, during jury selection, McKesson approached Rosenthal, put an arm around his shoulder and suggested that they talk. He had Perez give Rosenthal the barest sketch of a crime that he would confess to: the shooting of an unarmed suspect, and the planting of a gun on him. McKesson said that Perez wanted immunity on that charge and a reduced five-year term on the drug charges in exchange for exposing bad cops in the Rampart division. Gil Garcetti, the district attorney, approved the deal.

III—THE RAT

On the morning of September 10, 1999, Perez was secretly transported in handcuffs and shackles to a room in a downtown Los Angeles office tower. The unlikely meeting place, headquarters of the county transit system, had been chosen partly for security reasons, as there were concerns for Perez's life. Everyone on the law-enforcement side of the case, from Rosenthal to Chief Parks to district attorney Garcetti, had high expectations. Within a week, David Mack would be sentenced to fourteen years in prison, and he was being investigated in connection with the 1997 killing of Biggie Smalls, the rap singer managed by Sean (Puffy) Combs, Death Row Records' East Coast rival. The hope now was that Perez might shed light on that and other unsolved crimes, including the whereabouts of the bank-robbery money and the identities of Mack's accomplices. "We didn't know if he was going to talk about Biggie Smalls's murder, the bank robbery involving David Mack, home-invasion robberies, other additional narcotics, maybe rip-offs," Detective Tyndall says. "We just weren't sure."

Rosenthal reminded Perez that if he failed to tell the complete truth the plea deal was off. "Yes sir," Perez said, and he began to tell a story that would stun everyone in the room, except for his own attorney. Kevin McKesson knew what Perez was going to tell, and he knew that it wasn't a story about a criminal cadre of black cops. He knew that Perez, who by now had become a personal friend, was going to tell a story that confirmed what Johnnie Cochran, the brutality bar and McKesson had been proclaiming for years about the L.A.P.D. "It hurts me to say it, but there's a lot of crooked stuff going on with L.A.P.D., especially L.A.P.D. specialized units," Perez told the investigators.

Perez said that he had gone bad while making his first drug bust on the CRASH team. He said that he and his partner, Nino Durden, had seized money from a drug dealer, and decided to keep some for themselves. Perez also described the botched police shooting, a 1996 confrontation with a nineteen-year-old gang member who'd surprised Perez and Durden during a stakeout. The two officers shot the man, Javier Francisco Ovando, hitting him in the head and chest before they realized that he was not carrying a weapon. As Ovando lay bleeding, Perez recounted, Durden wiped clean a "drop" gun they carried with them for just such an event, and placed it near the body. Then Perez and Durden began to concoct their cover story—that Ovando was a cop killer who had burst in on their observation post, intent on assassination.

Ovando had survived the shooting, only to find himself facing trial on felony-assault charges for trying to kill the two police officers. Ovando, a Honduran who speaks little English, was partially paralyzed in the incident and confined to a wheelchair; he protested that he had no gun, but in the trial Perez took the stand and calmly testified otherwise, convincing the jury of Ovando's guilt. The judge rebuked Ovando for lacking remorse, and sentenced him to twenty-three years in state prison.

Rosenthal and the officers were horrified by what Perez was telling them, but there was more. Perez said that the practice of keeping a drop gun for framing suspects was quite common in CRASH. "Everybody . . . kept one," he said. "Everybody." Bogus arrests and the writing of false police reports, he said, were the rule. "I would say that ninety percent of the officers that work CRASH, and not just Rampart CRASH, falsify a lot of information," Perez said. "They put cases on people."

Rosenthal was hearing a prosecutor's nightmare. He had to find out one thing: was there anyone else sitting in jail for a crime he did not commit? Perez didn't quite answer the question, saying that he would first need to see the CRASH "recap books"—logs of all activities undertaken by the unit.

"Did it happen that frequently that you can't remember?" Rosenthal asked Perez.

"I am really going to need to see those books," Perez replied.

Perez talked for three hours in that first session, and he was eager to keep going ("There's still a lot of things that we have not talked about," he told them), but Rosenthal cut the session short. He was now desperate to get Javier Ovando out of prison, and he took the unprecedented step of filing a writ of habeas corpus (usually the work of a defense lawyer), asking for Ovando's immediate release. Ovando was freed from prison within a week

Ovando was only the first. Rosenthal had once thought that the debriefing sessions with Perez would be completed in a few weeks; they went on for more than a year, thirty-five sessions, which fill forty-five hundred pages of transcript. As Perez's story continued to unfold, the circle of alleged wrongdoers steadily widened. Perez spoke of some officers as being "in the loop"—countenancing, if not necessarily participating in, wrongdoing—so the task force compiled a list of every cop who'd been in the Rampart CRASH and narcotics divisions during Perez's time there, and had him "go through and identify who are the potential suspects," Rosenthal recalls.

Perez was also allowed to peruse fifteen hundred cases, including those in the CRASH recap books he had asked for. Detectives would deliver packages to the county jailhouse of a hundred cases at a time for Perez to go through, selecting cases to discuss at his next debriefing. Sometimes during the debriefings, Perez would volunteer a new memory that had come to him in jail. Rosenthal says that occasionally "we'd start off on an interview and he'd say,

'You know what? I was laying around last night, and I remembered that there was something we need to discuss.'" Other times, Perez would fill in the blanks on incidents that he hadn't witnessed himself, "but he knew what was going on," Rosenthal says.

"If we were to believe Officer Perez," Garcetti says, "we had a rogue group of cops who were totally out of control, who were unsupervised, who were their own little enforcement group." Indeed, Perez portrayed Rampart CRASH as a secret gang in blue, with its own logo (a white skull with a cowboy hat, flanked by playing cards arranged in the "dead man's hand'—aces and eights) and an awards system for shoot-outs with gangsters.

Investigators found that at least some of what Perez said about the Rampart CRASH culture was true. For example, at the time Perez was under investigation the department was also looking into a complaint against a Rampart CRASH officer named Brian Hewitt, who was accused of beating a handcuffed gang member while he was in custody at the station. Hewitt and another policeman, Ethan Cohan, who saw the beaten gang member but did not report the incident promptly, were fired by the department. Both officers were also accused by Perez of other wrongdoing. But how much of Perez's story was hype? Perez's eventual catalogue of misdeeds ranged from his own shooting and frame-up of Javier Ovando to allegations of guns being routinely planted on suspects, cops drinking beer on the job and cops allowing a suspect to lie bleeding rather than calling for medical attention.

The investigation was a messy process, because it had no precedent. Perez would tell the task force about a bad case, and the detectives would fan out to prisons or to a village in Central America or to wherever the wronged party could be found, trying to corroborate Perez's story. Rarely was Perez's account of an event fully verified—even Ovando's version of the shooting incident differed significantly from Perez's—but Chief Parks had declared early on,

"We take Rafael Perez at his word," and so, for the most part, the detectives did. In a way, they had no choice, because Perez's word was by itself enough to undermine confidence in any case in which he had made the arrest, written the report or testified in court.

"At that point, no one was seriously questioning the allegations that he was making," Judge Larry Paul Fidler, of the Los Angeles Superior Court, says. "It rocked everybody back on their heels." As supervising judge of the Superior Court's criminal division, Fidler was responsible for deciding whether or not to grant the writs and overturn the cases that Perez was identifying. Fidler held Rosenthal in high regard, and he felt that the court had no choice but to grant the writs—more than a hundred of them so far.

Inevitably, when transcripts of Perez's debriefings were leaked, his untested allegations became fixed in the public mind. Defense attorneys began to employ the "Perez defense," claiming that Perez's picture of what happened in Rampart might well have happened in the case of their client, and therefore the jury should acquit. "That was the standard, if you will, the battle cry in almost every case," Judge Fidler says.

When Javier Ovando was released from prison, on September 16, 1999, he was flown home to Los Angeles by the L.A.P.D. But before he even boarded the plane, he was approached by Gregory Moreno, a lawyer in the Los Angeles police-brutality bar, who a few days later landed Ovando as a client. In October, Moreno filed suit against the city, and the only real question was how much the settlement would be. "When this came out, it was the opportunity that many of us had waited for," Moreno says, "and we were blessed to be able to be at the forefront." Rodney King had received a settlement of $3.8 million, and Moreno had recently won a settlement of $5.3 million against the county sheriff's office. For Ovando, he says, "fifteen million dollars was the right figure."

In February 2000, Johnnie Cochran convened a Saturday summit meeting of the city's leading police critics and brutality-bar attorneys, to see how they might respond to what one lawyer called "a situation that is tailor-made for reform." Among those who spoke to the gathering was Cochran's protégé Kevin McKesson.

As more convictions were overturned, more lawsuits were filed. Ruben Rojas, a gang member whom Perez acknowledged having framed on a dope charge, won a settlement for $1 million. His attorney, Gregory Yates, eventually ended up with sixty Rampart clients. He bundled twenty-nine of those cases together for an eleven-million-dollar settlement last December, and the Beverly Hills branch of the Wells Fargo Bank stayed open late one Friday night just to handle all the deposits. Forty-three settlements have been made already, ranging from $25,000 to Ovando's $15 million.

Some have accused plaintiffs' lawyers of rank opportunism, and Yates has heard the charge of "police-car chasing." He is unmoved. "Who else is going to do it?" he asks. "Who else is going to seek redress for these people?"

In the wake of the Rodney King beating, Congress passed a law allowing federal oversight of local police departments that had been found guilty of a pattern of depriving citizens of their rights. The law has been used by the Justice Department to establish federal oversight of police forces in Pittsburgh, in New Jersey, and in Steubenville, Ohio, and was cited by those (such as the New York City mayoral candidate Mark Green) proposing federal oversight of the New York Police Department after the 1997 brutalizing of Abner Louima. The Justice Department opened a civil inquiry into the L.A.P.D. in 1996; it had no discernible result until the Rampart scandal lent it new impetus. In the waning days of the Clinton administration, the acting head of Justice's civil-rights division, Bill Lann Lee, threatened to sue Los Angeles to prove a "pattern or practice" of excessive force and rights abuses unless the city consented to federal oversight. Chief Parks and the city's mayor,

Richard Riordan, opposed the agreement, but Rampart sapped their political capital on the issue, and the city council relented to the feds.

Among the reforms imposed on the department are some that were first urged after the Rodney King incident, including a computerized "early warning" system for tracking problem officers. There is now also a mandate to maintain a running tally of all police stops, categorized by the subject's ethnicity and gender—an intended guard against racial profiling.

There were some topics on which Rafael Perez had very little to say, and they happened to be the subjects that the task force had hoped he might illuminate when he was given his immunity deal. He said he had not known Kevin Gaines, and that, contrary to Frank Lyga's assertion, he had never met Lyga while working narcotics, or anywhere else.

On the subject of his friend David Mack, Perez was similarly unhelpful. "I considered him a very good friend who saved my life," Perez said when the subject first came up. "Was I involved in that bank robbery? No. Was this a big coincidence that we both end up in this kind of trouble, or he ends up in that type of trouble, and I—" He stopped himself, then concluded, "It's a very big coincidence." Perez said he knew nothing about Mack's accomplices, or about what Mack had done with the stolen money.

"He seems to have a very strong relationship—I don't know if that's fear, or an affection—with Mr. Mack," Gil Garcetti says. "I'm absolutely convinced he knows something he has never told us."

That opinion is shared by police and prosecutors who have dealt with Perez. Suspicion grew among some of them that he had directed—or possibly misdirected—the course of the scandal investigation. "He's deflecting us everywhere else but where we should be," says one officer who is deeply involved in the case, and believes that he gave Perez too much credence. "The task force just went wherever he took them. He's counting on getting out in June."

Detective Tyndall says that he came to sense that Perez was almost taunting the investigators. "He was eating this up," Tyndall says. "He knew that, this whole production, he was the center, he was the star. And he was going to take advantage of it to the utmost."

When Perez directed the investigation toward other cops in Rampart CRASH, Garcetti hoped that at least some implicated officers would turn, and cooperate in exposing others. But that didn't happen. Instead, cops fought the charges in police Board of Rights hearings—proceedings argued before a panel comprising two command officers and a citizen. Most of the hearings found in favor of the officers. Still, there was enormous political and media pressure for a definitive outcome, and the district attorney's office felt most of it. Gil Garcetti had won another term after his team lost the O. J. Simpson case, but his standing with voters was precarious as he faced the November 2000 election. Chief Parks, determined to be seen as leading the fight against police corruption, criticized Garcetti publicly and often for not bringing criminal cases against Rampart officers, and Garcetti countered that there was no case yet to bring.

"My position is, all we have is Rafael Perez pointing the finger," he says. "That's all I have. A convicted perjurer, a liar, a thief. We get to a court, it will never even get to a jury. The judge will have to dismiss the case."

Eventually, as the pressure continued, Garcetti decided that he would have to go with what he had despite his own misgivings. "Once we could see we were not going to get any police officers from within the department, that's almost the end of the case," Garcetti recalls. "You take the little bits and pieces that are left, and you go forward with that prosecution."

IV—A VERY GOOD OFFICER

The criminal accusations that Garrcetti's office chose to prosecute came to trial last October 4, in the courtroom of Los Angeles Superior Court judge Jacqueline A. Connor. To the extent that the Rampart scandal had become a stain on the character of the L.A.P.D., the case could not have been more fitting. One defendant, a thirty-nine-year-old cop named Brian Liddy, was the perfect embodiment of the department of Daryl Gates and Joseph Wambaugh, for better and worse.

Like Perez, Liddy had always wanted to be a cop. His father kept bar at a tavern in the Bronx which was a hangout for off-duty cops. He joined his first civilian force in Norwalk, Connecticut, and quickly became a star. Dana McIndoe, his first captain in Norwalk, says, "He had a nose for finding the bad guys. . . . I don't know how to put it—he was just born to be a police officer, I guess."

Liddy, a burly man with a sardonic air, was an aggressive cop who "had his rough edges," McIndoe says, and a number of complaints were filed against him. "I talked to him a few times about minor indiscretions," McIndoe says, "and one thing I'll say about Brian, if he messed up, he said he did. He'd come out and say, 'Yeah, I did it. I lost my cool and yelled at the guy, called him a coupla names.'"

Like Frank Lyga, Liddy believed that the L.A.P.D. was the best force in the world, and after visiting a friend in California he determined to try to join the department he called "the varsity." But the L.A.P.D. first wanted to know about an incident in Liddy's private life, in which a woman he knew had accused him of sexual assault. Liddy had protested his innocence, and a jury acquitted him in a matter of minutes. The L.A.P.D. looked into the matter, and admitted Liddy into its ranks.

On April 29, 1992, when Liddy arrived for roll call at the Seventy-seventh Street station, in the heart of the city's South Central district, cops were congregating around a TV set watching a news report that a Simi Valley jury without any black members had just acquitted the L.A. cops accused in the Rodney King beating. A few blocks from the station, near Seventy-first Street, a young black man named Mark Jackson was changing the brakes on a friend's car when a neighbor came by and said she'd just heard the verdict reported. Jackson and his friends started grousing about the verdict, and soon other people came into the streets, shouting, "Rodney King! Rodney King!"

A short while later, Liddy and his partner, Terry Keenan, along with a third officer, were riding in their patrol car when, over the radio, they heard a call for help, signaling that officers were in trouble. They drove to the corner of Seventy-first Street and Normandie, where a boisterous crowd had encircled two cops who were in the middle of arresting a teenager after their patrol car was showered with rocks and bottles. The young man had tried to escape by climbing a fence. When the cops pulled him back down, the crowd began jeering, and chanted, "Fuck the police!" Liddy, Keenan and the other officer singled out two of the instigators, Mark Jackson and his friend Cerman Cunningham, and arrested them, but only after a struggle in which Jackson was slammed against the patrol car before finally being pushed inside.

The arrests further excited the crowd, and as Liddy was getting ready to drive away, Jackson's younger brother, Damian Williams, turned his back to the police and dropped his trousers, mooning the officers, to great cheers. About then, Liddy's lieutenant, Michael Moulin, arrived and ordered all the officers at the scene to retreat, leaving a vacuum in the streets that was quickly filled by the mob.

The crowd, Damian Williams among them, moved a block south, to the intersection of Florence and Normandie, where Tom's Liquor Store was soon overrun by looters. With booze flowing, people started throwing bottles at passing cars. Motorists were dragged out of their cars and beaten. Then a truck driver named Reginald Denny, en route to Inglewood with a load of sand and gravel, rolled into the intersection. A group of black youths pulled him from the truck, stomped him, hit him on the back with an oxygenator, clubbed him with a crowbar and smashed him in the face with a concrete block. As Denny lay on the street, bleeding and unconscious, one of the young men spat on him, and another rolled him over and picked his pocket. The man who hit Denny with the concrete block, and then spun into a dance over his body while flashing gang signs, was Damian Williams.

Two days later, the fires were still burning. As Liddy drove to work, a car pulled up next to his on an off-ramp near the station and one of its occupants fired at him. Liddy returned fire, and at the end of the gun battle one of the car's occupants was dead. Liddy survived the incident unhurt, and was awarded the department's highest honor, the Medal of Valor.

Brian Liddy had made the arrest that sparked the worst Los Angeles riot in a century, and won the Medal of Valor, but what made him really famous inside the force occurred a month after the riot, when Liddy was vacationing in New York. He was showing the city to his future wife, a fellow L.A. cop named Sandra Garcia (whom Liddy had met while standing over a corpse at a crime scene), when they heard a bank alarm go off near East Twenty-third Street by Third Avenue. Three men ran from the bank into a getaway car, smashed into another motorist, then fled on foot, in the direction of Liddy. He tackled one of the men, flipped him over into the "proned out" position, then held him with his arms pinned back until a New York cop arrived and handcuffed the suspect. Half a block away, Sandra Garcia had nabbed another of the suspects. Liddy and Garcia received a letter of commendation from the commander of the N.Y.P.D.'s Thirteenth Precinct.

Unlike Rafael Perez, Liddy was not a compelling presence in a courtroom. His recitation of events was coldly professional, and he didn't bother to mask his "coppers vs. assholes" attitude. This had been evident several months after the riot, in the joint trial of Mark Jackson and Cerman Cunningham. The racially mixed jury acquitted them, and jurors said afterward that they didn't like the demeanor of the husky cop. "Downtown jury" was Liddy's explanation.

Liddy and Rafael Perez came to Rampart CRASH on the same day in 1995. They weren't partners, or even friends, and when Perez left the unit for a time, Liddy argued against allowing his return. On the job, they tolerated each other.

Later, when Perez was going over lists of CRASH cops with Richard Rosenthal and the task force, rating officers as good or bad, he first mentioned Liddy as a pretty good cop with a nose for the bad guys. "I categorize him as a very good officer," Perez said. "A lot of good, uh . . . uh, Obs arrests. 'Obs' meaning observations arrests. . . . The most I've seen him do was fabricate some P.C." — probable cause for an arrest. "But could he be trusted? He could be trusted that if we told him the worst of the worst, he's gonna go, 'OK. I'm gonna go along with the story.' Uh, but he, himself, wouldn't, uh, really be involved in doing things."

Perez made that statement in one of his first sessions, in September 1999. By November, as his list of wrongdoers was growing, he had changed his mind about Liddy, accusing him of falsely arresting two members of the violent Temple Street gang after a raid. Perez later told Rosenthal that he'd heard that Liddy had spoken against him at CRASH, and said he thought Liddy (whom he described as "a very heavy officer who couldn't run half a block to save his life") was just jealous of him. Perez went on to implicate

Liddy directly in other misdeeds, ranging from making a bad gun-possession arrest to fabricating a report in a spray-painting incident.

By the time Perez was making those allegations, Liddy had been promoted out of Rampart CRASH, and was a sergeant in the Pacific division, near the beach. He held the dual ranks of detective and sergeant, and was pleased with his career status as he began to plot the next twenty years toward his pension.

Sandra was nine months pregnant, and on the morning she went into labor Liddy's badge, ID card and gun were taken from him by the police authorities in the delivery room when his son was being born. He was charged, with his CRASH partner, Michael Buchanan; his sergeant, Edward Ortiz; and another CRASH officer, Paul Harper, with various acts of perverting justice in the arrests that Perez had cited.

The most important allegation arose from a July 1996 CRASH raid on a meeting of the Temple Street gang, which was involved in a dispute with the Mexican mafia. One of the gangsters the CRASH cops hoped to run into that night was Anthony (Stymie) Adams, who was believed to have been the trigger man in the killing of a Mexican mafia man called Lizard in a dispute over "taxes" paid on the gang's street trade.

When the cops, including Liddy, Buchanan and Ortiz, arrived at the meeting place, the gang was all there—Stymie, Ghost, Diablo, Wicked, Speedy among them. A police helicopter illuminated the scene, and the gang members fled. Two of them jumped into a pickup truck and sped past Liddy and Buchanan, and down the alley. Liddy and Buchanan claimed they were struck by the escaping vehicle before the driver, Raúl (Prieto) Muñoz, was captured, in possession of a .357-magnum handgun, along with his passenger, Cesar (Joker) Natividad.

Liddy and Buchanan briefly went to the hospital, then filled out the paperwork on the arrest, charging Muñoz and Natividad with assault with a deadly weapon—the pickup truck. Both gangsters pleaded guilty, Muñoz was imprisoned and then deported to El Salvador, and in a plea deal, Natividad was released.

The issue in question was whether or not Muñoz had actually struck Liddy and Buchanan with the truck as they drove down the alley. Perez, who had been nearby at the scene, said the officers had fabricated that part of the story, even though they both had shown injuries at the time and had gone for treatment at the hospital. As the trial began, the talk around the courthouse was that the case seemed laughably insignificant, given the magnitude that the Rampart scandal had assumed.

Liddy gave his usual charmless witness-box performance. One of the *Los Angeles Times* reporters covering the trial wrote, "Liddy was so calm and deliberate that it appeared he had no stake in how he was perceived."

Even so, Judge Connor didn't seem to believe that the prosecution had much of a case—she consistently granted defense motions, and overruled the prosecution—and neither did anyone else. For one thing, Liddy and Buchanan hadn't needed to fabricate a charge in order to arrest Muñoz, who was illegally in possession of a gun and was violating parole. Technically, they could have charged him with assault with a deadly weapon for simply coming at the two officers in the truck, even if the truck hadn't struck them.

Not only had Muñoz pleaded guilty after the incident, but when the task-force detectives visited him in El Salvador to test Perez's allegations, he told them that he didn't know whether he had struck the officers that night, and that his passenger, Natividad, might well have opened the door of the truck, striking Liddy while trying to escape. But Muñoz's conviction was overturned, mostly on the word of Perez. From El Salvador, Muñoz had hired a lawyer—

Gregory Moreno, who also represented Javier Ovando—and filed a claim against the city.

Now Muñoz claimed that he'd pleaded guilty only because he didn't think anyone would believe a protest of innocence. He said that he hadn't struck the officers with his truck that night, and that the gang meeting was really just a "reunion." Indeed, he claimed that he was not really an active member of a gang (which Moreno likened to a social club for economically disadvantaged minority youths), and that he had never been involved in any criminal activity. Under cross-examination, he was obliged to admit to a 1989 shooting outside a high school when he was a juvenile.

The jury returned a verdict of guilty against Liddy, Ortiz and Buchanan. The jurors had focused not on the question of whether Liddy and Buchanan had been struck by Muñoz's truck but on a computerized report about the incident on which the letters "GBI"—great bodily injury—had been marked. The jurors said that Liddy and Buchanan didn't look greatly injured to them.

Judge Connor overturned the decision and, in an eighteen-page opinion, wrote that the prosecution had not presented sufficient evidence to warrant a conviction and that the jury had ruled on the wrong point of law. "While recognizing the enormous pressure on the community, on the police force, on the district attorney's office, and on the courts to 'fix' the Rampart scandal," she said, "this court is only interested in evaluating the fairness of the proceedings in this court and determining whether justice was done in this case."

A week before the jury rendered its verdict, the voters of Los Angeles County turned Gil Garcetti out of office; his successor, Steve Cooley, has appealed Judge Connor's ruling.

Rafael Perez, who has spent his entire incarceration in the Los

Angeles County Jail rather than in prison, had hoped to be freed in June. But that hope was cast into doubt in March, when Perez's former partner, Nino Durden, reached a plea agreement with federal and state prosecutors, promising to cooperate in an investigation of civil-rights abuses in the Rampart case. Sources indicate that the thrust of the federal effort is aimed at Rafael Perez.

Chief Parks's future at the L.A.P.D. is uncertain. Because of term-limit reform passed after the Rodney King episode, Parks must seek reappointment to a second term next year, and low morale within the force, as well as the Rampart developments, may become an obstacle.

Defense attorneys are still scrutinizing thousands of convictions that might have been tainted by Rampart wrongdoing, and plaintiffs' attorneys are awaiting settlement decisions in 150 lawsuits and claims against the city.

Of the gang members who received settlements from the city, at least two have been shot by rival gang members, and three others are known to be back in prison. On March 13, Javier Ovando, on his way to Las Vegas with friends from his old neighborhood, was arrested and charged with four felony counts of drug possession.

Brian Liddy is in personal and professional limbo, awaiting a ruling on the district attorney's appeal and possible federal charges related to Perez's accusations. He has been working at a private security firm, and has plans to start his own business when the Rampart case is resolved. "My new company is gonna be called Centurion Security and Investigations," he says.

Looking back, the people directly involved in uncovering and assessing the Rampart scandal now find themselves unable to take its measure—and that is mostly because of Rafael Perez. "I just think when you deal with the case as it appeared when it first broke, and what you have today, it is not what people thought would happen," Judge Fidler says. "Basically, it came down to Perez. What the prosecutor has is Perez and nothing else. And when you have all your eggs in one basket and the basket's starting to come apart at the seams . . . the case just doesn't have as much strength." Chief Parks contends that the Rampart case was exploited by the news media and police critics, and in the process became distorted beyond all proportion. "The media tried to make this the crime of the century," he says. "They began to talk about 'This is the worst corruption scandal in the history of L.A.P.D.' When it's all resolved, we'll have one-tenth of one percent of our officers involved in this issue."

In creating and, to some degree, directing the course of the Rampart scandal, Rafael Perez may have overtly lied or withheld the whole truth, and he may have protected his friends and settled old scores by implicating his enemies. Few now believe that the wrongdoing was as widespread as Perez once suggested—of the seventy officers eventually implicated by Perez, five were fired by the department and eight more resigned. What has been verified in Perez's allegations is nowhere near as serious as the crimes that he himself confessed to. Meanwhile, investigators find themselves no closer to answers about possible police involvement in the bank robbery, Death Row activities or the death of Biggie Smalls.

Yet there was in Perez's story a compelling element of truth—the revelation of a culture within the L.A.P.D. that, at the least, countenanced a strain of rough justice in the street. In that regard, the lasting significance of the Rampart scandal, perhaps, is the opportunity that it has afforded critics of the L.A.P.D. who have long been frustrated in their efforts to reform the department. "To the critics of the system," Judge Fidler says, "this gave them the ammunition they needed to say, 'See, we've always told you the system is corrupt, it only favors the prosecution or the police—we've proved it because Officer Perez has made these allegations.'"

*   *   *

Rafael Perez had a particular ending in mind when he began to tell his tale to prosecutors in September 1999, and nearly two years later, he got the conclusion he'd hoped for: the jail doors opened, and Perez became a free man. Perez, a dirty cop who'd stolen $1 million worth of cocaine, then shot a man and left him for dead and then lied under oath to send his victim to prison, had achieved an astonishing feat. He had deflected an outraged city's attention away from the crimes committed by a group of gangster cops, including Perez and his friend David Mack, turning it instead toward the culture of the L.A.P.D. itself. Largely on the word of Perez, convictions were overturned, millions of dollars in settlements were paid and seventy L.A. cops were investigated for wrongdoing—eight of them criminally charged. And after three years in jail, Rafael Perez walked free.

It was an ending that satisfied few beyond that group of lawyers who'd won millions in settlements with the city. It had become clear that the scandal Perez had loosed was nothing so pervasive as his story had suggested. In November 2001, the district attorney, Steve Cooley, announced that his office was bringing no further Rampart prosecutions. A few weeks later, Officer Brian Liddy, his conviction overturned by his trial judge, joined with his codefendants, Paul Harper and Edward Ortiz, in a federal lawsuit claiming they had been falsely arrested and maliciously prosecuted. That action is pending, as is the city's appeal of the judge's ruling overturning Liddy's criminal conviction. Liddy remains on unpaid "home assignment," awaiting the outcome of those actions.

Back in September 1999, his client cornered and facing certain conviction for stealing cocaine, the Johnny Cochran protégé Winston Kevin McKesson had correctly guessed that L.A. prosecutors would be impressed enough by Perez's stunning story to give him a cozy deal. McKesson apparently believed the deal also protected Perez from federal prosecution; he was wrong. The U.S. attorney in Los Angeles continued its own investigation of Perez, forcing him to make a new deal to avoid facing fifteen years in federal prison. In November, Perez agreed to plead guilty to federal civil rights violations and to serve two years in federal custody. The deal did not protect Perez from prosecution from any crimes other than those he has already confessed to.

THE CHICKEN WARRIORS
MARK SINGER

KINGSTON, OKLAHOMA

It's true that I hadn't absolutely made up my mind to join the Oklahoma Gamefowl Breeders Association. Still, I felt let down when,
preemptively, I was deprived of the opportunity. Ever since last winter, after I was nominated but failed to get elected to the Oklahoma
Journalism Hall of Fame, I've been looking for ways to pad my
résumé in my native state. Which explains, in part, how one Friday
morning in mid-December, in the wake of a sleet storm, I wound
up driving from Oklahoma City toward Kingston, on the Texas border. Specifically, I was on my way to a two-day cockfighting derby at
the members-only Texoma Game Club, where, as I understood the
protocols, I'd be expected to pay $20 and pledge allegiance to the
Gamefowl Breeders before being allowed inside—never mind that
the sum of my avian holdings is a couple of fainthearted parakeets.
As I pondered what sorts of friendship I might forge, I weighed
some conflicting information I'd received from two reliable sources,
both attentive students of the cockfighting subculture.

Janet Halliburton, the chairman of the Oklahoma Coalition
Against Cockfighting—a political-action committee pushing for an
initiative that, in all likelihood, would result in Oklahoma's becoming the forty-eighth state to outlaw this quaint pastime (Louisiana
and New Mexico are the other holdouts)—had suggested, "While
you're down there with the cockfighters, make sure you keep an eye

out for the guy who showed up to harass me at the state fair in Oklahoma City when I was trying to gather petition signatures. He had the tattoo of a headless nude female torso running from his shoulder to his elbow."

On the other hand, Gregory Albert, an Oklahoma Supreme Court referee who had recently spent a month listening to the sworn testimony of cockfighters determined to defend and preserve their way of life, had told me, "People who engage in cockfighting look just like everybody else. Cockfighters are like the couple next door, or the Waltons. They're just people."

After stopping for a maximum-cholesterol late breakfast—buttered hotcakes and sunny-side ups—at a place called Hobo Joe's, in the blink-and-you-miss-it town of Madill, I traveled ten more miles, until I came upon a gymnasium-size building, with a cream-colored metal exterior, set back about a hundred yards from the highway. No signs identified it as the Texoma Game Club, but I knew from the fence postings that said "Private Property" and "No Trespassing"—the unwelcoming scrutiny of a beady-eyed gatekeeper was another tip-off—that this was the place. Among the curious allurements of the Texoma Game Club is that it's a strictly-within-the-law establishment whose operators have cultivated the coy ambience of a speakeasy.

While I waited, the sentry went to find James Tally, the president of the Gamefowl Breeders. He materialized five minutes later, a sallow blond-going-gray fellow in his mid-fifties with a mustache and the slightly mournful demeanor of someone burdened by unwieldy responsibilities. We stepped into a narrow hallway lined with snapshots of cockfighters posing with tournament trophies, and before I realized what was happening—that is, before I had a chance to compromise my professional integrity or even to equivocate—he escorted me past a ticket booth. No one demanded to see proof of my membership in the Gamefowl Breeders Association or the Texoma Game Club. Just like that, dang, I'd been granted journalistic immunity.

Tally, a Union Pacific freight-train conductor who lives not far from Kingston with his wife, two stepchildren, two dogs, three hundred roosters and seventy-five hens, introduced me to the Texoma owners, a slender white-haired Alabama native named Roy and a straight-talking, compactly built brunette named Judy, who made it clear that they weren't eager to see their last names in print. Then we settled in the stands, where steeply raked rows of cushiony yellow theater chairs surrounded a dirt-floored, wire-enclosed, eighteen-by-twenty-six-foot fight pit. Occasions arise during the cockfighting season, which runs from November through July, when the Texoma crowds reach capacity—a little over seven hundred—but at the moment the place was less than half filled. Red and silver tinsel and Christmas lights had been strung along the top of the wire cage, a homey touch that went nicely, I thought, with the disingenuous "No Gambling" signs that had been affixed to each of its four sides.

Inside the cage, a couple of black roosters equipped with two-inch stainless-steel weapons on both legs were trying to perform surgery on each other. This was one of seventy or so bouts during what Tally described as "a prelim-type deal," a warm-up for the next day's Christmas Derby—a four-cock tournament followed by a seven-cock tournament. The way the scoring worked, not all the livestock would see action; cockfighters who fared poorly in the early rounds would be eliminated, and their remaining birds would, for the time being, be spared. The entry fee was $100 on Friday and $300 on Saturday, and the triumphant handlers stood to take home a few thousand dollars, plus or minus their ancillary winnings or losses if, like virtually everyone else on the premises, they neglected to obey the "No Gambling" injunction.

Not that cockfighting is mainly about, or really is in any way

about, money, I was repeatedly informed; it's about freedom—
nowadays, especially, the freedom not to get pushed around by the
anticockfighting lobby. "We don't solicit people to come to rooster
fighting," Roy, the proprietor, said. "People who come, ninety percent been doin' it all their lives. It's part of our national heritage.
I'm gonna bet you there's never been a rooster fighter asked an animal-rights activist to come to a rooster fight, and I'll bet you an animal-rights activist never invited a rooster fighter to one of their
events. And that's all right with me. All we want to do is break even:
they leave us alone, we leave them alone"— "they" being the Oklahoma Coalition Against Cockfighting and its fellow-travelers, the
sinister forces arrayed to try to put out of business Roy and Judy and
the forty-one other cockfight-pit operators in Oklahoma, along with
countless game-fowl breeders scattered around the state, many of
whom had emigrated from jurisdictions where the lawmakers took
a dim view of people who amuse themselves by watching animals
battle to the death.

I stuck around both days and did witness quite a few cockfights. At
one point, with a red Hatch Roundhead and a Hatch Grey cross
and their handlers standing poised for battle, and the cacophonous
gentlemanly wagering that precedes each fight getting under way
("Bet fifty on the red! . . . Lay a hunnerd to your eighty! . . . Call
eighty!"), I felt like an agnostic trying to ignore a gospel choir as I
resisted the temptation to do a little gentlemanly wagering myself.
But it was mainly the particulars of the fight over cockfighting,
rather than cockfighting itself, that interested me.

When Oklahoma joined the union, in 1907, its criminal code, a
vestige from territorial days, was generally understood to outlaw
cockfighting. Anyone "who maliciously, or for any bet, stake, or
reward, instigates or encourages any fight between animals, or insti-

gates or encourages any animal to attack, bite, wound or worry another" was guilty of a misdemeanor. (I recall, from an eighth-grade course in Oklahoma history, that the brave pioneers also made it illegal to get a fish drunk.) The cockfighting ban survived until 1963, when a decision by the Oklahoma Court of Criminal Appeals prevented a county judge from proceeding with the trial of a half dozen citizens who had been caught in flagrante. The defendants argued, among other things, that the law was insufficiently explicit, and the appellate panel unanimously agreed, establishing the foundation upon which the local cockfighting industry thrives to this day. The opinion, written by the chief judge, Kirksey Nix, remains noteworthy as a novel theological treatise. After quoting Genesis and its delineation of the distinctions between the "fish of the sea" and "the fowl of the air" and "every beast of the field," Judge Nix asked rhetorically, "Is a 'gamecock' an animal?" Though stopping short of a flat-out declaration that it wasn't, he nevertheless found that "persons of ordinary intelligence" could read the law and not necessarily grasp that it covered chickens. What the authors really intended to prohibit, he surmised, was organized dog fighting.

Nix concluded his opinion with the tongue-in-cheek observation "The Legislature is now in session and if it so desires, it can make a direct approach to the act complained of by making cock-fighting an offense against the state." Judge Nix knew the tenor of the legislature, an institution in the grip of rural logic, and he understood that a law against cockfighting was as likely to get adopted as a law making Russian the official language. In the decades since, not much has changed. During one memorable debate several years ago, a noble statesman from Muskogee named John Monks declared, "In every country the Communists have taken over, the first thing they do is outlaw cockfighting." The last time the question arose in the legislature, two years ago, it was dead on arrival: an anticockfighting bill proposed by a representative from Oklahoma City also would have outlawed such sacrosanct diversions as rodeos, coon hunts and rattlesnake roundups, and might as well have included football games and church suppers.

Lately, however, the cockfighters have come up against formidable opposition. Oklahoma is one of many states that allow citizen initiatives, a cumbersome constitutional provision that makes it possible to circumvent a recalcitrant legislature. In the fall of 1999, anticockfighting canvassers, concentrating their efforts in Oklahoma City and Tulsa, collected signatures endorsing a vote on a proposed new law that would define as felonious behavior just about everything I witnessed at the Texoma Game Club—except for the act of merely being a spectator, which would be a misdemeanor.

When the petition drive ended, the secretary of state certified that the canvassers had gathered thirty thousand more signatures than were needed to place the question on the ballot in the next statewide general election. (Public-opinion surveys, meanwhile, indicated that two out of three voters favored outlawing cockfighting.) The Gamefowl Breeders Association responded by challenging the validity of tens of thousands of signatures. That the proposed law wasn't voted upon in last November's general election—and may not be in the foreseeable future—is, if you ask most cockfighters, a consequence of their tenacity and organizational skills and the adroitness of their lawyers. The cockfighting opponents are more inclined to attribute the delay to the boorish behavior of certain cockfighters and, above all, foot-dragging by the Oklahoma Supreme Court. This past fall, after a month of hearings, Supreme Court referee Albert—he of the belief that cockfighters are just like the folks next door—upheld enough of the cockfighters' objections so that, in the end, the petition proponents came up almost eleven thousand short. The anticockfighters have formally challenged the referee's decision and are awaiting a hearing by the full Supreme Court. The cockfighters, naturally, don't see any reason to rush.

When Janet Halliburton agreed to become the chairman of the anticockfighting campaign, it had nothing to do with the fact that as a child she owned a pet rooster named Ichabod, which died a seminatural death after "a varmint, most likely a skunk or a badger," invaded the henhouse. Halliburton is somewhere in her forties and has streaked-blond hair and a seeming disinclination to smile. For twenty years—until last spring, when she opted for early retirement—she was the chief counsel of the Oklahoma State Bureau of Investigation, which probably accounts for her clipped, coplike diction. In our first conversation, she made a point of telling me, "I used to ride in rodeo barrel races. I love animals, but I regard them as property." She elaborated: "My father's side of the family is from southeastern Oklahoma. We have land there and we run cattle on it . . . steers that are going to be slaughtered. My brother-in-law hunts deer and turkeys on that land. He fishes there, too. I'm not a vegetarian and I don't believe that animals have rights."

Such sentiments might not seem to qualify her as the cockfighters' nemesis, but she is that nevertheless. In the fall of 1998, during a seminar organized by the Oklahoma Humane Federation, an animal-welfare coalition, Halliburton delivered a presentation on the links between violence against animals and human violence. The following spring, the federation, encouraged by successful anti-cockfighting crusades in Missouri and Arizona, decided to mobilize a similar effort in Oklahoma. Precisely because Halliburton didn't fit anyone's stereotype of an animal-rights activist, she was drafted to be chairman. Recently, when I asked whether she regretted having got involved, she said, "It seemed like a sensible thing to do. I thought the cockfighters just had the issue buttonholed in the legislature, and if you give the people a chance to vote they'll solve the problem. But I didn't realize that from A to B was so far."

The moments during the campaign that Halliburton least enjoyed, she says, occurred when petition gatherers were verbally menaced, threatened with physical harm and spat upon. More than once, her car was followed. One morning, she found a dead rooster in her backyard. She received so many harassing phone calls at home that she had to get an unlisted number. Harassing phone calls at work, including some to her superiors, contributed to her premature retirement. Early in the campaign, she gave an interview to a public-television station in which she alluded to reports that prostitution, illegal gambling and illicit drugs proliferated in the vicinity of cockfighting pits. These comments prompted two game-fowl breeders to sue her for slander, which she says came as a surprise, because "none of the cockfighters I met impressed me as being public-television watchers." When the anticockfighters tried to gather petition signatures at a crafts festival in a suburb of Oklahoma City, a group of cockfighters who didn't resemble the Waltons showed up and the festival manager asked them to leave. "They went away and came back carrying signs that said 'Don't Ban Cockfighting. Don't Ban Christmas in Schools,'" Halliburton said. "They told people about me, 'She's an atheist and head of the atheist movement in Oklahoma.' At the time, I was a deacon in my church. And my dad's a minister."

Much of this mischief was the handiwork of the Oklahoma Animal Coalition, a splinter faction of rather more militant cockfighters organized by a gung ho breeder named Chuck Berry, whose general estimation of the Gamefowl Breeders leadership was that it was "unprepared and unmotivated to deal with the problem." The Berry shock troops' standard tactic was to appear at anticockfighting rallying spots and intercept potential petition signers, urging them to read carefully what they were about to endorse. The coalition

also paid for newspaper ads stating that if the cockfighting opponents succeeded their next endeavor would be to make pet owner-
ship illegal. At Texoma, I met Anthony Villalobos Jr., one of Berry's
cohorts. During an Oktoberfest event at a park in Tulsa, Villalobos
recalled, he and a few fellow tricksters mingled with petition gatherers, some of whom carried "Ban Cockfighting" signs, and held up
signs of their own that said "Ban Hunting" and "Ban Fishing."

"They called me the Tulsa Area Harassment Coordinator," he
said. "If you want someone harassed in the Tulsa area in a coordinated fashion, I'm the man to see. Just before Thanksgiving, the
Tulsa World ran an editorial asking both sides to call their troops off,
to cool the rhetoric. But then the other side went out and started
collecting signatures on Thanksgiving Day. When we found out
about it, we had just enough time to finish our turkey and get back
out in the streets."

Such stratagems wouldn't have been necessary, the cockfighters
say, if their adversaries hadn't stooped to various forms of carpetbagging, including soliciting assistance from subversive organizations
like the Humane Society of the United States, raising money
from out-of-state animal-protection groups and employing so-called
petition gypsies—itinerant professional canvassers who weren't necessarily legal residents of Oklahoma. In his final report, Supreme
Court referee Albert more or less agreed, invoking the phrase "outside agitators." Despite such xenophobic flourishes, Albert appeared
to be evenhanded. He disqualified more than four thousand signatures collected by a petition gypsy who gave as his legal address
what turned out to be a vacant lot. But Albert agreed to accept more
than seventy-five hundred gathered by a hermit who gave as *his*
address an abandoned house. In the end, the majority of the disqualified signatures were tossed out on technical grounds, because
the signers' addresses, when compared with those listed in voter-
registration records, didn't precisely match.

.   .   .

Game-fowl breeders seem to derive perverse enjoyment from being accused, usually by animal-rights activists, of "training" otherwise pacifist birds to fight. The scientific explanation for combative rooster behavior, they're happy to point out, is rooted in Darwinism and DNA, an inbred male desire to control sexual territory—literally, an uncontrollable urge to impress chicks. And it's not only because humans, when they engage in approximately the same activity, tend not to have sharp weapons strapped to their limbs that their mortality rate is much lower. "A rooster's testosterone level, per body weight, is seventeen times greater than a male *Homo sapiens*'," a breeder named Jimmy Tyler told me. "So they can't help themselves. They're gonna kill one another." Or as another breeder, Kurt Oleksuk, said as he was on his way to collect his trophy and prize money after winning the four-cock preliminary tournament at Texoma, "Very rarely, you'll get a rooster that won't face, that won't show courage. And if you do an autopsy you'll find that he'll have only one nut or a deformed testicle, in almost every case."

The crowd-stirring action in a cockfight typically occurs in the first thirty seconds. That's when the birds, though aerodynamically ill equipped for sustained flight, actually do levitate, generally about as high as an average small-college Caucasian basketball player can jump. Most cockfighting pits offer combat with a variety of metal weapons—gaff (sharp point, no cutting edge, worn in pairs), short knife (one inch) and long knife (two inches). The knives are sickle-shaped, are worn on only one leg and usually have only one edge sharpened: knife duels usually end in swift death for the loser and, quite often, permanent disability for the ostensible winner.

At Texoma, whenever a fight lasted longer than about five minutes, the birds, their handlers and the referee would shift from the central pit to one of three contiguous combat areas, or drag pits, beneath the grandstand, trailed by spectators with financial interests in the outcome. Some fights went on for almost an hour, adhering to specific and complicated endgame rules. As often as not, the denouement was the equivalent of a technical knockout: one bird, through injury, fatigue, testosterone deficiency or perhaps existential despair, couldn't or wouldn't respond to his opponent, who was deemed to possess superior "gameness."

Shortly after nine o'clock the morning of the Christmas Derby, I found James Tally standing in one of the drag pits, looking more preoccupied than usual. He hadn't got much sleep the night before, he said; he had a lot of details on his mind, and at the moment he was struggling with a friend's lively Hatch Grey rooster. The cock wouldn't stop sexually harassing a couple of hens with which it had been sharing a cage, and Tally, wearing a crimson Oklahoma Gamefowl Breeders Association warm-up jacket, had the bird under one arm while someone hunted for an extra cage. Hens normally don't make appearances at cockfighting pits, but these were on hand because a brood-stock auction was scheduled for that morning. Several breeders had donated trios, a rooster and two hens, and the proceeds—the trios would bring prices ranging from $500 to $1,250—would go to the Gamefowl Breeders legal fund.

Before the auction, two attorneys who represented the cockfighters in the initiative-petition challenge, Larry Oliver and Lee Slater, entered the fighting pit and addressed the crowd. Oliver, a broadshouldered, gray-haired former police officer and the current vice chief justice of the supreme court of the Creek Nation, wore black jeans, black boots, a red turtleneck, a black ski vest and a broadbrimmed black cowboy hat with a turquoise hatband, and did most of the talking. "Let me tell you somethin' about my good friend James Tally," he began. "He got me a hotel room last night. I told him this morning I wasn't gonna complain about the water being cold. I wasn't gonna complain about the light that wouldn't turn off, so I had to fish around under the bed to unplug it. But I was gonna complain that there's no girls come with it. . . . Hey, what about those Sooners?"—a reference to the University of Oklahoma's undefeated, Orange Bowl–bound football team—"Tell me about 'em, huh? Aren't they great? Lemme ask you another question: What about those cockfighters? Aren't they great? When the Sooners started their season, nobody thought they'd get anywhere, did they? When y'all started this process, did anybody think you'd get anywhere with it? Both of you are world champions. I think the referee's decision will stand. I've often said, and it's no truer ever before than it is now, there ain't no lawyer any better'n his clients. And you people united and brought yourselves together, and you're the best clients a lawyer could ever expect to have."

In this upbeat and optimistic spirit, Oliver declined to dwell upon a suggestion he'd floated several months earlier—that in the event cockfighting was outlawed, the breeders should be compensated for their lost property, and the funds could come from a $25 million payment due Oklahoma as its share of a multistate tobacco-litigation settlement. On his way out, Oliver stopped by a table that was selling veterinary supplies—vitamins, hormones, antibiotics, parasite treatments—and picked up a jar of something called Cock Booster and another product called Pecker Wrecker. As he paid for them, he told me they were for "friends."

A scoreboard above the bleachers listed the Christmas Derby entries, which were identifiable by their fighting handles—Porkchop, Gunrunner, Showtime, Skeeter, Pinky & The Brain, Cold Blue Steel, Bad Company. There were 115 entries, which I gathered meant that something like fourteen hours of continuous cockfighting lay ahead. I had no illusions that I was game enough to go the distance.

I spent most of the day camped out in a seat in the top row, entertaining the fantasy that there was less cigarette smoke up there.

From that vantage point, I could see the feathers fly but couldn't really detect the moment when a spur pierced flesh. And I could avoid the glassy, opaque expression of a bird in extremis. (One breeder assured me that "a rooster doesn't have a fully formed brain, and he doesn't have a pain center." Another cockfighting bromide is that any bird battling for its life in a pit has, up to that point, led a far cushier existence, and possesses the potential for far greater glory, than a factory-raised supermarket-bound Perdue oven stuffer.)

Every ten or so fights, someone would enter the pit, rake the feathers, sprinkle the dirt with a watering can and draw fresh boundary lines with cornmeal. Somewhat less frequently, Judy would pick up a handheld microphone and threaten to put the hurt to whoever's truck was blocking someone else's out in the parking lot.

In the early evening, I decided to visit the drag pits, and as I passed the veterinary-supply table I heard a woman in lavender stretch pants and a matching sweater and curly red hair that originally belonged to someone else say, "I got me some Viagra. He better come home tonight." It felt like time to hit the road again. I thanked Judy and Roy and James Tally for their hospitality. On my way to my car, I came across an old Buick with the wordiest bumper sticker I'd seen in a long time: "If They Take Our Game Cocks, Next Time They Will Take Our Rodeos, Race Horses, Our Hunting Guns and Shotguns, and Maybe Even Our Fishing Poles!" For a variety of reasons, I doubted that.

*   *   *

When I fill in the blanks on a document that asks me to list my occupation, I write "journalist," though the truth is I regard myself as an uncredentialed cultural anthropologist. My subspecialty is my birthplace, Oklahoma—its habits and rituals. Well-meaning people in

Oklahoma are forever suggesting story ideas to me, but I happened upon the cockfighting drama when I spied a brief news item in USA Today. After a few phone calls, I hustled down to southern Oklahoma to write a story for The New Yorker *about the attempts of the pro- and anticockfighting forces to inflict mortal wounds upon each other. Being an eyewitness to such a rarefied public-policy debate was, as always, a happy exercise—a chance to observe my kinsmen, my fellow Okies, while, astonishingly, getting paid for the pleasure.*

At the time my story was published, in January 2001, the Oklahoma Coalition Against Cockfighting was appealing the decision of an Oklahoma Supreme Court referee who had disallowed several thousand petition signatures. Several months later, the full court overruled the referee, decreeing that the tossed-out signatures were in fact valid. This meant that a sufficient number had been gathered to put to a statewide vote a proposal to ban cockfighting. Most likely, the question will appear on a ballot during 2002, and if public-opinion polls are a reliable indicator, the anticockfighting partisans will prevail. As someone who, in principle, opposes cruelty to animals, I suppose the passage of such a law should be construed as progress. As someone who consumes a factory-bred chicken or two per week, I'm wary of my own hypocrisy. As one intoxicated by most things Okie-fied, I can't begin to plumb the depths of my ambivalence.

THE CRASH OF EGYPTAIR 990
WILLIAM LANGEWIESCHE

I remember first hearing about the accident early in the morning after the airplane went down. It was October 31, 1999, Halloween morning. I was in my office when a fellow pilot, a former flying companion, phoned with the news: It was EgyptAir flight 990, a giant twin-engine Boeing 767 on the way from New York to Cairo, with 217 people aboard. It had taken off from Kennedy Airport in the middle of the night, climbed to 33,000 feet and flown normally for half an hour before mysteriously plummeting into the Atlantic Ocean sixty miles south of Nantucket. Rumor had it that the crew had said nothing to air-traffic control, that the flight had simply dropped off the New York radar screens. Soon afterward an out-bound Air France flight had swung over the area and had reported no fires in sight—only a dim and empty ocean far below. It was remotely possible that flight 990 was still in the air somewhere, diverting toward a safe landing. But sometime around daybreak a merchant marine training ship spotted debris floating on the waves—aluminum scraps, cushions and clothing, some human remains. The midshipmen on board gagged from the stench of jet fuel—a planeload of unburned kerosene rising from shattered tanks on the ocean floor, about 250 feet below. By the time rescue ships and helicopters arrived, it was obvious that there would be no survivors. I remember reacting to the news with regret for the dead, followed by a thought for the complexity of the investigation that now lay ahead. This accident had the markings of a tough case. The problem was not so much the scale of the carnage—a terrible consequence of the 767's size—but, rather, the still-sketchy profile of the upset that preceded it, this bewildering fall out of the sky on a calm night, without explanation, during an utterly uncritical phase of the flight.

I don't fly the 767, or any other airliner. In fact, I no longer fly for a living. But I know through long experience with flight that such machines are usually docile, and that steering them does not require the steady nerves and quick reflexes that passengers may imagine. Indeed, as we saw on September 11, steering them may not even require much in the way of training—the merest student-pilot level is probably enough. It's not hard to understand why. Airplanes at their core are very simple devices—winged things that belong in the air. They are designed to be flyable, and they are. Specifically, the 767 has ordinary mechanical and hydraulic flight controls that provide the pilot with smooth and conventional responses; it is normally operated on autopilot, but can easily be flown by hand; if you remove your hands from the controls entirely, the airplane sails on as before, until it perhaps wanders a bit, dips a wing, and starts into a gentle descent; if you pull the nose up or push it down (within reason) and then fold your arms, the airplane returns unassisted to steady flight; if you idle the engines, or shut them off entirely, the airplane becomes a rather well behaved glider. It has excellent forward visibility, through big windshields. It has a minimalist cockpit that may look complicated to the untrained eye but is a masterpiece of clean design. It can easily be managed by the standard two-person crew, or even by one pilot alone. The biggest problem in flying the airplane on a routine basis is boredom. Settled into the deep sky at 33,000 feet, above the weather and far from an obstacle, the 767 simply makes very few demands.

Not that it's idiot-proof, or necessarily always benign. As with any fast and heavy airplane, operating a 767 safely even under ordinary circumstances requires anticipation, mental clarity and a practical understanding of the various systems. Furthermore, when circumstances are *not* ordinary—for example, during an engine failure just after takeoff or an encounter with unexpected wind shear during an approach to landing—a wilder side to the airplane's personality suddenly emerges. Maintaining control then requires firm action and sometimes a strong arm. There's nothing surprising about this: all airplanes misbehave on occasion, and have to be disciplined. "Kicking the dog," I called it in the ornery, old cargo crates I flew when I was in college—it was a regular part of survival. In the cockpits of modern jets it is rarely necessary. Nonetheless, when trouble occurs in a machine as massive and aerodynamically slick as the 767, if it is not quickly suppressed the consequences can blossom out of control. During a full-blown upset like that experienced by the Egyptian crew, the airplane may dive so far past its tested limits that it exceeds the very scale of known engineering data—falling off the graphs as well as out of the sky. Afterward the profile can possibly be reconstructed mathematically by aerodynamicists and their like, but it cannot be even approximated by pilots in flight if they expect to come home alive.

I got a feel for the 767's dangerous side last summer, after following the accident's trail from Washington, D.C., to Cairo to the airplane's birthplace, in Seattle, where Boeing engineers let me fly a specially rigged 767 simulator through a series of relevant upsets and recoveries along with some sobering replays of flight 990's final moments. These simulations had been flown by investigators more than a year before and had been reported on in detail in the publicly released files. Boeing's argument was not that the 767 is a flawless design but, more narrowly, that none of the imaginable failures of its flight-control systems could explain the known facts of this accident.

But that's getting ahead of the story. Back on October 31, 1999, with the first news of the crash, it was hard to imagine any form of pilot error that could have condemned the airplane to such a sustained and precipitous dive. What switch could the crew have thrown, what lever? Nothing came to mind. And why had they perished so silently without a single distress call on the radio? A total electrical failure was very unlikely, and would not explain the loss of control. A fire would have given them time to talk. One thing was certain: the pilots were either extremely busy or incapacitated from the start. Of course there was always the possibility of a terrorist attack—a simple if frightening solution. But otherwise something had gone terribly wrong with the airplane itself, and that could be just as bad. There are more than eight hundred Boeing 767s in the world's airline fleet, and they account for more transatlantic flights than all other airplanes combined. They are also very similar in design to the smaller and equally numerous Boeing 757s. So there was plenty of reason for alarm.

"EGYPTAIR NINE-NINETY, RADIO CONTACT LOST"

One of the world's really important divides lies between nations that react well to accidents and nations that do not. This is as true for a confined and technical event like the crash of a single flight as it is for political or military disasters. The first requirement is a matter of national will, and never a sure thing: it is the intention to get the story right, wherever the blame may lie. The second requirement follows immediately upon the first, and is probably easier to achieve: it is the need for people in the aftermath to maintain even tempers and open minds. The path they follow may not be simple, but it can provide for at least the possibility of effective resolutions.

In the case of EgyptAir flight 990 the only information available at first was external. The airplane had arrived in New York late on a flight from Los Angeles, and had paused to refuel, take on passengers and swap crews. Because of the scheduled duration of the flight to Cairo, two cockpit crews had been assigned to the ocean crossing—an "active crew," including the aircraft commander, to handle the first and last hours of the flight; and a "cruise crew," whose role was essentially to monitor the autopilot during the long, sleepy mid-Atlantic stretch. Just before midnight these four pilots rode out to the airport on a shuttle bus from Manhattan's Pennsylvania Hotel, a large establishment where EgyptAir retained rooms for the use of its personnel. The pilots had been there for several days and, as usual, were well rested. Also in the bus was one of the most senior of EgyptAir's captains, the company's chief 767 pilot, who was not scheduled to fly but would be "deadheading" home to Cairo. An EgyptAir dispatcher rode out on the bus with them, and subsequently reported that the crew members looked and sounded normal. At the airport he gave them a standard briefing and an update on the New York surface weather, which was stagnant under a low, thin overcast, with light winds and thickening haze.

Flight 990 pushed back from the gate and taxied toward the active runway at 1:12 A.M. Because there was little other traffic at the airport, communications with the control tower were noticeably relaxed. At 1:20 flight 990 lifted off. It topped the clouds at 1,000 feet and turned out over the ocean toward a half-moon rising above the horizon. The airplane was identified and tracked by air-traffic-control radar as it climbed through the various New York departure sectors and entered the larger airspace belonging to the en route controllers of New York Center; its transponder target and data block moved steadily across the controllers' computer-generated displays, and its radio transmissions sounded perhaps a little awkward, but routine. At 1:44 it leveled off at the assigned 33,000 feet.

The en route controller working the flight was a woman named Ann Brennan, a private pilot with eight years on the job. She had the swagger of a good controller, a real pro. Later she characterized the air traffic that night as slow, which it was—during the critical hour she had handled only three other flights. The offshore military-exercise zones, known as warning areas, were inactive. The sky was sleeping.

At 1:47 Brennan said, "EgyptAir Nine-ninety, change to my frequency one-two-five-point-niner-two."

EgyptAir acknowledged the request with a friendly "Good day," and after a pause checked in on the new frequency: "New York, EgyptAir Nine-nine-zero heavy, good morning."

Brennan answered, "EgyptAir Nine-ninety, roger."

That was the last exchange. Brennan noticed that the flight still had about fifteen minutes to go before leaving her sector. Wearing her headset, she stood up and walked six feet away to sort some paperwork. A few minutes later she approved a request by Washington Center to steer an Air France 747 through a corner of her airspace. She chatted for a while with her supervisor, a man named Ray Redhead. In total she spent maybe six minutes away from her station, a reasonable interval on such a night. It was just unlucky that while her back was turned flight 990 went down.

A computer captured what she would have seen—a strangely abstract death no more dramatic than a video game. About two minutes after the final radio call, at 1:49:53 in the morning, the radar swept across EgyptAir's transponder at 33,000 feet. Afterward, at successive twelve-second intervals, the radar read 31,500, 25,400, and 18,300 feet—a descent rate so great that the air-traffic-control computers interpreted the information as false, and showed "XXXX" for the altitude on Brennan's display. With the next sweep the radar lost the transponder entirely, and picked up only an unenhanced "primary" blip, a return from the airplane's metal mass. The surprise is that the radar continued to receive such returns (which show only location, and not altitude) for nearly another minute and a half, indicating that the dive must have dramatically slowed or stopped, and that the 767 remained airborne, however tenuously, during that interval. A minute and a half is a long time. As the Boeing simulations later showed, it must have been a strange and dreamlike period for the pilots, hurtling through the night with no chance of awakening.

When radar contact was lost, the display for EgyptAir 990 began to "coast," indicating that the computers could no longer find a correlation between the stored flight plan and the radar view of the sky. When Brennan noticed, she stayed cool. She said, "EgyptAir Nine-ninety, radar contact lost, recycle transponder, squawk one-seven-one-two." EgyptAir did not answer, so she tried again at unhurried intervals over the following ten minutes. She advised Ray Redhead of the problem, and he passed the word along. She called an air-defense radar facility, and other air-traffic-control centers as far away as Canada, to see if by any chance someone was in contact with the flight. She asked a Lufthansa crew to try transmitting to EgyptAir from up high. Eventually she brought in Air France for the overflight. The prognosis was of course increasingly grim, but she maintained her professional calm. She continued to handle normal operations in her sector while simultaneously setting the search-and-rescue forces in motion. Half an hour into the process, when a controller at Boston Center called and asked, "Any luck with the EgyptAir?" she answered simply, "No."

GOVERNMENT LITE MEETS GOVERNMENT HEAVY

Among the dead were one hundred Americans, eighty-nine Egyptians (including thirty-three army officers), twenty-two Canadians and a few people of other nationalities. As the news of the disaster spread, hundreds of frantic friends and relatives gathered at the airports in Los Angeles, New York and Cairo. EgyptAir officials struggled to meet people's needs—which were largely, of course, for the sort of information that no one yet had. Most of the bodies remained in and around the wreckage at the bottom of the sea. Decisions now had to be made, and fast, about the recovery operation and the related problem of an investigation. Because the airplane had crashed in international waters, Egypt had the right to lead the show. Realistically, though, it did not have the resources to salvage a heavy airplane in waters 250 feet deep and five thousand miles away.

The solution was obvious, and it came in the form of a call to the White House from Egyptian president Hosni Mubarak, an experienced military pilot with close ties to EgyptAir, requesting that the investigation be taken over by the U.S. government. The White House in turn called Jim Hall, the chairman of the National Transportation Safety Board, an investigative agency with a merited reputation for competence. Hall, a Tennessee lawyer and friend of the Gores, had in the aftermath of the TWA flight 800 explosion parlayed his position into one of considerable visibility. The Egyptians produced a letter formally signing over the investigation to the United States, an option accorded under international convention, which would place them in a greatly diminished role (as "accredited representatives") but would also save them trouble and money. Mubarak is said to have regretted the move ever since.

In retrospect it seems inevitable that the two sides would have trouble getting along. The NTSB is a puritanical construct, a small federal agency without regulatory power whose sole purpose is to investigate accidents and issue safety recommendations that might add to the public discourse. Established in 1967 as an "independent" unit of the Washington bureaucracy, and shielded by design from the political currents of that city, the agency represents the most progressive American thinking on the role and character of good government. On call twenty-four hours a day, with technical teams ready to travel at a moment's notice, it operates on an annual baseline budget of merely $62 million or so, and employs only about 420 people, most of whom work at the headquarters on four floors of Washington's bright and modern Loews L'Enfant Plaza Hotel. In part because the NTSB seems so lean, and in part because by its very definition it advocates for the "right" causes, it receives almost universally positive press coverage. The NTSB is technocratic. It is clean. It is Government Lite.

EgyptAir, in contrast, is Government Heavy—a state-owned airline with about six hundred pilots and a mixed fleet of about forty Boeings and Airbuses that serves more than eighty destinations worldwide and employs twenty-two thousand people. It operates out of dusty Stalinist-style office buildings at the Cairo airport, under the supervision of the Ministry of Transport, from which it is often practically indistinguishable. It is probably a safe airline, but passengers dislike it for its delays and shoddy service. They call it Air Misère, probably a play on the airline's former name, Misr Air (*Misr* is Arabic for "Egypt"). It has been treated as a fiefdom for years by Mubarak's old and unassailable air-force friends, and particularly by the company's chairman, a man named Mohamed Fahim Rayan, who fights off all attempts at reform or privatization. This is hardly a secret. In parliamentary testimony six months before the crash of flight 990, Rayan said, "My market is like a water pond which I developed over the years. It is quite unreasonable for alien people to come and seek to catch fish in my pond." His critics answer that the pond is stagnant and stinks of corruption—but this, too, is nothing new. The greatest pyramids in Egypt are made not of stone but of people: they are the vast bureaucracies that constitute society's core, and they function not necessarily to get the "job" done but to reward the personal loyalty of those at the bottom to those at the top. Once you understand that, much of the rest begins to make sense. The bureaucracies serve mostly to shelter their workers and give them something like a decent life. They also help to define Cairo. It is a great capital city, as worldly as Washington, D.C., and culturally very far away.

An official delegation traveled from Cairo to the United States and ended up staying for more than a year. It was led by two EgyptAir pilots, Mohsen al-Missiry, an experienced accident investigator on temporary assignment to the Egyptian Civil Aviation Authority for this case, and Shaker Kelada, who had retired from active flying to become a flight-operations manager and eventually vice president for safety and quality assurance. These men were smart and tough, and managed a team primarily of EgyptAir engineers, many of whom were very sharp.

The U.S. Navy was given the job of salvage, and it in turn hired a contractor named Oceaneering, which arrived with a ship and grapples and remote-controlled submarines. The debris was plotted by sonar, and found to lie in two clusters: the small "west field," which included the left engine; and, 1,200 feet beyond it in the direction of flight, the "east field," where most of the airplane lay. From what was known of the radar profile and from the tight concentration of the debris, it began to seem unlikely that an in-flight explosion was to blame. The NTSB said nothing. Nine days after the accident the flight-data recorder—the "black box" that records flight and systems data—was retrieved and sent to the NTSB laboratory in Washington. The NTSB stated tersely that there was preliminary evidence that the initial dive may have been a "controlled descent." Five days later, on Sunday, November 14, a senior official at the Egyptian Transportation Ministry—an air-force general and a former EgyptAir pilot—held a news conference in Cairo and, with Rayan at his side, announced that the evidence from the flight-data recorder had been inconclusive but the dive could be explained only by a bomb in the cockpit or in the lavatory directly behind it. It was an odd assertion to make, but of little importance, because the second black box, the cockpit voice recorder, had been salvaged the night before and was sent on Sunday to the NTSB. The tape was cleaned and processed, and a small group that included a translator (who was not Egyptian) gathered in a listening room at L'Enfant Plaza to hear it through.

"I RELY ON GOD"

Listening to cockpit recordings is a tough and voyeuristic duty, restricted to the principal investigators and people with specific knowledge of the airplane or the pilots, who might help to prepare an accurate transcript. Experienced investigators grow accustomed to the job, but I talked to several who had heard the EgyptAir tape, and they admitted that they had been taken aback. Black boxes are such pitiless, unblinking devices. When the information they contained from flight 990 was combined with the radar profile and the first, sketchy information on the crew, this was the story it seemed to tell:

The flight lasted thirty-one minutes. During the departure from New York it was captained, as required, by the aircraft commander, a portly senior pilot named Ahmad al-Habashi, fifty-seven, who had flown thirty-six years for the airline. Habashi of course sat in the left seat. In the right seat was the most junior member of the crew, a thirty-six-year-old copilot who was progressing well in his career and looking forward to getting married. Before takeoff the copilot advised the flight attendants by saying, in Arabic, "In the name of God, the merciful, the compassionate. Cabin crew takeoff position." This was not unusual.

After takeoff the autopilot did the flying. Habashi and the copilot kept watch, talked to air-traffic control and gossiped about their work. The cockpit door was unlocked, which was fairly standard on EgyptAir flights. Various flight attendants came in and left; for a while the chief pilot, the man who was deadheading back to Cairo, stopped by the cockpit to chat. Then, twenty minutes into the flight, the "cruise" copilot, Gameel al-Batouti, arrived. Batouti was a big, friendly guy with a reputation for telling jokes and enjoying life. Three months short of sixty, and mandatory retirement, he was unusually old for a copilot. He had joined the airline in his mid-forties, after a career as a flight instructor for the air force, and had rejected several opportunities for command. His lack of ambition was odd but not unheard of: his English was poor and might have given him trouble on the necessary exams; moreover, as the company's senior 767 copilot, he made adequate money and had his pick of long-distance flights. Now he used his seniority to urge the junior copilot to cede the right seat ahead of the scheduled crew change. When the junior man resisted, Batouti said, "You mean you're not going to get up? You will get up. Go and get some rest and come back." The junior copilot stayed in his seat a bit longer and then left the cockpit. Batouti took the seat and buckled in.

Batouti was married and had five children. Four of them were grown and doing well. His fifth child was a girl, age ten, who was sick with lupus but responding to treatment that he had arranged for her to receive in Los Angeles. Batouti had a nice house in Cairo. He had a vacation house on the beach. He did not drink heavily. He was moderately religious. He had his retirement planned. He had acquired an automobile tire in New Jersey the day before, and was bringing it home in the cargo hold. He had also picked up some free samples of Viagra, to distribute as gifts.

Captain Habashi was more religious, and was known to pray sometimes in the cockpit. He and Batouti were old friends. Using Batouti's nickname, he said, in Arabic, "How are you, Jimmy?" They groused to each other about the chief pilot and about a clique of young and arrogant "kids," junior EgyptAir pilots who were likewise catching a ride back to the Cairo base. One of those pilots came into the cockpit dressed in street clothes. Habashi said, "What's with you? Why did you get all dressed in red like that?" Presumably the man then left. Batouti had a meal. A female flight attendant came in and offered more. Batouti said pleasantly, "No, thank you, it was marvelous." She took his tray.

At 1:47 A.M. the last calls came in from air-traffic control, from Ann Brennan, far off in the night at her display. Captain Habashi handled the calls. He said, "New York, EgyptAir Nine-nine-zero heavy, good morning," and she answered with her final "EgyptAir Nine-ninety, roger."

At 1:48 Batouti found the junior copilot's pen and handed it across to Habashi. He said, "Look, here's the new first officers' pen. Give it to him, please. God spare you." He added, "To make sure it doesn't get lost."

Habashi said, "Excuse me, Jimmy, while I take a quick trip to the toilet." He ran his electric seat back with a whir. There was the sound of the cockpit door moving.

Batouti said, "Go ahead, please."

Habashi said, "Before it gets crowded. While they are eating. And I'll be back to you."

Again the cockpit door moved. There was a *clunk*. There was a *clink*. It seems that Batouti was now alone in the cockpit. The 767 was at 33,000 feet, cruising peacefully eastward at .79 Mach.

At 1:48:30 a strange, wordlike sound was uttered, three syllables with emphasis on the second, perhaps more English than Arabic, and variously heard on the tape as "control it," "hydraulic," or something, unintelligible. The NTSB ran extensive speech and sound-spectrum studies on it, and was never able to assign it conclusively to Batouti or to anyone else. But what is clear is that Batouti then softly said, *"Tawakkalt ala Allah,"* which proved difficult to translate, and was at first rendered incorrectly, but essentially means "I rely on God." An electric seat whirred. The autopilot disengaged, and the airplane sailed on as before for another four seconds. Again Batouti said, "I rely on God." Then two things happened almost simultaneously, according to the flight-data recorder: the throttles in the cockpit moved back fast to minimum idle, and a second later, back at the tail, the airplane's massive elevators (the pitch-control surfaces) dropped to a three-degrees-down position. When the elevators drop, the tail goes up; and when the tail goes up, the nose points down. Apparently Batouti had chopped the power and pushed the control yoke forward.

The effect was dramatic. The airplane began to dive steeply, dropping its nose so quickly that the environment inside plunged to nearly zero gs, the weightless condition of space. Six times in quick succession Batouti repeated, "I rely on God." His tone was calm. There was a loud thump. As the nose continued to pitch downward, the airplane went into the negative-g range, nudging loose objects against the ceiling. The elevators moved even farther down. Batouti said, "I rely on God."

Somehow, in the midst of this, now sixteen seconds into the dive, Captain Habashi made his way back from the toilet. He yelled, "What's happening? What's happening?" Batouti said, "I rely on God."

The wind outside was roaring. The airplane was dropping through 30,800 feet, and accelerating beyond its maximum operating speed of .86 Mach. In the cockpit the altimeters were spinning like cartoon clocks. Warning horns were sounding, warning lights were flashing—low oil pressure on the left engine, and then on the right. The master alarm went off, a loud high-to-low warble.

For the last time Batouti said, "I rely on God."

Again Habashi shouted. "What's happening?" By then he must have reached the left control yoke. The negative gs ended as he countered the pitch-over, slowing the rate at which the nose was dropping. But the 767 was still angled down steeply, forty degrees below the horizon, and it was accelerating. The rate of descent hit 39,000 feet a minute.

"What's happening, Gameel? What's happening?"

Habashi was clearly pulling very hard on his control yoke, trying desperately to raise the nose. Even so, thirty seconds into the dive, at 22,200 feet, the airplane hit the speed of sound, at which it was certainly not meant to fly. Many things happened in quick succession in the cockpit. Batouti reached over and shut off the fuel, killing both engines. Habashi screamed, "What is this? What is this? Did you shut the engines?" The throttles were pushed full forward—for no obvious reason, since the engines were dead. The speed-brake handle was then pulled, deploying drag devices on the wings.

At the same time, there was an unusual occurrence back at the tail: the right-side and left-side elevators, which normally move together to control the airplane's pitch, began to "split," or move in opposite directions. Specifically: the elevator on the right remained down, while the left-side elevator moved up to a healthy recovery position. That this could happen at all was the result of a design feature meant to allow either pilot to overpower a mechanical jam and control the airplane with only one elevator. The details are complex, but the essence in this case seemed to be that the right elevator was being pushed down by Batouti while the left elevator was being pulled up by the captain. The NTSB concluded that a "force fight" had broken out in the cockpit.

Words were failing Habashi. He yelled, "Get away in the engines!" And then, incredulously, ". . . shut the engines!"

Batouti said calmly, "It's shut."

Habashi did not have time to make sense of the happenings. He probably did not have time to get into his seat and slide it forward. He must have been standing in the cockpit, leaning over the seat-back and hauling on the controls. The commotion was horrendous. He was reacting instinctively as a pilot, yelling. "Pull!" and then, "Pull with me! Pull with me! Pull with me!"

It was the last instant captured by the on-board flight recorders. The elevators were split, with the one on the right side, Batouti's side, still pushed into a nose-down position. The ailerons on both wings had assumed a strange upswept position, normally never seen on an airplane. The 767 was at 16,416 feet, doing 527 miles an hour, and pulling a moderately heavy 2.4 gs, indicating that the nose, though still below the horizon, was rising fast, and that Habashi's efforts on the left side were having an effect. A belated recovery was under way. At that point, because the engines had been cut, all nonessential electrical devices were lost, blacking out not only the recorders, which rely on primary power, but also most of the instrument displays and lights. The pilots were left to the darkness of the sky, whether to work together or to fight. I've often wondered what happened between those two men during the 114 seconds that remained of their lives. We'll never know. Radar reconstruction showed that the 767 recovered from the dive at 16,000 feet and, like a great wounded glider, soared steeply back to 24,000 feet, turned to the southeast while beginning to break apart, and shed its useless left engine and some of its skin before giving up for good and diving to its death at high speed.

CONFLICTING REALITIES

When this evidence emerged at the NTSB, the American investigators were shocked but also relieved by the obvious conclusion. There was no bomb here. Despite initial fears, there was nothing wrong with the airplane. The apparent cause was pilot error at its extreme: Batouti had gone haywire. Every detail that emerged from the two flight recorders fit that scenario: the sequence of the switches and controls that were moved, the responses of the airplane, and the words that were spoken, however cryptic and incomplete. Batouti had waited to be alone in the cockpit, and had intentionally pushed the airplane to its death. He had even fought the captain's valiant attempt at recovery. Why? Professionally, the NTSB didn't need to care. It was up to the criminal investigators at the FBI to discover if this was a political act, or the result of a plot. Even at the time, just weeks after the airplane went down, it was hard to imagine that Batouti had any terrorist connections, and indeed, the FBI never found any such evidence. But in pure aviation terms it didn't really matter why Batouti did it, and pure aviation is what the NTSB is all about. So this was easy—Crash Investigation 101. The guy to blame was dead. The NTSB wouldn't have to go after Boeing—a necessary task on occasion, but never a pleasant prospect. The wreckage, which was still being pulled out of the ocean, would not require tedious inspection. The report could be written quickly and filed away, and the NTSB could move on to the backlog of work that might actually affect the future safety of the flying public.

When Jim Hall, the NTSB chairman, held a news conference to address the initial findings, on November 19, 1999, he was culturally sensitive, responsible and very strict about the need to maintain an open mind. There had been leaks to the press about the content of the cockpit voice recorder. It was being said that Batouti's behavior had been strange during the dive and that he had recited Muslim prayers. Hall scolded the assembled reporters for using unofficial information and exciting the public's emotions. He made a show of being careful with his own choice of words. He said that the accident "might, and I emphasize *might*, be the result of a deliberate act." He did not say "suicide" or "Arab" or "Muslim." He did not even say "Batouti." He said, "No one wants to get to the bottom of this mystery quicker than those investigating this accident, both here and in Egypt, but we won't get there on a road paved with leaks, supposition, speculation and spin. That road does not lead to the truth, and the truth is what both the American people and the Egyptian people seek." It was standard stuff, a prelude to a quick wrapping up of the investigation. The Egyptian delegation, which had moved into rooms at the Loews L'Enfant Plaza Hotel, might have felt grateful to have such a man at the NTSB to guide them through these difficult times. Instead the Egyptians were outraged.

At the NTSB this came as a surprise. Looking back, it's possible to see signs of a disconnect, especially the Egyptian government's baffling speculation about a bomb in the forward lavatory; but just the day before Hall's press conference the Egyptian ambassador had heaped praise on the NTSB and the investigation. Now, suddenly and with startling vigor, the Egyptian delegation went on the offensive. The leader of the charge, Shaker Kelada, later told me about running across one of the American investigators in the halls of the NTSB. When the investigator mentioned with satisfaction that the work might wrap up within a few weeks, Kelada brought him up short with the news that he'd better change his plans—because far from being over, the investigation had hardly begun.

First the Egyptians had to prepare the ground: the delegation started to loudly criticize the performance and intentions of Boeing, the FBI and the entire NTSB. Kelada said that Batouti was the scapegoat, and that this was happening because it was an *Egyptian* airliner that had gone down. It did not escape Kelada's attention that the legendary head of aviation investigations at the NTSB—a brilliant and abrasive engineer named Bernard Loeb, who was overseeing the flight 990 inquiry—was Jewish and something of a Zionist.

Loeb retired last spring; Kelada implied to me last summer that this was a deception, and that Loeb continued to pull the strings. Loeb laughed when I mentioned it to him afterward. He was looking forward to spending time with his grandchildren. But at the same time, he was angry that Egypt, after receiving $1.3 billion in American assistance every year, would have used any of its budget to cause the United States unnecessary expense by prolonging an investigation that for the NTSB alone had so far cost $17 million. As to Zionism, Loeb did seem bothered by aspects of the Egyptian culture. I got the feeling, though, that his opinion was fresh—that it stemmed from his contacts with EgyptAir, rather than from experiences that had preceded them.

But it didn't really matter who at the NTSB was in charge of the investigation. In faraway Cairo, inevitably, it was seen as unfair. From the day that flight 990's recorder tape was transcribed and word of its contents began to leak out, the feeling in Egypt was that all Arabs were under attack, and that the assault had been planned. More than a year after the crash I met a sharp young reporter in Cairo who continued to seethe about it. He said, "For many Egyptians it was a big example of this business of dictating the reality. What made many people question the authenticity of the U.S. claims was the rush to conclusions. . . . The rush, the interpretation of a few words, it left no chance. The whole thing seemed to apply within a framework of an American sort of soap opera, one of those movies you make. You know—this is a fanatic, he comes from the Middle East, he utters a few religious words, he brings the plane down." But what if Batouti really had brought the plane down— where did the reporter's reaction leave Egypt? Earlier the reporter had written critically about the corruption at EgyptAir, but he refused even to think critically about it anymore.

The reporter's anger was similar, at least superficially, to the anger that was seething through Shaker Kelada and the rest of the Egyptian delegation in November of 1999. For Jim Hall, Bernard Loeb and others at the NTSB, the source of the problem seemed at first to be the media coverage, which was typically overeager.

Rumors of suicide had circulated in the press almost since the airplane hit the water, but it was only after the voice recorder was recovered that the reports began to make uniformed reference to Muslim prayers. Three days before Hall's press conference the *Washington Post* ran a headline saying, PILOT PRAYED, THEN SHUT OFF JET'S AUTOPILOT. Television stations speculated that the "prayer" was the *shahada* ("There is no god but God; Muhammad is the messenger of God"), as if this were what one might say before slaughtering infidels. When the actual Arabic words—*Tawakkalt ala Allah*—became public, some news outlets gave the following translation: "I have made my decision. I put my fate in God's hands." This was reported so widely that the NTSB took the unusual step of announcing that "I have made my decision" had never been spoken. By implication, "I place my fate . . ." had.

When NTSB investigators explained their lack of control over the American press, the Egyptians scoffed and pointed out—correctly—that the reporters' sources were people inside the investigation. And anyway, the Egyptians added, what Batouti had said was not "I put my fate in God's hands"—as the NTSB's interpreter had claimed—but rather, "I rely on God." The investigators blinked at the subtlety of this distinction, and made the necessary changes to the transcript. Then the Egyptians produced a letter from an Islamic scholar in Cairo who certified that the meaning of *Tawakkalt ala Allah* is "I depend in my daily affairs on the omnipotent Allah alone." The Egyptians wanted the letter inserted into the record, but were willing to allow "I rely on God" to remain in the transcript. Again, the investigators blinked. This was not the sort of thing they normally dealt with. They tried sometimes to bridge the gap as they might have with Americans, with a nudge and a smile, but it got them nowhere.

In essence the Egyptians were making two intertwined arguments: first, that it was culturally impossible for Batouti to have done what the NTSB believed; second, that the NTSB lacked the cultural sensitivity to understand what was on the cockpit voice recorder. With those arguments as a starting point, the Egyptians tore into the complexities of the evidence, disputing any assumptions or conclusions the NTSB put forward and raising new questions at every possible turn—a process that continues to this day. They were tenacious. For example (and this is just a small sample of the Egyptians' arguments): When Batouti said, *"Tawakkalt ala Allah,"* he was not preparing to die but responding in surprise to something wrong with the flight. He said it quietly, yes, but with emotion that the Americans lacked cultural sensitivity to hear. When he started the dive, he was trying to avoid a plane or a missile outside. If not that, then the airplane went into the dive on its own. When he idled the engines, it was to keep from gaining speed. When he cut the engines, he was going through the required restart procedure, because he erroneously believed—on the basis of the low-oil-pressure warning light that flashed in the cockpit—that the engines had flamed out. Apparently Habashi made the same mistake, which is why he discussed engine cuts. When Habashi called, "Pull with me!" Batouti did exactly that. The split elevators were like the upswept ailerons—either an aerodynamic anomaly, resulting from the unknown pressures of ultrahigh-speed flight on the 767, or, more simply, an error in the flight-data recorder. Whichever way, the Egyptians argued that expensive wind-tunnel testing was necessary at high Mach numbers near the speed of sound.

Meanwhile, most of the wreckage had been recovered and spread out in a hangar in Rhode Island. A second salvage operation was mounted in the spring to coincide with a state visit by Mubarak to Washington. It went to the west debris field and brought up the left engine and a boatload of worthless scraps. At the NTSB a story circulated about Al Gore, who was said to have angered Mubarak by making a casual reference to "the suicide flight." There was a short flap about that. The investigation continued. The documentation grew. The possibilities multiplied and ran off in a hundred directions. An airline pilot observing the scene said to me, "It could have been this, it could have been that. Bottom line is, it could have been anything except their guy."

THE SEARCH FOR A MOTIVE

While the Egyptians were proposing theory after theory to absolve Batouti, the FBI was conducting a criminal investigation, collecting evidence that provided for his possible motive. Mostly through interviews with employees of the Pennsylvania Hotel, the FBI found that Batouti had a reputation for sexual impropriety—and not merely by the prudish standards of America. It was reported that on multiple occasions over the previous two years he had been suspected of exposing himself to teenage girls, masturbating in public, following female guests to their rooms, and listening at their doors. Some of the maids, it was said, were afraid of him, and the hotel security guards had once brought him in for questioning and a warning. Apparently the hotel had considered banning him. The FBI learned that EgyptAir was aware of these problems and had warned Batouti to control his behavior. He was not considered to be a dangerous man—and certainly he was more sad than bad. In fact, there was a good side to Batouti that came out in these interviews as well. He was very human. Many people were fond of him, even at the hotel.

But a story soon surfaced that an altercation may have occurred during the New York layover before the fatal departure. The FBI was told that there had been trouble, and possibly an argument with the chief pilot, who was also staying at the hotel. It was hypothesized that the chief pilot might have threatened disciplinary action upon arrival back in Cairo—despite the public humiliation that would entail. Was that perhaps Batouti's motive? Did the killing of 217 people result from a simple act of vengeance against one man? The evidence was shaky at best. Then, in February of 2000, an EgyptAir pilot named Hamdi Hanafi Taha, forty-nine, landed in England and requested political asylum, claiming that he had information on the accident. FBI and NTSB investigators flew immediately to interview him, hoping that he would provide the answers they needed. They were disappointed. Taha told a story that seemed to confirm that Batouti had been confronted by the chief pilot, and he added some new details, but he turned out to be an informant of questionable utility—a radical Muslim who, along with others in the ranks of EgyptAir pilots, had forced the airline to ban the serving of alcohol, and who now went on at length about corruption at EgyptAir, and also what he claimed was rampant alcoholism and drug use among his secular peers. The request for asylum was itself a little flaky. The American investigators flew home without solid information. Most of this came out in the press when the story of Batouti's sexual improprieties was leaked, further angering the Egyptians. They countered, eventually producing a Boeing 777 captain named Mohamed Badrawi, who had been with the other pilots in New York on the fateful night, and who testified at length that they were like a band of brothers—that Batouti and the chief pilot got along well and had had no direct confrontations. Rather, Badrawi said, he had acted at times as a "mediator" between the two men, cautioning Batouti on behalf of the chief pilot to "grow up" in order to avoid legal problems in the United States.

With that on the record, assigning a motive to Batouti became all the more difficult. For a variety of reasons, Bernard Loeb thought the FBI was wasting everyone's time. He did not really oppose the search for a motive, but he was against entering such speculative and easily countered discussions into the NTSB's public record. Privately he believed in the story of the fight. But as he later emphasized to me, "We just didn't need to go there."

Loeb thought the same about much of the investigation. Month after month, as the NTSB chased down the theories that EgyptAir kept proposing, Loeb worried about the other projects that were being put aside. He tried to keep a sense of distance from the work, driving from suburban Maryland to his office dressed in a sports jacket and tie, just like any other Washingtonian with a quiet job. But it was a hopeless ambition. Most mornings the Egyptian delegation was there too. Later Loeb said to me, his voice strangled with frustration, "You had to be there! You had to live through this! Day in and day out! It was as if these people would go back to their rooms at night and then identify some kind of reason. . . . And then it would start all over again. It was insane! It was just insane!"

To bolster their arguments the Egyptians had hired some former accident investigators and also the retired NTSB chairman Carl Vogt, whose willingness to legitimize the Egyptian campaign was seen by many within the NTSB as a betrayal. The Egyptians also turned to the American pilots' union — in principle to improve their communication with the NTSB, but in practice probably just to add weight to their side. In the spring of 2000 the union sent to Washington a man named Jim Walters, a U.S. airline pilot with long experience in accident investigations. Walters thought he could patch things up. Later he said to me, "The Egyptians appeared to be listening to me. But as it turned out, they weren't." Then he said, "I thought I was there to give them advice . . ." It was a disappointment. He liked the Egyptians personally, and remained sympathetic to their side even after he left.

I asked him to describe the scene in Washington. He said, "The NTSB isn't terribly tolerant of people who don't follow good investigative procedure. And they weren't used to dealing with a group like this, right in their backyard, with offices in the same building, there *every* day. I thought, the first thing we have to do is calm everybody down. I thought I could explain to the Egyptians, 'This is how the NTSB operates,' and explain to Jim Hall, 'Hey, these guys are Egyptians. You've got to understand who these guys are, and why they're doing things the way they are, and maybe we can all just kiss and make up and get along from here.'"

But it didn't work out that way. Walters was naive. Kiss and make up? The Egyptians no more needed his advice about investigative procedure than they had needed the NTSB's opinions about the nature of a free press.

A small war had broken out between Egypt and the United States on a battlefield called Loews L'Enfant Plaza Hotel. On one side stood Shaker Kelada and his men, fighting for the honor of their nation against the mysterious forces of American hegemony, and specifically against an agency whose famed independence they believed had been compromised. On the other side stood Bernard Loeb and his people, fighting just as hard—but to set a schedule, write the report and disengage. Jim Hall was scurrying in between. And Boeing was off in Seattle, not quite out of range, trying unsuccessfully to look small.

The irony is that Loeb, too, thought the agency's independence had been compromised, though for the opposite reason: there were meetings at the White House, and phone calls to Jim Hall, in which concern was expressed about accommodating the Egyptian view, and in which it was implied that there should be no rush to finish a report that inevitably would offend Mubarak. Loeb was disgusted and typically vocal about his opinion. When I asked him if the influence was necessarily so wrong, he said, "Next they ask you to *change* the report—to say Batouti didn't do it." He added, however, that no one had ever suggested such a change—and it was a good thing, too.

EGYPT VERSUS THE WEST

By late last May the fight had slowed, and Shaker Kelada was able to spend most of his time back home in Cairo. The NTSB had just issued a draft report, and Egypt was preparing an opposing response. I found Kelada in his expansive new office at the Cairo airport, where we talked several times over the course of a week. These were not good conversations. Kelada insisted on repeating the official Egyptian positions, and would go no further. At one point he began to attack the New York air-traffic controllers, and specifically Ann Brennan, for having walked away from her display. He implied that her absence had a bearing on the accident, or perhaps sparked a subsequent cover-up by the American government. He said, "It was very sloppy air-traffic control, and not what the U.S. wants to show. They're number one at everything, and they don't want *anyone* to know that they have a sloppy operation in New York."

I tried to reach him as one pilot to another. I said, "Come on, I think of that as being a normal operation, don't you?"

He said, "Well, if it is, I don't want to fly in the New York area!"

It was nonsense. And in aviation terms, a lot of what he said to me was equally unconvincing. Eventually I stopped taking notes.

Even when he was being reasonable, the party line kept showing through. He said, "I cannot say it's a mechanical failure. I don't have enough evidence, but I cannot dismiss the possibility of a mechanical failure . . . if I want to be careful."

I said, "On the other hand, you *do* have enough evidence to dismiss the human factor?"

And he said, "Yes."

"To dismiss the intentional act?"

"Yes." He paused. He said, "We search for the truth."

It was late in the day. Kelada sat behind his desk—a man in a big office with jets outside, a smart man, a careful man. I thought of the question that had plagued me all along: not whether the Egyptians were right or wrong but whether they really believed their own words. Loeb had said to me, "Do they *believe* it? I believe they believe in fear."

I went downtown, to an old coffeehouse near the Nile, and spent a few hours with Hani Shukrallah, a columnist and one of the more thoughtful observers of the Egyptian scene. Shukrallah is a small, nervous man, and a heavy smoker. He said, "I know that as far as the Egyptian government was concerned, the point that this was *not* pilot error, and that the Egyptian pilot did *not* bring it *down*—this was decided before the investigation began. It had to do with Egypt's image in the outside world. . . . The government would have viewed this exactly as it would, for example, an Islamic terrorist act in Luxor—something that we should cover up. So it got politicized *immediately.* And this became an official line: You are out there to prove that EgyptAir is not responsible. It became a national duty. It was us versus the West. And all the history played into it, from Bonaparte's campaign until now." In the minds even of people on the street, Shukrallah said, it became "an all-out war."

FOLLOWING FLIGHT 990'S PATH

If so, the United States was in such a strong position that it could lose the struggle only by defeating itself. This is why from the very start of the difficult process it was all the more important for the NTSB to consider the evidence fairly and keep an open mind. The problem was that so many of the scenarios the Egyptians posited were patently absurd—stray missiles, ghost airplanes, strange weather and the like. Yet that didn't mean that everything they said was wrong. As long as Batouti's motive could not be conclusively shown, the possibility remained that the dive of Flight 990 was unintentional, just as Kelada maintained. And in the background the Egyptians had some very smart engineers looking into the various theories.

The 767's elevator movements are powered by three redundant hydraulic circuits, driving a total of six control mechanisms called "actuators," which normally operate in unison. Given the various linkages and cross-connections, the system is complex. The Egyptians thought it through and realized that if two of the six actuators were to fail on the same side of the airplane, they would drive both elevators down, forcing the 767 to pitch into a dive that might match the profile that had emerged from EgyptAir 990's flight-data recorder. Furthermore, if such a failure happened and either pilot tried to right it, that could conceivably explain the "splitting" of the elevators that occurred during 990's attempted recovery.

As might be expected, the discussion about dual actuator failures grew complicated. It also grew political. The NTSB had salvaged most of the actuators from the ocean floor and had found no clear evidence of failure, but with perceptions of public safety at stake, the agency asked Boeing for further information. Boeing engineers calculated that a dual actuator failure would not have deflected the elevators far enough down to equal the known elevator deflections of flight 990, and that such a failure therefore would not have caused as steep a dive. To explore the question they performed a series of ground tests of a 767 elevator, inducing dual actuator failures and "splits" on a parked airplane in Seattle. After adjusting the measured effects, for the theoretical aerodynamic pressures of flight, they found—as they had expected—poor correlation with the known record of flight 990 elevator positions. They believed in any case that either pilot could quickly have recovered from a dual actuator failure by doing what comes naturally at such moments— pulling back hard on the controls.

The NTSB was satisfied; the Egyptians were not. They poked holes in the conclusions and requested basic and costly aerodynamic research, at speeds well beyond the 767's limits, toward Mach One. The question was, of course, to what end? But for Boeing this was a delicate thing, because Egypt kept buying expensive airplanes and was influential in the Arab world. A bit of additional research would perhaps be in order.

Meanwhile, the company's engineers had moved on to flight simulations of the accident, a series of dives set up to be flown in Boeing's highly programmable 767 engineering simulator—a "fixed cab" without motion, capable of handling extremes. These were the profiles that I flew when I went to Seattle last summer. On that same trip I went to Everett, Washington, where the airplanes are made, and in a cockpit with a company test pilot split the elevators in a powered-up 767, as the Egyptian crew presumably had. In order to do this we needed to break the connection between the left and right control yokes, which are mechanically joined under the floorboards, and usually move together. He pushed on his, I pulled on mine, and at fifty pounds of pressure between us the controls were suddenly no longer working in tandem. Far behind us, at the tail, the elevators separated smoothly. On a cockpit display we watched each elevator go its own way. The airplane shuddered from the movement of the heavy control surfaces. We played with variations. Toward the end the pilot laughed and said I was compressing his bones.

But when I got to the simulations, they felt too real to be a game. The simulator was a surrogate cockpit already in flight—humming and warm, with all the controls and familiar displays, and a view outside of an indistinct twilight. It was headed east at 33,000 feet and .79 Mach—just as flight 990 had been. The first set of profiles were "back-driven" duplications of the fatal dive, generated directly from flight 990's flight-data recorder. Another Boeing test pilot sat in Batouti's seat, and the engineers clustered around behind. I let the simulation run on automatic the first few times, resting one hand on the controls to feel the beast die—the sudden pitch and shockingly fast dive, the clicking of a wildly unwinding altimeter, the warbling alarm, the loss of most displays at the bottom after the engines were gone, and the dark, steep, soaring climb up to 24,000 feet, the control yoke rattling its warning of an aerodynamic stall, the airplane rolling southeast to its end. I watched this several times and then flew the same thing by hand, matching the pressure I put on the control yoke to a specially rigged indicator, which, after the elevators' split had occurred, allowed me to match the force required to achieve Habashi's "pull" and Batouti's "push" as captured by the flight-data recorder. First I stood and flew Habashi's "Pull with me!" from behind the seat—up to ninety pounds of force, which under those conditions seemed like not very much. It was the other intention, the pushing, that was dramatic. What was required was not only pushing but then pushing harder. The idea that someone would do that in an airplane full of passengers shocked me as a pilot. If that's what Batouti did, I will never understand what was going on in his mind.

The second set of simulations were easier to fly. These were the dual actuator failures, which EgyptAir proposed might have overcome Batouti when he was alone in the cockpit. The purpose was to test the difficulty or ease of recovery from such an upset. Again the simulations began at 33,000 feet and .79 Mach. I flew by hand from the start. The airplane pitched down strongly and without warning. I hauled back on the controls and lost 800 feet. It was an easy recovery, but not fair—I had been ready. The engineers then made me wait before reacting, as they had made other pilots— requiring delays of five, ten and finally fifteen seconds before I began the recovery. Fifteen seconds seems like an eternity in a 767 going out of control. Even so, by hauling hard on the yoke and throttling back, I managed to pull out after losing only 12,000 feet; and though I went to the maximum allowable dive speed, the airplane survived. This was not unusual. Airplanes are meant to be flown. During the original simulation sessions done for the NTSB every pilot with a dual actuator failure was able to recover, and probably better than I. So what was wrong with Batouti? The simplest explanation is that he was trying to crash the airplane. But if he wasn't, if the Egyptians were right that he couldn't recover from a dual actuator failure, what was wrong with him as an aviator?

I posed the question to Jim Walters, the airline pilot who despite his disappointment remained sympathetic to the Egyptians' position. He had a ready answer. He called Batouti "the world's worst airline pilot."

But how good do you have to be?

Bernard Loeb would have none of it. He said, "Sure. In the end they were willing to sell him down the river. They said, 'He panicked!' Bottom line is, if the actuator drops the nose, you can pull it up. They know that. They *admit* it. Pulling the nose up is the most intuitive, reflexive thing you can do in an airplane. So when you start hearing arguments like that, you *know* people are blowing smoke.

"Look, first we sit through this cockpit voice recording in which . . ." He shook his head. "How many cockpit voice recordings have I heard? Hundreds? Thousands? When someone has a problem with an airplane, you know it. One of our investigators used to say to me, 'These damned pilots, they don't tell us what's happening. Why don't they say, "It's the rudder!"' They don't do that. But I'll tell you what they do say. They make clear as hell that there's something really wrong. "What the *hell's* going on? What is *that*?' Every single one of them. When there's a control problem of some sort, it is so crystal clear that they are trying desperately to diagnose what is going on. Right to when the recorder quits. They are fighting for their lives.

"But this guy is sitting there saying the same thing in a slow, measured way, indicating no stress. The captain comes in and asks what's going on, and he doesn't answer! That's what you start with. Now you take the dual actuator failure that doesn't match the flight profile, and is also fully recoverable. Where do you want to go after that?"

The NTSB's final report on flight 990 was expected for the fall of this year, and it was widely presumed in aviation circles that the report would find no mechanical failure or external cause for the crash. It also seemed likely that the report would at least implicitly blame Batouti for the disaster—a conclusion that would, of course, be unacceptable within Egypt. Nonetheless, by last May, when I met him in Cairo, Shaker Kelada was looking pleased, and I later found out why. His engineers had gotten busy again, and had come up with new concerns—certain combinations of tail-control failures that might require further testing. Now Boeing had come to town for a quiet talk with its customers, and had agreed to do the tests. Boeing was going to inform the NTSB of the new work, and the end would again be delayed.

Sitting in his office, Kelada could not help gloating. He said, "Jim Hall told me, 'I've learned a very good lesson. When you deal with a foreign carrier in an investigation, before you go anywhere with it, you have to study the history and culture of the country.' These were his own words to me! He said, 'I knew nothing about Egypt or its culture before we got into EgyptAir 990.'"

I said, "What would he have learned?"

"Not to underestimate people. To think that he's way up there, and everybody's way down here."

Fair enough. But in the end there was the question of the objective truth—and there was the inclination not to seek real answers for even such a simple event as a single accident nearly two years before.

I knew that at the start of the investigation the Egyptian delegation had included a man named Mamdouh Heshmat, a high official in civil aviation. When the cockpit voice recording first arrived at L'Enfant Plaza, Heshmat was there, and he heard it through with a headset on. According to several investigators who listened alongside him, he came out of the room looking badly shaken, and made it clear he knew that Batouti had done something wrong. He may have called Cairo with that news. The next day he flew home, never to reappear in Washington. When NTSB investigators went to Cairo, they could not find him, though it was said that he was still working for the government. I knew I wouldn't find him either, but I wanted to see how Kelada would react to the mention of him. Kelada and I had come to the end. I said I had heard about a man who had been one of the first to listen to the tape—who could it have been? Kelada looked straight at me and said, "I don't recall his name." There was no reason to continue, from his perspective or mine.

✳   ✳   ✳

This piece was meant as a parable—an exploration of the distance between Egyptian and American political cultures, and at the risk of overgeneralizing, between the Arab and Western worlds. We used it as The Atlantic Monthly's *first response to the September 11 attacks, and with a huge effort rushed it through the magazine's exhaustive fact-checking process, and to completion within days. In fact, I had been working on the story intermittently for nearly six months—and had followed it through the United States into Boeing engineering simulators and to Egypt. The editors considered it to be natural for* me because of my experience as a working pilot, as well as my previous political reporting from North Africa and the Middle East.

Cairo is where the story came together. By the time I got there, I had read the documentation carefully, and I was inclined to believe that the American crash investigators were right when they said that the airplane had not failed: all the technical evidence supported the idea that Batouti, the copilot, had gone berserk in the cockpit and had pushed flight 990 out of control. Nonetheless, I was also inclined to believe that the Egyptians were sincere in their insistence that for personal as well as cultural reasons their friend and fellow Muslim could not have done such a thing. They had invited me to Cairo to hear their point of view. But then a strange thing happened. Rather than talking to me frankly—even off the record—as one pilot to another, they continued to repeat the technically silly claims that they had made to the general press. When I tried to move beyond such party lines, they stonewalled me in embarrassingly obvious ways. This went on for two weeks and became a sort of unintended confession: it became evident that they neither believed their own claims nor cared about appearing dishonest in my eyes. Despite all my experience in the Middle East, this took me by surprise. They were intelligent people, but they were operating entirely in their own world, by rules that were not mine. The distance between us grew greater with contact, not less. In the end we found no common ground at all. In a small way, of course, this is how wars begin.

JUDGMENT DAY
DOUG MOST

He knew what he had to say, but the words were stuck in his gut. And they weren't coming up. *Damned if I do,* he thought, *damned if I don't. Either way, I look like a liar.* So he sat there, silent, in his crisp white shirt, gold tie and neatly pressed charcoal suit. His bald head glistened. His salt and pepper beard and wire-rimmed glasses made him look professorial, but the shackles around his ankles, just above the black, tasseled shoes, told another story. The seconds passed, and the dull hum of the fluorescent lights filled the room. No one said a word. No one shifted, twitched or glanced at a watch. It wasn't that he didn't know the answer. This was his life they were asking about. Of course he knew. It was burned into his memory like his birth date, his granddaughter's name and the terrified face of that young woman he had shot and killed while robbing a liquor store in Dorchester.

For three hours, twenty-three people had been sitting in this small, windowless rectangle of a room on the third floor of a building in South Boston, and now one question had everyone leaning forward. Aside from the American flag, the video camera perched on a tripod and the expressionless faces of four men and two women, there wasn't much to look at. Fifty-three-year-old Lewis Dickerson sat perfectly still, wrestling with the most important decision of his life. He could stick by his story, and hope that no one caught him in the lie, or finally face the truth and come clean in front of his loved ones. "I was crying inside," his sister, Rose, recalls of watching her brother struggle. "I wanted him to tell the truth." The silence lasted all of fifteen seconds, but when a man's life is riding on the next sentence he utters, time ticks by slowly.

The story of how Lewis Dickerson found himself on the morning of June 29 sitting before six people who will determine his future is a sad one. Watch him speak. See the emotion spill out. Listen to others sing his praises, call him "extraordinary," "a gentle soul," "a good person." Only then will his twenty-six years in prison for first-degree murder seem puzzling. But for him to become the man he is today, Dickerson first had to be the man that he was. And that man was a coward who lived the life others wanted him to lead, not the life he wanted. That man took hold of a gun in the backseat of a car because someone handed it to him. That man pointed it at the chest of a harmless store clerk, pulled the trigger and ran.

"I was weak back then," Dickerson says now. "I took the gun and went into the store. I was scared. I knew it was wrong, but I went anyway. I'm sorry."

He's said those words before — "I'm sorry" — but it's taken him so long to mean it, to believe it. Now he's hoping the Governor's Advisory Board of Pardons will believe him, too, and make him that rarest of inmates to have a life sentence commuted so he can start anew.

On February 7, 1975, Dickerson was lost. He was twenty-seven and living in Mattapan, earning $125 a week working for Lee's Auto Body in Dorchester, but he had no focus, no purpose, no direction.

The third eldest of seven children raised in a small West Virginia coal-mining town, he says his father beat him with belts, cords and fists before dying in a fight. His mother moved her children to Newark, New Jersey, a city that in the 1960s resembled a black-and-white cookie: blacks on one side, whites on the other. Race riots in 1967 left twenty-six dead, fifteen hundred injured and the city in ruins. It was here that Dickerson's life began to crumble. He was arrested for breaking and entering, and he experimented with heroin. He wasn't out looking to rob and steal, or score some drugs, but if the drugs were there, he did them. If a friend asked for his help breaking into a building, he tagged along. He wasn't the troublemaker, he was simply ripe for trouble to find him. And it did.

Dickerson graduated from high school at the height of the Vietnam War. In 1968, the draft board called, and he was shipped overseas. He was honorably discharged in 1970. A short marriage produced a baby girl but little happiness, and in 1974, separated and frustrated about seeing his daughter so infrequently, he followed another woman north to Boston. It was here, a few months later, while living in a rooming house and working at an auto repair shop, that he landed one night in the backseat of a car with a woman, two men and a .38 automatic.

It's 9:10 A.M. as Dickerson shuffles into the room behind two guards from the Massachusetts Department of Corrections. His lawyer, Bruce Taub, sits to Dickerson's right. Behind them are a few reporters and interested lawyers, along with Dickerson's friends and relatives. "The board needs to look at what you were as a person compared to what you've become," Michael Pomarole, the chairman of the advisory board, says to open the hearing.

Each member of the panel has a thick file filled with every detail of Dickerson's life: from his childhood, to his crimes, to the ways he's improved himself in prison by taking college courses, tutoring other inmates, working with schizophrenic patients, joining the

Nation of Islam, learning to bake and restoring antique furniture. Each has letters from people who have come to know him over the years and say he's earned his freedom. Some are even penned by prison guards who befriended Dickerson. And there is the story about the day, when he was on work release at Metropolitan State Hospital in Waltham, that one of his patients hanged himself. Dickerson was distraught, and one of the unit directors was struck by how much he cared. "He was very gentle and kind," that woman, Kris Dodson, says from her home in Winchester. Within weeks of meeting Dickerson, Dodson had quit her job, begun dating him and fallen in love, eventually sponsoring his weekend furloughs. "He's dedicated his life to being helpful," Dodson says.

That's what helped Dickerson get his first commutation hearing eleven years ago. But predictably for a first-degree murder convict, not even the backing of some Concord homeowners whose furniture he had restored or a clinical specialist who oversaw his work with the mentally ill could convince the board to release him. "There was a gentleness about him," says Margaret Edmands, a Concord resident and professor of nursing at University of Massachusetts/Lowell who met Dickerson when he refinished her antique wood chair. He cooked a meal for her and her husband at the prison in the early 1980s, and she later invited him over for dinner on one of his furloughs. "He brought flowers," she remembers. Even though he was denied release in 1990, it was by a narrow, 4-3 decision, giving everyone hope he would get another hearing. Back at the Bay State Correctional Center in Norfolk, he picked up where he left off and patiently waited for this next shot.

Taub is first to speak as the hearing begins. His long legs crossed in his chair, he speaks slowly, emphasizing every sentence. He, too, was working at Metropolitan State Hospital when he met Dickerson. "In rare instances," Taub begins, "a person convicted of first-degree murder felony without the possibility of parole gets this chance. The board has the capacity, and indeed the duty, to make a recommendation to the governor as to whether there are exceptional circumstances that would warrant the commutation of a sentence." That recommendation, he says, should be to reduce Dickerson's sentence to second-degree murder, making him eligible for release with lifetime supervised probation. In the next few hours, he tells them, they will discover that although Dickerson "is a person who is guilty of first-degree murder, he is a gentle soul, a responsible and respectful human being, who has been transformed by this experience, and presents absolutely no danger to the community."

And then he turns to his client.

A "gentle soul"? It's difficult to hear someone who blasted a hole in another person's chest for $752.10 be called a "gentle soul." Eva Dodds was thirty-two when she died of that gunshot wound. Little is known about her. She was from North Carolina. She had a son and was separated from her husband. She was the common-law wife of the store owner, Cyril Miller. And she was working behind his register at Cy's Variety and Package Store on Erie Street in Dorchester just after 10 P.M. when two men walked in.

One with a beard and mustache asked for a pint of Wild Irish Rose wine to distract her, before pulling out a gun and pointing it at her chest. The other shouted, "All right, give it up. Give up the money," then jumped over the counter to grab the cash, emptying the register of all but a few quarters. Back in the store's cooler, Miller heard the commotion and peered through a peephole. He had two guns to his right—a six-shot rifle and a twelve-gauge shotgun—and he reached for the shotgun while watching the men. But before he could point the tip through the hole a single shot ripped through the store and Dodds slumped over the counter. Miller quickly aimed and fired, striking the shooter in the back and tearing some scraps off his jacket.

Dickerson ran out and Miller rushed to the front to find the woman he loved dying on his floor. Miller lives in Florida now, his memory and speech ravaged by two strokes. Eva Dodds is dead. The only person today still whole from the shots fired that night is Dickerson.

"I am so, so sorry for all the pain and suffering I caused Mrs. Dodds and her family," he tells the board. He walks them through his life, from the beatings by his father to his failed marriage to his arrival in Boston. He's not eloquent. He stutters, at a loss for words. He tells them about his timely returns from dozens of unsupervised furloughs. He talks about his granddaughter, Canice, who just turned three, the same age his daughter, Nicole, was when he went to prison. He begins to sob. "On February 7, 1975, I shot and killed Eva Dodds. She was shot and killed during an armed robbery. Her death was totally my responsibility. Nothing I do can ever change that. I panicked. I live with the consequences of my actions every day of my life."

His lips are quivering. "I am immensely ashamed of myself. I'm here today to ask for your forgiveness and mercy. I will never act in any way to draw negative attention to embarrass the board. I am a changed man after twenty-five years in prison, and a trustworthy human being."

To everyone in the room, Dickerson seems to be saying all the right things. Finally. His defense at trial in 1975 had been that he had no involvement in the killing, that he'd been shot while watching a fight on a street nearby. The jury didn't buy it and sent him away for life. His story changed fifteen years later at his first commutation hearing. He admitted shooting Dodds but said the gun went off accidentally after Miller shot him. "A muscle spasm," he called it. Again, he was not convincing, and his request was denied. Parole boards want to hear admissions, confessions and apologies, not excuses. At last he's given them what they want. He didn't walk into that store intending to shoot someone. But with his barrel aimed at Dodds, and a creaking sound stretching his nerves, his finger eased back on the trigger in fear.

He looks down at the table as the board members begin to question him. Those who know him say he's shy, and that's becoming apparent.

"Where did your life start to go wrong?" Pomarole asks. The downhill began with his discharge from the military, Dickerson answers, followed by the failed marriage. "I didn't feel good about myself." Pomarole asks why he committed that breaking and entering in New Jersey, and why he used heroin, hammering away at the friends he made. "I knew they were involved in illegal things," Dickerson says. "They made me feel okay."

Maureen Walsh, seated next to Pomarole, continues the theme, addressing the shooting. "Why would you bring a loaded handgun into the shop that day?"

"I was a very weak individual and was easily influenced at the time. I'm not making excuses. I was scared. I knew it was wrong, but I went anyway. I'm sorry."

Daniel Dewey goes next, but veers off in another direction. A Vietnam veteran, he's curious why Dickerson made no mention in his petition of his military service. At his 1990 hearing, Dickerson included in his request a detailed description of his service, writing, "I came to view Vietnam as one of the most violent places of my life." He wrote that he was driving a tank when he was struck in the head by shrapnel, suffered a gash from his temple to his mouth and spent the remainder of his stint in Germany.

"Is all of that true, any of that true, or what?" Dewey asks.

"It's true," Dickerson answers.

"You had six months in Vietnam?"

"A little less than six months."

"Why doesn't it show up on your forms?"

"I have no idea, sir."

Dewey is annoyed. He tells Dickerson, "Part of the basis of your petition is your credibility, and some things from your early days can't be verified."

The issue fades when board member Doris Dottridge, a Mashpee detective, takes Dickerson back to the shooting. "I had no intention of hurting anyone," he says. He says he fired the shot only when he started to hear noises—Miller, in the cooler. He says the other people involved that night dropped him off at Boston City Hospital, where he was arrested, and he knew them only as Will, Tony and Lou. That's why he couldn't help police find them. He didn't know their last names. Dottridge looks skeptical.

The questioning grows more intense with John Kivlan, who returns to Dickerson's service record. Vietnam is a touchy subject with the board. In 1995, the board released convicted killer Joseph Yandle after he won members' sympathies with stories about being a decorated Vietnam veteran. He lied, and when the embarrassed board found out, it revoked his parole and returned him to prison. Now, with Dickerson sitting before them, the board members can't fathom that he might be trying the same ruse, knowing they'd hunt down the truth. Finally, Kivlan asks the question.

"If it turns out that it's not true, what action do you think the board should take on your petition?"

Dickerson hears the tone in Kivlan's voice. He knows what he has to say, but can't get the words out. He desperately wants to put an end to this charade and admit what's become obvious to everyone in the room. The problem is he's told this story so many times, the hole is too deep now. Having his family sitting right behind him only makes it tougher. He's caused them so much anguish already with his crime. The idea of causing them more pain is too much. He looks up at Kivlan through his glasses.

"The board should look at what I did while I was incarcerated."

"But if your statements are not verified, what action do you think this board should take?" Kivlan repeats.

Again, silence.

"I don't know."

In a heartbeat the opportunity is gone, but then the questioning continues. Where would he live if released? "I would live in Worcester with family." But he doesn't have family in Worcester—his relatives are in New Jersey—and the board knows that. The reason Dickerson says Worcester is because Paul King, a corrections officer who has been pushing for his release, lives there, and has offered to help Dickerson. But Dickerson never mentions King, so the board is left to think he'd be thrown into the world without any support nearby.

"Why should we extend you this extraordinary remedy to your case?" Kivlan says.

"I'd be a positive person. All I want to do is give back some of what I've taken away."

And then he's done. After almost three hours of grilling, he stands up and walks to the side of the room, where he sits and listens.

His brother, Robert, speaks. "I know a life was taken," he says. "But he's a good person. I wish I could take his place."

Kathleen Puckett speaks. With pale skin, red hair, a long skirt and a motherly way about her, she hardly looks like someone who'd stand up for a killer. But she's known Dickerson as long as anyone in the room, other than his family. They met back in the eighties, when Puckett was a nurse at the quarterway house on Fenwood Road in Boston. It was part of a mental health facility, where inmates on work release helped schizophrenic patients. Willie Horton spent time there. So did Dickerson. "He was just extraordinary," Puckett tells the board. "An incredible person to work with. He stood out from the other inmates. I have no doubt Lewis would be an upstanding member of the community. Lewis is ready to come out. You'll never regret your decision."

A few others speak. A Los Angeles woman who wanted to write a screenplay. A therapist who worked with Dickerson in prison.

Charles Bartoloni is last. At Dickerson's 1990 hearing, no one spoke out against his release. Not a relative or friend of Eva Dodds or Cyril Miller. Not the police. Prosecutors only wrote a letter. But eleven years later, the Suffolk County District Attorney's Office wants to be heard. "First Mr. Dickerson lied at his trial and said he wasn't involved," says Bartoloni, an assistant district attorney. "Then he said the weapon went off involuntarily. His credibility is very important. He still has not come to terms with what he did in 1975."

That Dickerson has been a model prisoner who has improved himself while behind bars is hardly enough to grant him freedom, Bartoloni says. "Someone should not be rewarded for doing the things that are expected of them."

Pomarole asks Taub if he has anything else, and Taub takes a moment with Dickerson. He walks over, sits next to him and begins whispering in his left ear. Dickerson whispers back. They stare at each other while everyone in the room stares at them. They might as well be using bullhorns. Their conversation is hardly a mystery. Two minutes pass and Taub walks back to his table. He tells a rambling story about how sometimes people lie, and sometimes people get caught lying, and then become too ashamed to admit it. Dickerson, he says, got caught, and now he wants to undo the mess he's created. Dickerson walks back to the center of the room and takes his seat.

"It's not true about the Vietnam part. The truth of the matter is I was in Germany and that's how I got the scars, when I was in Germany, and I apologize to the board."

"Why did you lie to the board ten years ago?" Pomarole asks.

"I was in the military and Vietnam was the thing and everyone had been there. And I so much wanted to be a part of that so I put it in the packet."

"But why would you lie to the board today knowing the significance of that?"

"I just got caught up in the moment. I was very nervous."

Pomarole thanks Dickerson and Taub and the witnesses, and closes the hearing. The board members stand, but just as the room is breaking up Kivlan offers Dickerson a sliver of hope. "Even though we were going to find out anyway, I still want to say I think it took some courage in front of your family and colleagues to acknowledge that you lied."

Dickerson is escorted away and the room clears out. There is no deadline for the board's decision. After his 1990 hearing, nearly three years passed before his release was denied. But back then, the memory of Willie Horton and the rape and murder he committed while on a weekend furlough was still vibrating through the state's prison system. Times have changed. Dickerson has changed. "I cannot imagine him jaywalking now," says Puckett.

For the people who sat through the hearing, it was like watching the air rush out of a balloon. Dickerson had been so sincere, finally taking responsibility for the killing. He'd never done that before. That was his downfall in 1990. But in 1990 Vietnam was not an issue. Ironically, in the year he created the lie, no one questioned it, but eleven years later, when he tried to quietly make it go away, it tripped him up.

"I knew the whole thing was a lie," his sister, Rose, says later. "He was ashamed. At least he finally admitted it."

But was he too late? Three weeks after the hearing, Dickerson types a letter to his lawyer.

"When the board asked me their questions about Vietnam, I was so shaken up I didn't know what to do," he wrote. "If I said I wasn't in Vietnam they'd think I was a liar. And if I said I was in Vietnam they'd think I was a liar. I tried to escape their questions about Vietnam, but then I felt I had no choice but to say I had been in Vietnam. I was wrong."

He closed with the only words he could find after a hearing that had left him tortured. "What will be will be. I'm praying and have my fingers crossed."

* * *

So many crime stories are about the crime itself that too often the criminal is forgotten about as a person once they disappear from society behind bars. Lawmakers claim that the purpose of incarceration is twofold: punishment and rehabilitation. But is it really? Because if that's true, Lewis Dickerson should surely be a free man, more than twenty-five years after he committed murder. The entire story "Judgment Day" came out of one four-hour hearing at which he begged the Massachusetts Parole Board for a second chance at freedom. It was a fascinating look inside the criminal justice system: a scared and nervous black man with little education, struggling to articulate his thoughts, sitting before an almost entirely white, college-educated panel of officers who will determine his fate. Something about it seemed wrong. The deck was stacked before he walked in the door. Is that the best we can do for justice?

THE KILLING OF ALYDAR
SKIP HOLLANDSWORTH

He was a beautiful, proud Thoroughbred, headstrong and demanding, the kind of horse who would snort impatiently if he decided the grooms were not paying him enough attention. Each day, his oak-paneled stall was swept, mopped and replenished with fresh straw. His richly colored chestnut coat was constantly brushed. For his daily exercise sessions, he was taken to his own three-acre paddock, where he could frolic alone in perfectly tended bluegrass.

His name was Alydar. To sports fans, he was known for the thrilling duels he staged with his rival, Affirmed, for the 1978 Triple Crown. But to the world's wealthiest horse breeders, he was revered for a different reason altogether. Alydar was one of the greatest sires in Thoroughbred history—a 1,200-pound genetic wonder whose offspring often became champion racehorses themselves. Each spring, the breeders would come with their convoys of horse trailers to Kentucky's Calumet Farm, one of the country's premier horse-racing operations, willing to pay hundreds of thousands of dollars to have Alydar mount their finest mares. Day after day, more than two hundred times a year, he would strut into the breeding shed, eye his latest prize, rise up on his hind legs, and begin to dance forward. Within seconds, his tail would swoosh up, signaling the end of his encounter, and he would be washed and then led away, back to the stall with his name emblazoned on the brass doorplate.

But on a chilly November night in 1990, the great stallion was found in shock in his stall, his coat glistening with sweat, his right hind leg hanging by tendons, a shaft of white bone jutting through his skin. J. T. Lundy, the rotund, blustery head of the farm, told veterinarians that Alydar had shattered his leg by kicking his own stall door. He had kicked it so hard, Lundy said, that he had knocked loose a heavy metal roller that had been bolted into the floor just outside Alydar's sliding door.

In emergency surgery, veterinarians were able to set the bone and put a cast on his leg. But within twenty-four hours, Alydar, hearing the whinnying of some mares in a nearby pasture, turned to look out a window in the Calumet clinic, put too much weight on the leg, and this time broke his femur. The sound of the break was like a gunshot. As he lay on the floor, an uncomprehending look in his eyes, Alydar was put down, and his body was taken to the Calumet cemetery, where he was buried with the farm's other racing champions. Eight months later, Calumet itself unraveled, forced to declare bankruptcy with more than $127 million in debts. According to the stories splashed on the sports pages of almost every newspaper in the country, the farm could not begin to pay its immense bills and bank loans without the millions of dollars it had been deriving from Alydar's stud fees. Calumet was so broke that its horses and equipment were going to be sold at public auction.

It was difficult for Kentucky horse people to believe that such a calamity could have happened. A few of them quietly said they were haunted by the strange circumstances of Alydar's death. A foreman from the stallion barn, for instance, couldn't remember Alydar having ever kicked anything hard enough to do any damage to his leg. And it was difficult to understand how even a powerful horse could have kicked that solid oak door with enough force to knock it off its hinges. Yet there was never an official investigation into the events of that night. No public accusations were made. As everyone in the horse business knew, horses could be unpredictable, and they could also be fragile. Alydar's death, no doubt, was one of those accidental, heartbreaking tragedies that no one could have done anything about.

And that, by all accounts, was the end of the story—until one afternoon in 1996, when a young assistant U.S. attorney in Houston was sitting in her downtown office, flipping through some bank records. The attorney's name was Julia Hyman (she now goes by her married name, Julia Tomala), and she knew nothing about horse racing. She spent her days investigating one of the worst financial scandals in American history: the widespread failure of hundreds of Texas financial institutions. Her job was to unearth the most complicated of white-collar crimes, such as money-laundering schemes and check-kiting operations.

On that particular afternoon, Tomala was studying the documents of the defunct First City National Bank of Houston, looking for evidence of fraud. She paused when she came to a document that mentioned Calumet Farm. She paused again when she came to a document that mentioned Alydar.

At the time, Tomala, an elegant woman with thick dark hair and a fondness for stylish black pantsuits, had no idea who or what Alydar was. She had never even been to a horse race. But by the summer of 1997, she was on her way to Kentucky to ask questions about how that horse had lived and died. She was accompanied by a rookie FBI agent out of the Houston office, Rob Foster, a former college baseball player who had never conducted a field investigation and who also knew nothing about horse racing.

Quickly, the word spread among the Bluegrass aristocracy that a couple of outsiders intended to pry into their private business. Tomala and Foster had been seen in Alydar's stall at Calumet, at a veterinary clinic, even at a construction site, where a former Calumet groom had gone to work as a laborer.

What, people wondered, did this prosecutor think she was going to learn about Alydar that wasn't already known? And why, after all this time, did it matter?

It would not be until October 2000, almost ten years after Alydar's death, that Tomala would finally reveal what she had been doing. At a little-publicized hearing in a nearly empty federal courtroom in Houston, she stood before a judge and said that the death of Alydar was no accidental tragedy. Alydar, she proclaimed, had been murdered.

THE HORSE FARM

It is a blockbuster of a story, a sweeping saga of greed, fraud and almost unimaginable cruelty that could have been lifted straight from a best-selling Dick Francis horse-racing novel. The settings range from the raucous pageantry of the Kentucky Derby to the hushed, baronial offices of Lloyd's of London in England, and even the minor characters—from an uneducated, chain-smoking Kentucky farmhand tormented by a secret to a corrupt Texas banker living in luxury at Houston's Four Seasons Hotel—seem right out of central casting. "This story has got blood and money, scandal and intrigue, and one hell of a beautiful horse," says Allen Goodling of Houston, one of the many lawyers who became involved in the case. "What more does anybody want?"

The story begins at the fabled Calumet Farm just outside Lexington, Kentucky—a picture postcard of a place consisting of some eight hundred acres of lavish pastureland crisscrossed with pristine white fences. Horse-racing fans once regarded Calumet the same way baseball fans view the New York Yankees—as an almost sacred institution, its horses having won eight Kentucky Derbies, two Triple Crowns and more than five hundred stakes races. Founded in 1924 by William Wright, who made his fortune as the head of the Calumet Baking Powder Company, and later run by his son Warren Wright, it was already a racing dynasty by the early forties, producing such champions as Whirlaway, Citation and Tim Tam. In 1950, after Warren's death, the farm was taken over by his widow, Lucille, an imperious grande dame who, like all proper Bluegrass ladies, wore white gloves to the track on racing day. She was devoted to the horses. She was not, however, devoted to her only child, Warren Wright Jr., the sole heir to the farm. A likable but scatterbrained young man, he apparently forgot to pay his income taxes for a couple of years and was sent to prison. What earned him his mother's deepest wrath, however, was his lack of interest in the horse business. When he died before she did, she mostly ignored his widow and his four children—the new heirs to the farm—because they too showed little interest in working at Calumet. They seemed more interested in the farm's dividends.

But in the early sixties, one of Lucille's grandchildren, her own namesake, Lucille "Cindy" Wright, made a decision that would have an enormous impact on Calumet's future. She decided, at the mere age of sixteen, to marry a rambunctious good old boy who liked racing his souped-up car down the narrow two-lane roads that ran past the horse farms. J. T. Lundy, the twenty-one-year-old son of a tenant farmer who worked a piece of land in an adjoining county, was to the Kentucky horse gentry what Jett Rink was to the Texas ranchers in the movie *Giant*—the classic outsider who dressed in old work clothes and usually couldn't get through a conversation without letting loose a few choice cusswords. With a head the size of a gasoline can and a nose that looked as if it had been busted and reset by a plumber, he looked like a country bumpkin. As one disgusted Kentucky blueblood would later tell Austin journalist Carol Flake, who wrote an absorbing profile of Calumet Farm in 1992 for the now-defunct *Connoisseur* magazine, a big night for Lundy was "sitting in front of the TV with a bucket of buffalo wings watching reruns of *The Dukes of Hazzard*."

Yet underneath that salt-of-the-earth personality lay a surprisingly fierce ambition. Lundy often told his friends that his dream was to run Calumet. Some of those friends even remember him boasting that he was going to marry young Cindy Wright just so he could get into Calumet's founding family. If so, he made the right choice. Those who know Cindy say she was never much of a society girl—"She didn't like those parties where people sipped mint juleps," says a Lundy relative—and that she always preferred the company of plainspoken rural boys rather than the college-bound sons of Lexington's aristocrats. To her, the down-home Lundy was ideal.

After their marriage, Lundy bought a small farm and started a breeding program to produce racehorses, perhaps to show Cindy and her family that he was serious about his desire to head Calumet. Throughout the sixties and seventies, however, the farm remained firmly in the hands of its matriarch, who by then had married a dashing retired U.S. Navy admiral named Gene Markey. Though approaching eighty, Lucille Wright Markey had not lost her resolve to produce one more Kentucky Derby winner. In 1976 she hired a brilliant young trainer, John Veitch, who began watching a horse named Alydar that had been born at Calumet the year before. At the Blue Grass Stakes in the early spring of 1978, Lucille Markey stood next to the outside rail, gripping it with her white gloves, as Alydar introduced himself to the world, sweeping around the final turn and racing victoriously to the wire. Then, at the Kentucky Derby, the Preakness and the Belmont—the races that make up the Triple Crown—Alydar and another Kentucky Thoroughbred, Affirmed, staged what turf writers still describe as the greatest duel in horse-racing history. They literally raced side by side, eyeball to eyeball, their hooves pounding like cannon fire as they hit the home stretch. In their fight to the finish at Belmont, they ran dead even for the final seven furlongs.

To Lucille Markey's deep disappointment, it was always Affirmed who got to the wire just ahead of Alydar. Yet once the two horses were retired to their stallion barns back on the farms where they were born, it was Alydar that everyone wanted to see. In the Thoroughbred-breeding business, there is no way to tell which stallion, regardless of its own pedigree, will be able to produce a new generation of winners at the track. The business is a crapshoot, based almost purely on luck. So when Alydar's initial progeny turned out to be strong, fleet-footed foals, the word quickly spread that the most famous second-place finisher in the Triple Crown had semen as valuable as gold.

Initially Alydar's stud fee was $40,000. J. T. Lundy told his in-laws that Calumet's management team was forfeiting the chance to make millions off Alydar. His message to the heirs was clear: Calumet needed a new leader. And who better than Lundy himself? There was no question that he was a hard worker who knew how to make money in the horse business. At the time, Lundy's farm was said to be worth several million dollars.

According to a history of Calumet, *Wild Ride*, by Ann Hagedorn Auerbach, Lucille Markey despised the overly ambitious tenant farmer's son. She refused to let Lundy breed his horses with Calumet horses, and she even tried to keep him from visiting the farm— which only reinforced Lundy's resolve to take over her kingdom. One story that circulated through Bluegrass circles was that Lundy had taken up jogging to stay in good enough shape just to outlive her. "Here was somebody who may have felt inferior his entire life," says Gary Matthews, Calumet's former chief financial officer. "And he wanted to get to the top just to show everybody he could do it."

He got his chance on July 24, 1982, when Lucille Markey died at the age of eighty-five. Soon afterward, the Calumet heirs announced an agreement with forty-one-year-old J. T. Lundy, granting him "full discretionary management powers" over the farm. The country bumpkin was now the lord of Calumet Farm.

THE EMPIRE BUILDER

Almost immediately, Lundy began a multimillion-dollar restoration of Calumet. He had workers install iron gates across the main entrance, as if to signify to the world that a new man was in charge, and he had the farm's twenty-three miles of fence repainted. He ordered the construction of a state-of-the-art veterinary clinic, complete with a treadmill and an equine swimming pool, which alone cost $1 million. He added new freeze-proof water troughs and a five-eighths-mile turf track, and he bought new stallions and race-horses, all in the hope that Calumet would regain the glory of its early days.

Lundy was in such a hurry to get his projects under way that in 1983 he took out a $13.2 million loan. His bankers could not possibly have been worried about Lundy's paying it back. The farm was then debt free. What's more, Lundy soon raised Alydar's stud fee to $250,000. He also did something never before heard of in the Thoroughbred business: he started selling what he called lifetime breeding rights to the stallion. For $2.5 million, an owner could send one mare to Alydar's breeding shed each year for as long as Alydar was able to breed.

Lundy's timing couldn't have been better. In the early eighties the Bluegrass world was awash in money. Multimillionaire bidders—from Saudi sheiks to Japanese industrial titans and American oil barons such as Dallas's Nelson Bunker Hunt—attended yearling auctions at Keeneland Park, waving their hands to push the prices higher and higher. And when a son or daughter of Alydar was led into the ring, the bidding occasionally topped $2 million—for a single, unproven young horse. In 1983 Alydar was the industry's champion first-year sire: his offspring sold for an average of $760,000 each, at that time a record for a first crop.

Horse breeders who once rolled their eyes at J. T. Lundy were now slapping him on the back—hoping that he would look favorably on them when it came time to pick the new mares who would get to visit Alydar's breeding shed. Lundy even found himself the object of adulation by a respected columnist for the industry's journal, the *Blood-Horse*, who wrote, "While there has been some criticism of the methods of Lundy in his direction of Calumet, it seems to be based more on envy than fact. Lundy, in my opinion, is doing a great job in rebuilding a grand heritage."

But Lundy didn't just want to rebuild a heritage. He wanted to create a Thoroughbred empire unlike any other. He too joined the bidding frenzy for new horses—spending between $20 million and $30 million for a half interest in a stallion named Secreto. He continued renovating the farm, installing a gazebo and a tennis court and a swimming pool (this one for humans). He renovated his office, adding a second story with a balcony from which he could survey the farm. Although he still wouldn't buy nice clothes for himself—he continued to wear open-collar shirts, corduroy pants and Top-Siders to formal events at which every other horseman was dressed in a jacket and tie—he did spend $30,000 a month of Calumet money to lease a private jet, which he didn't hesitate to use for personal trips. (He once flew a group of friends to Maine for a lobster dinner.) He bought property for himself in the Florida Keys. In one of his most perplexing ventures, he made Calumet a sponsor of the Indy race car of A. J. Foyt, one of Lundy's longtime heroes.

Suddenly, J. T. Lundy was a jet-setting wheeler-dealer, sitting in the finest boxes at the nation's finest racetracks, cutting deals with other horse farm owners for horses and breeding rights, and paying himself a reported 10 percent sales commission on every deal he made. Perhaps because Lundy's wife, Cindy, had realized that she would never be able to compete with her husband's obsession with the farm, she began spending most of her time in the Virgin Islands, Scotland and Colorado—which apparently was just fine with Lundy. He soon had a girlfriend, a young woman he had hired to work in the main office at the farm.

To pay for his newest ventures, Lundy took out a $20 million mortgage on the farm and received another $15 million line of credit from a Kentucky bank. Even in 1986, when the horse-racing industry went into a steep economic slump, due in large part to the collapse of the oil market and the restructuring of tax laws that eliminated one of the tax breaks for the purchase of horses, Lundy kept spending. He received an extra $10 million from the Kentucky bank that already had loaned him $15 million. And in 1988, just as the Thoroughbred market was really souring, Lundy got another bank loan for a staggering $50 million. It came from the flagship bank of Houston's First City Bancorporation, one of the state's largest bank holding companies, with more than sixty banks and $12 billion in assets.

Kentucky horse breeders who were scrambling to stay afloat were baffled. How did Lundy get a loan from a bank in Texas, where no one knew anything about horse racing? What bank officer did he find to approve that deal?

Actually, it was no ordinary bank officer. The banker behind the Calumet loan was none other than the powerful vice chairman of First City, a big, burly cannonball of a man named Frank C. Cihak.

THE TEXAS BANKER

According to stories Frank Cihak has told his friends, he was raised in an orphanage on the South Side of Chicago and became an amateur boxer. He must have been a formidable opponent: a *Wall Street Journal* reporter once wrote that Cihak was built like a Chicago Bears lineman. After college he entered banking, worked his way up the ladder at First Chicago Corporation and in 1976 took control of a string of smaller banks, where he developed a reputation for his relentless pursuit of profits.

In 1988 his old boss, A. Robert Abboud, the freewheeling former chairman at First Chicago, made a deal with the FDIC to take over First City in Houston, which then was on the verge of collapse because of hundreds of millions of dollars of bad real estate and energy loans. (FDIC officials, thrilled someone wanted the bank, agreed to spend nearly $1 billion to bail out First City if Abboud would raise $500 million in new capital.) Abboud asked Cihak, then forty-five years old, to go to Texas and be his "right hand." The two had a lot in common. Like Abboud, who once had been named one of the nation's "ten toughest bosses" by *Fortune* magazine, cigar-smoking Cihak was aggressive and abrasive—and he didn't like to be second-guessed. "His employees knew if they questioned what he was doing, they'd likely get fired," says an attorney who knew him. "His modus operandi was to call in a loan officer to his office and say, 'You are going to make the following loan to this guy. I'm vouching for him.'"

Cihak came barreling into Texas. His salary, as vice chairman, was $450,000 a year (he also got a $1 million bonus for taking the job), and most of his expenses were paid for, including an apartment at the Four Seasons Hotel and his dinners and $200 bottles of wine at the pricey Cafe Annie. He hired various consultants, many of them old friends, to work on various bank projects. He also started looking to make very large loans. According to the deal Cihak had made with Abboud, he could authorize a loan of up to $120 million without having to go through a traditional loan committee. And one of the first loans he made, less than four months after First City was recapitalized, was for almost $50 million to Calumet.

When Cihak told the First City loan officers not to check Calumet's credit reference at the Kentucky bank where it already had a loan, they didn't consider the demand unusual. First City certainly didn't want to tip off the bank that it was trying to lure away a big client. But they were perplexed that he told them not to audit the financial statements or appraisals of the farm presented by Lundy and Gary Matthews, Calumet's chief financial officer. Nevertheless, when the deal was completed, in July 1988, Cihak was treated as a hero by Abboud and the other executives. Texas had just legalized pari-mutuel betting, and First City officials believed the Calumet loan would bring them a host of new horse-racing clients. They even took out an advertisement in the *Wall Street Journal* trumpeting the bank's addition of Calumet to its loan portfolio.

But within weeks, First City loan officers received a phone call from Matthews, asking for even more money. The officers couldn't believe what they were hearing. Matthews was telling them that Calumet was already unable to make its loan payments. Cihak suddenly stepped in, signed off on the larger Calumet loans, and said the farm just needed more time to weather the depressed horse market. Cihak also said he was going to transfer the Calumet loan to Structured Financing, a bank section created by Cihak and headed by one of his handpicked associates.

And that seemed to take care of that. For the next two years, the loan was handled by Cihak himself. As for Calumet, no one could have imagined that it was already veering toward bankruptcy. As 1990 rolled around, the farm had new white fences and more than one hundred Calumet horses at racetracks all over the country. One of the horses, a son of Alydar named Criminal Type, was on his way to winning seven times in eleven starts that year, earning $2.2 million for the farm. Meanwhile, Alydar remained indefatigable in the breeding shed. Lundy had his great stallion serving one hundred mares a year, which meant Alydar went to the shed about two hundred times: it took him an average of two mounts per mare to get her pregnant. A normal stallion goes through only fifty to seventy mares a year. Alydar was known around Kentucky as J. T. Lundy's ATM, a constant source of cash. The Calumet grooms called him the "cock of the walk." Ironically, his old rival, Affirmed, was also at Calumet in 1990, leased by the farm to be one of its stallions. When the two chestnut-colored horses were out in their paddocks, they would stare at each another, their manes flicking in the breeze. Occasionally, Affirmed would start running on his side of the fence, and Alydar would take off after him on the other side. Even then, twelve years after their races, they remained competitors.

It was hard to imagine that anything could have shattered such an idyllic scene, certainly not the little piece of news that came out of Houston in October 1990 that one Frank C. Cihak had resigned as vice chairman of the First City Bancorporation. In the twenty-nine months since First City had been restructured, the bank's pool of bad loans had grown from nothing to $433 million. According to stories in the Houston newspapers, the bad loans had been generated by Cihak. Although he was being given a graceful exit—the bank would continue to pay him $450,000 a year as a consultant—other officers would be taking control of the loans he had made.

But Cihak's resignation was to have immediate and catastrophic effects on Calumet. Lundy and Matthews were contacted by a First City vice president who told them their loan was being restructured. The time had come for Calumet to pay, he said. If Calumet didn't come up with $15 million by February 28, 1991, then First City would foreclose, taking all the farm's horses and assets.

That conversation took place on October 25, 1990. Less than three weeks later, Alydar was dead.

THE YOUNG PROSECUTOR

Julia Hyman Tomala missed the news that Alydar was dead. She also missed the news, eight months later, that Calumet Farm was declaring bankruptcy and that its president, J. T. Lundy, had resigned. She was then thirty, consumed with her career as a white-collar-crime prosecutor for the U.S. attorney's office in Tampa, Florida, where she had been born and raised. In late 1991 she moved to the U.S. attorney's office in Houston, which desperately needed prosecutors to deal with numerous criminal allegations that were flooding into the office regarding the huge number of Texas bank failures. For her, Texas was where the action was: from 1986 through 1992, 485 banks and 238 savings and loans in Texas went under, including First City Bancorporation. And the first case she was handed concerned the activities of the infamous Frank Cihak.

Tomala began investigating the transactions between Cihak and his cronies whom he had hired as bank "consultants." Within months, she had bank documents not only piled up on her desk but also stacked in the hallway outside her office. "What's required in this kind of work is a tenacity to follow very complex paper trails," says Jim Powers, a chief prosecutor at the U.S. attorney's Houston office who initially supervised her First City work. "And Julia was about as tenacious as they come."

Tomala discovered that Cihak had set up a complex scheme to steer more than $4 million in First City loans and fees to his consultants, who then gave Cihak part of the money as kickbacks. At Cihak's 1993 trial she told the jury that he had come down to Texas to use First City as his "personal piggy bank," which in turn helped lead to First City's own failure, putting thousands of people out of work. Although the once-swaggering Cihak, wearing a gray suit, royal blue tie and unlaced white athletic shoes, offered a rambling courtroom plea for leniency, even mentioning that he had made a halfhearted suicide attempt, an unsympathetic federal judge sentenced him to prison for twelve years and seven months. Tomala immediately went back to work investigating Cihak, and in 1995, she had him indicted again for another series of multimillion-dollar kickback schemes with other "consultants." This time, he got a twenty-two year sentence. Cihak was probably going to prison for the rest of his life.

Still, Tomala wasn't finished. After Cihak's second trial, she decided to find out why Cihak, a racehorse investor himself and a Kentucky Derby fan, had been so determined to get the bank into the equine-lending business. She knew that a few months after the First City loan to Calumet was funded, Cihak had received a personal $1.1 million loan from a Kentucky entity called Equine Capital Corporation (ECC). Curious, she started retracing the money coming in and out of the ECC and learned that the money had not come from the ECC at all. Through a series of convoluted check-kiting maneuvers, Lundy and Gary Matthews had provided the $1.1 million to the ECC, which was run by Lundy associates, and the ECC had then passed on the money to Cihak, which he wasn't asked to repay. Cihak then used that money to lease two Calumet mares and pay for them to get into the breeding shed with Alydar. He also had arranged a deal with Lundy to buy one-time breeding rights to another Calumet stallion, Secreto, which were worth $125,000 on the open market, for a mere $1.

In return for access to Calumet's best horses—and the possibility of getting a foal of his own that might someday be a successful racehorse—Cihak agreed to become J. T. Lundy's financial patron, pushing through the $50 million loan at First City and then protecting Lundy when loan officers became anxious about Calumet's financial condition. To Cihak, it must not have seemed like a particularly perilous deal. He no doubt assumed, as everyone else did in the horse business, that Alydar's stud fees would generate the money necessary to pay back any bank loan. Calumet itself had drawn up a document showing that Alydar's "stud fee revenue potential" could be nearly $25 million a year.

Actually, it was journalist Carol Flake who first learned that Alydar's earnings were not even close to what Lundy suggested they were. After poring over Jockey Club records, she discovered that Alydar was often performing on mares for free. Either the mares' owners had already paid for the trips to the breeding shed years earlier through one of the lifetime breeding rights that Lundy had been selling, or they had received free breeding rights from Lundy in exchange for something Lundy wanted. To pay for a stallion, for instance, Lundy offered that stallion's owner a series of visits to Alydar's breeding shed. In other instances, Lundy simply gave his closest buddies free passes to Alydar. By 1990 the free passes to Alydar were outnumbering the ones that were paid for with stud fees.

In her 1992 *Connoisseur* story, Flake hinted that Alydar's death might not have been accidental. After learning that the farm's insurance policies on Alydar totaled $36.5 million, making him the most heavily insured horse in history, she went so far as to suggest that Alydar might have been worth more dead than alive. Yet no law enforcement official had shown any interest in pursuing the issue—until Tomala began flipping through records about Calumet in 1996.

What she realized was that Lundy had to have been frantic in the months before Alydar's death. There was no way he was going to be able to come up with that $15 million payment to First City by February 1991. An accountant who had studied Calumet's records told Tomala that the farm was then losing almost $1 million a month. Lundy was unable to find new bankers to loan him money, and he was equally unsuccessful in persuading investors from as far away as Japan to purchase a minor interest in Calumet. What's more, Lundy couldn't get any more income out of Alydar, who was already being bred so often that, according to one veterinarian, the muscles of his hind end were constantly sore. And Lundy suffered another blow in 1990 when his best horse that year, Criminal Type, who was favored to win the Breeders' Cup, the most lucrative purse in horse racing, was injured just before the race, depriving a clearly distraught Lundy of the chance to receive millions.

Tomala also verified that Lundy had a big problem with the insurance companies that held multimillion-dollar "equine mortality" policies on Alydar. In 1990 they were threatening to cancel those policies because of Calumet's slowness in paying its premiums. Lundy had been forced to send Matthews and his own sister, who handled the insurance on Calumet's horses, to London to beg exasperated Lloyd's representatives to give them one more chance — which they did. But the head of another equine insurance company, Golden Eagle Insurance out of California, told Lundy's sister in the early fall of 1990 that he had reached the end of his patience with Calumet's delinquent payments. He said the company's policy on Alydar would not be renewed when it expired in December.

Tomala realized that if there was a perfect time for Alydar to die, it was precisely in November 1990, just after Frank Cihak's resignation and just before one of Alydar's insurance policies expired. She looked at another record. Calumet had indeed used Alydar's insurance proceeds to make its payment to First City Bancorporation and staved off foreclosure for a few more months.

For Tomala, there was only one person who could have had Alydar killed: J. T. Lundy. And she was determined to prove it.

THE KENTUCKY INVESTIGATION

The question was, how could anyone prove, seven years after the fact, that a racehorse had been murdered? Tomala had no experience investigating murders. Neither did Rob Foster, the young FBI agent assigned to work with her. Yet here they were in Kentucky, and it didn't take them long to understand that they were not welcome. Few people wanted to speak to them. Those who did said that Lundy couldn't possibly be a horse killer. They pointed out that on the night of Alydar's injury, November 13, 1990, Lundy got on the phone and begged the best veterinary orthopedic surgeon in Kentucky, Larry Bramlage, to try to save Alydar's life.

One of the first people Tomala and Foster interviewed was Tom Dixon, a mild-mannered, churchgoing Lexington insurance adjuster who had been hired by Lloyd's of London to handle its equine claims. Dixon was one of the first non-Calumet employees to arrive the night Alydar was injured, and according to the notes he took, it was Lundy who told him that Alydar was known to kick his stall violently and that he had no doubt broken his leg kicking the stall. Dixon had taken some photos and had conducted a few interviews, including one with the night watchman, Alton Stone, a muscular farmworker with shaggy blond hair. Sitting in on that interview was one of Lundy's assistants, Susan McGee, who occasionally interrupted Stone to explain to Dixon what Stone meant to say. Dixon asked few follow-up questions of Stone or anyone else. He was a sympathetic man who felt bad for what had happened to the horse. He quickly filed a report saying the death was accidental, and he had Lloyd's of London's money to Calumet within thirty days. "The fastest payoff in history," he later said proudly.

There was another Lexington insurance adjuster who had tried to get into the farm the night of the injury, but he was prevented from getting past the front gates by a security guard, who said he was not allowed to let anyone in. When Terry McVey, representing Golden Eagle (the company that was not renewing its coverage of Alydar), was finally allowed in the stallion barn the next afternoon, he was amazed to find that Alydar's stall had been mopped and swept and that the heavy roller outside the door, the one that supposedly had been knocked loose from Alydar's kicks, had already been repaired and rebolted to the floor.

Why, he wanted to know, would Calumet employees so quickly clean up the evidence that suggested how Alydar had died? And why, if Alydar had been such a kicker as Lundy had said, were there no marks on the stall door consistent with heavy kicking? All horse farms would regularly add padding to the stalls of horses that kicked. Surely if the prized Alydar had been a kicker, Lundy would have had pads on Alydar's walls for his own protection.

Yet in the end, Golden Eagle officials decided not to challenge the circumstances regarding Alydar's death, and they too paid off the claim. "It was as if those who made a living off the big horse farms—like the insurance adjusters and the veterinarians—realized it was not in their best interests to rock the boat," Tomala says now. "Why risk losing any future business by asking too many questions?" Even breeders from competing farms were hesitant to talk about an event they knew could make the entire industry look bad. "There was this fear that a scandal about Alydar would deeply hurt the public's perception of horse racing," says Tomala. "So people started circling the wagons."

The veterinarians who had examined Alydar said they were firmly convinced that his injury was accidental: the horse had kicked the door, and the busted roller was proof. The roller was contained in a heavy metal bracket, about six inches long, that was bolted to the floor just outside Alydar's sliding stall door. The roller kept the stall door on its track. Because Alydar's fracture was the "torquing" type that happens when a horse twists its leg, the veterinarians theorized that when he knocked the roller loose with his kick, the stall door moved outward, thus opening a gap between the dislodged door and the wall of the stall. Alydar must have caught his leg in that gap, and in his struggle to get free, twisted his leg until it broke.

When Tomala and Foster asked to see an X ray of Alydar's fracture, Lynda Rhodes Stewart, a former veterinarian at Calumet, told them it had mysteriously disappeared from her files less than a year after Alydar's death. They asked her if she remembered anything else about that night that seemed unusual. Well, she said, when Alton Stone had called her to say that something was wrong with Alydar, he had never indicated that Alydar's condition was serious. He told her only to come up when she had a chance.

On June 4, 1997, when Foster and Tomala finally tracked down Stone at a construction site where he was working, he nervously recounted for them the same story he had told insurance adjuster Tom Dixon. He said the regular night watchman, Harold "Cowboy" Kipp, had asked him to work for him that evening so he could have a night off. Between eight-thirty and nine-thirty in the evening, Stone said, he was sitting on a turned-over five-gallon bucket in an office of the stallion barn, talking to a security guard whose job it was to drive the perimeter of the farm. Around nine-thirty, they drove over to the canteen to buy some sodas and returned ten to fifteen minutes later. Stone went back inside the stallion barn while the security guard returned to his rounds. It was then that he saw Alydar.

To verify Stone's story, Foster interviewed the security guard, Keed Highley, who told him he had never been interviewed by anyone about Alydar's death. Foster was stunned when Highley told him that he had not sat in that office with Stone but that he had stopped by the stallion barn at about ten to call his wife from a telephone there. When he approached the barn, he said, he saw Stone leaving. Highley noticed that the lights were on in the farm office—Lundy's office—which was attached to the barn. As he spoke to his wife on the phone, Highley heard the stallion whinny. He investigated, saw the horse's leg dangling, and then radioed Stone to call a veterinarian. For the first time, Foster realized there was a cover-up going on. It was Highley, not Stone, who had found Alydar.

Foster also found the original night watchman, Cowboy Kipp. Kipp's primary job was to take care of the stallions, specifically Alydar, and he had rarely missed a night of work since starting at the farm. He loved his job so much that he wouldn't even take vacations. In fact, when Foster found him, Kipp was still working as a night watchman at Calumet. (After filing for bankruptcy, the farm had been sold at auction for a mere $17 million to a Polish-born investor named Henryk de Kwiatkowski, who lived there only part-time and who maintained a skeletal staff.)

Once again, no one—no insurance adjuster or reporter—had talked to Kipp. If they had, they would have been told a chilling story. About five days before Alydar's injury, Kipp said, he was at work on the farm when a dark blue Ford Crown Victoria with tinted windows drove up. A large man got out of the car. Kipp said he had seen the man in the main office a couple of times, but he didn't know his name or what he did for Calumet. The man told Kipp that the farm's management was worried he was getting burned out. Kipp needed to take a day off. "How about Tuesday, November 13?" the man said. Although Kipp didn't think he needed a break, he was the kind of employee who followed orders and didn't cause trouble. He did take that evening off, but he insisted to Foster that he never asked Stone to substitute for him.

Throughout 1997, Tomala had several of the witnesses—including Alton Stone, Keed Highley and Cowboy Kipp—flown separately to Houston to tell their stories to a federal grand jury that had been secretly convened just to hear evidence about Alydar. In January 1998 that grand jury indicted Stone for perjury for telling numerous false stories to federal agents and to the grand jury itself. Obviously Tomala's strategy was to squeeze Stone (few people are indicted for perjury in federal court) to see if he would reveal what else he knew. Stone's court-appointed defense attorney said Tomala had become obsessed with conspiracy theories about Alydar's death. It was a charge Tomala could not deny. In a trial brief, she said that Stone was part of a plot to harm the horse.

As for Lundy, he had kept a low profile since his resignation from Calumet, staying mostly in Florida, where he was training horses at a small farm. Although he had declared personal bankruptcy in 1992, few people imagined he was really broke. An accountant who had studied the Calumet books said Lundy had paid himself nearly $6 million during his tenure. He did show up at a Lexington lawyer's office for a deposition regarding his bankruptcy. He took the Fifth Amendment more than two hundred times while fidgeting, rubbing his eyes and chewing on his fingernails. Irritated, an attorney asked Lundy if he would just tell him the color of the shirt he was wearing. "I think it's red," Lundy said after consulting with his attorney.

Lundy had been subpoenaed by the defense to testify at Alton Stone's perjury trial, but U.S. marshals couldn't find him. Still, he was hardly ignored during the trial. Outside the presence of the jury, Marsha Matthews, who was married to Lundy's chief financial officer at the time of the horse's death, took the stand to say that she had overheard Lundy say during a conversation at the Matthewses' home about Calumet's deep debts, "There are ways to get rid of the horse." The judge ruled the testimony was inadmissible. But he did allow writer Carol Flake to testify that Alton Stone, whom she went to see again in 1992 after her magazine story was completed, suddenly had become very emotional in her presence and blurted out that J. T. Lundy "knew something was going to happen to Alydar."

Yet Tomala didn't get what she really wanted from that trial. Stone didn't cooperate with her, and he didn't testify. He decided to take his lumps, which weren't that bad: he received only five months in prison and five months of home confinement.

By 1999, it seemed, Tomala's investigation had run out of gas. After more than two years of interrogations and grand jury hearings, she hadn't been able to prove Alydar had been murdered. She had been able to prove only that Alton Stone couldn't keep his stories straight.

But she still had one more card to play.

THE KILLING OF ALYDAR

In March 1999 Tomala persuaded a Houston federal grand jury to indict Lundy, who was finally found in Florida, and Gary Matthews, who was working as a lawyer in Lexington since his resignation from Calumet, on charges of bank fraud, conspiracy, bribery and lying about the $1.1 million bribe they had offered to Frank Cihak. When the trial finally got under way, in February 2000, the most interesting case for Lundy's innocence was made by Dan Cogdell, one of Houston's most colorful defense attorneys. During his closing argument, he told Lundy, who was sucking on candy, to stand up and face the jury. Cogdell then asked jurors if they thought this man looked smart enough to pull off a massive fraud. The jurors did. They took less than three hours to find Lundy and Matthews guilty.

The story was barely covered by the press. By then the financial shenanigans involving Cihak, Calumet and Lundy were old news. At Lundy's sentencing this past October, only a handful of spectators were in the courtroom gallery. But Tomala suddenly called FBI agent Foster to the stand to recount the questions and suspicious stories regarding Alydar's death. Then she called a surprise witness: a tall, silver-haired man with a deep Bostonian accent.

His name was George Pratt, and he was a full professor of electrical engineering and computer science at the Massachusetts Institute of Technology. He also was an avid horseman and the chairman of the National Association of Thoroughbred Owners Racetrack Safety Committee. Pratt testified that he had been contacted by Foster about a year earlier asking if he would analyze some evidence. Soon, a large box arrived at Pratt's cluttered MIT office. Inside was a section of concrete, about one square foot in size. It was a piece of the floor that had been cut out from the front of Alydar's stall.

Foster and Tomala had always been bothered by the busted roller story. There had been two bolts that had connected the roller to the floor, which a Calumet maintenance supervisor had told Foster were broken in half from the force of the kick. The supervisor had said he threw the top half of the bolts away, then he simply moved the roller over from its original location, drilled new holes in the floor and installed new bolts. He had told Foster that the bottom portions of the broken bolts were still embedded in the floor.

Foster noticed later that Tom Dixon, the insurance adjuster, had taken a photo of that roller while it was still lying on the floor. Clearly visible in the photo were the top halves of the bolts. It occurred to Foster that the upper part of the bolts should match the bottom part of the bolts. If they didn't, then there was finally physical evidence that the bracket had been removed before Alydar's accident, with the intention that it later be found to serve as an explanation of how Alydar broke his leg. With other agents, Foster cut out the section of the floor that included the original bolts, and he sent it to Pratt along with Dixon's enlarged photograph.

Almost immediately, Pratt noticed that the bottom half of the bolts were cut off evenly at the same height, while one of the top bolts was a little long and the other a little short. Then he noticed that the top parts of the bolts in the photograph were rusty and heavily corroded, while the bottom parts of the bolts had little or no corrosion. There was no way the upper and bottom halves of those bolts matched. He also noticed that if the concrete block was put back in its proper place in the floor, the shear on the bottom part of the bolts was parallel, not perpendicular to the stall door—which meant the force applied to them had to have come from somewhere outside the stall, not from inside.

Then Pratt flew to Calumet, studied the stall, took measurements and went back to MIT to devise an equation to determine how much force would be required from a horse to kick that roller off its hinges. He determined that 6,600 pounds of force would have to hit the stall door exactly three feet off the floor. The strongest stallion, Pratt concluded, could generate only 1,000 to 2,000 pounds with a kick.

Alydar, Pratt said in his Houston testimony, had to have been killed. He speculated that someone had tied the end of a rope around Alydar's leg and attached the other end of the rope to a truck that could easily have been driven into the stallion barn. The truck then took off, pulling Alydar's leg from underneath him until it snapped.

There was a long, long silence when Pratt finished. At the defense table, Lundy, who was wearing a poor-fitting sports coat, a thin tie and soft brown walking shoes, kept his head down, writing on a notepad. From the government's table, Tomala, in her black Prada pantsuit, gave Lundy a lingering look, her eyes squinting in disgust. She had presented the evidence hoping the federal judge would tack a much larger sentence to Lundy's bribery conviction. In her summation, she said that only Lundy had "the motive and opportunity" to have the horse killed. He wanted the horse dead, she said, to collect the insurance windfall to forestall First City's takeover of the farm. And his false statements to the insurance adjusters, as well as the lies told by Stone, only confirmed that Lundy was responsible for the injury. "To believe otherwise, one would have to accept a string of coincidences that defy common sense," she declared.

There were still many unanswered questions. If Lundy had wanted Alydar dead, then wouldn't he have made sure the horse was killed that first night? And didn't the fact that Lundy was apparently so distraught throughout that night, begging doctors to operate on the horse, suggest that Lundy wanted Alydar to live? Tomala later said, "What was he supposed to do at that point—cheer?" It could also be assumed that Lundy had to have known from the extent of that first injury that it was unlikely Alydar would survive. Thus, he could pretend to be distraught to mislead others.

Still, the death of Alydar didn't accomplish anything for him in the long run. Calumet still went under. Lundy still lost his job. Yet as Gary Matthews himself says, Lundy had to have been terrified of going down in racehorse history as the man who ruined Calumet. "I can't imagine him doing something so drastic as to kill his best horse," Matthews told me after his trial. "J.T. loved animals. But he was in a desperate situation. I remember we discussed that if the First City debt was cut in half, the Japanese would be far more interested in investing. Maybe he thought this was the thing to do. I just don't know."

The federal judge overseeing the case eventually decided he didn't know either. He said he wasn't comfortable about a whole new criminal case being introduced at a sentencing hearing, and in his final ruling he said, "Although there is evidence Mr. Lundy had the motive and opportunity to injure Alydar, and although there is some physical evidence, I am not able to conclude by the preponderance of the evidence that Mr. Lundy is responsible for the death of Alydar." The judge sentenced Lundy to four years in prison for the bribery; Matthews received twenty-one months.

For more than an hour after the hearing, Tomala and Foster hung around the courtroom, packing up their exhibits and their files filled with a decade's worth of notes about Alydar's death. Although they hadn't won, they said they felt some satisfaction in getting their allegations into open court so that everyone would know that Alydar's death was no accident. I asked Tomala if she felt a sense of sadness that her long obsession with Alydar had come to an end. The statute of limitations on an insurance fraud case is ten years, which would make it unlikely that she'd ever be able to bring charges again regarding the horse's demise.

Tomala gave me a confident smile. "Actually, there are ways to expand that statute and keep the case going for a little longer," she said. "Somehow, someday, the whole truth is going to come out."

Meanwhile, Lundy, who had been given a few months to get his affairs in order before reporting to prison, headed out of the federal courthouse, saying he needed to get back to Florida to take care of horses and visit his sick mother. I saw him standing at the curb, his hands in his pockets, his shoulders hunched. For a moment I thought about the young Lundy from the sixties, the rambunctious, hot-rod-driving son of a tenant farmer, dreaming of the day he would run Calumet. Nearly forty years later, the dream had turned his life into a shambles. "That Tomala knows she's full of bull——," he said. "All she wants to do is get her name in the paper."

"You didn't have anything to do with that horse's death?" I asked him.

Lundy looked at me, his face turning red. I realized it was the first time he publicly was going to answer a question about his alleged involvement. "Hell, no," he said. "I loved that horse. Loved him." He paused and shook his head, as if he couldn't believe he would be living for the rest of his life with the reputation as Alydar's killer. "I tell you, I'd give anything if Alydar was still at Calumet, heading off to his breeding shed," Lundy said. And then he jumped into a cab, and he was gone.

✳ ✳ ✳

When I first began to hear that a long bank-fraud inquiry of a failed Houston bank was looking at the operations of the fabled Calumet

Farm in Kentucky, I assumed the story would concern discrepancies in loan documents. But it turned out to be an old-fashioned true crime tale—with one fascinating twist. This tale centered on the death of one of the most famous horses in the history of Thoroughbred racing. I don't know if the mystery surrounding Alydar's demise will ever completely be solved, but the quixotic investigation into Alydar's life by an assistant U.S. attorney in Houston and a rookie FBI agent, both of whom knew nothing about horse racing, certainly put a lot of pieces into the puzzle.

THE CHICAGO CRIME COMMISSION
ROBERT KURSON

On Grand Avenue in Chicago, a man sits in a car, watching and waiting. Afternoon becomes evening becomes night, and still he waits. Outside a quaint Italian restaurant, gentlemen open doors for their dates, puff after-dinner cigars and tip valets handsomely. None of them notice the Camry parked across the street, or that its driver hasn't moved in hours.

This man, Wayne Johnson, is the chief investigator, the only investigator, for the Chicago Crime Commission, a private organization funded by local business and civic leaders that dates to 1919—the year Al Capone came to town. In a city notorious for political complicity in organized crime, the commission's enduring mandate has been to act as the eyes of the people—to name names, inform the media and prick the conscience of government. In its heyday, between 1928 and 1970, it was even more than that. Run by bona fide gangster haters, the CCC forced sit-downs with Capone, leaned on U.S. presidents and gave mayhem back to the bad guys, sponsoring secret vigilante armies of machine gunners and sluggers to take down the mafia by whatever means necessary, including shoot-outs in the street. When the hoodlums owned Chicago's cops, judges and politicians, the Chicago Crime Commission was often the only incorruptible line between them and us.

Today, the commission operates with a total of six employees, spartan offices and a budget of about $500,000. If not for an unexpected bequest by an elderly board member, it would have folded five years ago. Like many businesses, the commission has taken stock of the changing times and brought itself into the twenty-first century. Its sensible board now favors contemporary causes such as early juvenile intervention, battling girl gangs and monitoring the messages in rap music. Given that the commission can afford only one investigator, some people in Chicago think that it might be nice if Wayne Johnson would consent to work on any of these issues.

Instead, outside this restaurant on Grand Avenue, Johnson waits in his car for reputed mafia boss Joey "the Clown" Lombardo. An informant swears that Lombardo breaks bread here with the city contractors close to Mayor Daley, and in Johnson's world, this cannot stand. If he can get a photo of Lombardo with these scumbags, Jesus, it'll blow the roof off Chicago. With his heavily starched white business shirt, solid red tie and Russian-weight-lifter chest, he screams narc from here to the Sears Tower, but Johnson's not budging. With his left hand, he steadies a thirty-five-millimeter camera on the front door. Holstered under his right arm is a loaded nine-millimeter pistol. Attached to his hip in a buttery black leather wallet rests a shiny gold badge that carries precisely the same weight as the Junior Lone Ranger stars on sale at Toys "R" Us. Six hours later, no Lombardo, just a waitress locking up for the night. Johnson secures his gun, puts the camera on the passenger seat and drives home. Every block, he checks his rearview mirror. Every block, there is no one there.

Here in Chicago, the mafia is known as the Outfit. Since 1994, there has not been a single Outfit murder in the city—not a shooting, not a stabbing, not a swing of a Louisville Slugger. Chicagoans, raised on corpses and *Godfather* movies, have come to conclude that the Outfit has died. In Chicago, the Outfit does not die.

Today the organization still makes millions the Capone way— gambling, juice loans, labor racketeering, political fixing, street tax and vice—but it has learned to enforce by innuendo and cunning. Delinquent bettors and juice-loan borrowers are now blackballed rather than beaten or murdered; the Outfit has discovered that depriving an addicted gambler of his fix is even sharper punishment than killing him. Euphemisms stand in for threats. Now, instead of "Pay me or I'll hack off your head," as Outfit extortionist Mario Rainone was said to have told a restaurateur, collectors might say, "This could be very serious," or, "You don't want to see me again." With no more deadbeats floating down the Chicago River, law enforcement stopped worrying about Outfit muscle and directed its limited manpower elsewhere. The result is a mob so tightly woven into ordinary city living as to be virtually transparent. This new approach is eerily in line with the 1992 dying wish of Anthony "Joe Batters" Accardo, perhaps the Outfit's greatest boss. The Outfit, he said, should seek to become invisible, to camouflage itself in quiet until the public had concluded that the organization had vanished. When people stopped believing in gangsters, Accardo knew, anything would be possible. These days, Chicagoans laugh when someone stands up and tells them that the Outfit still prowls the city and that it's more dangerous than ever and that it's doing wrong in our society. Still, someone must tell them. Someone must show them that these scumbags have become chameleons among the law-abiding and good citizens of Chicago. Someone must do something, because Accardo's dying wish is coming true.

This is the face of organized crime in modern-day Chicago. Silent. Invisible. Dangerous.

Or maybe this is all just Wayne Johnson's fantasy.

.   .   .

Chicago is a city of unspoken understandings, a place where the cultural mandate is mixed into sidewalk cement and atomized into playground air: go with the flow; play the game; get what's yours. Quaint notions of right and wrong are museum pieces in Chicago, a great museum town.

Every so often, a kid grows up who doesn't get it. He will likely lead a frustrating life, straining to do right and railing against injustice, a sad spectacle in a city where right and wrong all depends. Most of these innocents eventually develop a skin of savvy and learn to fit in. They never had Major Johnson for a father.

Joe Johnson was built for his era. A man of unwavering principle, he seemed delivered by destiny into General Patton's fabled Third Army, where the major conferred with Patton and served proudly as his tank commander, fighting the noblest of causes. By the time Wayne was born, in 1951, Major Johnson had been transferred to an Illinois military base, but he carried with him all the airs of his overseas glory. In Wayne's first memories of his father, Major Johnson is on that military base, holding Wayne's hand, and they are going for haircuts—the same haircut. Along the way, uniformed men salute Major Johnson, which means that Wayne's father is boss.

What a glorious stroke of luck to have a father like Major Johnson! The world speeds by a child in a blur of wondrous faces, ominous sounds and close calls, but Major Johnson was immutable, a six-four, 240-pound collection of muscle and morals who could not be shaken by mere events. When his insurance company unjustly refused to pay an accident claim, Major Johnson parked the car in a faraway garage and didn't drive any car again for ten years. When a colonel wrongly accused him of a petty mistake on the base, Major Johnson spoke up, respectfully, whereupon the two stepped outside to settle things like men. Major Johnson knocked out the colonel's teeth, and oh, boy, did the neighborhood kids love that part of the story—Christ, Wayne's dad could kick ass! That was never the part Wayne liked best about that story. He loved that his dad stood up for what was right.

By high school, Wayne had earned a reputation as the toughest—and sweetest—kid in the neighborhood, a guy who had taken to stepping between legendary street bullies and whatever poor mope they had chosen to victimize. The Summer of Love rolled into his life when he was sixteen, but Wayne wasn't buying it. While other guys spent 1967 growing their hair, smoking pot and making out to Sgt. Pepper's, he spent every night at St. Hilary's play lot near California and Bryn Mawr, shooting hoops and cutting up with pals until the place closed at ten o'clock. He sported a crew cut, a Major Johnson barrel chest and straight-leg slacks, never bellbottoms. He played ball and built his body and stuck to his guns, and when the Chicago police started kicking the asses of troublemakers at the '68 Democratic Convention, Wayne and his jock buddies backed the cops—it was a matter of principle. When it came time to choose a career, there was little thinking to be done. Where else but in the Chicago Police Department would a city kid get paid to do right and fight wrong?

Johnson spent twenty-four years on the force, seven as a homicide detective. Colleagues still tell Wayne Johnson stories, tavernquality stories that fall into two categories. First, Johnson was a great policeman, especially as a member of the department's volunteer Task Force, a collection of true believers who blitzkrieged Chicago's deadliest neighborhoods—Cabrini Green, Cragin, the Fifteenth District—areas where cops died regularly. And when they saw someone or something they didn't like—hell, when they smelled it—boom, they'd take down the scumbag by whatever means necessary. Johnson won't deny that the Task Force had a reputation for brutality, but what caught his attention was a different prerequisite for membership: it was not enough simply to despise the bad guy; a Task Forcer had to cherish doing right—he had to be in love with justice. The guys on the Task Force took to calling Johnson Captain America for his black-and-white ethical outlook. "Hey," they'd announce before roll call, "here comes Captain America!" Johnson and his partner also earned the nickname Black and Blue. That moniker needed no explanation.

The second kind of Wayne Johnson story always comes back to his not understanding the game. Intellectually, sure, he could tell you that in Chicago, nobody gets anywhere without political connections, without a rabbi, without someone to grease the way. But the game never computed for him, he never breathed it, so while a connected woman who had played Officer Friendly was promoted ahead of him, Johnson waited two years for his call to homicide, all the while kicking the asses of street monsters, all the while looking at the world through Major Johnson's eyes. When he finally made detective, Johnson became known for an obsessive refusal to let go of certain murder cases, the kind that seemed particularly unfair to the victim. He worked homicide for seven years, taking night classes at local colleges because his father valued education and no one in his family had ever earned a college degree. He even moved into the intelligence division, where he was assigned to investigate organized crime and discovered that since 1919, there had been 1,106 suspected Outfit murders, only twenty-nine of which had been solved. This was embarrassing to the CPD, Johnson thought. But he began to sense, as the years passed, that this was the end of the line for a guy without connections. When he left the department to join the Chicago Crime Commission in 1997, friends understood the motivation. At a private organization founded by true believers, he would be free from rabbis, free from politics, free to track the city's most dangerous criminals—the Outfit.

.   .   .

If you look out the windows of the Chicago Crime Commission's offices, you can see a building where Capone's boys ran one of the city's biggest bookmaking operations. They did it in broad daylight. The cops? Hell, they were the best customers.

Today is a big day for Johnson, maybe the biggest since he joined the commission. He's expecting a phone call, and by 7:30 A.M. he is past the always-locked inner door and into the commission's offices. His uniform, as always, is standard issue: business suit, starched shirt, muted tie, gun, that badge. In the morning light, at just the right angle, his right hand flashes a scar from the long-ago bite of a gangbanger. The doctor wanted to amputate that hand while Johnson lay doped up and nearly unconscious. Johnson's wife, Donna, told the doctor that you don't amputate hands of men like him, men who still have important things to do. Today, his handshake crushes, but he still can't move his fingers as he'd like.

The secretary won't arrive for an hour, so Johnson pours himself a mug of coffee, tunes in the classical-music station on his boom box (he loves rock 'n' roll but can work only to classical), and scans the back rooms for . . . whomever. Along the walls are rows of green metal filing cabinets crammed with hundreds of thousands of index cards and blue carbon-copied notes, eyewitness accounts by Johnson's heroic predecessors of Chicago's roguish past. Johnson's office is the first one in the place. On the far wall, next to a portrait of his two sons, hangs an ancient organized-crime chart checkerboarded with the mug shots of Outfit hoods, tough guys whose eyes seem designed by God to tell police photographers to go fuck themselves. On a near wall is a framed *Chicago Tribune* front-page story about patrolman Johnson arresting a cop killer in 1977—pulled the gun-flashing son of a bitch by his hair through the window of his pimpmobile not twenty minutes after hearing the call—the arrest of a lifetime. Cops still talk about that one, not just the brute force or the instinct that led him to the suspect, but the fact that Johnson left his squad car and *walked* up to the Lincoln. How many cops would have walked up to that Lincoln? Those days were beautiful, Johnson says in his stocky Chicago accent, and you can see it in his eyes on that yellowing front page; you can see him say in that downward glance, even with all the reporters around, You did wrong, motherfucker.

When Johnson joined the commission, he brought with him a golden piece of intelligence from the Chicago Police Department. As a detective, he had investigated three suspected Outfit murders. One man, it turned out—a North Side gas-station manager named Pierre Zonis—had been questioned in all three homicides. Johnson dug into the guy's past, and he did not find, as he says, the story of Snow White. Zonis's name had appeared on an Outfit "juice" list showing that he owed $14,000-plus juice—at 3 percent a week—to Outfit loan shark Mario Rainone. Hours before the last murder, a call had been placed from a pay phone at Zonis's gas station to the victim's home. An FBI contact swore Johnson to secrecy, then told him this: Zonis was a bookmaker and up to his neck in Outfit associates, a real mobbed-up character. Johnson dug deeper and discovered one more piece of information, a wrecking ball that swung into his stomach and jerked the world off its axis. Zonis had since become a uniformed Chicago police officer.

To Johnson, the police department was sacrosanct, a Platonic ideal of good wedged into a stained and suspect world. Outfit guys might run gas stations or be decent fathers or host generous block parties, but they could not be Chicago policemen. Johnson prepared to strike.

He would write a new organized-crime chart, the pyramid-shaped hierarchy of Outfit power invented by the commission in 1930, when it coined the term "public enemy" and listed Capone as its first number one. But he would do more than that. He would push all of the commission's chips into the middle of the table, offer up its last shard of credibility and relevance, by listing Zonis as an Outfit associate—meaning a nonmade man who did the daily work of organized crime. Never in the commission's history had a uniformed cop made the list. The commission's president and board grilled him—a single lawsuit could wipe out the organization. Johnson stuck to his guns. He was listing the cop.

Johnson called a press conference, ready to unleash a scandal the likes of which Chicago hadn't seen since Summerdale in 1960, when newspapers ran front-page stories for weeks about a team of city cops who had pulled a series of major heists. The media showed up. Johnson made his presentation. The papers ran a few stories. Then, nothing—no public outcry, no City Hall protests, no editorials, no comment. A month later, the police department moved to fire Zonis. After two years, the police board ruled in Zonis's favor; even the FBI testified that while Zonis had been questioned, he had never been a suspect in the murders—the crux of the charge against him. Today, a year after that police-board decision, a court of law will rule on the police department's appeal—and in a sense rule on the legitimacy of Johnson and the Chicago Crime Commission.

The phone starts ringing around 8:30 A.M. Each time, Johnson forces calm as he reaches for the receiver; each time, it's just a friend or an informant or Donna. Finally, the right call comes. For a minute, Johnson listens and says nothing, but the veins in his treetrunk neck—first red, then bulging, then throbbing—tell an old Chicago story. Zonis has been exonerated; he will continue to serve on the force.

Johnson thanks the caller and hangs up the phone. He turns his chair to the window and stares out at the building Capone once operated. After forever, he reaches into his desk drawer and pulls out a business card. Printed on the card is a caricature of an Italian mafioso, a gun in his hand, a slot machine and handcuffs by his side. The card reads, PIERRE ZONIS, CHICAGO CRIME COMMISSION'S MAN OF THE YEAR. "This was being passed out at his precinct," Johnson says. "It's a big joke." Johnson takes the card and studies it, this time with the same downward glance as in the *Tribune* photo on his wall. "I'll tell you this," Johnson says, "I'm not done with this scumbag. I'm not going to let this one go."

Just before Christmas in 1999, a yellow rental truck pulled up alongside a man walking near his home in Chicago. A man in the truck's passenger seat got out, pointed a gun at him and shot him eight times in the face and chest. The shooter then got back in the truck, and it drove away. The victim was Ronnie Jarrett, reputed to be a longtime Outfit burglar, juice man, hijacker, fence and bodyguard. His wallet wasn't touched. The killers torched the rental truck in a nearby alley, a classic post-whacking Outfit move. The first person to reach Jarrett's body was not his wife or a neighbor or even the police; it was an FBI agent. The most remarkable aspect of the crime, however, was not the brazenness of its execution or its public nature. The most remarkable aspect of the crime is that, in 2001 Chicago, investigators have yet to call it an Outfit murder.

Johnson is almost unrecognizable at his home on Chicago's far North Side. In sweatshirt and jeans, gun and badge inert on the kitchen counter, he appears slightly weakened, the way a relative does in those backward dressing gowns during checkups at the doctor's office.

Johnson rarely invites strangers to his house or even reveals the neighborhood in which he lives. He worries for his family's safety;

the fewer people who know about their lives, the better. But it is also important that people know that there is fun in this house, that not every cop is drunk and walking sanity's tightrope like the ones on *NYPD Blue* and all the other cop shows he and Donna can't stop watching.

Major Johnson did not believe in owning houses. A man, he thought, ought not go around owing money. This is Wayne Johnson's second house. He still mists up at the mention of his father, downright sobs when he recalls how old Major Johnson looked the last time he saw him, which was the first time his father ever looked old. But as Johnson tells about buying this house, the part he seems to savor the most is that he took a chance on the place, put a bid in for a fixer-upper no one seemed to want, the kind that could blow up in a man's face. Then he went ahead and spent more money, made it beautiful and even built a new rec room, where he and Donna plan trips to Disney World and split pizzas and talk longingly of the day this summer when Johnson finally completes his doctoral thesis on training homicide detectives. Dr. Johnson. Imagine that.

It is obvious from the sporting trophies and outdoor gear here that Johnson's exhale comes from sports. His mother was a professional basketball player who toured the world with a championship women's team, and since he was a kid, Johnson has not been himself without a golf club or a football or a tennis racket in hand. In a typical week, he'll work out with his kids at a local gym, walk miles with Donna past the new neighborhood mansions—Outfit guys live in some of these, you know—then polish things off with a little basement power lifting.

There are memories in this house, lots of them. Downstairs by the dumbbells is a framed photo of patrolman Johnson, all chest and neck and grimace, winning a medal in the 242-pound power-lifting championship of the Illinois Police Olympics. Upstairs is a photo of the Johnson men: Major Johnson, Wayne and his two brothers, Joel and Gary, at Wayne's wedding. It is the only photo of Gary in the house, and that is by design. The brothers do not speak today, even though Gary served with Wayne on the police Task Force and is just two years Wayne's senior. Growing up, Gary pummeled Wayne regularly while Major Johnson was away at work, landing vicious combinations of punches to Wayne's face before his younger brother could manage a single body blow in defense. Still, Wayne fought back every day, not because he was a fool but because Gary was wrong to bully him, and wrong could not go unchallenged in the Johnson household any more than a false accusation from a colonel or a show of bad faith by an insurance company could. More than three decades later, Johnson's friends still wince when recalling those fights. A long time ago, Johnson promised Donna that the brutality of his childhood home would never be tolerated here, and he wants you to see his sons' room—the karate posters, the Bulls plaque from the first championship, especially the photo of the boys together smiling—the way a room looks when brothers are best friends. "My dad was wrong to allow that," Johnson says, closing his sons' door. It is the only time Johnson attributes a mistake to his father.

Donna is home now, a department-store bag in one hand, a box of doughnuts for Wayne in the other. A pretty and petite brunette, she becomes a toy against Johnson's chest in their kiss hello, then retires to the rec room to watch television. In the living room, Johnson checks his files for a list he has prepared—"people who hate me," as he puts it, who might provide perspective on his life and times. With the word *hate*, the volume on Donna's television drops slightly, and she shifts her position on the couch so that now she is sitting closer to the living room and her husband, though she continues to watch her program. Johnson talks about the story his old homicide colleagues still tell about a double murder and arson case in which Johnson had the scene and the only survivor was a young girl who had been raped and left for dead. The crime sickened everyone in the department but after months passed with no productive leads, the other detectives had to pull Johnson aside, put an arm around his shoulder and level with him: Wayne, we know how you feel about that little girl. But you gotta let it go. We don't have these luxuries in homicide. You can't stay on a murder for months. Johnson wouldn't hear them. He pulled in suspects, one a week, it seemed, for six months. He formulated scenarios, drew diagrams on McDonald's napkins, called in favors—still nothing. He never solved the case. Homicide detectives still remember him working that double murder and thinking, Jesus, pity the poor bastard he's gonna look for next.

Johnson writes in one additional name on his enemies list, then hands it over, explaining that none of the men will likely return a phone call. The television voices in the rec room go mute. Donna, fists clenched and eyes puffy, walks into the living room. For a moment, she simply stands in front of her husband, her back to him, barrier as much as a wife or the woman of the house.

"I'm sorry. I was listening," Donna says. "That's a true story about the girl. I'm glad someone told you that. I don't know how these interviews work or what you're looking for, but I have to say, I heard you ask for a list of Wayne's enemies. I wish Wayne hadn't given it to you."

The house again goes silent. In Major Johnson's home, a wife did not interrupt a husband's business conversations. Donna stands there, staring at the piece of paper, and it is clear that she wants the names returned to her husband. "They've got agendas," she says. "They're not good people, you know? Why do you need to talk to his enemies? This is the most honest, noble man in the world. He shouldn't have enemies."

Donna apologizes again and only then begins to move away

from her husband and to a living-room couch, where she sits cross-legged and asks to add one more thought, then she'll go back to the television, and this time the volume will be loud, she promises. She fears for Wayne's life, she says. For her kids' lives, too. Yes, that's a good story about Wayne not letting go on that double murder, but it's a bad story, too, because, can't you see, Wayne doesn't let go of anything, and now he's chasing people who are famous for striking back, and she doesn't care how many years it's supposedly been since the Outfit has murdered anyone, this is the sweetest, most loving husband and father in the world, so why in God's name do you need to talk to his enemies? For the first time, Johnson speaks to his wife, and it is in a near whisper. "I've got nothing to hide," he tells her. "You can't arrange for a writer to only talk to people with good things to say—it doesn't work." For another minute, no one moves or says anything. Then Donna apologizes and turns to leave. "Please stay," Johnson tells her. "This stuff is important. You should be here." And Donna stays.

There are few corollaries for Wayne Johnson in the taxonomy of modern law enforcement. He is a private citizen funded by private donations and as such is not bound to support his opinions with the kind of irrefutable, demonstrable evidence required of his government colleagues. He can neither subpoena nor indict. At the same time, the commission's staid name lends it a whiff of state imprimatur—few in Chicago would guess that the commission does not belong to the Illinois government. In the commission's glory days, before the vogue in defamation lawsuits and before damaged reputations could get much of a fair hearing, the commission could print with impunity the names and home addresses of those it suspected. Today, slinging accusations without file cabinets of supporting evidence has a way of pissing people off.

Pierre Zonis is pissed off. On the coldest day of the year, he has come to a local hamburger joint—no, thanks, he does not want a pop or a burger—to defend his name. Yes, he is bitter about Wayne Johnson and the Chicago Crime Commission. No, he is not a mobbed-up bookmaker. How do you put someone's name on a list, have a big press conference accusing him of terrible things and insinuating worse, without presenting a shred of evidence? Where does this happen in America? Newspapers don't do it. The government doesn't do it. Only Wayne Johnson does it, just writes down a name.

Zonis cannot understand why Johnson never consulted him, never came to him man-to-man and put it out, just said, "I think you're a suspect." "Real detectives," Zonis says, "right away, they want to interview a guy they suspect. If this guy Johnson had any balls, he would have come talk to me."

No one gives a rat's ass about the commission's organized-crime chart, Zonis says. Even coppers don't know who they are, and coppers know everyone in law enforcement. "They might as well be a group of ladies who meet for coffee and cake," he says.

Was he questioned in those three homicides? Sure, he was questioned. Let's say you have a neighbor murdered. The police will question you, too—"Did you hear anything? Did they have any enemies?" Does that make you a suspect? Yes, he knew two of the victims, so of course he was questioned. Doesn't make him a suspect—even the FBI said so at his hearing. Was a phone call placed from his gas station to the third victim hours before the murder? "Let's say it's true. Do you know how many people used those pay phones in those days, before cell phones? Am I supposed to be responsible for everyone's phone calls?"

Zonis still is without his police powers; he can't carry a gun or a star, which he says is in direct violation of the judge's orders. He thinks Wayne Johnson has the department's ear, and that's why he's still doing desk duty.

He has considered suing Johnson and the commission but has been told that it's pointless to pay a fortune to go after a nonprofit agency that won't end up coughing up a dime. And what might he tell Johnson if he met him today?

"I'd tell him to go fuck himself."

Since Mayor Daley took office, Chicago has awarded nearly $100 million in affirmative-action contracts to businesses controlled by seventy-four-year-old John Duff and his sons. The Duffs are West Side Irish whites. The Duffs are also longtime pals of the mayor's. According to court records, John Duff was an associate of slain Outfit enforcer Tony "the Ant" Spilotro. He also testified in 1960 on behalf of Tony Accardo, the greatest Outfit boss of them all. In 1982, Duff pleaded guilty to federal embezzlement charges and served seventeen months in prison. One of Duff's sons also has been linked to Outfit associates. Among the contracts awarded to the Duffs was a multiyear deal to clean the offices of the 911 center, storehouse for sensitive police records. This March, according to reports, the Duffs were in line for a new $10 million contract at McCormick Place, the convention center, where Daley is the boss.

Thomas Kirkpatrick has been the president of the Chicago Crime Commission for six years. Asked to list the organization's most important accomplishments during his tenure, Kirkpatrick cites three: the reports on girl gangs, the report on street gangs and a study of new manifestations of organized crime, such as Asian and Russian gangs. "Of course girl gangs fit into the reputation of the commission," he says. "They're a serious threat to the public safety! You know, violence, crime."

"There are no girl gangs," says Bob Feusel, Kirkpatrick's predecessor. "The commission has lost its whole sense of direction. Wayne is knocking his head against the wall there. No one listens to him."

"Kirkpatrick would have a heart attack if he saw a hood in a restaurant—he has no real experience with crime," says John Flood, president of the Combined Counties Police Association—a union for Illinois law-enforcement officers—and a commission member. "They had a housewife as the chairperson until last year. A *housewife*. This was a great organization once; it was revered by everyone from the mayor to the lowest beat cop. Now it's a joke. No one knows who they are. If it weren't for Wayne, the commission would be kaput. But Wayne will never tell you that. He still believes in the chain of command—it's psychological with him. It's his father—it's respect for his father and the military. Ask him. You'll see."

Johnson's office is stuffed with books on the Outfit—*Capone, Accardo. Man Against the Mob. Barbarians in Our Midst. Spilotro.* There is not a book on girl gangs anywhere. While the commission board continues to champion what Bob Feusel calls "crap," Johnson keeps to his office, fielding phone calls from the media ("Angelini died? My comment is that he was one of the, I hate to say, great minds within organized crime"); checking with sources and informants ("He's been seen in which Vegas strip joint?"); drafting new publications ("The Mob in Cicero"); firing off faxes and e-mails to the media; even arranging for an ex–Outfit bookmaker—now in witness protection—to warn Northwestern University students about the evils of sports betting. If he finds spare time, he packs his camera and attends an Outfit wake or stakes out a suspicious card room.

In a few weeks, Johnson will undertake a battle even larger than the one he waged against Zonis. The Illinois Gaming Board is scheduled to hold hearings on a request to place a casino in suburban Rosemont, next to O'Hare Airport. To the average citizen of

Illinois, it will be just another smoky riverboat. To Johnson, it is the Outfit's dream come true: a casino at O'Hare, he says, is a casino right in Chicago, a nirvana beyond the wildest dreams of Capone, Giancana and Accardo.

Are girl gangs and juvenile intervention really the business of the venerable Chicago Crime Commission? The organization whose president once walked past machine gunners into Capone's marbled Lexington Hotel headquarters and demanded—and was granted—a square election? The organization that Senator Kefauver asked, instead of Chicago police, to serve subpoenas on Outfit killers? The organization that once published not just the names of Outfit hoods but also their addresses? John Flood is right—Johnson will not answer. He sits silent in his chair, lips pursed, neck reddening, as the question hangs. Kirkpatrick is his superior, he outranks Johnson, and where would the world be without rank and order?

And then Johnson begins to speak, and in his measured words, in the hard *aw* in his *Chicaw-go,* he is Major Johnson on that military base, respectfully telling the colonel that despite the colonel's rank, he is wrong, sir, and if it is necessary to step outside to make things right, he will do so, respectfully, sir. Social programs, Johnson says, are well-intentioned, but they are not the legacy of the Chicago Crime Commission, and fund-raising is crucial, yes, but fund-raising is not his job; his job is to be the eyes of the public, because the enemy is turning invisible, and he loves the Chicago Crime Commission, girl gangs or no, even if it doesn't necessarily love him.

Later, in his office, Kirkpatrick is visibly uncomfortable discussing Johnson's focus on the Outfit. "How do I say this . . . he's filling a need," Kirkpatrick says. "We have some obligation to our eighty-one-year history of being a repository of up-to-date knowledge of organized crime, and he's on top of that. Did you know there are clubs who debate all this organized-crime stuff? Who killed Giancana? Who was really hanging from that meat hook? It's like those Civil War buffs moving their pieces around on a miniature battlefield. This is the twenty-first century—nobody's going to give you money to do that."

In 1997, a thirteen-year-old black youth made the mistake of riding his bicycle into Chicago's predominantly white Bridgeport neighborhood. There, three young white men pulled the boy from his bike, yelled racial epithets, kicked him, slammed his head into concrete and left him for dead. The black youth suffered severe brain damage and memory loss but lived.

One of the attackers identified by eyewitnesses was eighteen-year-old Frank Caruso. The Caruso name was familiar to Outfit watchers. Caruso's father had resigned his post in the Laborers' International Union during an investigation into Outfit infiltration. Caruso's uncle had been ousted from his union position after the same investigation linked him to Outfit bosses.

Among the key witnesses scheduled to testify against the perpetrators was nineteen-year-old bystander Michael Cutler. Six weeks before the trial was to begin, Cutler was shot and killed by two masked men while sitting alone in his car. Police never determined if anything was taken from Cutler. To date, the murder is still classified as nothing more than an attempted robbery.

On the afternoon of January 30, as the Illinois Gaming Board prepares to convene in a downtown-Chicago office building for hearings on the proposed casino in Rosemont, Johnson locks his gun and badge in his commission office (there will be a metal detector at the hearings) and walks the half mile to state his case. He will have five minutes to speak against the plan.

When he first heard of the casino project, Johnson talked to law-enforcement sources, absorbed forty years of newspaper clippings, studied the handwritten notes of his predecessors stuffed into those endless rows of green metal filing cabinets and memorized arrest and business records. He did not care for what he found. Johnson has come to believe that Rosemont mayor Donald Stephens—the key operative in delivering the casino to Rosemont and one of Illinois's most powerful politicians—has a smorgasbord of Outfit connections. And in his estimation, a casino in Rosemont overseen by the powerful Stephens would be nothing short of a Chicago catastrophe.

Today, he intends to name names.

The meeting is standing-room only and is packed with well-heeled attorneys, media and celebrity investors like Mrs. Roger Ebert and Mrs. Walter Payton. Known as a rubber stamp for gambling interests, the board is expected to automatically approve the casino—a Chicago lock if ever there was one. The mood is celebratory. A minister speaks on the evils of gambling and is tolerated politely. A man from the Sierra Club urges respect for the wetlands, and he is tolerated politely. Another man reads a letter from former Illinois governor James Thompson in support of Stephens's credibility: "Mayor Stephens is respected by his peers, as well as the citizens of Rosemont, who have continuously reelected him over a forty-five-year career. I consider him a fine public servant and friend. I hope this letter will serve as a testament to my personal support for the village of Rosemont and its mayor, Don Stephens." Bingo. Just a few more minutes before everybody gets rich.

Then Johnson pushes to the podium, sorts his stack of notes and addresses the assembled.

"Members of the Illinois Gaming Board, staff, ladies and gentlemen. I'm Wayne Johnson of the Chicago Crime Commission. . . ."

Perhaps there is something in Johnson's stocky accent, or maybe it is his old-fashioned wrestler's grip on the podium, or the commission's name: something announces to the audience that this is not another carpetbagging do-gooder desperate to save some tree or soul but a Chicagoan, the real deal, up to bat in his own city. Whatever the reason, the room falls silent with Johnson's introduction, so that the hum of his microphone dominates the room through the breaks in his speech.

"What I find most troubling in this case," Johnson says, "is the litany of associations Mayor Stephens has accumulated over the years." A woman gasps from the audience. Lawyers exchange here-it-comes glances. Then Johnson utters a sentence that dates to the founding instincts of his predecessors, to the glory days when the commission meant something, when it was respected and law and order held sway not because it was convenient but because it was right. "Those associations," Johnson says, "include the following individuals. . . ."

He tells the board about William Daddano Jr., "a business partner of the mayor, a business associate of organized crime in Chicago, who was listed on no less than three organizational charts produced by the commission and local law enforcement, and son of the late North Side Outfit boss Willie 'Potatoes' Daddano." He warns the board about Nicholas Boscarino, "a business associate of the mayor, a suspected union racketeer—his father was the victim of an Outfit assassin"; about Anthony "Jeeps" Daddino, "a Rosemont employee and convicted Outfit member and extortionist who drew such admiration from the mayor that the mayor wrote a letter to a judge on his behalf."

In another time, the crowd would have risen to applaud such a bold stance—who else would have the courage to name such dangerous names? A different sound comes from this crowd. The sound of giggling. "Who let this fool speak?" whispers one attorney. "I can't wait for the defamation suits to roll in on this one!" says another. From seated spectators to those standing along the wall dressed in fur and Armani, people are either smiling or giggling or mouthing the word *potatoes* to each other or screwing their faces into who-is-this-guy expressions. Johnson doesn't hear them.

"Peter DiFronzo, an established Outfit lieutenant who was listed on no less than three organizational charts, is the brother of current Outfit operating director John 'No Nose' DiFronzo, is a contributor to Don Stephens's political coffers, is the owner of D&P Construction, and remains a benefactor from no-bid contracts with Rosemont."

More snickering. Much whispering. Scattered *Bullshits* from the back of the room.

"Willie 'the Beast' Messino, an established Outfit lieutenant who has been listed on numerous organizational charts since the 1960s, has been involved in gambling and extortion in the past, and is the uncle of two Outfit associates and a lifelong friend and associate of Mayor Stephens.

"The late Sam 'Momo' Giancana; known nationally as the former operating director of the Outfit, he previously appeared at the very top of many Outfit organizational charts until his assassination in 1975 and had business dealings with Mayor Stephens."

Johnson thanks the board and urges them to reject the Rosemont casino. Few pretend to listen to the final speaker, opting instead to compare notes about the "jerk" from where-was-it-again? Moments later, the board adjourns to discuss its decision. Johnson stands in the back of the room, briefcase at his feet, soldier-straight, the same stance he used as a cop outside courtrooms awaiting the verdict on whatever bad guy he was helping to put away. The people who stood next to him earlier now stand safely down-room. In a hall where every shoulder seems to rub another, Johnson has room to stretch out his arms and twirl.

A few minutes later, the board returns with its decision. By a vote of four to one, the Rosemont casino is denied. And while some board members strain above the din to absolve Stephens and Rosemont, the words of board administrator Sergio Acosta seem to mute all the voices and shuffling and camera snapping, so that, to Johnson's ears, the room falls silent, as if it were just he and Major Johnson at the dinner table, ready for another story about Patton. The board's investigation, Acosta says, shows the insidious presence of organized-crime elements." The board's investigation, Acosta says, shows "organized-crime elements associated with this proposed project that cannot be ignored." The board's investigation, Acosta says, shows "known members of organized crime who control at least one firm that has done work at the Rosemont site."

While reporters leap from their chairs with stop-the-presses urgency and attorneys speed-dial millionaire-investor clients, Johnson stands frozen against a back wall, the board's *denied* seeping into his pores. The Outfit is different in twenty-first century Chicago, quiet and invisible. But today the ghosts of Capone and Accardo and Giancana pace this room, and you can feel them here, guests of honor on the occasion of the Outfit's eighty-one-year dream. And you can hear them mutter, as they look upon a Chicago kid who still doesn't get it, "You son of a bitch. We'll be back." That night, after the dust has settled and he has answered every reporter's questions, Johnson walks to his Camry for the drive home. Every few blocks, he checks his rearview mirror. Every few blocks, there is no one there.

*   *   *

When I last saw Wayne Johnson, in the summer of 2001, he was preparing to defend a defamation lawsuit filed against him by Rosemont mayor Donald Stephens, one of Illinois's most powerful politicians. The litigation arose from remarks Johnson made to the Illinois

Gaming Board in which Johnson invoked—by name and nickname—
a litany of Chicago mob, or Outfit, members with whom he alleged
Stephens to have had contact. This speech, which froze a packed
meeting hall in a city where nothing shocks anymore, formed the
basis for the conclusion to my Esquire piece on Johnson. It also may
have been the undoing of Johnson's career at the Chicago Crime
Commission.

I recently received an e-mail from Johnson announcing that, effective January 1, 2002, he had left the commission to take a position
with a private security firm in the Chicago suburbs. Despite Johnson's near religious commitment to the purpose, history and goodness
of the CCC, I can't say that such a move surprised me. During my
reporting, I got the sense that the commission's president—and perhaps even some of its board—viewed their outspoken chief investigator as a potentially expensive anachronism. I don't know for certain,
but I suspect that the Stephens lawsuit—which Johnson was eager to
defend—became the last straw for the suits at the CCC; without
internal support, my bet is, Johnson knew his time was up there and
called it quits, marking the effective end of one of Chicago's most sto-
ried and muscular institutions.

UNDER SUSPICION
ATUL GAWANDE

In 1901, a professor of criminal law at the University of Berlin was lecturing to his class when a student suddenly shouted an objection to his line of argument. Another student countered angrily, and the two exchanged insults. Fists were clenched, threats made: "If you say another word . . ." Then the first student drew a gun, the second rushed at him and the professor recklessly interposed himself between them. A struggle, a blast—then pandemonium.

Whereupon the two putative antagonists disengaged and returned to their seats. The professor swiftly restored order, explaining to his students that the incident had been staged, and for a purpose. He asked the students, as eyewitnesses, to describe exactly what they had seen. Some were to write down their account on the spot, some a day or a week later; a few even had to depose their observations under cross-examination. The results were dismal. The most accurate witness got 26 percent of the significant details wrong; others up to 80 percent. Words were put in people's mouths. Actions were described that had never taken place. Events that *had* taken place disappeared from memory.

In the century since, professors around the world have reenacted the experiment, in one form or another, thousands of times; the findings have been recounted in legal texts, courtrooms and popular crime books. The trick has even been played on audiences of judges. The implications are not trivial. Each year, in the United

States, more than seventy-five thousand people become criminal suspects based on eyewitness identification, with lineups used as a standard control measure. Studies of wrongful convictions—cases where a defendant was later exonerated by DNA testing—have shown the most common cause to be eyewitness error. In medicine, this kind of systematic misdiagnosis would receive intense scientific scrutiny. Yet the legal profession has conducted no further experiments on the reliability of eyewitness evidence, or on much else, for that matter. Science finds its way to the courthouse in the form of "expert testimony"—forensic analysis, ballistics and so forth. But the law has balked at submitting its methods to scientific inquiry. Meanwhile, researchers working outside the legal establishment have discovered that surprisingly simple changes in legal procedures could substantially reduce misidentification. They suggest how scientific experimentation, which transformed medicine in the last century, could transform the justice system in the next.

For more than two decades now, the leading figure in eyewitness research has been a blond, jeans-and-tweed-wearing Midwesterner named Gary Wells. He got involved in the field by happenstance: one morning in 1974, a packet from a Cincinnati defense attorney arrived at the department of psychology at Ohio State University, in Columbus, where Wells was a twenty-three-year-old graduate student. The attorney had written to see if anyone there could help him analyze a case in which he believed his client had been wrongly identified as an armed robber. Inside the envelope was a large black-and-white photograph of the lineup from which his client had been picked out. Digging around a little in his spare time, Wells was surprised to discover that little was known about how misidentification occurs. He corresponded with the attorney several times during the next year, though he never came up with anything useful. The suspect was tried, convicted and sent to prison. Wells never did find out whether the client had been falsely identified. But the case got him thinking.

Some months later, he put together his first experiment. He asked people in a waiting room to watch a bag while he left the room. After he went out, a confederate got up and grabbed the bag. Then he dropped it and picked it up again, giving everyone a good look at him, and bolted. (One problem emerged in the initial experiment: some people gave chase. Wells had to provide his shill with a hiding place just outside the room.) Wells knew from all the previous demonstrations that people would often misidentify the perpetrator. Still, he figured, if they did it without great assurance it wouldn't matter much: under directions that the Supreme Court laid out in 1972, courts placed strong weight on an eyewitness's level of certainty. Wells found, however, that the witnesses who picked the wrong person out of the lineup were just as confident about their choices as those who identified the right person. In a later experiment, he assembled volunteer juries and had them observe witnesses under cross-examination. The jurors, it turned out, believed inaccurate witnesses just as often as they did accurate ones.

Wells tried variations on these experiments, first at the University of Alberta and later at Iowa State, where he's now a professor of psychology, but after a time even he found the work discouraging. He did not just want to show how things go wrong; he wanted to figure out how they could be improved. His first clue came after several years, when he noticed an unexpected pattern: having multiple witnesses did not insure accurate identifications. In his studies, a crime might be witnessed by dozens of people, yet they would often finger the same wrong suspect. The errors were clearly not random.

To investigate further, Wells staged another crime, over and over, until he had gathered two hundred witnesses. The subjects were seated in a room, filling out what they thought were applications for a temporary job, when a loud crash came from behind the door to an adjacent room. A stranger (a graying, middle-aged, mustached local whom Wells had hired) then burst through the door, stopped in his tracks in evident surprise at finding people in the room and retreated through the same door. Apparently finding a dead end that way, the man rushed in again, dropped an expensive-looking camera, picked it up and ran out through the exit at the opposite end of the room. Everyone got several good looks at him. At this point, another person dashed in and said, "What happened to my camera?" Wells tested each witness, one by one. Half the group was given a photo lineup of six people—a "six-pack," as the police call it—which included the actual perpetrator. (Police use photo lineups far more frequently than live ones.) In a group of a hundred individuals, fifty-four picked the perpetrator correctly; twenty-one said they didn't think the guy was there; and the others spread their picks across the people in the lineup.

The second group of witnesses was given the same lineup, minus the perpetrator. This time, thirty-two people picked no one. But most of the rest chose the same wrong person—the one who most resembled the perpetrator. Wells theorizes that witnesses faced with a photo spread tend to make a relative decision, weighing one candidate against the others and against incomplete traces of memory. Studies of actual wrongful convictions lend support to the thesis. For example, in a study of sixty-three DNA exonerations of wrongfully convicted people, fifty-three involved witnesses making a mistaken identification, and almost invariably they had viewed a lineup in which the actual perpetrator was not there. "The dangerous situation is exactly what our experiments said it would be," Wells says.

Once this was established, he and others set about designing ways to limit such errors. Researchers at the State University of New York at Plattsburgh discovered that witnesses who are not explicitly warned that a lineup may not include the actual perpetrator are substantially more likely to make a false identification, under the misapprehension that they've got to pick someone. Wells found that putting more than one suspect in a lineup—something the police do routinely—also dramatically increases errors. Most provocative, however, were the experiments performed by Wells and Rod Lindsay, a colleague from Queen's University in Ontario, which played with the way lineups were structured. The convention is to show a witness a whole lineup at once. Wells and Lindsay decided to see what would happen if witnesses were shown only one person at a time, and made to decide whether he was the culprit before moving on. Now, after a staged theft, the vast majority of witnesses who were shown a lineup that did not include the culprit went through the set without picking anyone. And when the culprit was present, witnesses who viewed a sequential lineup were no less adept at identifying him than witnesses who saw a standard lineup. The innovation reduced false identifications by well over 50 percent without sacrificing correct identifications. The results have since been replicated by others. And the technique is beautifully simple. It wouldn't cost a dime to adopt it.

It has now been fifteen years since Wells and Lindsay published their results. I asked Wells how widely the procedure has been followed. He laughed, because, aside from a scattered handful of police departments, mainly in Canada, it was not picked up at all. "In general," he told me, "the reaction before criminal-law audiences was 'Well, that's very interesting, but . . .'" A Department of Justice report released in 1999 acknowledged that scientific evidence had established the superiority of sequential-lineup procedures. Yet the report goes on to emphasize that the department still has no preference between the two methods.

.   .   .

Among the inquisitive and scientifically minded, there are a few peculiar souls for whom the justice system looms the way the human body once did for eighteenth-century anatomists. They see infirmities to be understood, remedies to be invented and tested. And eyewitness identification is just one of the practices that invite empirical scrutiny. Unfortunately, only a handful of scientists have had any luck in gaining access to courtrooms and police departments. One of them is Lawrence Sherman, a sociologist at the University of Pennsylvania, who is the first person to carry out a randomized field experiment in criminal-enforcement methods. In 1982, with the support of Minneapolis police chief Anthony Bouza, Sherman and his team of researchers completed a seventeen-month trial in which they compared three tactics for responding to non-life-threatening domestic-violence calls: arrest, mediation, and ordering the violent husband or boyfriend to leave the home for eight hours. Arrest emerged as the most effective way to prevent repeated acts of violence. The research was tremendously influential. Previously, it had been rare to arrest a violent husband, at least where the assault was considered "nonsevere." Afterward, across the country, arrest became a standard police response.

Such cooperation from law enforcement has proved rare. In Broward County, Florida, researchers started a randomized study to see whether counseling for convicted wife beaters reduced repeat violence — and prosecutors went to court to stop the study. The state of Florida had granted judges discretion in mandating such counseling, and there was a strong belief that it should be assigned broadly, to stop violence, not randomly, for the sake of study. ("No one is suggesting counseling is a panacea and will solve everyone's problems," the lead prosecutor told the local newspaper, "but I think everyone will agree, in a certain percentage of cases it works.") The researchers managed to get most of the men through the study before it was shut down, though, and they discovered not only that counseling provided no benefit but that it actually increased the likelihood of rearrest in unemployed men. (Probably that's because the women misguidedly believed that counseling worked, and were more likely to agree to see the men again.) In the field of law enforcement, people simply do not admit such possibilities, let alone test them.

Consider the jury box. Steven Penrod, a professor of both psychology and law at the University of Nebraska at Lincoln and another lonely pioneer in this area, is happy to rattle off a series of unexplored questions. Are there certain voting arrangements that make false convictions or mistaken acquittals less likely? (Most states require jurors to reach a unanimous verdict for a criminal conviction, but others allow conviction by as few as eight out of twelve jurors.) How would changing the number of jurors seated— say, to three or seventeen or eight—affect decisions? Do jurors understand and follow the instructions that judges give them? What instructions would be most effective in helping juries reach an accurate and just decision? Are there practical ways of getting juries to disregard inadmissible testimony that a lawyer has brought in? These are important questions, but researchers have little hope of making their way into jury rooms.

Lawrence Sherman points out that one of the most fertile areas for work is that of prosecutorial discretion. Most criminal cases are handled outside the courtroom, and no one knows how prosecutors decide whom to prosecute, how effectively they make these decisions, how often they let risky people go, and so on. But he reports that prosecutors he has approached have been "uniformly opposed" to allowing observation, let alone experimental study. "I've proposed repeatedly, and I've failed," Sherman told me. He has a difficult enough time getting cooperation from the police, he says, "but the lawyers are by far the worst." In his view, the process of bringing scientific scrutiny to the methods of the justice system has hardly begun. "We're holding a tiny little cardboard match in the middle of a huge forest at night," he told me. "We're about where surgery was a century ago."

Researchers like Sherman say that one of their problems is the scarcity of financial support. The largest source of research funding is an obscure government agency called the National Institute of Justice, which was modeled on the National Institutes of Health when it was established, in 1968, but has a budget of less than 1 percent of the N.I.H.'s. (The government spends more on meat and poultry research.) The harder problem, though, is the clash of cultures between the legal and the scientific approach, which is compounded by ignorance and suspicion. In medicine, there are hundreds of academic teaching hospitals, where innovation and testing are a routine part of what doctors do. There is no such thing as an academic police department or a teaching courthouse. The legal system takes its methods for granted: it is common sense that lineups are to be trusted, that wife beaters are to be counseled and that jurors are not to ask witnesses questions. Law enforcement, finally, is in thrall to a culture of precedent and convention, not of experiment and change. And science remains deeply mistrusted.

"The legal system doesn't understand science," Gary Wells told me. "I taught in law school for a year. Believe me, there's no science in there at all." When he speaks to people in the justice system about his work, he finds that most of his time is spent educating them about basic scientific methods. "To them, it seems like magic hand waving and—boom—here's the result. So then all they want to know is whose side you're on—the prosecutor's or the defendant's." In an adversarial system, where even facts come in two versions, it's easy to view science as just another form of spin.

.   .   .

For a scientist, Gary Wells is a man of remarkable faith; he has spent more than twenty-five years doing research at the periphery of his own field for an audience that has barely been listening. When I point this out to him, it makes him chuckle. "It's true," he admits, and yet it does not seem to trouble him. "This may be my American optimism talking, but don't you think, in the long run, the better idea will prevail?"

Lately, he has become fascinated with the alibi. "You know," he told me in a recent conversation, "one of the strange things that pop up in DNA-exoneration cases is that innocent people often seem to be done in by weak or inconsistent alibis." And it has got him thinking. Alibis seem so straightforward. The detective asks the suspect, "Where were you last Friday around 11 P.M.?" and if the suspect can't account for his whereabouts—or, worse, gives one story now and another later—we take that as evidence against him. But should we? Wells wonders. How well do people remember where they were? How often do they misremember and change their minds? What times of the day is a person likely to have a provable alibi and what times not? How much does this vary among people who are married, who live alone, who are unemployed? Are there better ways to establish whether a suspect has a legitimate alibi? "No one knows these things," he says.

※　　※　　※

It has struck me how different legal and medical cultures are. When the reports of the disconcertingly large number of DNA exonerations of death row inmates came out, however, I began to understand what the core difference was: it was our different history and feelings about the role of science in what we do. It did not take much searching to find Wells's pioneering but ignored work trying to bring science to the design of methods in the law—and his seemed a story that needed to be told.

X FILES

JULIAN RUBINSTEIN

In the early evening of April 7, 2000, one of the strangest and most lucrative careers in the history of American drug smuggling was coming to an end. Twenty undercover agents, most from the U.S. Customs Service and the Drug Enforcement Administration, fanned into position outside a plush midtown Manhattan high-rise waiting for Jacob "Cookie" Orgad, the enigmatic Israeli king of ecstasy, to return from dinner.

When he arrived, at around nine-thirty—a babe on each arm and reeking of cologne— the former "Beeper King" of Los Angeles calmly consented to a search of his three-bedroom penthouse. What would a forty-three-year-old self-described former rabbinical student have to hide? But with Cookie, nothing was ever the way it seemed. As the search commenced, one of his girlfriends entertained the agents by showing them the marijuana leaf tattooed on her ass.

Such was the bizarre and incongruous world of Jacob Orgad— a.k.a. Tony Evans—a man feared by some and considered a joke by others, whose rise to prominence on the Hollywood scene as a close associate of Heidi Fleiss gives new meaning to the immigrant ideal of the self-made man. Was Cookie the Pablo Escobar of ecstasy? If so, he went down without so much as a splash. "Wait up for me," he told the girls through his thick Israeli accent as he was cuffed and put into a waiting car. "I'll be back in a few hours."

But Cookie wasn't going to be coming home for a long, long time. There were too many people—from the notorious former Gambino-crime-family underboss Sammy "the Bull" Gravano down to the Las Vegas strippers and Brooklyn Hasidic teens employed as drug mules—who had been convicted for working in the worldwide ecstasy empire Cookie shrewdly came to rule. "It was one of the most sophisticated and complex operations we've seen," says Dean Boyd, a spokesman for U.S. Customs. It was also one of the most unlikely.

Cookie's rise and fall traces a precipitous Wall Street–like graph: his fortunes boomed spectacularly in the mid-to-late nineties—when the emergence of a massive market for ecstasy reconfigured the power structure of the world drug market—before crashing at the tail end of an investigation that spanned three continents and tore up the lives of scores of the most unlikely pushers imaginable. Take nineteen-year-old Simcha Roth, a Hasidic Jew from Brooklyn who pleaded guilty to ecstasy-smuggling charges in a related case. At his bail hearing, he was released to the custody of two rabbis.

As much as 90 percent of the world's ecstasy supply is manufactured in secret, high-tech labs scattered throughout the Netherlands, where the materials to make the hallucinogen are not as closely regulated as they are in the rest of Europe and the United States. For years, a cabal of Israelis have used Holland as a base for diamond smuggling through the ports in Antwerp and Rotterdam. In the mid-nineties, some of them noticed that an even more lucrative trade had blossomed around them, one with few players as well positioned to cash in as they were. "Israelis are everywhere, and they get to know each other very fast because of the language and the tradition," says an Israeli intelligence official familiar with his countrymen's stranglehold on the world ecstasy market. "It doesn't take long for a guy like Cookie to get big."

Authorities say that by the time of his arrest, Cookie had brought in more ecstasy to the United States than any other individual ever has: an estimated nine million pills with a street value of more than $270 million. A former discount-electronics salesman, Cookie climbed to the top of the world drug trade chiefly by lying with such élan that emboldened associates were eventually threatening to "whack" mafia made man Gravano. But in the end, Cookie's sex-filled gangster paradise grew too big for its own good.

"I was stupid," Cookie told me through his lawyer from a federal detention facility in Brooklyn—one of the few comments he agreed to make for this story. "It was a macho thing."

What most people who knew Cookie in his early L.A. days remember is that he was a member of Mossad, Israel's elite intelligence organization. Cookie grew up in Israel—in a big Moroccan Jewish family in the north of the country—and followed his ex-wife, Sigal, and six-year-old daughter, Ravid, to the United States in 1985. He spent a few years in Fort Lauderdale before moving to Los Angeles in 1989. And though he has been able to keep many of the facts about his life a mystery even to the authorities who tracked his case for years, one thing is certain: Cookie was never an intelligence agent.

Cookie might never have amounted to more than a street-level salesman if it hadn't been for his extraordinary ability to exploit opportunity—the southern California equivalent of good genes. An opportunity presented itself to Cookie in the form of Heidi Fleiss, who showed up at his electronics store one afternoon in 1990, look-ing for a bargain on a big-screen television. Not that Fleiss needed a bargain. She was already running what she brags was the best oper-ation of its kind in the world—a $1,500-a-night call-girl service. (The "Hollywood Madam" eventually drew three years in prison.) "I dealt with the richest people in the world and the best-looking girls," Fleiss crows from her Los Angeles home, where she remains sequestered as part of her parole agreement.

Cookie knew who Fleiss was; a mutual Israeli friend had told him that she would be coming in for a deal on a TV. Law-enforcement officials here and in Israel believe Cookie was already involved in drug dealing—cocaine, mostly—but it was small-time stuff; it's unlikely that's why Fleiss sought him out. What is clear is that Cookie sold Fleiss a television and drove it to her now-infamous $1.6 million Benedict Canyon pleasure palace himself.

"Next thing you know, Cookie's doing favors, running errands," says Ivan Nagy, Fleiss's boyfriend at the time. The call-girl market, much like the ecstasy scene that would soon explode, was fiercely competitive. With demand exceeding supply, many girls were looking to use Fleiss as a springboard to their own service.

Cookie didn't look like much—short, pudgy, hairy, with a sartorial style reminiscent of Steve Martin's Wild and Crazy Guy: tight pants, shirts unbuttoned to his navel, lime green Valentino jackets, and chest-nesting gold chains. But Cookie recognized Fleiss's need for someone to protect the business, and the Mossad tale was born. "Heidi and I looked at him like he was a moron," says Nagy. "But at that time, anyone who suggested they could be some kind of an enforcer was valuable."

Fleiss (who has little bad to say about Cookie) says she never believed his Mossad yarn but did make use of it. "I had a lot of enemies," she says. "Sometimes I needed to find out something about a girl, and he'd help me."

He and his friends would wait around for the girls to come home and then sneak up on them and say, "When are you going to go see Heidi?' " recalls one source. "They killed one girl's cat."

·   ·   ·

As Fleiss's "enforcer," Cookie had found a place for himself in the Hollywood scene. But he quickly came to realize that the role was limiting. He had a legendary libido—"He could fuck all day," says one source—but being feared didn't get you much action that you didn't have to pay for. Nor did it command respect. While dapper johns like Charlie Sheen were whisked into the clubs with the Fleiss posse, Cookie had to stand in line with the rest of the losers.

But not for long. If there was one thing his days with Fleiss seems to have drilled into Cookie's head, it was this: girls are the universal currency; they're accepted anywhere, and the more you have the more powerful you become. Soon, Cookie's services to Fleiss involved more than just security. He began recruiting women for her, picking one girl up outside a Western Union by offering to shoot modeling photos. Cookie also ingratiated himself with women by providing them with drugs. "Sometimes guys would request drugs from the girls," says the source, "mostly coke and 'ludes."

The official federal case against Cookie, which charges him as the leader of an international ecstasy-smuggling conspiracy, involves offenses committed only between 1998 and 2000. But law-enforcement sources say he was operating well before that. "He began moving a lot of cocaine in the early nineties," says one source at Customs.

Fleiss refuses to comment on the drug allegations, but doesn't deny Cookie was pimping for her. "He knew a lot of really cute girls," she says. "Some needed money, a little makeover. I turned these girls into millionaires, and they loved Cookie for the intro-duction. I paid him, on average, $500 a girl."

Around this time, Cookie moved out of his dingy apartment and into a swanky high-rise just off Sunset Boulevard. He was now in the heart of Hollywood, where self-invention is standard operating procedure. But he soon learned that trying to prove you're legit in an illegitimate world can also be dangerous. Within a year, his new twelfth-floor bachelor pad became the scene of an incident that nearly sidelined him before he became a true contender.

In February 1993, Cookie began spending time with a beautiful twenty-two-year-old named Laurie Dolan. They'd known each other about two weeks when Cookie showed up at her apartment one evening in a limousine and whisked her and another young woman to dinner at the popular fashionista hangout Tatou. "She called me from there," remembers her father, Paul. "It was obvious that she was out partying, but she said, 'Dad, I'll be all right.'"

After dinner, the group showed up at their regular hangout, Bar One, where Cookie was now a part owner—no more waiting in line for him. He made a show of buying buckets of the best champagne before heading back to his apartment with Dolan and two other women. ("He always liked three or four women in his bed," says one former associate. "It was like Caligula every night.")

Dolan surfaced around 5 P.M. the next day, when Cookie left her comatose body at Cedars-Sinai Medical Center. She never regained consciousness and three days later was pronounced dead, the victim of a massive drug overdose. An investigation into the death didn't begin in earnest until four months later, in the wake of Fleiss's June arrest. When the media put together the Fleiss-Cookie-Dolan connection, the mysterious death of one of Heidi's supposed call girls became fodder for *Hard Copy* and tabloid headlines all the way to London.

Fleiss claims that she never met Dolan. But perhaps it would have been only a matter of time. "A girl like Laurie Dolan was worth fifty thousand dollars to Heidi," says Nagy. "She was gorgeous, natural, young." Nonetheless, the investigation into her death was dropped after witnesses refused to speak to authorities, and Cookie was never charged. That fact hasn't changed the mind of her father. "He should have been arrested for murder," says Paul

Dolan. "He took away Laurie's innocence, her beauty, her life. This is what he did for a living. He drugged girls up, got them hooked and turned them into prostitutes."

As the Fleiss affair filled the tabloids in the fall of 1993, casual acquaintances began to reconsider their association with the woman the New York Post called "the Heidi Ho." For Cookie, who appeared by that time to be using the Fleiss scene as cover for his growing drug business, their relationship meant danger.

As L.A. burned, Cookie split town. For several months, he began showing up nightly in the high-end strip clubs in New York City and Las Vegas, throwing his money around like a sultan. "He would drop ten thousand to twenty thousand a night," says the owner of a New York club.

But in 1994, three clubs he frequented barred him from their premises. "He was soliciting the women," says one of the New York managers who banned him. "He liked the bisexual ones with big tits. He'd tell them, 'I'll take you shopping tomorrow. We'll go out to eat.' Soon, they were on his payroll and not coming to work anymore. I thought he was a pimp, not a drug dealer."

With Cookie, who left almost no paper trail and few documents registered to his name, it was always hard to tell. While he appeared to be angling to succeed Fleiss—at least outside California—back in L.A., he was returning to his straight sales roots. A year earlier, he'd opened a pager store called J&J Beepers, and in 1994, he began a major promotional campaign. According to his own newspaper and radio ads, Cookie was now the "Beeper King" of Los Angeles.

But if Cookie was really looking to go clean, he chose an odd location for his headquarters. J&J Beepers—a narrow storefront in a small strip mall—was at the corner of Sunset and La Brea, ground zero for drugs and prostitution. "There could only be two reasons he would open a store there," says a source close to the Fleiss investigation. "One, he wanted to move in on the drug market, or two, he wanted to become a police informant to stay out of trouble."

Neither Cookie's lawyers nor the federal government will address the rumors that Cookie was an informant, but it's clear that he was able to track the phone calls of every pimp, floozy and drug pusher he sold a beeper to. "They had some technology that enabled them to monitor the phone numbers of all the calls coming in and out," says a source who saw "these huge call logs."

Cookie's connections to strippers and small-time pushers may not seem significant, but within a few years, court papers show, many of them had become part of a multitiered, multinational organization that would blow away its competition in the ecstasy trade. And like any successful businessman, Cookie wasn't only looking for help from below. By utilizing all of his new connections— from Fleiss's moneyed associates to the Israeli community on both coasts to his ever-growing stable of strippers—he began to shore up ties to big money. In Los Angeles, he befriended Judah Hertz, a multimillionaire developer, who paid Cookie hundreds of thousands of dollars in the mid-nineties in what he says were real-estate-broker fees. And in New York, Cookie was frequently seen at the fancy flesh pits with Sholam Weiss, a New York–based Israeli plumbing magnate who would later be convicted, along with John Gotti Jr., in a $450 million life-insurance scam. Weiss was sentenced to 845 years in prison, the longest federal sentence in U.S. history.

"Cookie had access to big, big money," says a Customs agent close to the investigation. "We suspect this was one way he funded his drug purchases."

.   .   .

By 1996, ecstasy had become the drug of the decade, and Hollywood was the world's biggest market for the love pills. The area known as Sunset Plaza turned into a showroom for the world drug trade's new aristocracy. On a typical afternoon, Ferraris and Porsches were lined up along the street, and a group of immigrants, including the young Egyptian cousins John and Tamer Ibrahim, would be dining out in the sun under bright-colored umbrellas, fighting for the check.

At the time, according to Customs and DEA sources, Cookie was still primarily a coke dealer. But it was this younger group that got in on the ecstasy trade first, and they flaunted the rewards, flashing $50,000 Rolex watches. Cookie seemed to view these upstarts as a threat. One night, he hired a cameraman to film him presiding over a lavish dinner party at the model lounge the Gate, and he bought his own VIP table at the popular dance spot the Key Club.

Cookie burnished his godfather reputation away from the clubs as well. According to a source close to the investigation, he kept a safe in his apartment stacked with cash; selected female guests were invited to grab as much as they could with one fist in exchange for sexual favors. But, Cookie quickly realized, it was ecstasy, not cocaine, that could keep your coffers stocked. What could be bought from a lab for a dollar could be resold for eight times that amount to street dealers (who then resold the pills at clubs for as much as $40 each).

According to documents seized by the feds, Cookie began making frequent trips to Amsterdam, where he set up a connection with a Dutch chemist who had a lab in an industrial building north of the city. The ecstasy trade was quickly consolidating as well-connected players staked out their markets. The alleged smuggler Oded Tuito, an Israeli, was already said to control much of Miami. Tuito also had a major piece of the New York market, along with

Ilan Zarger (also an Israeli), who was the head of BTS, the notorious Brooklyn Terror Squad infamous for beating and robbing clubgoers and other dealers to insure their dominance of the market.

But as ruthless and conniving as those players were, Cookie would ultimately outwit and outplay them. Several people contacted for this story claim Cookie was "all bark and no bite." But sometimes his bark was enough. "Blackmail is a powerful tool," says one, and Cookie wasn't above using it against even his mightiest money connections. In 1996, he shook more than $200,000 out of one wealthy associate by threatening to show his wife videotapes of the man having sex with prostitutes.

The deposition of one of the members of his organization, forty-four-year-old Melissa Schwartz, shows how Cookie roped in lower-level deputies while squashing the competition. Schwartz met Cookie through another acquaintance in the fall of 1998 in Amsterdam, according to a sworn statement she later made to French authorities. She was deeply distressed at the time over the fact that a man she called Victor had asked her to smuggle ecstasy back to the States. "Cookie told me not to transport the package, and that he would take care of me," she stated. "He sent someone to take the package from me."

When Schwartz returned to New York sans ecstasy, Victor and his contacts were furious. "They threatened to mutilate me, to hurt my family," Schwartz told investigators. They robbed her and told her to stay in her hotel room. She called Cookie in Europe, who persuaded her to call the police. When Victor returned to the hotel, he was arrested. "This made me feel closer to Cookie," Schwartz said. "From then on, he took care of me financially, but also morally."

Cookie invited Schwartz to Paris, where they stayed at the Hôtel California, a luxury bed-and-breakfast off the Champs-Elysées. "We spent a few weeks together, had a good time going to discos, nice restaurants," Schwartz told investigators. "But one day Cookie became mean, and he even told me that without him I would be dead, and that I owed him for everything he had done for me."

Schwartz became one of as many as fifty people who went to work for Cookie's organization, which federal investigators say started smuggling and selling ecstasy in the summer of 1997. "Cookie's organization had three layers of people who were tasked to do different things," says a source at Customs. "He removed himself from actually touching the drugs but not from knowing what was coming in and where it was going." The drugs would be picked up in Amsterdam from contacts for Cookie's chemist. Someone would then drive them to Paris, where they would be packed inside socks and toys by people like Schwartz. About sixty thousand pills were hidden in each false-bottom suitcase that couriers carried on flights into Los Angeles, Houston and New York.

But it wasn't until early 1999 that Cookie's business began to boom, soon after a confidential tip led authorities in France to arrest Oded Tuito. Coincidentally or not, a beeper Tuito carried was traced back to Cookie's store in Los Angeles.

Cookie's operation quickly expanded to Tuito's territory on the East Coast, primarily in Miami, where he was soon a regular on the club scene. He also made significant inroads in New York by hooking up with the Zarger/BTS organization, some of whose members came to believe that Cookie was the "head of the Israeli mafia." When Sammy Gravano, then living in the witness-protection program in Arizona as Jimmy Moran, got into the ecstasy business and had one of his men beat up Zarger's connection in Arizona, the response was appropriately moblike. Cookie's associates sent a hit man nicknamed Macho to Phoenix, according to court documents, where he was "standing by to whack Gravano"—a man who has confessed to killing nineteen people himself. But ultimately, at a Cosa Nostra–style powwow, it was Cookie's men who blinked first. "I own Arizona—it's locked down," Gravano is said to have told his

Israeli rivals. They agreed to give Gravano a 25-cent tariff on every pill sold on his turf.

It was a drop in the bucket compared with what was coming in. "Cookie made millions," says the Customs source. "A lot of it went back to his mother in Israel. He owns some apartment buildings there."

After an anonymous tip in 1999 led feds to take down L.A. ecstasy king Tamer Ibrahim (who has not been tried), rumors began flying through the L.A. scene that Cookie was a rat. And as anyone in the underworld can tell you, when that happens, it's a slippery slope to the end.

On July 4, 1999, a stripper carrying pills for Cookie was busted by Customs coming into LAX. Five days later, two more went down, and the Customs-led "Operation Paris Express" went full tilt with cooperation from the DEA as well as officials in the Netherlands, France and Israel.

Cookie should have quit while he was ahead, but it doesn't appear he considered that to be an option. "You know, there's a reason we always get them," says a DEA agent who worked the case, "and that's greed. They have a million, they want two million. They have ten, they want twenty. They have control in Los Angeles, they want New York. The only way that they get out of this business is when we arrest them. They don't retire."

Cookie could feel the heat. Around this time, he applied for and was granted U.S. citizenship. The name he gave himself on his new papers: Tony Evans. He also changed all his phone and beeper numbers and relocated himself to a high-rise in New York. But he wasn't quitting.

Instead, Cookie overhauled his organization from top to bottom, putting in new lieutenants who knew less about his involvement and masterminding a new plan for the couriers. If they were looking for strippers, he figured, he would send strippers. Only this time, they would be decoys. Meanwhile, the same flights, from Paris to JFK and LAX, would have people on them he thought would never be suspected of toting drugs: Hasidic Jews in black jackets and high hats, and hillbillies with kids. "Cookie knew how to play the game," admits the Customs source. One couple from Texas was nabbed traveling with their retarded teenage son. "They said we'd get more money if we took a kid," says a twenty-five-year-old woman who turned herself in after smuggling drugs with her infant son in tow.

In March 2000, Cookie made his last trip to L.A., where he led a Passover service and feast for forty friends and family in the conference room of his apartment building. The same week, French authorities raided the stash house he'd leased (under another name) in Paris, and three of the highest-ranking members of Cookie's organization—including Melissa Schwartz, who had worked her way up the ladder—were arrested. "Our investigation started from the bottom and worked its way all the way up," says Boyd, the Customs spokesperson. "All paths led back to Cookie."

On June 27, 2001, after fifteen months in custody, Cookie finally decided to give up his game and plead guilty to the seemingly unbeatable charges of operating a continuing criminal enterprise and conspiracy to distribute ecstasy.

As he was led into the courtroom at the federal courthouse in Brooklyn, Customs and DEA agents clucked at the sight of the almost unrecognizable religious penitent before them. There was Cookie, a short wisp of a guy with dark olive skin, a fishlike face with bulging green eyes, a well-trimmed salt-and-pepper beard and a yarmulke. Were it not for the fact that he wore drab, blue federal-issue clothing, he could have been going to temple for a prayer service.

Cookie stood motionless with his hands clasped behind his back as Judge John Gleeson, who'd presided over dozens of cases involving Israelis and ecstasy, handled the thirty-minute proceeding. Nothing Cookie had done in years seemed so bland and uninteresting. But in the world of drug trafficking, this was as symbolic a moment as any. "It's the end of an era," says Cookie's former attorney Ronald Richards, who has represented more ecstasy cases than anyone. "You'll never see individual dealers getting this much power in the ecstasy trade again."

While Gleeson sternly read the charge, Cookie actually seemed to be shrinking. There were no family members or friends in attendance, and he made no statement other than a brief acknowledgment of his role in the conspiracy for which he would be sentenced to between fourteen and seventeen years in the States, after which he will be extradited to France, where he stands to serve another twenty. At one point while Cookie read his statement, his voice was so quiet and heavily accented that the judge had to ask him to move closer to the stenographer.

Los Angeles's boisterous sugar daddy was dead and gone. But he hadn't retired. "I just want to make things right for myself, my family, and my God," Cookie tells me later through his lawyer. After all he'd been through, he wasn't going to be just another inmate. Cookie, a.k.a. #54737053, was now also a rabbi.

* * *

Sometime between 1999 and 2000, I began to take notice of newspaper reports detailing the increasing number of federal ecstasy seizures. But what caught my eye was not just that large-scale ecstasy distribution had become a business with a higher profit margin than even that of cocaine, but also that, oddly, a disproportionate percentage of the biggest dealers who were being nabbed were Israeli. So when my editor at Details *called and asked what I thought about pursuing a piece on Israeli immigrant and Hollywood scenester Jacob "Cookie" Orgad—reported to be the largest-ever importer of the love drug into the United States—I signed on immediately.*

Cookie's story turned out to be even more intriguing than I'd expected. Aside from his connections to Heidi Fleiss and Sammy "the Bull" Gravano, my head was spinning from the get-go because of the incredible dichotomy of impressions I was getting about the enigmatic drug lord. Many who knew Cookie practically trembled at the mention of his name, often refusing to speak to me for fear of their own safety. They believed he was the head of the Israeli mafia, an associate of Pablo Escobar, a member of Mossad, Israel's elite intelligence agency. Yet others roundly dismissed him as a lowlife, a cheeseball, a hanger-on. With any story, it's imperative to size up your sources in order to determine their disposition and reliability, and with this story that was made more confusing—but ultimately more interesting—by the fact that much of the West Hollywood scene Cookie inhabited exists in an almost half-conscious state that doesn't distinguish between rumor and truth. Cookie's genius, I soon realized, was his ability to exploit the opportunities that this vapid world offered. Like a slick Madison Avenue image maker, he slowly began, in the early-to-mid-nineties, to simply invent himself as a godfather-like kingpin on the basis of nothing but hot air. Within several years it paid off: he was running a multimillion-dollar empire that controlled much of the ecstasy coming into the United States. When I finally got to see Cookie (a.k.a. Tony Evans) up close, at the June 2001 hearing in Brooklyn Federal Court in which he pleaded guilty (a hearing that took place while I was still in L.A. and for which I jumped on a red-eye within an hour of being notified of his decision to plea), Cookie looked so small and unintimidating that I couldn't help but think of a helium balloon that had leaked and shriveled back to its original size.

THE DAY OF THE ATTACK
NANCY GIBBS

If you want to humble an empire it makes sense to maim its cathedrals. They are symbols of its faith, and when they crumple and burn, it tells us we are not so powerful and we can't be safe. The Twin Towers of the World Trade Center, planted at the base of Manhattan Island with the Statue of Liberty as their sentry, and the Pentagon, a squat, concrete fort on the banks of the Potomac, are the sanctuaries of money and power that our enemies may imagine define us. But that assumes our faith rests on what we can buy and build, and that has never been America's true God.

On a normal day, we value heroism because it is uncommon. On September 11, we valued heroism because it was everywhere. The firefighters kept climbing the stairs of the tallest buildings in town, even as the steel moaned and the cracks spread in zippers through the walls, to get to the people trapped in the sky. We don't know yet how many of them died, but once we know, as Mayor Rudy Giuliani said, "it will be more than we can bear." That sentiment was played out in miniature in the streets, where fleeing victims pulled the wounded to safety, and at every hospital, where the lines to give blood looped round and round the block. At the medical-supply companies, which sent supplies without being asked. At Verizon, where a worker threw on a New York Fire Department jacket to go save people. And then again and again all across the country, as people checked on those they loved to find out if they were safe and then looked for some way to help.

This was the bloodiest day on American soil since our Civil War, a modern Antietam played out in real time, on fast forward, and not with soldiers but with secretaries, security guards, lawyers, bankers, janitors. It was strange that a day of war was a day we stood still. We couldn't move—that must have been the whole idea—so we had no choice but to watch. Every city catalogued its targets; residents looked at their skylines, wondering if they would be different in the morning. The Sears Tower in Chicago was evacuated, as were colleges and museums. Disney World shut down, and major league baseball canceled its games, and nuclear power plants went to top security status; the Hoover Dam and the Mall of America shut down, and Independence Hall in Philadelphia, and Mount Rushmore. It was as though someone had taken a huge brush and painted a bull's-eye around every place Americans gather, every icon we revere, every service we depend on, and vowed to take them out or shut them down, or force us to do it ourselves.

Terror works like a musical composition, so many instruments, all in tune, playing perfectly together to create their desired effect. Sorrow and horror, and fear. The first plane is just to get our attention. Then, once we are transfixed, the second plane comes and repeats the theme until the blinding coda of smoke and debris crumbles on top of the rescue workers who have gone in to try to save anyone who survived the opening movements. And we watch, speechless, as the sirens, like some awful choir, hour after hour let you know that it is not over yet, wait, there's more.

It was, of course, a perfect day, seventy degrees and flawless skies, perfect for a nervous pilot who has stolen a huge jet and intends to turn it into a missile. It was a Boeing 767 from Boston, American

Airlines flight 11 bound for Los Angeles with eighty-one passengers, that first got the attention of air traffic controllers. The plane took off at 7:59 A.M. and headed west, over the Adirondacks, before taking a sudden turn south and diving down toward the heart of New York City. Meanwhile, American flight 757 had left Dulles; United flight 175 left Boston at 7:58; and United flight 93 left Newark three minutes later, bound for San Francisco. All climbed into beautiful clear skies, all four planes on transcontinental flights, plump with fuel, ripe to explode. "They couldn't carry anything—other than an atom bomb—that could be as bad as what they were flying," observed a veteran investigator.

The first plane hit the World Trade Center's north tower at 8:45, ripping through the building's skin and setting its upper floors ablaze. People thought it was a sonic boom, or a construction accident, or freak lightning on a lovely fall day; at worst, a horrible airline accident, a plane losing altitude, out of control, a pilot trying to ditch in the river and missing. But as the gruesome rains came— bits of plane, a tire, office furniture, glass, a hand, a leg, whole bodies, began falling all around—people in the streets all stopped and looked, and fell silent. As the smoke rose, the ash rained gently down, along with a whole lost flock of paper shuffling down from the sky to the street below, edges charred, plane tickets and account statements and bills and reports and volumes and volumes of unfinished business floating down to earth.

Almost instantly, a distant wail of sirens came from all directions, even as people poured from the building, even as a second plane bore down on lower Manhattan. Louis Garcia was among the first medics on the scene. "There were people running over to us burnt from head to toe. Their hair was burned off. There were compound fractures, arms and legs sticking out of the skin. One guy had no hair left on his head." Of the six patients in his first ambulance run, two died on the way to St. Vincent's Hospital.

The survivors of the first plot to bring down the Twin Towers, the botched attempt in 1993 that left six dead, had a great advantage over their colleagues. When the first explosion came, they knew to get out. Others were paralyzed by the noise, confused by the instructions. Consultant Andy Perry still has the reflexes. He grabbed his pal Nathan Shields from his office, and they began to run down forty-six flights. With each passing floor more and more people joined the flow down the steps. The lights stayed on, but the lower stairs were filled with water from burst pipes and sprinklers. "Everyone watch your step," people called out. "Be careful!" The smell of jet fuel suffused the building. Hallways collapsed, flames shot out of a men's room. By the time they reached the lobby, they just wanted to get out—but the streets didn't look any safer. "It was chaos out there," Shields says. "Finally we ran for it." They raced into the street in time to see the second plane bearing down. Even as they ran away, there were still people standing around in the lobby waiting to be told what to do. "There were no emergency announcements—it just happened so quickly nobody knew what was going on," says Perry. "This guy we were talking to saw at least twelve people jumping out of [the tower] because of the fires. He was standing next to a guy who got hit by shrapnel and was immediately killed." Workers tore off their shirts to make bandages and tourniquets for the wounded; others used bits of clothing as masks to help them breathe. Whole stretches of street were slick with blood, and up and down the avenues you could hear the screams of people plunging from the burning tower. People watched in horror as a man tried to shimmy down the outside of the tower. He made it about three floors before flipping backward to the ground.

Architect Bob Shelton had his foot in a cast; he'd broken it falling off a curb two weeks ago. He heard the explosion of the first plane hitting the north tower from his fifty-sixth-floor office in the south tower. As he made his way down the stairwell, his building came under attack as well. "You could hear the building cracking. It sounded like when you have a bunch of spaghetti, and you break it in half to boil it." Shelton knew that what he was hearing was bad. "It was structural failure," Shelton says. "Once a building like that is off center, that's it." "There was no panic," he says of his escape down the stairs. "We were working as a team, helping everyone along the way. Someone carried my crutches, and I supported myself on the railing."

Gilbert Richard Ramirez works for the BlueCross BlueShield on the twentieth floor of the north tower. After the explosion he ran to the windows and saw the debris falling, and sheets of white building material, and then something else. "There was a body. It looked like a man's body, a full-size man." The features were indistinguishable as it fell: the body was black, apparently charred. Someone pulled an emergency alarm switch, but nothing happened. Someone else broke into the emergency phone, but it was dead. People began to say their prayers.

"Relax, we're going to get out of here," Ramirez said. "I was telling them, 'Breathe, breathe, Christ is on our side, we're gonna get out of here.'" He prodded everyone out the door, herding stragglers. It was an eerie walk down the smoky stairs, a path to safety that ran through the suffering. They saw people who had been badly burned. Their skin, he says, "was like a grayish color, and it was like dripping, or peeling, like the skin was peeling off their body." One woman was screaming. "She said she lost her friend, her friend went out the window, a gust sucked her out." As they descended, they were passed by fire fighters and rescue workers, panting, pushing their way up the stairs in their heavy boots and gear. "At least fifty of them must have passed us," says Ramirez. "I told them, 'Do a good job.'" He pauses. "I saw those guys one time, but they're not gonna be there again." When he got outside to the street there were bodies scattered on the ground, and then another came plummeting, and another. "Every time I looked up at the building, some-body was jumping from it. Like from 107, Windows on the World. There was one, and then another one. I couldn't understand their jumping. I guess they couldn't see any hope."

The terror triggered other reactions besides heroism. Robert Falcon worked in the parking garage at the towers. "When the blast shook it went dark and we all went down, and I had a flashlight and everyone was screaming at me. People were ripping my shirt to try and get to my flashlight, and they were crushing me. The whole crowd was on top of me wanting the flashlight."

Michael Otten, an assistant vice president of Mizuho Capital Markets, was headed down the stairs around the forty-sixth floor when the announcement came over the loudspeakers that the south tower was secure, people could go back to their desks or leave the building. He proceeded to the forty-fourth floor, an elevator-transfer floor. One elevator loaded up and headed down, then came back empty, so he and a crowd of others piled in. One man's backpack kept the doors from closing. The seconds ticked by. "We wanted to say something, but the worst thing you can do is go against each other, and just as I thought it was going to close, it was about nine, nine-oh-three, whenever it was that the second plane crashed into the building. The walls of the elevator caved in; they fell on a couple people." Otten and others groped through the dust to find a stairway, but the doors were locked. Finally they found a clearer passage, found a stairway they could get into and fled down to the street.

Even as people streamed down the stairs, the cracks were appearing in the walls as the building shuddered and cringed. Steam pipes burst, and at one point an elevator door burst open and a man fell out, half burned alive, his skin hanging off. People dragged him out of the elevator and helped get him out of the

building to the doctors below. "If I had listened to the announcement," says survivor Joan Feldman, "I'd be dead right now."

Felipe Oyola and his wife, Adianes, did listen to the announcement. When Oyola heard the first explosion in his office, on the
eighty-first floor of the south tower, he raced down to the seventy-
eighth floor to find her. They met at the elevator bank; she was terrified. But when the announcement came over the loudspeaker
that the tower was safe, they both went back to work. Oyola was
back on eighty-one when the second plane arrived. "As soon as I
went upstairs, I looked out the window, and I see falling debris and
people. Then the office was on top of me. I managed to escape, and
I've been looking for my wife ever since."

United flight 175 left Boston at 7:58 A.M., headed to Los Angeles.
When it passed the Massachusetts-Connecticut border, it made a
thirty-degree turn, and then an even sharper turn and swooped
down on Manhattan, between the buildings, to impale the south
tower at 9:06. This plane seemed to hit lower and harder; maybe
that's because by now every camera in the city was trained on the
towers, and the crowds in the street, refugees from the first explosion, were there to see it. Desks and chairs and people were sucked
out the windows and rained down on the streets below. Men and
women, cops and firefighters watched and wept. As fire and debris
fell, cars blew up; the air smelled of smoke and concrete, that smell
that spits out of jackhammers chewing up pavement. You could
taste the air more easily than you could breathe it.

P.S. 89 is an elementary school just up the street; most of the
families live and work in the financial district, and when bedlam
broke, mothers and fathers ran toward the school, sweat pouring off
them, frantic to get to their kids. Some people who didn't know if

their spouse had survived met up at school, because both parents went straight to the kids. "I just wanted to find my kids and my wife and get the hell off this island," said one father. And together they walked, he and his wife and young son and daughter, sixty blocks or so up to Grand Central and safety.

The first crash had changed everything; the second changed it again. Anyone who thought the first was an accident now knew better. This was not some awful, isolated episode, not Oklahoma City, not even the first World Trade Center bombing. Now this felt like a war, and the system responded accordingly; the emergency plans came out of the drawers and clicked one by one into place. The city buckled, the traffic stopped, the bridges and tunnels were shut down at 9:35 as warnings tumbled one after another; the Empire State Building was evacuated, and the Metropolitan Museum of Art, the United Nations. First the New York airports were closed, then Washington's, and then the whole country was grounded for the first time in history.

At the moment the second plane was slamming into the south tower, President Bush was being introduced to the second-graders of Emma E. Booker Elementary in Sarasota, Florida. When he arrived at the school he had been whisked into a holding room: national security adviser Condoleezza Rice needed to speak to him. But he soon appeared in the classroom and listened appreciatively as the children went through their reading drill. As he was getting ready to pose for pictures with the teachers and kids, chief of staff Andy Card entered the room, walked over to the president and whispered in his right ear. The president's face became visibly tense and serious. He nodded. Card left and for several minutes the president seemed distracted and somber, but then he resumed his interaction with the class. "Really good readers, whew!" he told them. "These must be sixth-graders!"

Meanwhile, in the room where Bush was scheduled to give his

remarks, about two hundred people, including local officials, school personnel and students, waited under the hot lights. Word of the crash began to circulate; reporters called their editors, but details were sparse—until someone remembered there was a TV in a nearby office. The president finally entered, about thirty-five minutes late, and made his brief comments. "This is a difficult time for America," he began. He ordered a massive investigation to "hunt down the folks who committed this act." Meanwhile the bomb dogs took a few extra passes through Air Force One, and an extra fighter escort was added. But the president too was going to have trouble getting home.

Even as the president spoke, the second front opened. Having hit the country's financial and cultural heart, the killers went for its political and military muscles. David Marra, twenty-three, an information-technology specialist, had turned his BMW off an I-395 exit to the highway just west of the Pentagon when he saw an American Airlines jet swooping in, its wings wobbly, looking like it was going to slam right into the Pentagon: "It was fifty feet off the deck when he came in. It sounded like the pilot had the throttle completely floored. The plane rolled left and then rolled right. Then he caught an edge of his wing on the ground." There is a helicopter pad right in front of the side of the Pentagon. The wing touched there, then the plane cartwheeled into the building.

Two minutes later, a "credible threat" forced the evacuation of the White House, and eventually State and Justice and all the federal office buildings. Secret Service officers had automatic weapons drawn as they patrolled Lafayette Park, across from the White House. Police-car radios crackled with reports that rogue airplanes had been spotted over the White House. The planes turned out to be harmless civilian aircraft that air-traffic controllers at National Airport were scrambling to help land so they could clear the air space over the nation's capital.

But that was not all; there was a third front as well. At 9:58 the

Westmoreland County emergency-operations center, thirty-five miles southeast of Pittsburgh, received a frantic cell-phone call from a man who said he was locked in the rest room aboard United flight 93. Glenn Cramer, the dispatch supervisor, said the man was distraught and kept repeating, "We are being hijacked! We are being hijacked!" He also said this was not a hoax, and that the plane "was going down." Said Cramer: "He heard some sort of explosion and saw white smoke coming from the plane. Then we lost contact with him."

The flight had taken off at 8:01 from Newark, New Jersey, bound for San Francisco. But as it passed south of Cleveland, Ohio, it took a sudden, violent left turn and headed inexplicably back into Pennsylvania. As the 757 and its thirty-eight passengers and seven crew members blew past Pittsburgh, air-traffic controllers tried frantically to raise the crew via radio. There was no response.

Forty miles farther down the new flight path, in rural Somerset County, Terry Butler, forty, was pulling the radiator from a gray 1992 Dodge Caravan at the junkyard where he works. He had been watching the news and knew all flights were supposed to be grounded. He was stunned when he looked up in the sky and saw flight 93 cutting through the lingering morning fog. "It was moving like you wouldn't believe," he said.

The rogue plane soared over woodland, cattle pastures and cornfields until it passed over Kelly Leverknight's home. She too was watching the news. Her husband, on his regular tour of duty with the Air National Guard's 167th Airlift Wing in Martinsburg, West Virginia, had just called to reassure his wife that his base was still operating normally when she heard the plane rush by. "It was headed toward the school," she said, the school where her three children were.

Had flight 93 stayed aloft a few seconds longer, it would have plowed into Shanksville-Stonycreek School and its 501 students, grades K through twelve. Instead, at 10:06 A.M., the plane smashed into a reclaimed section of an old coal strip mine. The largest pieces of the plane still extant are barely bigger than a telephone book. "I just keep thinking—two miles," said elementary principal Rosemarie Tipton. "There but for the grace of God—two miles."

CIA director George Tenet was having a leisurely breakfast with his mentor, former senator David Boren, at the St. Regis Hotel, when he got the news. Their omelettes had just arrived when Tenet's security detail descended with a cell phone. "Give me the quick summary," Tenet said calmly into the phone. He listened a few moments, and then told Boren: "The World Trade Center has been hit. We're pretty sure it wasn't an accident. It looks like a terrorist act." He then got back to the phone, named a dozen people he wanted summoned to the CIA situation room. "Assemble them in fifteen minutes," he said. "I should almost be there by then."

Vice President Dick Cheney was in his West Wing office when the Secret Service burst in, physically hurrying him out of the room. "We have to move; we're moving now, sir; we're moving," the agents said as they took him to a bunker on the White House grounds. Once there, with members of the National Security staff and administration officials, they told Cheney that a plane was headed for the White House. Mrs. Cheney and Laura Bush were brought in as well. Staff members in the Old Executive Office Building, across the street from the White House, were huddled in front of their TV screens when they heard from TV reporters that they were being evacuated. Then the tape loop began. "The building is being evacuated. Please walk to the nearest exit." "The looks were stone-faced," a staff member to the vice president said. "They were just zombies," said another.

Senator Patrick Leahy of Vermont was heading to the Supreme

Court building to speak to a group of appellate judges. He had already heard the news from New York City. As he walked into the court building, he heard a muffled boom outside. It was the plane attacking the Pentagon. "I've got to tell you before we start there's some horrible, horrible news coming in," Leahy told the roomful of judges. By the time he was leaving the building, there were already twenty cops surrounding it. As he neared the Russell Senate Office Building, a Capitol policeman walked up. "Senator, I don't know if you want to go back to your office," he warned. "They're evacuating the buildings."

"I've got a lot of staff still working there," Leahy snapped. "I'm not going to leave them in the building."

Washington was supposed to have contingency plans for disasters like this, but the chaos on the streets was clear evidence that plans still needed work. By 10:45 A.M. the downtown streets around the Capitol, government buildings and White House were laced with cars pointing in every direction, unable to move. A security officer for one of the buildings sat on a park bench. He had been locked out of his building, so he didn't have a clue if the senior officials inside were out and in a safe place. "I'm not surprised at this," he said. "We aren't prepared. We were supposed to have a plan to evacuate our Cabinet officer to a place fifty miles out, but none of that has been done." Capitol police were slow to move as well. There was no increased security, no heightened alert around the Capitol for fully half an hour after the New York attack. Senate minority leader Trent Lott was drafting a press release to condemn the attack when he looked outside his window and saw black smoke billowing up from across the Potomac. He didn't wait for an evacuation order. He gathered up his top staff and security detail and headed out of the Capitol, shocked to find that tourists were still walking into the building while he was fleeing it.

Senator Robert Byrd, the Senate's president pro tempore and

fourth in line to the presidency, was put in a chauffeured car and driven to a safe house, as were Speaker Dennis Hastert and other congressional leaders. There were rumors flying that the fourth plane, the one that went down in Pennsylvania, had been headed for the Capitol or Camp David. The safe houses are scattered throughout the Washington, northern Virginia and southern Maryland area. The Secret Service has similar safe houses where they can take the vice president and other top administration officials as well. They are homes, offices, in some cases even fire stations, that have secure phones so that the leaders can still communicate.

By 11 A.M., the streets in Washington were gridlocked with people trying to get out. In a place that doesn't tend to carpool, coworkers had stuffed themselves into available vehicles. Both the Fourteenth Street Bridge and Arlington Memorial Bridge, leading to Virginia and past the Pentagon, had been closed, as were the airports and Union Station. On the corner of Constitution Avenue and Fourteenth Street, day-care workers from the Ronald Reagan Building clutched frightened toddlers in a tight bunch. Hysteria was gripping the city: senior generals at the Pentagon phoned children and other relatives, warning them not to drink tap water for the next thirty-six hours. They feared reservoirs might be poisoned.

Fed chairman Alan Greenspan was flying back to the United States from Switzerland when his airliner was ordered to turn back. He reached vice chairman Roger Ferguson by phone as soon as he could, and Ferguson coordinated contacts with Reserve banks and governors both in Washington and around the country. The goal: to make sure U.S. banks would keep functioning.

Meanwhile, the mood on board Air Force One could not have been more tense. Bush was in his office in the front of the plane, on the phone with Cheney, national security adviser Rice, FBI director Robert Mueller and the First Lady. Cheney told him that law-enforcement and security agencies believed the White House and Air Force One were both targets. Bush, the vice president insisted, should head to a safe military base as soon as possible. White House staff members, air force flight attendants and Secret Service agents all were subdued and shaken. One agent sadly reported that the Secret Service field office in New York City, with its two hundred agents, was located in the World Trade Center. The plane's TV monitors were tuned in to local news broadcasts; Bush was watching as the second tower collapsed. About forty-five minutes after takeoff, a decision was made to fly to Offut Air Force Base in Nebraska, site of the nation's nuclear command and one of the most secure military installations in the country. But Bush and his aides didn't want to wait that long before the president could make a public statement. Secret Service officials and military advisers in Washington consulted a map and chose a spot for Bush to make a brief touchdown: Barksdale Air Force Base, outside of Shreveport, Louisiana. In Bush's airborne office, aides milled about while Bush spoke on the phone. "That's what we're paid for, boys," he said. "We're gonna take care of this. We're going to find out who did this. They're not going to like me as president." The handful of reporters aboard were told not to use their cell phones—and not even to turn them on—because the signals might allow someone to identify the plane's location.

Air Force One landed at Barksdale at 11:45 A.M., with fighter jets hovering beside each wing throughout the descent. The perimeter was surrounded by air force personnel in full combat gear: green fatigues, flak jackets, helmets, M-16s at the ready. The small motorcade traveled to building 245. A sign on the glass windows of several doors, in large black type, read DEFCON DELTA. That is the highest possible state of military alert. Bush made his second remarks at 12:36 from a windowless conference room, in front of two American flags dragged together by air force privates. "Freedom itself was attacked this morning by a faceless coward," he began, then spoke for two minutes before leaving the room.

In New York, the chaos was only beginning. Convoys of police vehicles raced downtown toward the cloud of smoke at the end of the avenues. The streets and parks filled with people, heads turned like sunflowers, all gazing south, at the clouds that were on the ground instead of in the sky, at the fighter jets streaking down the Hudson River. The aircraft carriers U.S.S. *John F. Kennedy* and U.S.S. *George Washington*, along with seven other warships, took up positions off the East Coast.

Jim Gartenberg, thirty-five, a commercial real estate broker with an office on the eighty-sixth floor of 1 World Trade Center, kept calling his wife, Jill, to let her know he was OK but trapped. "He let us know he was stuck," says Jill, who is pregnant with their second child. "He called several times until ten. Then nothing. He sounded calm, except for when he told me how much he loved me. He said, 'I don't know if I'll make it.' He sounded like he knew it would be one of the last times he would say he loved me." That was right before the building turned to powder.

The tower's structural strength came largely from the 244 steel girders that formed the perimeter of each floor and bore most of the weight of all the floors above. Steel starts to bend at one thousand degrees. The floors above where the plane hit—each floor weighing millions of pounds—were resting on steel that was softening from the heat of the burning jet fuel, softening until the girders could no longer bear the load above. "All that steel turns into spaghetti," explains retired ATF investigator Ronald Baughn. "And then all of a sudden that structure is untenable, and the weight starts bearing down on floors that were not designed to hold that weight, and you start having collapse." Each floor drops onto the one below, the weight becoming greater and greater, and eventually it all comes down. "It didn't topple. It came straight down. All floors are pancaking down, and there are people on those floors."

The south tower collapsed at ten, fulfilling the prophecy of eight years ago, when last the terrorists tried to bring it down. The north tower came down twenty-nine minutes later, crushing itself like a piston. "I know that the rescue people who were helping us didn't get out of the building," said security official Bill Heitman, who worked on the eightieth floor. "I know they didn't make it." And he broke down and sobbed. All that was left of the New York skyline was a chalk cloud. The towers themselves were reduced to jagged stumps; the atrium lobby arches looked like a bombed-out cathedral." A huge plume of smoke was chasing people, rushing through those winding streets of lower Manhattan," says Charlie Stuard, thirty-seven, an Internet consultant who works downtown. "It was chaos, a whiteout. That's when people really started to panic. You could see it coming. A bunch of us jumped over a rail, onto the pilings on the East River, ready to jump in."

The streets filled with masked men and women, cloth and clothing torn to tie across their noses and mouths against the dense debris rain. Some streets were eerily quiet. All trading had stopped on Wall Street, so those canyons were empty, the ash several inches thick and gray, the way snow looks in New York almost before it hits the ground. Sounds were both muffled and magnified, echoing off buildings, softened by the smoke. You could hear the chirping of the locator devices the firefighters wear, hear the whistle of the respirators, see only the lights flashing red and yellow through the haze.

Major Reginald Mebane, who heads security for one of the state court buildings, organized a group of about ten officers. They grabbed some medical equipment and hopped a court bus to help evacuate people. But when one tower began to collapse, they raced for cover inside Building Five of the Trade Center complex. The smoke made it so dark they could see only a few feet in front of them, even with flashlights. They felt their way along the walls and windows to get out. "The building just blew," says Bill Faulkner, fifty-three, a Vietnam veteran who was part of the group. "I would be dead if I hadn't jumped behind a pillar." Another court officer, Ed Kennedy, who also hid behind the pillar, says he grabbed the arm of a woman in an effort to pull her behind the pillar with him. But he didn't grab her fast enough. Suddenly he realized he was holding just an arm. It was only when a fireman broke the window in the Borders bookstore that the men were able to escape.

Firefighters pushed people farther back, back up north. Mayor Giuliani took to the streets, walking through the raining dust and ordering people to evacuate the entire lower end of the island. Medical teams performed triage on the street corners of Tribeca, doling out medical supplies and tending the walking wounded. Doctors, nurses, EMTs, even lifeguards were recruited to help. Volunteers with the least training were diverted to blood-donation centers or the dreaded "black teams," where they would not be called upon to save a life, just handle dead bodies during triage. The color code: black for dead, red for immediately life-threatening wounds, yellow for serious, non-life-threatening and green for the walking wounded. Police and firefighters realized even as they worked that hundreds of their colleagues, the first to respond, were dead. Each looked as if someone had kicked him in the stomach. A looter was arrested: he had two fire department boots on his feet, and the cops looked as if they were going to kill him.

The refugee march began at the base of the island and wound up the highways as far as you could see, tens of thousands of people with clothes dusted, faces grimy, marching northward, away from the battlefield. There was not a single smile on a single face. But there was remarkably little panic as well—more steel and ingenuity: Where am I going to sleep tonight? How will I get home? "They can't keep New Jersey closed forever," a man said. Restaurant-supply companies on the Bowery handed out wet towels. A cement mixer drove toward the Queensboro Bridge with dozens of laborers holding on to it, hitching a ride out of town. Overcrowded buses, one after another, shipped New York's workers north. Ambulances, some covered with debris, sped past them, ferrying the injured to the waiting hospitals.

All over the city, people walked with radios pinned to their ears. One man had the news on his car radio turned up as close to a hundred people surrounded the car listening to the reports. Just before noon, a radio commentator said, "Inarguably, this is the worst day in the history of New York City." No one argued.

Churches opened their sanctuaries for prayer services. St. Bartholomew's offered water and lemonade to everyone passing by. The noon Mass at St. Patrick's was nearly full. "We pray as we have never prayed before," said Monsignor Ferry. "Remember the victims today. Forgive them their sins, and bring them into the light." Posted defiantly in every window of one restaurant was the sign WE REFUSE TO GIVE IN TO TERRORISM. CIBO IS OPEN FOR BUSINESS. GOD BLESS AMERICA. A well-dressed man in a suit sat on a bench in Central Park, his head bowed, his hands clasped between his knees. A carousel of quiet toys turned in the darkened windows of FAO Schwarz.

There were no strangers in town anymore, only sudden friends, sharing names, news and phones. Lines formed, at least twenty people long, at all pay phones, because cell phones were not working. Should we go to work? Is the subway safe? "Let's all have a good look at each other," a passenger said to the others in her car. "We may be our last memory." The passengers stranded at La Guardia Airport asked one another where exactly they were supposed to go and how they were to get there. Bridges, tunnels and ferries to Manhattan were not running. Strangers were offering one another a place to wait in Queens, giving advice on good diners in Astoria. Limousine drivers offered to take passengers to Boston for a price. A vendor dispensed free bottles of water to travelers waiting in the hot sun.

Dr. Ghoong Cheigh, a kidney specialist at New York Presbyterian Hospital, was handed an "urgent notice," along with other arriving staff: "The disaster plan for New York Presbyterian Hospital is currently in effect, and an emergency command center has been established." All elective surgeries were canceled, and any patient well enough to be discharged was released to make room for the incoming wounded. At Bellevue, the city's largest trauma center, an extra burn unit was set up in the emergency room. The night shift was called in early. The psychiatric department staff, the biggest in the world, was mobilized to meet the survivors and families. "We actually have too many doctors now," chief medical officer Eric Manheimer reported in midafternoon. "We thought we would have more patients." By 5:40, only 159 patients had been admitted—which suggested not how few had been injured, but how few could be saved.

Security guards were turning all cars away from New York Weill Cornell Medical Center, allowing only emergency vehicles through. Around 10:40 a taxi pulled up, bearing three women and a man. Security tried to stop them, but a woman yelled, "We have a woman in labor here!" The guards waved them through.

At St. Vincent's Hospital in Greenwich Village they were running out of Silvadene to treat burn victims, and began raiding the local drugstores. A hospital staff member wheeled around a grocery cart with a sign on the side reading, WE NEED CLOTHING DONATIONS. Within the hour, local residents had brought dozens of shopping bags full of blazers, shoes and pants, for patients whose clothes had been burned off. Edward Cardinal Egan led a team of priests to begin giving last rites. At one point he emerged from the emergency room, wearing blue hospital scrubs. His purple robes peeked out at the collar, and over one of his blue rubber gloves he had placed his enormous gold cardinal's ring. He said, quite formally, "I am amazed at the goodness of our police and our firefighters and our hospital people."

When English teacher Karen Kriegel heard the news, she couldn't just stay in her downtown office; she had to do something. So she printed up some handmade signs that said GIVE BLOOD NOW, photocopied them at a copy shop and headed for St. Vincent's. As she started walking and handing out flyers, a hundred people started walking with her. When they reached the hospital, the gurneys were everywhere, and rolling desk chairs covered with white sheets had been brought out to the pavement to handle bodies. The chairs already looked like ghosts.

Outside the N.Y. Blood Center, the lines of prospective donors stretched halfway down the block, around the corner, all the way to Sixty-sixth Street and around that corner—more than a thousand, all told. Type O donors, the universal donors, were handed little yellow movie tickets and asked to form a separate line. Eventually some blood centers turned everyone else away, told them to come back another day. "It's just amazing," said nurse Anne Taylor, standing in the donors' line. "There'll be a three- or four-hour wait, and just look at all of these people standing here. They can't scare us." Bellevue Hospital had so many donors, it ran out of plastic bags.

The warlike mobilization was by no means left to the stricken zones. At Chalkville Elementary School near Birmingham, Alabama, more than seven hundred calls had been received from worried parents, many of whom came at midmorning to pick up their children.

Churches and schools and civic groups all around the country offered to help anyone stranded by the grounding of the nation's planes. All over Los Angeles, offices and government buildings were shut down and surrounded by police: city hall, the Federal Building in Westwood, even shopping malls. At the Federal Building, armored rescue vehicles and Ford cars ringed the entrances and exits, with FBI staffers decked out in black and brandishing MP5 assault rifles. Even Express Mail trucks were searched by the FBI before they were allowed onto the premises. Gas pipeline companies were beefing up security at key transmission stations. Grand Coulee Dam in central Washington State was locked down. Gasoline stations around the country were running out of gas as motorists rushed to top off their tanks.

In Chicago, Steve Bernard was huddled around the TV with colleagues on the thirty-sixth floor of Chicago's Sears Tower, shortly after 8 A.M., watching the smoke billowing from the World Trade Center after the first attack. When the second plane hit, bewilderment at a faraway spectacle turned into a much more personal, creeping panic. The Chicago staff of the Piper Jaffray investment firm suddenly redirected their gazes toward the windows, quietly searching for jets on their own horizon. The 110-story Sears Tower, even taller than the World Trade Center, is the tallest building in the United States; a vulnerable target. Bernard's wife called him and insisted he come home. Within an hour, the building was evacuated.

Across the country, houses of all kinds of worship filled with grieving Americans singing "America the Beautiful," wiping away streams of tears. "Humanity came apart in lower Manhattan today, and each of us is wounded. We mourn the loss of our innocence," declared Rabbi Gary Gerson at Oak Park Temple, a Reform Jewish congregation outside Chicago. "Terror has struck us, but it will not destroy us. Now we are all Israelis," he added.

Indeed, there were many Americans who refused to be intimidated by the tragedy, rightly or wrongly. They were reassuring, if not necessarily reasonable. The order to close the U.S. Courthouse in Little Rock, Arkansas, came shortly before 10 A.M., and it was promptly heeded by everyone except a solitary federal district judge. There sat Henry Woods, age eighty-three, his lined face framed by a mane of white hair, beneath a replica of the seal of the United States. Around him, at his insistence, a jury and lawyers carried on in a damage suit stemming from, of all things, a 1999 American Airlines crash. "This looks like an intelligent jury to me," Woods said, explaining his refusal to grant a mistrial to the defense after getting word of the disaster. "And I didn't want the judicial system interrupted by a terrorist act, no matter how horrible."

If people all over the country had a sense of being suddenly at war—chat boards on Yahoo filled up with people wanting to volunteer for military service—it was with an enemy they could not see and not easily touch.

Meanwhile the U.S. government reassembled and mobilized. Secretary of State Colin Powell cut short his trip to Latin America to return to the United States. By midafternoon, members of Congress were calling on their leaders to summon a special session, to show the world the government was up and running. About half of the Senate convened in a conference room at the Capitol Hill police station to hear from their leaders—some to vent their outrage at President Bush. Both Democrats and Republicans wanted to know, Where is he? Why isn't he here? Why isn't he in New York? Why isn't he talking to the country? The answer: Bush had been told by the Secret Service, the military and the FBI that it was not yet safe to return to Washington. Only twenty-four hours later, after absorbing a wave of criticism for his delayed return, did aides claim there had been "credible evidence" that the White House and Air Force One were targets.

Some Republicans on the Hill wanted to know why Counsellor Karen Hughes was the highest government official anyone saw on television all day, other than Bush's brief, unsettling appearance in Louisiana. They wanted to see Bush stride across the south lawn and show that this is not a country that can be sent into hiding by cowards. "He better have the speech of his life ready tonight," sighed one Republican strategist. Bush did return a few hours later, did stride across the south lawn and did deliver a reasonably effective national address from the Oval Office. But it wasn't until the following day that he stepped up the intensity of his rhetoric and declared the attacks "acts of war."

Tucked inside the shock and fury was dismay at the performance of others whose job—perhaps impossible—was to prevent this from happening. There were quiet calls for the heads of CIA chief Tenet and FAA boss Jane Garvey for allowing so appalling a breach of security on their watch. And there was an equal determination to find those who were behind it.

Only God knows what kind of heroic acts took place at 25,000 feet as passengers and crews contended with four teams of highly trained enemy terrorists. But it is clear that the hunt for the culprits began way up in the sky, by the doomed passengers and crews themselves, minutes before the attacks took place. In their final good-byes, on brief and haunting calls from their cell phones, the victims on board at least two of the four planes whispered the number and even some of the seat assignments of the terrorists. A flight attendant on board American flight 11 called her airline's flight operations center in Dallas on a special airlink line and reported that passengers were being stabbed.

That gave investigators a heads-up that something had gone terribly wrong, but there were plenty of other clues. Even before the smoke had cleared, it was obvious that the culprits knew their way around a Boeing cockpit—and all the security weaknesses in the U.S. civil aviation system. The enemy had chosen the quietest day of the week for the operation, when there would be fewer passengers to subdue; they had boarded westbound transcontinental flights—planes fully loaded with fuel. They were armed with knives and box cutters, had gained access to the cockpits and herded everyone to the back of the plane. Once at the controls, they had turned off at least one of the aircraft's self-identifying beacons, known as transponders, a move that renders the planes somewhat less visible to air traffic controllers. And each aircraft had gone through dramatic but carefully executed course corrections, including a stunning last maneuver by flight 77. The pilot of that plane came in low from south of the Pentagon, and pulled a 270-degree turn before slamming into the west wall of the building.

And though everyone wanted to be prudent, there weren't a lot of suspects to round up. Palestinian terror groups are experienced at suicide missions, but have never attempted an operation this large. Groups with links to the Iranian government took down the Khobar Towers in Saudi Arabia in 1996, killing nineteen, but that target was a long way from the United States. Libya has lost its taste for terror, most experts believe, and Iraq's Saddam Hussein has always favored loud, brutish force over quiet finesse. Besides, no group other than Osama bin Laden's loose-knit network of operatives in dozens of countries worldwide has ever shown the will, wallet or gall to attack the United States before. Bin Laden is responsible for the attacks on U.S. embassies in Kenya and Tanzania. Three weeks ago he told an Arab journalist he would mount an unprecedented attack on the United States. "This was well funded and well planned," said Senator Pat Roberts, who sits on the Senate Intelligence Committee. "It took a lot of planning. The weather had to be just so on the East Coast. They used sophisticated tactics where they hijacked planes, killed the crew, and they had to have aviators or navigators who knew what they were doing."

Deputy secretary of state Richard Armitage gathered his senior aides in the State Department's seventh-floor secure facility shortly after 9 A.M. Tuesday for a videoconference with the administration's top national security aides. National security adviser Rice and her top counterterrorism coordinator, Richard Clark, were on one screen, with FBI director Mueller and his senior aides, the CIA's counterterrorism director and FAA officials on others. Vice President Cheney was supposed to be in on the teleconference, but the Secret Service had already spirited him off to a safe house. "We knew we were in trouble," says one official who was present. "We've got suicide attacks here."

Rice stayed silent as the meeting progressed; Clark did most of the talking. Finally at around 9:45 A.M., aides behind Mueller started murmuring and whispering into his ear. Mueller interrupted everyone. "The Pentagon has been hit by an airplane," the FBI chief announced. All the State Department officials turned their heads to Armitage, who was running the building in Powell's absence. "Let's increase security outside the building," Armitage said calmly, seeming unperturbed. Another aide piped up. "We probably need to think about getting the hell out of here," he said. Armitage decided to evacuate, and an alternate command center was set up at the Foreign Service Institute in Arlington, Virginia. Senior State Department aides jumped in staff cars to race to Arlington but immediately ran into clogged traffic in Washington.

By Tuesday afternoon, the spooks were making progress. Eavesdroppers at the supersecret National Security Agency had picked up at least two electronic intercepts indicating the terrorists had ties to bin Laden. By nightfall, less than twelve hours after the attacks, U.S. officials told *Time* that their sense that he was involved had got closer to what one senior official said was 90 percent. The next morning, U.S. officials told *Time* they have evidence that each of the four terrorist teams had a certified pilot with them; some of these pilots had flown for an airline in Saudi Arabia and received pilot training in the United States. It's not yet clear whether the pilots were trained in the United States or in Saudi Arabia or both. Intelligence officials believe each team had four to six persons. Some team members, it is thought, crossed the Canadian border to get into the United States. Sources told *Time* that within the past few months, the FBI added to the U.S. watch list two men whom the bureau believed to be associated with one of the Islamic Jihad terror groups. Through a screwup, the suspects were lost. The two men appear to have been on the American Airlines flight 77, the plane that crashed into the Pentagon, sources told *Time*. Boston appears to have been a central hub for the operation; U.S. intelligence believes a bin Laden cell in Florida was a support group helping with the aviation aspects of the attack.

Intelligence officials poring over old reports believe they got their first inkling of planning for the attack last June, although at the time the intelligence was too vague to indicate the scale of the operation. In the summer U.S. embassies, particularly those in the Middle East, were put on heightened alert, as was the U.S. military in the region. The CIA was getting vague reports "of some kind of spectacular happenings" by terrorists, said a U.S. intelligence official, but the reports were too vague as to timing. "A lot of this reporting we had in the summer that gained our attention and had us concerned, but wasn't specific, could have been tied to this," said a U.S. intelligence official.

Even had they known more, could officials ever have contemplated the scale of this thing? The blasts were so powerful that counterterrorism teams have begun asking the airlines for fuel loads on the plane; aviation experts have been asked to calculate the explosive yield of each blast—in kiloton terms. The reason? Washington wants to see if the planes amounted to weapons of mass destruction. "What we want people to realize is they've crossed a line here," said a U.S. intelligence official. In fact, some senior administration officials are considering drafting a declaration of war, although the State Department is leery since nobody knows precisely who the war would be against.

By contrast, as the day unfolded, it looked awfully easy to declare war on us. The attack was the perfect mockery of the president's faith in missile defense: what if the missile is an American Airlines plane, and the pilot wants to kill you? It was only eight years ago that a group of zealots led by Ramzi Yousef tried to take the towers down from the bottom, with a rented Ryder truck full of homemade explosives. Their goal, as an unsigned statement presented later at trial put it, was no less than toppling "the towers that constitute the pillars of their civilization."

U.S. officials learned a great deal from that attempt, notes retired ATF investigator Baughn. But the terrorists also learned. "They learned that they had to come at it from a different attitude," Baughn says. "What they've done today was the easiest thing they could do. They didn't have to bring in any explosives. They didn't have to put a group of people together. They didn't have to go find a safe house. They didn't have to go construct anything. They didn't have to rent a truck. They didn't have to load the truck. They didn't have to drive it to some place. All they had to do was hijack an airplane." They made it look so easy, you wondered if the only reason the U.S. has not seen a hijacking in twenty years was that hardly anyone was trying. It's a wonder why not; the Microsoft flight simulator and Fly! II— the two most popular simulators for personal computers—allow you to pretend to fly between the World Trade Center towers, and into them. Anyone looking to practice can buy the software off the shelf.

. . .

At 7:30 P.M. Tuesday, with the Pentagon still in flames, the congressional leadership, with a crowd of senators and congressmen behind them, stood on the Capitol steps. "When Americans suffer and when people perpetrate acts against this country, we as a Congress and as a government must stand united, and stand together," said an angry Dennis Hastert, Speaker of the House, with Democrat Dick Gephardt standing stony silent beside him. Both parties "will stand shoulder to shoulder to fight this evil," Hastert promised. He asked everyone to bow their heads in a moment of silence. Afterward the congressmen and Senators, Republicans hugging Democrats, broke out into a chorus of "God Bless America."

As patriotism swelled, the day threatened to loop us into the kinds of barbaric blood feuds from which we've always been able to stay away. So people lashed out, getting angry at our not very humble foreign policy, complaining about a culture of ironic detachment that made us unmoved by a threat that was very real. (Though in the immediate aftermath of the attacks, pollsters found that by a huge proportion, 80 percent, Americans were ready to go to war, and prepared for the body bags that go with it.)

Whatever the outcome, it was clear that some things had changed forever. The attacks will become a defining reference point for our culture and imagination, a question of before and after, safe and scarred. By 10:30 Tuesday morning, four tourists from the Czech Republic were at the Empire State Building, buying up all the postcards with pictures of the World Trade Center on them. "Soon there will be no more of these cards also," one explained.

When one world ended at 8:45 on Tuesday morning, another was born, one we always trust in but never see, in which normal people become fierce heroes and everyone takes a test for which they haven't studied. As President Bush said in his speech to the nation, we are left with both a terrible sadness and a quiet unyielding anger. He was wrong, though, to talk of the steel of our resolve. Steel, we now know, bends and melts; we need to be made of something stronger than that now—not excluding an unseasoned president new to his job.

Do we now panic, or will we be brave? Once the dump trucks and bulldozers have cleared away the rubble and a thousand funeral Masses have been said, once the streets are swept clean of ash and glass and the stores and monuments and airports reopen, once we have begun to explain this to our children and to ourselves, what will we do? What else but build new cathedrals, and if they are bombed, build some more. Because the faith is in the act of building, not the building itself, and no amount of terror can keep us from scraping the sky.

*   *   *

I was at home in Westchester on the morning of September 11, preparing to head down into Manhattan, when the phone rang. It's a call I've gotten before, and invariably dread. No greeting. Just, "Turn on your TV."

Like the rest of the world, I didn't turn off the TV for the next thirty hours, which was roughly the window I was given to write Time's *story of the attack. The magazine's editor, Jim Kelly, called around ten. "You busy?" He was trying to figure out whether it would be possible to find enough printing capacity around the country to produce about 8 million magazines on Wednesday night, in order to get a special issue to our subscribers and newsstands on Thursday. In the meantime, every reporter, every photographer, every single member of* the magazine's staff was working the story. A squad of reporters, many of them young staff members who had not signed on as war correspondents, headed to lower Manhattan, toward Ground Zero, to the firehouses, the hospitals, the armory where victims' relatives assembled.

One of our White House correspondents, Jay Carney, was traveling on Air Force One with President Bush; he was initially not allowed to tell us exactly where he was, but he was filing through the day and night. Correspondents in bureaus around the country and overseas were deployed as well, as no one knew the scope or nature of the attack at this point.

And my assignment? Jim Kelly had an extraordinary instinct about the nature of this story. Rather than dividing it up in the interests of speed—one person does the World Trade Center, another the Pentagon, someone writes about Islamic militancy, another on Bush's possible responses—he decided that the special issue would be a single story, and carry no advertising, with a cover printed with the first black border ever. "Think of it as a Time Capsule," he told me. "You don't have to speculate on who did this, or why, or how we will respond. We have a lot of time to do that. Just tell the story of what happened today."

I also began receiving calls from neighbors, wondering whether they should go take their kids out of school, or trying to track down husbands who worked downtown and had not yet been heard from.

That was noon on Tuesday 9/11. I was told I had until 6 P.M. Wednesday to write the story. "Don't worry about the length," Kelly said, "write whatever feels right." I began working in my office at home: there was no way to get into the city, as all the bridges and tunnels had been closed. Our reporters and editors in our midtown headquarters were advised to evacuate; there were reports of bomb threats all around the city. They stayed all through the night, through the next day.

By noon Wednesday I had received somewhere in the neighborhood of nine hundred e-mail files from colleagues around the world. Other writers and editors were helping to comb through them for the most striking details and stories.

That was when word came that our printing window suddenly changed; instead of a 6 P.M. deadline, the editors needed the story "Right now."

I bought an extra two hours or so by sending it in in chapters; rather than have a single editor edit the entire story, it was chopped into pieces and divided among four of them. As I kept writing, I suspect it was being edited, fact checked and copyread simultaneously.

By 6 P.M. it was well out of my hands. We rounded up neighbors, including some who had been in the second tower and made it out safely. Someone called it a trauma picnic. It was another of those uncannily gentle September nights. We sat outside, and drank a lot, and began the conversation about whether anything would be the same again.

ANATOMY OF A VERDICT
D. GRAHAM BURNETT

Last year I served as the jury foreman in a Manhattan murder trial. The culmination of this ordeal—twelve idiosyncratic individuals thrown into tight quarters for sixty-six hours of sequestered deliberations—pushed civics into a realm normally reserved for extreme sports. A clutch of strangers yelled, cursed, vomited, whispered, embraced, sobbed and invoked both God and necromancy. There were some moments when the scene could have passed for a graduate seminar in political theory, others that might have been a jujitsu class.

A man's fate hung in the balance. And we, the jury—closed in our crucible; shuttled about in the dark like shades by armed officers; cut off suddenly and indefinitely from our families, friends, news, regular life—shouldered the strange double burden of jury service. We wielded fearsome power (over the young man brought before us) and yet were rendered totally powerless (before the judge, the guards and the system that had drafted us as the foot soldiers of justice). Strung between these poles, we gained perspective and understood things in new ways. Understood intimately, for instance, the great power of the state. Understood glancingly, at least, the weakness and fear of a defendant standing before it. Understood feelingly, in the end, the great, disturbing truth that lies beneath the niceties of daily life: deep down, civics *is* an extreme sport; the ultimate, primordial and extremest sport of all.

What do I mean? I mean that lives are lost and won in the courts, lost and won in the law—every day, everywhere. Most of us seldom really think about this. But in the jury room, the thought cannot be avoided, since there you learn that justice doesn't merely happen (neatly, reliably, like a crystal taking shape in a distant vacuum); justice is, rather, done, made, manufactured. Made by imperfect, wrangling, venal and virtuous human beings, using whatever means are at their disposal. In the jury room, you discover that the whole edifice of social order stands, finally, on handicraft—there is no magic, no mathematics, no science, no angelic fixer who checks our juridical homework. This is a frightening thing, not least because any one of us could be accused of a crime.

We punish one another. To live together, we must. But it is a messy business when you get up close. The jury room is as close as you can get. We expect much of this small cell, and its door seldom stands open.

AUGUST 1998

Two N.Y.P.D. patrolmen kicked in the door. (Or said they did: later evidence would show that the jamb and latch, strangely, remained intact: moreover, each officer testified that he, and not the other, had been the one to get it to give.) When the door opened—in and to the right, stopping against a low coffee table—the two men surveyed the scene: a small, dark studio apartment.

Draped over the futon couch, and trailing onto the floor to the right, were two blankets, one a cream-colored knit coverlet, the other a cheap, quilted bedspread. Blood spatters stained both. The curtain of the single, street-facing, ground-level window was closed, with the exception of a small opening in the lower left corner.

Causing this aperture was the lifeless hand of an African-American male, about six feet tall and just under two hundred pounds. The body lay facedown, the head wedged between the arm of the couch and the radiator under the window, the legs splayed into the middle of the room. Rigor mortis had caught and preserved the victim's final gesture: his right arm reaching up to the sill—surely an effort to pull himself to the window and call for help. Under the left arm lay a wig of long, dark, kinky hair. The body was naked.

The officers did not approach the figure or check for vital signs. A multitude of stab wounds (it would turn out there were more than twenty altogether) along the right side of the victim's spine, neck and head enabled them to surmise from the doorway what the medical examiner would confirm several hours later: the man—a habitué of the West Village nightlife and a familiar face in the homey gay bar at the corner—was definitely dead.

Not until later, however, when crime-scene investigators rolled the body over, did anyone see the wound that actually killed him— a thin and nearly bloodless slit through his sternum, which, reaching two and a half inches into the thoracic cavity, had just nicked the upper arch of the aorta. Within minutes of his receiving the blow, blood would have filled the sac around the heart, a condition known as an "acute traumatic cardiac tamponade." It is as if the heart drowns.

Also revealed when the body was moved: two braided leather whips and two unrolled condoms, one inside the other.

JANUARY 2000

I passed through the metal detectors at 100 Centre Street. My juror card instructed me to appear at 9 A.M., but it was later than that when I finally cleared the line and the low-ceilinged lobby of the dingy court building and found my way upstairs. I caught a fragment of a conversation between two older Hispanic women in the elevator: "Just two ounces! Not some kilo or noth'n. . . . But he didn't care."

From the outset I had resolved to treat the unwelcome intrusion of jury duty as something like a vacation, a three-day visit to a foreign country of bureaucratic languor and vast waiting rooms, a linoleum land inhabited by a genuine demographic cross section of the Big Apple. Most of all, I was looking forward to getting some reading done.

I am a college professor, a historian of science, but that year I had been awarded a one-year fellowship in a well-appointed humanities center at the New York Public Library—books everywhere, a silent and bright office without a phone, distinguished colleagues, catered lunches. My only formal responsibilities were to read and to write. But things piled up on the desk—student evaluations, article proofs needing attention, endless e-mail—so the New York State Criminal Court began to look like an opportunity to hide in plain view.

Actually ending up on a jury never crossed my mind. The day before I reported for duty, I had a conversation with a friend, a logician, who claimed that the magic word was "philosophy": once the lawyers heard it, you were kindly asked to leave. I figured that introducing myself as an academic ought to have the same effect. With a lawyer wife who had worked for a public defender's office, I promised to give any healthy prosecutor hives.

In the twice-exhaled air of the jury waiting room, about two hundred disgruntled New Yorkers had arranged themselves like a tray of magnetic monopoles: maximum space between each particle and its neighbors. Some read newspapers, others books; a few students had staked out desks in the corner and had begun to study, wearing Walkmans. Most people simply stared into space.

This hostile levee was called to attention by the senior court clerk, who seemed a New York institution-in-the-making, to judge from the gallery of inscribed celebrity head shots on the wall outside his office. (Gwyneth Paltrow! Stephen Jay Gould?)

"Any convicted felons in the room?" he boomed happily. Snickers. "No need to jump up," he added, with the honed timing of a natural stand-up. "Just wander into the clerk's office down the hall a little later, and I'll let you go."

"Anybody not understand English?" he jawed, waving his arm over us.

He mumbled this so fast I hardly caught it. But quite a few people promptly rose and began making their way to the front to get their release cards. Out they filed.

The joke grew on everyone. Amused murmuring.

"I'll never understand it," he stage-whispered to the rest of us, over a knot of duty dodgers bulling for the double doors.

After details (locations of rest rooms, water fountain, snack machine; an exhortation not to steal the magazines), we settled in to watch the preparatory video, narrated by Ed Bradley and Diane Sawyer. In addition to offering canned testimonials to the effect that we were going to have a great time and learn a lot about our government, the program set jury duty in its historical context. This was compressed in the extreme and got under way with a memorable flashback to the dark days of trial by ordeal: as Sawyer's woodwind voice soothingly narrated the bleak realities of justice in a benighted age, a knot of stringy-haired plebes, smirched and scrofulous, dragged a bound man through the woods and cast him into a deep lake. A papist factotum solemnly made the sign of the cross over the disappearance of the accused, and we learned that he would be found innocent if he did not resurface. Not an outtake from Monty Python, but an educational film prepared by the state of New York, the dramatization ended with the suggestion that the accused was innocent and that his kinsmen might have succeeded in recovering him from the bottom.

The movie put everyone in a good mood and strongly suggested the possibility of human progress in matters of jurisprudence. The Centre Street court building was grim and forbidding in a Stalinist sort of way (towering, gray, squint-windowed), but it clearly beat the heck out of the Inquisition. I went back to my book.

Complacency was unwise. The next afternoon, my name came up.

THE CASE

How complicated was the case that absorbed my life for the weeks to come? That depends on how closely you look. For those weeks I looked very closely, so to me it seems immensely complex. And yet, the tale can be briefly told: two men are in a room; one stabs the other, first in the chest, then in the back, many times; the stabber says he was acting in self-defense. There are no witnesses.

But the plot thickens. This man, the defendant, claims that when he went into the room with that other man, the victim, he believed the victim to be an attractive woman who wanted eagerly to have sex with him. In fact, he says, it was only when they both undressed for this very purpose that he discovered something disturbing: his date's idea of sex placed the defendant on the receiving end of anal intercourse, like it or not. His date was a man.

Prevented from fleeing the room, pressed to the floor, grappling for his clothes and the exit, the defendant took a lock-blade pocketknife from the pocket of his overalls, opened it and stabbed his attacker once, in the chest. When the assault continued, so did the stabs—until, eventually, the attacker relented and the defendant gathered up his belongings and ran from the room into the street, drenched in blood, his pinkie nearly severed from the zealous swinging of the knife.

This is what the defendant says.

But the plot thickens. The defendant didn't tell any of this to the police when they picked him up in the street and took him to the hospital to have his finger sewn back on. He told them a lie, namely that he had just been mugged by a gang of "five white males." The defendant is black.

This might have worked. Except, when the police found the victim, they did what the police do when they find a person who has been stabbed to death: they canvassed area emergency rooms for patients admitted with suspicious cuts on their arms or hands. It is hard to stab someone many times, in haste and agitation, and avoid a slip or two. The defendant slipped.

His name came up in this search, and the police paid him a visit in the hospital to ask him some pointed questions about those five white males. The detectives didn't like his answers—too vague. They asked him to come down to the station—to help jog his memory. Within a few hours he admitted to stabbing the victim (copious DNA evidence from blood at the scene would have made it hard to deny). Only now did the police hear the story of the drag seduction and the desperate fight in the small, dark room.

But the plot was thicker still by the time I and eleven other Manhattanites took up our seats in the jury box of New York State Supreme Court, Criminal Term. Because by that time the district attorney's office had sniffed around and turned up a handful of witnesses ready to testify that the victim and the defendant had long been lovers, and that they had spent the evening of the killing together in the apartment. Also, the forensics team had noticed traces of semen on the penis of the victim and the underwear of the defendant. Whose semen? They couldn't say.

INTO THE OPEN COURT

We heard this evidence in the bright, high-ceilinged courtroom, under the stern eye of a sour-humored judge. Then, on a television wheeled up beside the witness stand, we were shown a grainy video of the defendant's confessional statement. After some back-and-forth between the judge and a court officer, the lights had been dimmed; it proved impossible to lower the shades, despite several attempts. The gallery had filled in for the showing—various clerks, assistants, a visiting class from John Jay College of Criminal Justice.

A large cockroach emerged from under the prosecution's table, creating a minor disruption. It escaped the stomp of a female guard and wedged itself into an invisible crevice at the foot of the bench.

The taped statement, taken the night the police picked the defendant up from the hospital, made the evening of the killing feel immediate. In the video, the assistant district attorney—young, handsome, Asian, wearing a tie—sits across from the suspect, a narrow table between them, as in a chess tournament. As the camera frame tightens on the defendant, the A.D.A. becomes a disembodied voice, inquisitive, measured. Each question, outwardly straightforward, seems to conceal complex structures: legal implications, potential charges, due-process considerations. The A.D.A. takes his time, making it clear he has to think before he speaks. The defendant responds quickly, telling the story, his intonation rising restlessly at the end of each phrase, as if he is looking for some confirmation from his inquisitor, as if he himself is asking question after question, in an eager tumble. The difference in pace, in caution, stands out.

Asked to show how he handled the knife, the defendant obliges, raising his right arm (in a cast, from his surgery) and supporting it with his left at the elbow, through the sling. He mimes an overhand grip and makes small, apologetic pecking gestures.

He has a high voice and a Southern accent, which together give him a curiously solicitous air. He has a lisp that seems nearly a hiss; he puts his mouth around words in haste, gobbling them. "Yessir," he replies, often.

When he quotes himself as having blurted out, "What the [expletive] is this?" (on spying the male sex of his erstwhile date), he excuses himself for his language, quickly, instinctively, in a whisper.

By the end of the tape, he is holding his bandaged right arm and wincing; he sucks air through his teeth in pain. Asked if he wishes to add anything to his statement, he responds, reasonably, "What's going to happen next?" And then, "Can I go home tonight?"

The A.D.A. pauses and repeats his question: Does he wish to add anything to his statement at this time?

He declines.

The high contrast of the image erases the features of his face, making him a silhouette.

Defendants in murder trials seldom take the stand. They are under no obligation to do so, and a jury is instructed to make no inferences from their choice. For one thing, testifying generally means exposing any criminal record they might have, information that is otherwise rigorously withheld from the jury.

Again and again I found myself sitting in court looking across at the defendant. Only he knew what had happened in that apartment. Day after day, I looked at the defendant, and I saw a cipher.

That changed on the last day of testimony, when, with a shrug (after requesting, unsuccessfully, more time from the judge in order to contact a no-show witness), the defense attorney called his client to the stand. As he went, long-legged, lankier than I had expected, I realized I had not yet seen him stand up. By taking the stand, he voluntarily settled the question of his criminal record. There wasn't much: some unspecified "participation" in a nonviolent robbery at the age of thirteen or fourteen. He had graduated from high school (where he had been something of a track star) and had attended marine corps boot camp, from which he had been dismissed after dislocating his shoulder in a boxing competition, aggravating an older injury. After this he had apparently held several regular jobs, one at a sporting-goods store in midtown, the other doing data entry for a medical records company. He lived with his fiancée (who was pregnant at the time of his arrest, and had since borne him a child) and her mother.

In the end, the bulk of the defense case hung on these minutes of testimony. Without hesitation, even forcefully, the defendant told his story again: he insisted that he had acted in self-defense, that he had been the victim of a sexual charade. After briefly rehearsing this account under direct examination (where he seemed shy, but clear and calm, and said that he had lied in his early statements), the defense turned him over to the prosecution for the cross.

A prosecutor cannot be successful without a strong sense of how to play such a moment. This prosecutor elected to use a badgering tone and a sneeringly sarcastic mien. He dived in by accusing the defendant of being a perjurer, for having "lied on his application" to the marines. But it appeared that this meant nothing more than that he had not alerted the corps to his having once hurt his shoulder in high school. Since the military assesses its recruiters on the basis of how many bodies they sign up, it is easy to imagine that no one pressed him to disclose an overly detailed medical history on the forms.

Given a defendant apparently so benign—young and slight, well spoken, with a handsome, dark face and bright white in his almond eyes—the prosecutor's combative strategy ran the risk of a backfire. And that, I would say, is what happened: when the defendant maintained his composure, the prosecutor had no place to go but up, escalating his belligerence in hope of cracking this composure. By the end, the prosecutor had pulled out all the stops and found himself furiously dramatizing the state's version of the victim's final moments, as he lay helpless on his face, with the defendant poised above him, repeatedly driving the knife into his head, neck and back.

Acting all of this out a few feet from the witness stand, directly in front of the jury box, the murder weapon in his hand, the prosecutor again and again swung the open knife, rolling his head and shoulders into each exaggerated stroke as he growlingly challenged the witness to deny that this, in fact, was how the victim met his death.

"And didn't you then—like this!—stab him? And then, again! Like this? As he tried to crawl away? And—again!"

But the sensational dramatization—which the judge refused to interrupt and which sent the victim's family howling from the room as several of the jurors squirmed in disgust—built to a crashingly flat climax. To the blistering assertion that this was how it had happened, the defendant offered a simple answer.

"No."

And yet, it seemed, if anything was going to shake him, it would have been that.

So egregious did I find the whole performance that, as the defendant returned to his seat, slightly hunched, as if afraid of bumping his head on something, I felt a deep desire to see the prosecutor lose the case. How did that whisper of a thought affect what followed? It is difficult to say.

INTO A CLOSED ROOM

Walking us down the hall and into the small jury room, the short, jovial sergeant said he would take care of us. "There's water there." He nodded at a thermos. "And this is the buzzer you press if you need anything, and there's no smoking, of course, but there's windows in the bathroom. . . . That's all I'm saying, OK?

"Oh, and, uh, you know, if you order up the knife, right? You know I bring it in, but we don't leave it with you, see? . . . I gotta carry it around, and you can look at it, but nobody can talk till I leave. And the knife goes with me."

He gave us a kidding smile as he prepared to close the door. "You know, we need twelve jurors for a verdict, eh?

"Anybody want cigarettes?"

Throwing a defendant into a lake seems barbaric to us, or blackly funny: we are heirs of the Enlightenment, after all; we are modern, thank God. But throwing a defendant to a jury has a medieval quality all its own. Things can come out different ways: large decisions hinge on small points. People are quirky, idiosyncratic, even strange. Place a dozen individuals together in tight quarters for long enough, and nearly anything can happen.

Who were we? Four men and eight women. Perhaps as many as half of us were thirty or younger. We were white (nine), black (two) and Hispanic (one); we were, for the most part, professionals (in advertising, software development, marketing). We seemed—milling about in the hall at breaks, chatting as we took the slow elevator to the street after a long day of testimony—to get along perfectly well. Once the door to the jury room closed, I asked that we begin with a moment of silence.

How did the deliberations unfold? I am sure each of us would remember things differently; if you learn anything from a criminal trial under the adversary system, it is that sincere people can differ vehemently about events, and that there is seldom any easy way to figure out what actually went on.

This is the way I remember things: On the first day we went around the room and people said whatever they wanted about the case. That taught us two things: first, that we didn't agree; and second, that there was a great deal of confusion about the different charges we had been asked to consider (murder in the second degree under two different "theories," as well as the lesser charge of manslaughter). Did we all have to achieve unanimity on a *single* charge before we could even consider the claim of self-defense? (This made no sense to me, but it would be days before everyone was convinced that it would never work.) Could a finding of self-defense trump all of the charges? (It seemed obvious to me that it could, but we had to hash this one out too and seek clarification by means of written queries to the judge.)

By the second day a straw poll indicated we were still all over the place: a handful wanted us to find the defendant guilty of the most severe charge, and another handful voted for each of the lesser charges; but about half the room also said they had not ruled out self-defense. (Some of these people, though, had also put in a ballot for guilt, which left me scratching my head.)

We began requesting evidence we wanted to review. I had initially been reluctant to drag these items into the room (it seemed to me it would be hard enough to have a serious conversation around the table without photographs, videos and other tidbits to play with), but a pair of striking discoveries followed. One juror, looking at a video taken of the crime scene, noticed that it was impossible to see the futon couch from the hallway outside the apartment door—the angle was wrong. A small point, but one with large implications, since this meant that a key prosecution witness had lied. He had testified to seeing the defendant on the victim's couch that night. But he had also insisted he had been standing in the hall.

The other discovery turned up in one of the crime-scene photographs: a pair of what looked like panties on the corner of the couch by the body. These corroborated the defendant's story, and in doing so cast doubt on the testimony of almost all of the police and crime-scene investigators who had testified for the prosecution: they uniformly claimed that no women's clothing had been found in the searches of the apartment.

But casting niggling doubt on various witnesses was one thing. The deeper issue lay in realizing just how much the state had to prove before we could find the defendant guilty: when someone claims to have killed in self-defense, the presumption of innocence extends to this claim; in other words, the prosecution must prove, beyond a reasonable doubt, not only that the defendant killed but also that he did not do so in self-defense. When there are no witnesses, is this even possible?

It took us some time to work out just how heavy the burden of proof was. Over four days we wrestled with this problem and struggled to understand not only what happened in that cramped apartment but also what the law demanded of us. Three moments were decisive in this long debate, and each of them hinged on a different juror, each of whom spoke clearly at a difficult juncture and shifted the course of our deliberations.

JUROR 10: MEN CAN BE DATE-RAPED, TOO

Juror 10 was a raspy, dyed-blond twenty-something tough girl in tight black jeans who spoke loudly and much, often well. An actress, apparently, with the hard edges of a barmaid in a Back Bay Boston Irish pub, she knew how to make herself heard and was not afraid to hold the floor. She leapt into the fray from the start, composing a long list of all the evidence that she wanted to hear again, a list that grew so long that I, as the foreman, finally felt I had to discourage her, because sending it in to the court would have obliged us to sit through nearly a week of readings from the transcript. My stalling on her requests caused trouble later: was I stringing her along? she wanted to know. She let me know that I'd better not try to jerk her around.

As the days wore on I increasingly got the sense that Juror 10's sudden, explosive interjections signaled someone quick to trigger. In addition, she was apparently taking some sort of heavily regulated prescription drug, and by the third day of deliberations she had run out. That spelled trouble.

Her moment of glory, though, came after lunch on the second day, at the end of an hour we had spent collectively trying to reconstruct the fatal fight from snippets of contradictory description given by the defendant in his videotaped statement. Replaying the tape of the defendant's account of the fight, several jurors got down on the floor and acted out the moves the defendant was describing. Juror 10 was on the floor on her back calling for someone to lie down between her legs. This and the subsequent wrangles occasioned a certain amount of joking, but our conclusion after this boisterous tangling was that the fight almost surely could not have happened in the way the defendant said. The wounds to the victim's back certainly looked as if they had been delivered from behind, when the victim was nearly motionless, lying on his face, dying, presumably, from the first blow to the chest. (The incisions in the back had the wrong penetrating angle to have been made as the defendant claimed—from underneath the victim, as the defendant struggled in his embrace.)

We pressed the evidence. Had this been a drag seduction? Unlikely. Look at the size of that victim. Who could get within ten feet of him and think he was a woman, wig or no?

Rape? We had lots of evidence that these men knew each other (a parade of witnesses who could have come straight out of "Paris Is Burning" swore to it), and the semen traces suggested they had just had some sort of sex before things went bad. Didn't this have all the marks of a crime of passion? Who could say why the defendant got so angry at his lover, but hadn't he clearly attacked and killed him in some sort of rage?

But not everyone agreed. Several people pointed out that even if the men had been sexually involved, that didn't prove it was murder. Juror 10 pushed this point: What difference did it make if they had just been fooling around before things got ugly? Did this make it impossible that the defendant was defending himself from rape when he swung the knife? Wasn't *that* the only question? "No means no," Juror 10 announced sharply, "even if they just had oral sex, and then his lover said he wanted more, if he said no, then it was rape."

This declaration — categorical, a little edgy, a little holier-than-thou — visibly irritated several of the people around the table. But as the conversation continued into the afternoon, we found ourselves coming back to it. Maybe the defendant was lying about a lot of things, but if he had been cheating on his pregnant fiancée and experimenting with a homosexual relationship, his reluctance to tell the truth about much of what had happened made sense. We all agreed that a woman could be raped by a lover, could kill to protect herself in that situation; could we reject that possibility here? Place it beyond a reasonable doubt? Did we have any more reasonable account for why an apparently mild-mannered young man with no history of violent crime would have committed such a monstrous act? We did not. Then didn't self-defense remain at least a possibility? Could it be ruled "beyond a reasonable doubt"? Those were powerful words.

Juror 10's analogy to date rape cut away much of the prosecution's case and focused us on that one fatal moment—when the knife came out.

JUROR 7: LAW OR JUSTICE?

Juror 7 was less impressed by this argument than most of us, and because she herself was a very impressive woman, this was a problem. Juror 7 was a professor, a historian like me. From day 1 she had been the clearest voice for the defendant's guilt, under the most severe murder charge, and she seemed a bit shocked that so many of the rest of us were hesitating. Very smart and articulate, she was evidently accustomed to holding the attention of a room. Her aspect was serious, though not at all unfriendly. Dressed comfortably—in sneakers and a shapeless sweater with loose sleeves that she pushed above her elbows—she moved with a kind of force, often lifting her short brown hair off her temples and fixing it behind her ears, rubbing her chin thoughtfully as she listened to others. Because she gave all indications of being temperamentally inclined to a prodefendant position (urban, bookish, seemingly left-liberal), her advocacy of a guilty verdict weighed heavily.

Juror 7 simply nudged us toward a conviction with her good arguments. As a number of people were rallying round Juror 10's point, Juror 7 spoke up: "But the only evidence for that moment"—the moment the defendant said no to sex—"is this guy's word, and what's that worth?" she asked.

She proposed an exercise. "Let's make a list of everything this guy has told us, and then let's cross off everything that has turned out to be a lie. What's left on the list? Only that one moment. How can you be ready to let him walk out of here on the basis of that?" How reasonable was it to doubt that a liar was lying? And with his neck on the line?

With the room increasingly polarized, a new idea began to circulate in the wake of this strong argument for a conviction: a compromise. Since about half the jury thought the defendant should be found guilty of the most serious crime, and the other half seemed to want a total acquittal, why couldn't we agree to convict on the lesser charge of manslaughter? That way we would ensure the defendant got some punishment for all the bad things he clearly did do: abandon the scene, lie to police, etc.

"I think it would be a violation of our duty as jurors, which is to apply the law," I said. "We weren't asked to consider whether this guy is guilty of abandoning the scene. The law says we can only convict if we're persuaded, beyond a reasonable doubt, that the defendant killed this man and did not do so in self-defense. So that's the only issue. We aren't allowed to fudge the law because we'd like to see the defendant get punished."

Conversation around the idea of a compromise heated up, as we debated whether this was a legitimate way to resolve the case.

"I keep coming back to this same question," she said, "the relationship between law and justice. What I keep wanting here is for us to figure out some way to do justice, but I am starting to realize that the law itself may be a different thing. What is my real responsibility? The law? Or the just thing? I'm not sure what the answer is. We've been told that we have to 'uphold the law.' But I don't understand what allegiance I should have to the law itself. Doesn't the whole authority of the law rest on its claim to be our system of justice? So if the law isn't just, how can it have any force?"

She had gone to the heart of the matter, directly, and with great equanimity and gentleness. Gradually this new formulation—justice versus law—began to take hold. Justice: compromise on a verdict so the defendant gets some punishment. Law: admit that it had not been proved, beyond a reasonable doubt, that this could not have been self-defense (nearly all of us agreed that the prosecution's case had failed to meet this very heavy—absurdly heavy?—burden of proof).

Thanks to Juror 7, a new question lay before us. How could we justify applying the law if we decided that the resulting verdict was itself unjust? Were we responsible to the law? Or to our idea of justice?

It would take a born-again, formerly Crystal-Meth-addicted ex-bull-riding-rodeo-cowboy to answer this question for us—the improbable Juror 9.

JUROR 9: JUSTICE AND GOD

Juror 9 was a big man: a six-foot-three-inch, God-fearing veteran of the United States armed forces who now repaired vacuum cleaners for a living. When I first noticed him, in the early days of jury selection, he was spitting tobacco juice behind the radiator by the elevator during a break. He had thin, brown hair slicked back and a manly mustache, and wore a weathered pair of work boots. A contractor of some sort, I assumed, and I pegged him, without much thought or interest, a prime example of Susan Faludi's tragic tale of the white working-class male—big chest, big gut, big debt. I called him, irreverently, "the Faludiman" in my diary. What did I know? Before the trial ended he had blown my stereotype (indeed, any stereotype) wide open.

From the start of the trial, I thought it very likely he would take the lead in pushing for a guilty verdict, if not a hanging. I think I figured anyone wearing, apparently in earnest, a large belt buckle reading "Rodeo" had to be a law-and-order type and quite possibly a bigot too.

But at breakfast on the second day (at the hotel out by J.F.K. Airport where we had been sequestered), we got into a conversation, at first about the food, then about fasting, then about the approach of

Lent and finally about the good Lord. In addition to telling us about his victory over drugs, he began to explain that he had become a domestic missionary of his California "mother church" (of recovered addicts), part of a small cell charged to found a new community in Spanish Harlem. Almost a decade had passed since this group took up residence in the community and began pursuing its mission: wandering in and out of the heroin galleries and the crack dens of the neighborhood, handing out literature, praising the Lord, preaching the possibility of recovery and redemption. They held their first meetings in an empty storefront and circled in prayer around vomiting addicts delirious from the struggle to go cold turkey. The church now had well over one hundred families, and Juror 9 had become one of its leaders, a deacon sometimes called upon to preach. He had married into the community, and he and his Guatemalan wife had two kids of their own; they were also rearing his daughter from a previous marriage.

All this helped explain his accommodating and gentle voice in our deliberations; his obvious ability to speak with authority and lead the group; his sympathy for the defendant. From the beginning, Juror 9's attitude had been that the defendant had done the wrong thing, that he had almost certainly gotten involved in something risky and stupid, but that this alone was not grounds for a conviction.

"The Lord knows," he would add, "I myself have been in the wrong place more than once."

By midafternoon on the third day, the debate over a compromise verdict of manslaughter had become testy, and several positions had hardened. We were tired, some personalities had clashed, we all felt increasingly trapped: without a verdict, would we ever be released? Could we ever agree? At least four people still pressed for a guilty verdict. About the same number seemed committed to acquit. The rest wavered. I thought we were a hung jury.

Those pushing for the compromise idea argued that the law's only purpose was justice; therefore justice had to be the higher principle. It followed, then, that an appeal to justice must trump the mincing details of the law itself. The law might prohibit us from compromising on a manslaughter verdict unless we could all agree that the burden of proof had been met (which we could not). But we agreed that it was not just to let the defendant go unpunished for what he had done. Conclusion? The dictates of justice demanded that we circumvent the law. Q.E.D. Momentum for a guilty vote gained, even though most people in the room had by now agreed that they felt some "reasonable" doubt, however small, about the self-defense issue.

It was an odd situation. We seemed ready to ignore the law in an effort to get the verdict that so many people wanted: guilty. Or this was how I saw it.

Then Juror 9 rose to speak. "I've been listening," he began, "to these things people are saying, and I have tried to pray about all this. Now I've decided what I have to do. I believe this young man did something very, very wrong in that room. But I also believe that nobody has asked me to play God. I've been asked to apply the law. Justice belongs to God; men only have the law. Justice is perfect, but the law can only be careful."

The statement centered the room.

Here was a repudiation of sophistication that suddenly seemed overwhelmingly sage. No one spoke for several moments. He did not try to explain, or to say more. He sat down.

There was silence.

To my right I heard a whisper. Looking over, I saw brimming eyes. "He's convinced me," someone whispered. It was close to a sob. No one else spoke.

Acquit before the law; leave justice to God—could we do this? Was this like throwing the defendant in a lake? A lake in the sky?

A SETBACK

We knew we were close. We took a poll, and the numbers hovered at the brink of an acquittal: ten to two. Juror 9's powerful declaration had played a role in killing the drive for a compromise conviction and had won converts. But the day did not end there.

Juror 10, missing her medication and exhausted by the stresses of the past three days, had been looking worse and worse. The pharmacy she had asked the court to contact claimed her prescription could not be refilled. She had been struggling with a bad cold sore for several days, and a number of ulcers could be seen on her face. Though she had applied heavy daubs of makeup to conceal them, several had opened, and she had been forced to stanch them with tissue. Her makeup bottle lay open on the table, and she had slumped into morose silence after complaining of a coming migraine.

Now from the men's bathroom came the strangled sounds of gags. She was throwing up.

At that, one juror stood up and said that he wanted to leave, and that he would vote for anything that would get us out of the room — he didn't care.

When the judge was informed of Juror 10's illness, he called us into the courtroom. He had decided to have Juror 10 taken to the hospital: we would suspend deliberations until further notice and were strictly prohibited from discussing the case until the full jury could reassemble.

It was shortly before 5 P.M. on Friday evening.

The hours that followed were the most painful of the whole trial. A new complement of court officials took charge, paunchy weekend cops who had oversize highway patrol sunglasses and gonzo equipment belts. They exuded a palpable sense of armed delight.

On the judge's orders they herded us into a cavernous empty court-room down the hall, where, for almost three hours, we waited without any sense of what to expect. Could the deliberations be suspended indefinitely? Could we be kept in custody all weekend? What if Juror 10 got worse? Would the judge ever let us go?

Several jurors began to lose their composure. One, increasingly desperate, wanted to contact her own lawyer, in the hope of winning release. No chance. The judge later apparently threatened the same juror with contempt. The powerlessness of her situation—indeed, the powerlessness of our shared situation—had been made painfully clear. We, it seemed, had become the prisoners.

So this was what incarceration felt like. No wonder the burden of proof set the bar so high. When Juror 10 rejoined us later that evening, there was a feeling that the ordeal had to end, and soon.

THE LAST DAY

It was Saturday, the fourth day of our deliberations. I took twelve index cards out of my pocket and passed them around. There was silence as they started to come back, each folded in half.

I counted the cards. Nine. We waited, and two more came in. Eleven. We waited. Still eleven.

At this point there was no confusion about who still held a card. Juror 7, my fellow historian, the eloquent voice for justice, sat at the corner of the table to my left, where she had sat for four days. She had a pencil in her hand, and the card on the table in front of her. She was looking fixedly away, up, behind her, out the window.

No one spoke. One juror adopted a contemplative posture, her fingers prayerfully arranged at her brow. Several others closed their eyes and clasped their hands to wait. One man put his head down on his folded arms. There was the sense that everyone in the room was concentrating on the blank card in rapt meditation. Juror 7 breathed audibly, wrote something rapidly on the card, closed it on itself and pushed it into the middle of the table.

I placed it, consciously, and more or less conspicuously, at the bottom of the pile. I wanted the full dismay of the room to land on her if she had voted for a conviction in this, the first poll of the fourth day. We knew we were close on the previous evening, but Juror 10's trip to the hospital had forced us to suspend deliberations right at that critical moment.

I began to open the cards and read them: not guilty, not guilty, not guilty, not guilty, not guilty, not guilty, not guilty, not guilty, not guilty, not guilty, not guilty. And the last one: not guilty.

The taut silence of the room broke in a gust of relief. There was absolutely no joy, no celebration, no delight. There was only an imprecise emotional surfeit. People were overwhelmed. I think there were only a few who were not crying, though I cannot remember everyone's face, because I was choked up myself.

Rapidly, I went to the wall next to the door and buzzed for the bailiff. I returned to my seat only for a moment, to take out a sheet of the paper we used for corresponding with the court and to write on it the message I had been told to give when our deliberations had ended: "The jury has reached a verdict."

I looked around the room. Several people were embracing, and two of the young women were gathered around Juror 7, saying encouraging things to her. She looked around over the shoulder of someone giving her a supportive hug, and she said suddenly, tearfully, "If we are doing the right thing, why are we all crying?"

At that instant, the knock came solidly at the door, followed by the requisite bark, "Cease deliberations!" The officer swung the door open, and I stood there with the sheet in my hand.

But as I reached to hand it to him, Juror 7 cried out: "No! Wait, we're not ready! Not yet."

I stood there dumbly, with my arm outstretched. I hesitated and then turned to him, apologized and asked him to leave.

With this back step, the room teetered on the brink of an unrecoverable collapse. At the prospect of snatching defeat from the jaws of victory like this, several jurors looked ready to go wild. I returned to my place and remained standing, asking for people to stay calm, if they could, and to hear a proposal.

"What we might do," I said, "is write a message to the court that makes explicit that we are unhappy, in a way, with our own verdict, that we feel we are doing the right thing before the law, but something that is not, in the end, really *just*."

I proposed a message, a sort of disavowal of our own verdict: "What if we wrote something like, 'We the jury wish it to be known to the open court that we feel most strongly that the strict application of the law to the facts established by the evidence in this case docs not lead to a truly just verdict.'" I had scribbled this statement in my diary, early that morning, as an expression of despair.

I looked up. A nod here and there. Yes. Several others. Yes. No onc said no, not even Juror 7.

So that was what we did. I wrote out that statement, concluding by saying that we had, nevertheless, reached a verdict. People consoled one another, and conversation turned to how this, at least, would be a way we could communicate our struggle to the family of the victim (who had sat mournfully through every day of the trial) and let them know that we had not accepted the demonized portrait the defense painted of him, but rather that we found ourselves bound by the strictures of the law. We could tell them that we were not unsympathetic toward their plea for justice.

In the half-hour it took for the court to assemble, our gray solemnity gradually brightened into the camaraderie of a parting of the ways. Laughter broke here and there, as the idea that it was over began to sink in. People started exchanging business cards, and someone had the idea that we ought to circulate an address sheet, so that we would all be able to stay in touch.

After we had taken our seats in the courtroom, the judge read my note aloud, without the least trace of inflection, slowly, mechanically, pausing momentarily after each word as if to strip the sentences of meaning.

"Have I read that correctly, Mr. Burnett?"

I said he had.

"Has the jury reached a verdict?"

I said yes.

The judge turned to the clerk and asked him to begin.

"On the charge of murder in the second degree with intent," the clerk began, "how finds the jury?"

"Not guilty."

I looked at the defendant, whose head was resting against his hands, clasped in front of him, his elbows on the table. His head dropped when the answer came.

"On the charge of murder in the second degree under the theory of depraved indifference, how finds the jury?"

"Not guilty."

His head dropped farther, and a distinct wailing went up from the back of the room.

"On the charge of manslaughter, how finds the jury?"

"Not guilty."

And the young man looked straight up, with tears streaming down his face, and his fists clenched at his throat.

The wailing from the back of the room grew louder.

The defense attorney showed no emotion; the prosecutors sat impassive.

I could hear sobbing in the jury box behind me and to my left. The judge spoke more words, the clerk spoke more words. I was asked a question. Was this the verdict of the jury? I said it was, aware that the moment was collapsing for me, that I was not able to maintain any distance from what was happening, that I was no longer seeing what was going on.

The attorneys approached the bench for a conference, and we were told that the jury would be polled. Each of us would be asked to affirm the verdict individually. Did I speak? I do not remember. I heard the voices around me. Yes. Yes. . . .

And so it went. I watched the defendant, who had again frozen in a posture of silent expectation, his hands clasped in front of him. Tears were visible, dripping down his nose, onto the table. His head again dropped, slightly, each time an answer came: Yes. Yes.

Once Juror 7, behind me, had spoken, the thing felt done. But five answers remained. Yes. Yes. Yes. Yes. Yes.

And it was over. We had let him go.

EPILOGUE

We let the defendant go.

Several weeks later, at a party on the Lower East Side, I fell into conversation with someone who turned out to be a cop. He pumped me for the story, and then, in a good-natured way, expressed his dismay that we had voted for acquittal. How had we decided to do that, when it sounded to him as if we all basically thought it had probably been a murder?

I thought about trying to explain. Trying to explain what it means to say you are convinced beyond a reasonable doubt. Trying to explain that not guilty doesn't mean innocent. Trying to explain that after four days of sequestration, you have a new understanding of the power of the state, and of the reason that the people's burden of proof is so heavy—to protect citizens from this thing, this leviathan. Trying to explain how you might think you were probably looking at a murderer but decide the law would not permit you to convict him. Trying to explain what it felt like to go home in tears, to sit in the dark, wondering if you had done the right thing.

I thought about trying to explain. Because if I explained all that, I could tell him the remarkable thing that happened next, that first night at home, in the dark. The phone rang, and I answered it, and heard the voice of a fellow juror, a young woman who had stayed around the court to talk to the lawyers after it had all ended. She told me, her voice trembling, that she had learned of additional information we had not been allowed to hear because it had been ruled inadmissible by the judge. Evidence that the victim had been in trouble with the police before—for a sexual-misconduct charge. Once upon a time, he was accused of dressing like a woman, luring a young man to his apartment and pressing sex on him.

It was a great deal to explain. The party was loud. I nodded again. "Do you want to hear the whole story?" I shouted.

*   *   *

"Anatomy of a Verdict" was drafted in July of 2001, while my wife and I were packing up our apartment in New Haven for a move to Princeton, where I was to take up a position in the history department as a junior professor. I did not enjoy writing it. This was mostly because the piece is a redaction from a book entitled A Trial by Jury *(Knopf, 2001), which was in press at the time. I had worked hard on the book, and every sentence in it was just so—each one had rung in my head a dozen times, and by the end I couldn't imagine changing a word. But the* New York Times Magazine *editors, though they liked the book manuscript, decided that no ten-thousand-word excerpt from it would really work as a stand-alone piece. So I shuffled my feet for a while, unwilling to take scissors to the thing, and hoping the editors would settle for a chapter. Eventually, I screwed myself to the*

task, resolving to spend three days on it and to drop the whole project if I couldn't make it work.

The result has its own strengths. Composing the opener, I found myself saying what the whole experience had meant to me more clearly and concisely than I do anywhere in the book itself. At the same time, there were costs to the compression: Characters (including me) are stripped in "Anatomy of a Verdict"; we are more complex in A Trial by Jury. This shorter version is built around three decisive "turning points," but these fudge the drawn-out wrangling of the deliberations, which are more faithfully portrayed in the book. The ending here (very different from the book) still feels rushed to me.

All that said, the piece received strong critical response, and my first days at the new job brought a swamping load of e-mail and phone calls, quite a few from lawyers, several from judges and many from people who wanted to share their own jury stories (letters from convicts came later).

Jury service is as close as many Americans get to crime; the summons invites every citizen to play an active role in that timeless and primordial drama—the righting of wrongs. It is, as I say in the piece, a messy business.

CONTRIBUTORS

CHARLES BOWDEN lives in Tucson, Arizona. He has just finished a book on the murder of Bruno Jordan, Sal's late cousin, to be published in the fall of 2002 by Simon & Schuster. His book *Blues for Cannibals: The Notes from Underground* was published by North Point in February 2002. He continues to correspond with Sal Martinez and continues to believe he is a casualty of the border drug wars and of the demands of serving in DEA.

PETER J. BOYER has been a staff writer at *The New Yorker* since 1992. His work as a correspondent on the PBS documentary series *Frontline* has been honored with a Peabody Award, an Emmy and two Writers Guild Awards. He lives in upstate New York with his wife, Kari Granville, and his children, Samuel and Eleanor Jane.

D. GRAHAM BURNETT is an assistant professor of history and a member of the Program in History of Science at Princeton University. He works on the history of geography, exploration and cartography, and is the author of *Masters of All They Surveyed* and *Trial by Jury*.

E. JEAN CARROLL appears on CBS's *The Early Show*. She writes for *Esquire, Rolling Stone, Spin,* is the advice columnist at *Elle,* and is the author of several books, including *Hunter: The Strange and*

Savage Life of Hunter S. Thompson. E. Jean was drawn to the topic of "The Cheerleaders" in part because she herself was a cheerleader and, indeed, was a Miss Cheerleader USA.

ROBERT DRAPER is a writer at large for *GQ* magazine and the author of *Hadrian's Walls,* a novel, as well as of *Rolling Stone Magazine: The Uncensored History.*

ATUL GAWANDE, a staff writer for *The New Yorker* and a resident in surgery in Boston, is the author of *Complications: A Surgeon's Notes on an Imperfect Science.*

NANCY GIBBS is editor at large at *Time* magazine. She joined *Time* in 1985 and has since written close to a hundred cover stories. In 1993 she served as the Ferris professor at Princeton University; her writing is included in *The Princeton Anthology of Writing,* edited by Carol Rigolot. A native New Yorker, Gibbs graduated from Yale in 1982, summa cum laude, Phi Beta Kappa, with honors in history; in 1984 she received a second B.A., in politics and philosophy, from Oxford, where she studied as a Marshall scholar.

SKIP HOLLANDSWORTH, an executive editor for *Texas Monthly,* has been writing true crime stories about Texas for more than twenty years. When he was a cub reporter for a Dallas newspaper, he wrote about the murder of a college friend, and since then he has written about everything from a Dallas socialite whose husbands kept mysteriously dying, to a brilliant NASA scientist in Houston who became the object of a witch-hunt after the bodies of young women were found buried on his land, to a young, dreamy-eyed couple who became the greatest jewel thieves of our time, to Texas's Jack the Ripper, a man who meticulously cut out the eyes of prostitutes.

PAT JORDAN has been a freelance writer since 1962. He's written eleven books, two of them novels, and hundreds of magazine articles for such publications as *The New York Times Magazine, The New Yorker, Time, Life, GQ, Sports Illustrated* and *Rolling Stone.* His most successful book was the memoir *A False Spring,* and his most recent book was the memoir *A Nice Tuesday.* His novel *A.k.a. Sheila Doyle* will be published next fall by Carroll & Graf. He lives with his wife, Susan, also a writer, their six dogs and a parakeet, Francis, in Fort Lauderdale, Florida.

ROBERT KURSON is thirty-eight years old and a graduate of the University of Wisconsin and Harvard Law School. He is a senior editor at *Chicago* magazine, a frequent contributor to *Esquire,* and has written for *Rolling Stone, The New York Times Magazine* and other publications.

WILLIAM LANGEWIESCHE grew up in the greater New York area and was for many years a professional pilot. For the past twelve years he has been a full-time correspondent, mainly for *The Atlantic Monthly.* His most recent books are *Inside the Sky* and *Sahara Unveiled.*

DAVID McCLINTICK, a former investigative reporter for *The Wall Street Journal,* is the prize-winning author of three books, including the best-selling *Indecent Exposure,* a chronicle of scandal in Hollywood and Wall Street, and *Swordfish,* the anatomy of a U.S. government espionage operation against the Latin American drug mafia.

DOUG MOST is thirty-four, grew up in Rhode Island and after a brief career as a sportswriter switched to news. He worked for papers in South Carolina and New Jersey, was named 1998 Journalist of the

Year in New Jersey and wrote a true-crime book called *Always in Our Hearts: The Story of Amy Grossberg, Brian Peterson, and the Baby They Didn't Want*. A story he wrote for *Sports Illustrated* about a racial profiling incident with four basketball players appeared in *Best American Sports Writing 2001*.

ALEX PRUD'HOMME has written on crime, business, politics and the arts for such publications as *The New Yorker*, *The New York Times*, *Time*, *People* and ARTnews and was a senior writer at *Talk* magazine.

PETER RICHMOND, a staff writer for *GQ*, has been a sportswriter for newspapers and magazines for twenty-five years. His work has appeared in such publications as *The New Yorker*, *Rolling Stone* and *The New York Times Magazine*. The author of two books, he was a Nieman fellow at Harvard University, and his work has been anthologized in various publications, including *Best American Sportswriting of the Twentieth Century*.

JULIAN RUBINSTEIN is a contributor to *The New York Times Magazine*, *Rolling Stone*, and *Details*. He is currently working on his first book, *The Ballad of the Whiskey Robber*, to be published by Little, Brown. He can be reached at www.julianrubinstein.com.

MARK SINGER was born in Tulsa, Oklahoma, in 1950. Since 1974, he has been a staff writer for *The New Yorker*. His books include *Funny Money, Mr. Personality* and *Citizen K*.

PERMISSIONS ACKNOWLEDGMENTS

THOMAS H. COOK is the author of eighteen books, including two works of true crime. His novels have been nominated for the Edgar Allan Poe Award, the Macavity Award and the Dashiell Hammett Prize. *The Chatham School Affair* won the Edgar Allan Poe Award for Best Novel in 1996. His true crime book, *Blood Echoes*, was nominated for the Edgar Allan Poe Award in 1992, and his short story "Fatherhood" won the Herodotus Prize in 1998 and was included in Best Mystery Stories of 1998, edited by Otto Penzler and Ed McBain. His works have been translated into fifteen languages.

OTTO PENZLER is the proprietor of The Mysterious Bookshop in New York City. He was publisher of *The Armchair Detective*, the founder of the Mysterious Press and the Armchair Detective Library, and created the publishing firm Otto Penzler Books. He is a recipient of an Edgar Award for *The Encyclopedia of Mystery and Detection* and the Ellery Queen Award by the Mystery Writers of America for his many contributions to the field. He is the series editor of *The Best American Mystery Stories of the Year*. His other anthologies include *Murder for Love, Murder for Revenge, Murder and Obsession, The 50 Greatest Mysteries of All Time*, and *The Best American Mystery Stories of the Century*. He wrote *101 Greatest Movies of Mystery & Suspense*. He lives in New York City.

NICHOLAS PILEGGI was born and raised in New York. He was a reporter for the New York City Desk of the Associated Press for seventeen years before moving to *New York* magazine. He is the author of *Blye, Private Eye; Wiseguy;* and *Casino. Wiseguy* (aka *Goodfellas*) and *Casino* were both turned into films which Pileggi cowrote with director Martin Scorsese. Pileggi lives in New York City.